Abolitionist.

Remember

JULIE ROY JEFFREY

Antislavery Autobiographies & the Unfinished Work of Emancipation

THE UNIVERSITY OF

NORTH CAROLINA PRESS

CHAPEL HILL

Library of Congress
Cataloging-in-Publication Data
Jeffrey, Julie Roy.
Abolitionists remember: antislavery
autobiographies and the unfinished work of
emancipation / Julie Roy Jeffrey.   p. cm.
Includes bibliographical references and index.
ISBN 978-0-8078-3208-0 (cloth: alk. paper)
ISBN 978-0-8078-5885-1 (pbk.: alk. paper)
1. Abolitionists — United States — Biography.
2. African American abolitionists — Biography.
3. Fugitive slaves — United States — Biography.
4. Autobiography. 5. Autobiography — African
American authors. 6. Slaves — Emancipation —
United States. 7. Antislavery movements — United
States — History — 19th century. 8. African
Americans — Civil rights — History — 19th century.
9. Memory — Social aspects — United States —
History — 19th century. 10. United States —
History — Civil War, 1861–1865 — Causes.
I. Title.
E449.J455   2008   326′.8092′2 — dc22
[B]   2007045616

cloth   12 11 10 09 08   5 4 3 2 1
paper   12 11 10 09 08   5 4 3 2 1

CONTENTS

ILLUSTRATIONS

ACKNOWLEDGMENTS

As everyone who has undertaken a major research and writing project knows, the completed book would never have been possible without support and critical feedback from colleagues, friends, librarians, family members, students, and, in my case, unnamed readers for the University of North Carolina Press. I wish to thank all those who helped to make the book better; any flaws are due to me, not to those who gave me such good advice.

Two experiences helped to plant the idea for this study. One was The History of the Book Seminar that I attended at the American Antiquarian Society in Worcester, ably led by Ann Fabian and the AAS's staff. Without this seminar, I would never have thought to consider the publication and circulation of the books that form the heart of my study. I appreciated being pushed hard to expand this aspect of my work by one of the press's readers. The second experience was teaching a course titled "The Personal Narrative in American History and Culture." In preparing for this course, I read widely about first-person narratives, and this reading stimulated me to think in new ways about abolitionist autobiographies. I also wish to thank students at Goucher College, the University of Southern Denmark, and Utrecht University who participated in lively discussions about many different American autobiographies. They helped keep my interest and enthusiasm strong in my research project.

During research trips, kind friends Peter and Wrexie Bardaglio and Kennie Lyman and Andrew Harper provided generous hospitality and willing ears to hear the latest ideas I had about my project. At more times than I care to remember, Chris Clark, Elizabeth Clapp, Michael Pierson, and Stacey Robertson listened to my attempt to explain what I was trying to do and encouraged me to keep on thinking and writing. The generosity of several people in sharing their research and expertise with me continues to astound me. Stacey Robertson provided me with ample material about Parker Pillsbury. Michael Winship helped a scholar whom he did not know personally understand some key Houghton Mifflin records. Thomas Hamm, whom I met just before the book was complete, plied me with helpful information on Levi Coffin. Donald Yacovone alerted me to the fact that Samuel J. May's diary was at Cornell and that it indeed covered the period during which he was writing his book. Finally, I want to express my appreciation to my colleague Jean Baker and former colleague Peter Bardaglio who spent part of a summer reading and marking up my manuscript.

I received important institutional support from Goucher College. Funds from the Todd Professorship helped to alleviate many of the costs associated with this study. The Goucher College Library gladly undertook the task of procuring necessary materials through interlibrary loan.

The staff of other libraries also contributed to my work. Working at the Houghton Library was a delightful experience, and I benefited from the expertise of staff who retrieved materials for me that they thought would be helpful. I also want to thank librarians at the Bentley Library at the University of Michigan, at the Historical Society of Pennsylvania, at the Cornell University Library, and at the Witherle Library, in Castine, Maine.

Finally, I want to thank my family, who had to live with my obsession with this project for more years than they must have expected.

CHRONOLOGY OF THE PUBLICATION OF ABOLITIONIST AUTOBIOGRAPHIES AND ANNIVERSARY PROCEEDINGS

1869   Samuel J. May, *Some Recollections of Our Antislavery Conflict*

1872   William Still, *The Underground Rail Road*
       John Quincy Adams, *Narrative of the Life of John Quincy Adams, When in Slavery, and Now as a Freeman*

1873   William Webb, *The History of William Webb, Composed by Himself*

1875   *Centennial Anniversary of the Pennsylvania Society for Promoting the Abolition of Slavery, the Relief of Free Negroes Unlawfully Held in Bondage: and for Improving the Condition of the African Race*

1879   *North Into Freedom: The Autobiography of John Malvin, Free Negro, 1795–1880*

1880   Levi Coffin, *Reminiscences*
       Jane Grey Swisshelm, *Half A Century*

1881   Frederick Douglass, *Life and Times of Frederick Douglass Written by Himself*
       Laura Haviland, *A Woman's Life-Work: Labors and Experiences of Laura S. Haviland*

1883   Parker Pillsbury, *Acts of the Anti-Slavery Apostles*

1884   *Commemoration of the Fiftieth Anniversary of the Organization of the American Anti-Slavery Society in Philadelphia*
       George Julian, *Political Recollections, 1840 to 1872*

1887   Henry B. Stanton, *Random Recollections*

1890   Calvin Fairbank, *During Slavery Times: How He "Fought the Good Fight" to Prepare "The Way"*

1891   Elizabeth Buffum Chace, *Anti-Slavery Reminiscences*
       Lucy N. Colman, *Reminiscences*

1892   Frederick Douglass, *Life and Times of Frederick Douglass*

Abolitionists Remember

In our cause, of all others, we cannot afford to dispense with any means of getting the truth before even a *limited* audience. No one can calculate how fast or how widely a great truth will spread, although at first told to but two or three. — This is the entire secret of the progress of the Anti-Slavery Cause in this Country.

SAMUEL J. MAY, 1858, quoted in Taylor, ed., *British and American Abolitionists*, 430

Introduction

In 1874, John Greenleaf Whittier, one of the poets of the abolitionist movement, contributed an article to the *Atlantic Monthly* in which he recalled the founding of the American Anti-Slavery Society (AAS) forty-one years earlier. The small group forming this organization, one of the most important bodies committed to eliminating American slavery, realized that it was probably undertaking what Whittier called a "life-long struggle." The idea of ending slavery, of course, threatened existing political, social, and economic arrangements, and it would take three decades of agitation and four years of war before the AAS's goals of providing freedom to the enslaved and political rights to freed black men would be realized.[1]

Such a vast transformation of social, political, and racial realities left some northerners convinced that the nation would never forget the abolitionists. As George W. Curtis, the editor of *Harper's Monthly Magazine*, declared, "Neither you, indeed, nor any sensible man will expect that we shall forget the causes or circumstances of the struggle. They must of necessity be remembered that they may be of use." Whittier shared these general sentiments and, in particular, the conviction that the abolitionists' participation in the struggle would be remembered. He confidently predicted that "their memories . . . will be cherished when pyramids and monuments shall have crumbled to dust."[2]

Such confidence in national memory was misplaced. Indeed, in 1874, the very year in which Whittier's piece appeared, Josiah Holland, editor of *Scribner's*, the most widely read and perhaps most influential of the monthly magazines, declared that it was time to end the process of reconstructing the South. Without referring to emancipation, Holland insisted that the war had been fought to reestablish the "old" relationship of union. "The moment the military power of the confederacy was crushed," he asserted, "it was the business of our government . . . to reclaim their affectionate loyalty." In a statement that entirely rejected the abolitionist perspective of slavery as a sin, the editor declared, "We have nothing to do with the question whether . . . [southerners] sinned, and deserved punishment."[3]

Clearly Whittier and *Scribner's* editor held very different views of the causes and nature of the Civil War and its goals. Each was crafting a memory of the past that had implications for how, and if, abolitionists would enjoy an honored place in the nation's history and whether their goals for black people would be realized or shunted aside. At a deeper level, whatever understanding of the past prevailed would affect the very meaning of the country's political ideals. Abolitionists had insisted that the Declaration of Independence's offer of liberty and freedom should apply to both white and African American men. Their efforts to bring about emancipation and then to secure black citizenship, they believed, had realized the promises implicit in the American Revolution. But unless others were persuaded of this expansive vision of civic equality and participation, Americans would easily revert to the traditional view that national ideals applied to whites only.

Like Whittier and *Scribner's* editor, historians have recognized the importance of memory and the forces that affect what nations, groups, and individuals remember or forget. As Michael Kammen points out, "Societies . . . reconstruct their pasts rather than faithfully record them." On the one hand, this effort to "manipulate the past" can "mold the present." On the other hand, the creation of a compelling or convincing vision of the past also has the power to shape the future.[4]

Because the racial, political, and cultural stakes of the interpretation of the past were so high in the post–Civil War years, the period has attracted considerable scholarly attention. Historians such as David Blight, W. Fitzhugh Brundage, and Nina Silber have explored the ways in which northerners and southerners after the Civil War constructed their cultural memories about these great events. As they have pointed out, the creation of different versions of the past took place not only in formal histories of the period but also in different cultural mediums: stories, poems, novels; autobiographies and biographies; monuments, images, and rituals. The process engaged editors, writers, and artists as well as readers, viewers, and those who participated in commemorative exercises. The process was a "collaborative," one in which writers, artists, editors, and planners of collective events created and promoted visions of past and present that satisfied or reflected what audiences wanted or would support.[5]

Among the competing versions of history that circulated, the one that ultimately prevailed smoothed the process of reconciliation between North and South. History was remade. Rather than a struggle over slavery, the Civil War became a conflict to preserve the Union. Although one side triumphed, noble white soldiers from both the North and the South were now seen as heroes who had bravely fought to defend their vision of the country. Romantic views of the Old South and its benign plantation class undermined the idea that slavery was evil and mitigated the need for national or regional guilt. With slavery gone as a primary cause of war, the abolitionists lost any claim to historical importance. They suffered the fate of many radical groups in American history and were viewed as misguided or malignant troublemakers irrelevant in the larger scheme of the nation's past. Emancipation no longer appeared as a noble or realistic goal. Black suffrage was increasingly regarded as a mistake, and southern efforts to curb black political rights were applauded. Freed people were depicted as so debased and primitive that they were incapable of exercising the rights of free citizens. In the long run, this "history" legitimated forgetting the commitment to black rights that resulted from war and reconstruction and forgetting African Americans as a group. As one scholar has suggested, this history allowed Americans to avoid acknowledging slavery as "a historical evil" and atoning for it.[6]

This summary captures the broad outlines of the cultural transformation that occurred, but scholarly studies have overemphasized the historical narrative that triumphed. The process of creating historical memories was less determined and more contentious than this suggests, and the efforts to present alternative interpretations were more vigorous. Abolitionists challenged every important point of the reconciliation narrative, trying to salvage the nobility of their work for emancipation and African Americans and defending their own participation in the great events of their day. One of this book's goals is to restore the history of those who struggled against the creation of what they saw as a false and dangerous understanding of the past.[7]

By focusing on the alternative narratives that were created and presented to the public, whether written by abolitionists who supported moral suasion or political action to eliminate slavery, the dynamics and nature of the cultural contest over memory and history become more apparent. Frederick Douglass's role in maintaining an abolitionist interpretation of the past has been fully explored, but other abolitionists who joined him in the public debate are less well known. Some chose to play a modest role, confining themselves to making occasional speeches or writing articles. The disappearance of abolitionist newspapers and organizations limited their influence. But from the end of the Civil War into the twentieth century, a succession of white and black abolitionists tried to reach a large audience by writing and publishing personal accounts that assessed their reform achievements and interpreted the significance of their life's work. They explained the reasons that led them to embrace abolitionism, described their reform colleagues, and portrayed the opposition they encountered as they pursued immediate emancipation. Collectively, their narratives suggest the rich mix of activities that reformers pursued. Not surprisingly, they analyzed the nature of slavery and the slaves and exposed the character of slaveholders. Explicitly or implicitly, their narratives offered an analysis of the causes of war.[8]

Whether abolitionists conceived of their narratives as recollections, autobiographies, or memoirs, they had much at stake in the cultural struggle. Many had devoted years to the antislavery movement. Both personal and professional identities, indeed the very meaning and survival of their achievements, depended upon how Americans would remember and write about the past. Their commitment to the difficult tasks of composing a life narrative and then to ensuring its publication highlights their determination to enter the public debate in a manner that would attract serious consideration of their point of view.[9]

I first became interested in abolitionist memoirs when I was writing about ordinary women in the antislavery movement. At that time, I used the autobiographies as sources that revealed the activities of women active in reform and their understanding of its meaning in their lives. Subsequently, I taught a course on personal narratives and began to think about how people went about making sense of and writing about their lives and events that had taken place many years earlier. Critical literature as well as common sense suggested that the ways in which people depicted their past were affected by the moment they began to write and the events that were occurring in their world. Such a realization raised a host of questions about abolitionist recollections. How did the end of Reconstruction and the growing indifference to the situation of freed people influence how writers wrote about their reform work and structured their narratives? Did emancipation still seem to be the victory that it had once seemed? Did abolitionist autobiographers remain faithful to the ideals that had animated their efforts for African Americans, or did they turn away from their early commitments? Writing decades after the end of organized antislavery, did they see their lives as failures or successes?

Scholarship by Blight and others prompted additional questions. The cultural efforts to shape the memory of the Civil War changed not only its meaning but also the character of those who fought it and the events that led up to it. The new interpretations that were generated and circulated, especially through popular monthly magazines, challenged who the abolitionists were and what they had done as well as the cast of characters—slaves, masters and mistresses, slave hunters, fugitives—who had populated abolitionist rhetoric in the decades before the war. Did abolitionist writers recognize the cultural transformation that was taking place? If so, were their recollections an attempt to respond to the new climate of opinion and refute new "truths" about the past? How might the cultural climate have affected the reception of abolitionist recollections? These are some of the questions that this study seeks to answer.

Composing an autobiography is a challenging enterprise, of course, and most abolitionists did not undertake it. William Lloyd Garrison, despite agreeing with a Boston publishing house in 1866 to write a two-volume history of the antislavery movement in which he had spent most of his life, never could settle down to do it. He finally returned the $5,000 advance. Abby Kelley Foster, the fiery female abolitionist and woman's rights lecturer, was encouraged to write her reminiscences, and she began the project in 1885. But she, too, abandoned the task. A life of action, perhaps, had prevented her from keeping a diary and collecting the articles and letters that would be helpful in reconstructing her life. But the personal discomfort caused by remembering her early years of activism proved to be just as important as the lack of primary sources. As she told her daughter, the act of recollection brought "a rush of blood to my head which is very distressing and puts an end to all thought."[10]

Difficult though the task was, a surprising number of black and white abolitionists embraced the challenge of composing and publishing the story of their lives. Most of their work could technically be classified as a form of memoir, for the writers emphasized the ways in which they had witnessed the unfolding of the antislavery movement and participated in its activities. They believed that their lives and stories were meaningful not because of worldly achievements or a rich and ever developing internal life but because of the reform they espoused. Many described a conversionlike "moment of truth" when they embraced the cause but then suggested that their identity was essentially fixed after this crucial experience. They presented themselves as simple, direct, uncomplicated people who pursued reform with a single-minded devotion. Their personal examples of commitment provided a sharp contrast to the self-interest and greed so obvious during the Gilded Age and exemplified the personal character needed by anyone claiming the title of reformer.[11]

This moral vision of the past restated many of the essential elements of abolitionist prewar arguments against slavery and, of course, justified abolitionists' efforts to end it. But as I analyzed each autobiography, it became clear that each narrative was also responding to the events and the changing cultural perspectives of the postwar period. While writers may not have carried their accounts up to the present, the ways in which they told their stories and the themes they chose were colored by what they saw going on around them. Especially as time passed, events made many writers realize that their work was incomplete. While still insisting that emancipation represented a central event in the nation's past, they now saw it as only a milestone in the ongoing struggle to ensure black equality. If slavery had corrupted the nation's conscience, prejudice, its stepchild, continued to blight national life. Some abolitionists had always emphasized the need to eliminate prejudice, but for most it had been a secondary goal. Now it assumed its fundamental importance as the means to bring about racial justice.[12]

As these perspectives became less and less popular, abolitionists felt increasingly anxious to acquaint the younger generation with the nature of the reform that had consumed so many years. They rejected the notion that it was futile to try to speed up the slow process of social change and insisted that feeling and emotion, not cold reason, drove a reform commitment. They urged young people to embrace the important work still unfinished.[13]

While autobiographies written and published by abolitionists are the most obvious example of efforts to "fix" a mutable past and to pass on the spirit of reform, others reformers were also intermittently engaged in this work when they came together after the war. Abolitionists had always appreciated the value of collective gatherings, whether they were political conventions, antislavery meetings, or fairs. In the late 1860s and early 1870s, as the major antislavery societies began to consider the question of dissolution, members used this familiar forum to begin the collective effort to define abolitionism's place in history. Sharp disagreements over basic abolitionist goals, which had not seemed so important in the heat of the battle to destroy slavery, made the victorious interpretation of the movement offered by some very unstable. Almost as soon as the societies stopped functioning, different groups of abolitionists began to hold reunions and commemorative assemblies. Many ordinary people seized the opportunity to take part in shaping memory by offering their own recollections of the past. Their recollections solidified both individual and group identities. But the construction of a "community of memories" was not the only focus of the reunions. Participants also registered their dismay at contemporary events, North and South, and called for renewed activism in response to them.[14]

Several of these reunions published their proceedings in an effort to influence those who had not attended the event. Like the authors of antislavery recollections, "veteran" abolitionists realized the need to enter the printed debate over the past that had such powerful implications for the present.

The circulation of reunion reminiscences was probably limited, but formal abolitionist autobiographies faced obstacles in reaching the readership for which their authors hoped. Despite the popularity of memoirs and autobiographies, the construction of the past embedded in abolitionist recollections struck many as irrelevant or tedious. The *New York Times*'s comments about William Lloyd Garrison could easily be applied to his less famous colleagues. "Does he really imagine . . . that outside of small and suspicious circles any real interest attaches to the old forms of the Southern question," they asked? Moreover, abolitionists constructed autobiographies that were increasingly out of step with prevailing views of autobiographical excellence. Prominent publishing houses were not interested in printing or promoting their work, leading some authors to publish and market their own books. Few received critical attention or sold very many copies. But disappointing sales did not prevent others from adding their own stories to the store of narratives that appeared in print. Even as the numbers of abolitionists dwindled and their message seemed more and more out of step with the times, reformers persisted in addressing the public. In one of the very last of these autobiographies, published in 1902, Ednah Dow Cheney, a Boston reformer in her late seventies, insisted on the noble character of abolitionism and lashed out at the South (and by implication the North). Their denial of the truth about the past had had terrible consequences that must be reversed. "It is of the first importance that all legislation sanctioning such [racial] distinctions should be abolished," she wrote, warning that "we cannot have permanent peace and a true republic with a body of millions of people who are not heartily one with us. The process of the entire fusion of different races will be slow and attended by many sufferings and wrongs and cruelties, but the result must be accomplished if the American republic is to be perfected and perpetuated."[15]

In this book, I explore all the autobiographical narratives abolitionists wrote and published from the end of the Civil War to 1900 that I have been able to locate. I have adopted a generous definition of abolitionist to include all those who worked to eliminate slavery. In the decades leading up to the Civil War, abolitionists themselves often drew sharp lines between those who believed in moral suasion and those who supported antislavery political parties. The recollections that appeared in print sometimes reflected prewar divisions and attitudes. But war and emancipation had helped to mute differences, and abolitionist gatherings often noted that veterans representing all facets of the abolitionist movement were in attendance. From the point of view of making history, the most important truth was that all had worked in their own way to end slavery when most of their fellow Americans opposed their efforts.

While an analysis of published narratives forms the heart of this study, I have also investigated the collective events in which more ordinary abolitionists voiced their concerns and shared their memories. These short sections, titled "Ritual Remembrances," are interspersed throughout this book. They illuminate a process of constructing the past that was less formal and structured than the production of a written autobiography.

Although the ways in which abolitionists conceived of their work and the reasons for it naturally drew on familiar abolitionist conceptions and arguments, what they chose to emphasize had much to do with contemporary events and cultural currents. I have, therefore, placed each narrative work within a framework that clarifies the dynamic relationship between autobiography, history, culture, and memory. In particular, I have explored the short stories, articles, humorous poetry, and occasionally illustrations published in literary monthlies. Since the monthlies had thousands of readers, the interpretations of the past and the depiction of black people, southern slave owners, and occasionally abolitionists appearing in these magazines created the context in which abolitionists wrote and the climate in which their work would be read.

Few of the abolitionist autobiographers were masters of style. Indeed, their books, often long and repetitive, are difficult to read today. Their work receives no extended literary analysis here. Nevertheless, because the authors were engaged in the familiar task of moral suasion, as well as recollection, it seems important to consider some of the literary devices they used to engage their readers and to try to assess the general impact of form and style on the audience.

Abolitionist writers were trying to get their work in as many hands at a time when Americans had an increasing array of published materials from which to choose. To determine how well they succeeded in reaching readers, I have explored the publication history and critical reception of their books. This part of the story is incomplete, for often information about publication and sales is nonexistent. Critics, for the most part, ignored abolitionist autobiographies, perhaps considering them too clumsy and artless to be worth a review. But what is clear is that few of the books had the impact for which their authors had hoped.

This study draws several conclusions about the nation's failure to hold onto the abolitionists' vision of the past. In the age of print media, those who had the power to reach large numbers of people, especially through the powerful and influential literary monthly magazines, were far better placed to propagate their ideas than abolitionists who did not have this outlet and whose modest financial means limited their ability to reach a broad audience. Furthermore, unlike those writing for the monthlies, few of the abolitionists had much literary talent. Their narratives not only were clumsy but often raised uncomfortable questions that many readers would probably prefer to avoid.

While accounts of the past by writers with talent and exposure have a much better chance of shaping memory than those that are awkwardly written and not widely distributed, organizations also played a critical role in the struggle over history and memory. Writers who overlooked emancipation as a war goal and ridiculed abolitionists or who romanticized slavery and the Old South had an institutional home in the monthlies. They were paid for their work, given editorial help, and could rely on the magazine to circulate their views aggressively. As Richard Watson Gilder, editor of *Century* (the successor of *Scribner's*), pointed out in 1886, his magazine had both "editorial and business sagacity." He observed, "It is of great use that a northern periodical should be so hospitable to southern writers and Southern opinion."[16]

Having disbanded their antislavery societies and representing only a minority in the Republican Party, abolitionists were forced to reach out to the reading public as individuals. In contrast to British abolitionists, American abolitionists lacked an organizational base that could sustain and promote their point of view, contribute to publication costs, help publicize and circulate their work, or serve as a repository for memory. Occasional reunions allowed collective reminiscences and calls for action, but they were too brief to have a lasting impact. From this perspective, the decision to dissolve antislavery societies was a crucial error, not just because they might serve as watchdogs for former slaves and as political lobby groups, but also because they could support and advocate ideas and memories that promoted civil and political equality. Those ideas and memories were, for the most part, lost, only to be rediscovered many decades later during the civil rights movement.[17]

The Dissolution of the Antislavery Societies

In 1865, only weeks after the Civil War's end, reform, religious, and benevolent organizations held their annual meetings in New York City. Long one of the high points of the benevolent and reform calendar, Anniversary Week, as it was called, had traditionally drawn throngs of outsiders to the city. Conversations and debates with old and new acquaintances, the transaction of society business, and attendance at one or more society meetings provided fellowship, information, direction, and excitement for supporters of benevolent causes. In the aftermath of war, Anniversary Week in 1865 was "celebrated with unusual vigor," although the editor of *Harper's Monthly Magazine*, George W. Curtis, who was reporting on some of the week's events, sensed that the prewar benevolent and reform world that Anniversary Week represented was changing and its importance "declining."[1]

Of all the meetings that took place, Curtis regarded the American Anti-Slavery Society's gathering as the most interesting. For decades, abolitionists had gathered not only for national and local antislavery society meetings but also for antislavery meetings of all kinds, ranging from sewing circles to political and religious conventions and antislavery fairs. There, with others who agreed upon the necessity of ending slavery, abolitionists discussed current events, debated strategy, devised projects, and assessed progress in the cause. These gatherings, repeated often enough to take on a ritualistic quality, had served the vital purpose of sustaining and renewing loyalty to the movement and creating a sense of community among reformers. They had also publicized the antislavery understanding of events and presented a picture of collective commitment to reform. Now that emancipation had become a reality, however, those organizational structures were in danger of collapsing.[2]

Indeed, the discussion over the possibility of dissolution among members of the AAS was one reason why *Harper's* editor had found the proceedings of interest. Abolitionists had failed to come to an agreement. William Lloyd Garrison argued that the society had achieved its goal and that work for the freed people could now become a joint effort between abolitionists and the rest of the country, which was "thoroughly alive to the question."

Wendell Phillips, Frederick Douglass, Samuel J. May, and others disagreed, arguing that the society had "not yet accomplished" its broad goals. Eventually Phillips and Douglass, and their supporters, carried the day when Garrison and his followers withdrew from the Anti-Slavery Society.

The question of dissolution, of course, was an open one as abolitionists who belonged to the major antislavery societies continued to meet to decide their postemancipation future. As part of that process, they evaluated the great changes that had already taken place and reflected upon the part they had played in bringing them about. Speaking to the annual meeting of the AAS in 1869, Wendell Phillips painted a broad canvas. Recent events had taught the world a historical lesson, he suggested, by demonstrating "how a nation shall eradicate its own narrowness." The idea that the United States had lived up to its noblest ideals established emancipation and rights for blacks as critical moments in the nation's history and implied an honored place for abolitionists in historical memory. Despite Phillips's confident assertion about history's lesson, however, the late 1860s and early 1870s posed practical and ideological challenges for abolitionists. Within prominent antislavery societies like the American Anti-Slavery Society, the New England Anti-Slavery Society, and the Pennsylvania Anti-Slavery Society, members considered how to respond to the changing political and racial landscape of the postwar era and debated whether it was time to disband their organizations. Their discussions revealed significant differences about the original goals of the abolitionist movement even among those who had cooperated for decades. These disagreements, often sharp, complicated attempts to decide upon an organizational future and to establish a coherent historical legacy. Although the *New York Times* had proclaimed that "an anti-slavery society has no more business to be stirring now-a-days than a dead man to be walking about his coffin," the end of collective gatherings also had a serious practical result. It robbed abolitionists of an organized base for further reform activities and a forum from which to spread their views.[3]

When the *Philadelphia Press* maintained that abolitionism would live on in the hearts of both whites and blacks and that veneration for abolitionists' accomplishments would prove more permanent than a marble monument, the paper was expressing the common view of the immediate postwar years. But broad political and cultural changes were influencing how the recent past would be remembered. "Whatever the negro has or may have," the *Brooklyn Eagle* snapped in 1870, "there is indeed small thanks to Wendell Phillips and men of his school." The presidential campaign of 1872 highlighted how much the political climate had changed since 1865. One Democratic newspaper claimed that blacks had been happy as slaves, while

Horace Greeley, the Liberal Republican candidate who also was the Democratic nominee, suggested the outsider status of blacks by labeling them the "African race in America." The Liberal Republican platform included reconciliation with the South and a termination of Reconstruction.[4]

Such circumstances encouraged members of existing antislavery societies to reexamine their own founding documents and goals. For more than three decades, abolitionists had agreed on the necessity of immediate emancipation, although they disagreed about the means to bring it about. This radical objective attracted the most public attention, but many abolitionists also harbored the equally radical belief that it was their duty to battle against the racial prejudice that bolstered slavery and promoted the discriminatory treatment of northern free blacks. The (1832) constitution of the New England Anti-Slavery Society highlighted the comprehensive nature of changes in racial relations sought by a core of abolitionists. Pledging itself to improve "the character and condition of the free people of color," the society agreed on the importance of informing and correcting "public opinion in relation to their situation and rights," and obtaining for northern free people "equal civil and political rights and privileges with whites."[5]

With the primary goal achieved but with continuing violence in the South and a struggle over the ratification of the Fifteenth Amendment, abolitionists confronted issues barely considered during thirty years of activism. Many abolitionists had believed that emancipation would occur because the moral sensibilities of the nation would be transformed and racial prejudice weakened. But instead emancipation was the consequence of war and the political action of a victorious North. What then could or should be done about race prejudice? Would white views about the inferiority of blacks disappear as freed people learned to live as free Americans? What, in fact, was the nature of the freedom that emancipation had brought, and what did it entail? Were the rights once sought for northern blacks to be awarded to former slaves? Was the Fifteenth Amendment, which forbade federal and state governments from curtailing suffrage on the basis of race but said nothing about black officeholding or tests that might limit the franchise, a suitable guarantee for black rights? What future role, if any, did antislavery societies have? To such questions there were no simple answers. The different positions abolitionists took would influence their understanding of abolitionism's contemporary purpose and its historical significance.[6]

Running through the discussions carried on in letters, meetings, and reports was a sense that some abolitionists, at least, were eager to end their work. As Mary Grew, secretary of one of the oldest northern antislavery organizations, the Philadelphia Female Anti-Slavery Society (PFAS), founded in 1833, explained, a number of the society's members in 1865 had already "fancied that the close of four years of war would consummate our work and the glorious triumph of freedom in our land." After thirty years of activity, their desire to see the successful conclusion of their efforts was understandable. But as she ruefully explained, "Our ardent hope outran our judgment." As events in the North and South highlighted the limitations of the Thirteenth and Fourteenth Amendments, the Philadelphia women chose a new and tangible goal that would signal when the society had realized its mission: the right of black men to the vote must be "secured . . . by the Federal Constitution, and not left to the poor protection of the laws or Constitutions of restored rebel States." Agreeing with the Philadelphia society, the women sponsoring the 1869 National Anti-Slavery Festival in Boston, a descendant of Boston's famous antebellum fair, saw the passage of the Fifteenth Amendment as "the crowning guaranty and necessary close of our movement." The following February, as the passage of the Fifteenth Amendment became more assured, the Boston women declared that the 1870 fair was "probably the last we shall hold" because "the Anti-Slavery battle, so long and faithfully fought, would at last be won." Rejoicing that they had lived long enough to see "the results" of their labors, the women took the time to pay brief tribute to "the moral grandeur and heroism" of those who had devoted so much to the cause. With the approaching end of organized antislavery, the time for memorializing had arrived.[7]

Yet even those who believed that the passage of the Fifteenth Amendment concluded the antislavery struggle acknowledged that race prejudice and hatred flourished in both the North and the South. These abolitionists, pinning their hope on the persistence of an activist state and the power of law, the latter perhaps a dubious position given their own past defiance of the law, suggested that the constitutional amendment could overcome race hostility. The "positive, irrevocable recognition of . . . [black] equality before the law" and time would "surely" bring "the country to obey it." Mary Grew considered the amendment the most powerful protection for blacks that the government could provide since three-quarters of the state legislatures would have to agree in order to revoke it. For Wendell Phillips, the amendment represented the nation's pledge to protect black suffrage. And, as he had long argued, the ballot made a man the master of all situations. Agreeing with Phillips, another commentator declared that the amendment represented "the most important victory for the Abolitionists . . . yet . . . recorded upon the statute-books of the nation." The vote would deliver the deathblow to the old southern elite because black voters would outnumber white voters.[8]

Given their recognition of the persistence of prejudice, those who supported an 1869 resolution offered at the AAS's annual meeting declaring the Fifteenth Amendment the "capstone" of abolitionism and the fulfillment of its pledge to secure equal political rights, had to square that position with the reality of prejudice. All agreed on the necessity of battling racial intolerance once the antislavery movement had ended. But their words suggested how uneasy they were about the future. Social and civil influences would eventually conquer prejudice, according to one resolution at the AAS meeting, leaving open the question of exactly how and when this transformation might occur. Wendell Phillips acknowledged that prejudice would linger a "long while" but argued that history was moving in the right direction. At the meeting of the Pennsylvania Anti-Slavery Society, Charles Burleigh was more specific, setting the timetable for change as a generation, a period he considered short in the history of the nation. Taking a much longer view, Thomas Higginson bluntly told those attending the annual meeting of the Massachusetts Anti-Slavery Society that it would be centuries before the blacks were "where they should be." As for the freedman, he "must bide his time."[9]

The persistence of virulent prejudice in both the North and the South and the election of Grant, interpreted as the victory of the Republicans' "conservative element," convinced other abolitionists that it was hardly the time to disband organized antislavery. During 1869, a core of abolitionists argued that their mission was incomplete and that much remained for abolitionists to do. As E. D. Hudson, among others, pointed out, the abolition of slavery had been a wartime measure rather than a moral act. Southerners were unrepentant, and an "excrescence of hate and cruel proscription" bubbled up in social, religious, and political matters. Speaking to the Massachusetts Anti-Slavery Society, Methodist minister Gilbert Haven reminded his audience that while slavery was gone, "political" slavery and "social slavery" still remained. In a letter to the *National Anti-Slavery Standard*, Samuel Johnson argued that people who were ready to say that abolitionism had outlived its day were mistaken. An important role for moral agitation remained: "The Abolitionist has that which can illuminate public events to-day as it did yesterday." It was just this moral role that Wendell Phillips himself had played with the Republican Party in 1866 and 1867.[10]

Stephen Foster, a well-known Garrisonian lecturer, and Cora Daniels Tappan, wife of abolitionist Samuel F. Tappan, the cousin of Lewis and Arthur Tappan, offered some of the most spirited defenses of the need to continue organized antislavery at the 1869 annual meeting of the AAS. (Cora Tappan also spoke on the same topic at the annual meeting of the New

England Anti-Slavery Society.) Foster disagreed that the Fifteenth Amendment fulfilled the abolitionists' pledge to slaves. Urging the importance of winning a bigger victory than ending slavery, Foster pointed out that the first need of the freed people was for land. Agreeing with Foster, Tappan supported a proposal offered by Republican congressman George Julian for the creation of a Department of Home Affairs. Black people, she continued, needed not only land but also equipment like plows. Disagreeing with the argument that the ballot had the power to transform black life, she pointed out that voting would not prevent starvation. At the business meeting, Foster tried to force the society to take action. The resolution he offered committed the society to lobby Congress to break up the holdings of the southern "aristocracy" in order to put a homestead within the reach of all. Foster stated that the right to a homestead was one of the "natural right[s]" of all human beings.[11]

Wendell Phillips had once hoped to provide southern blacks with not only the ballot but also land and education. The nomination and election of Grant had convinced him the year before that "at Present, it [land] is not to be hoped for." Now, he and Charles Burleigh proposed amendments that changed Foster's resolution so drastically, by omitting references to land confiscation and landownership as a natural right, that even Foster voted against it, saying that the changes had robbed it of all life. As Mary Grew had tartly pointed out, conveniently forgetting the AAS constitution's third article dealing with race prejudice, the society stood for the abolition of slavery and nothing else.

Foster's action and the support from others like Cora Daniels Tappan, however, brought the issue of land back into the discussion. Adopting a realistic point of view, Thomas Higginson declared that confiscation should have occurred but its moment had passed, while Republican senator William Stewart, true to his free labor ideology, said that former slaves knew how to labor and were therefore capable of getting land on their own. But there was enough anxiety in antislavery societies over the viability of black freedom without land that discussion and resolutions continued into the latter part of 1869 and 1870. Having opposed Foster's reference to the landed aristocracy of the South, Phillips now presented a resolution to the New England Anti-Slavery Society that demanded that Congress "break up the landed monopolies of the South" in order to put a homestead within the "reach" of the humblest. Phillips once again argued that the nation owed former slaves land, and clearly others agreed. At meetings and in the *National Anti-Slavery Standard*, other schemes for providing southern poor whites and blacks homesteads that were less controversial than confiscation were presented, including government loans and installment-plan purchases. Perhaps they were not only expressing their concern but also trying to salve their consciences, for Higginson and the politicians were right that the moment for land confiscation was long past. President Johnson had already returned most confiscated lands to their former owners, and various legislative attempts to provide blacks with land had failed. The Southern Homestead Act, passed in 1866, had offered blacks preferential treatment in acquiring public land, but that special status for black land acquisition ended in 1868. In any case, public lands in the South were poor, and most blacks had no money to buy a homestead. While there was ample political will to furnish railroads with land, the political will to provide blacks with land was absent.[12]

As the process of ratifying the Fifteenth Amendment finally concluded in the winter of 1870, the issue of disbanding the AAS became pressing. The AAS held its last meeting on March 24, 1870, declaring that "white man and black man stand, side by side, as a result of the amendment," agreeing that "the work for which the society had been organized was complete." But since some of the members of the AAS rejected the idea that the Fifteenth Amendment fulfilled the society's mission, the meeting was discordant and heated. At what had been advertised as the final commemorative exercises, Unitarian minister John Sargent stated his position at the very beginning of the public session: "If this were to be the close of the efforts for the progress by those whose labors have hitherto been devoted to the abolition of slavery, it would be the saddest funeral" he had ever witnessed. Yet most of the subsequent speakers at the public session, populated largely by women, were upbeat and jubilant. Lucretia Mott spoke several times. During one speech, she told the audience she had never expected the victory that abolitionists had won and that "they should be cheerful and happy at their success." At another point, she reminded everyone "that the Anti-Slavery Society was the cause of the abolition of slavery."

At the executive meeting, the tone was dramatically different, and abolitionists argued. Although those who favored disbanding the society won the day, their opponents proved prescient. As he had at the public session, Sargent focused immediately on the issue that abolitionists had not finished their work. As evidence, he read the third article of the society's constitution that referred to the elimination of prejudice as one of its goals. Cora Tappan and Stephen Foster gave vigorous support. Tappan was annoyed that the gathering had been advertised as the society's last meeting. It seemed, she remarked correctly, that the society's leaders had already made up their mind to dissolve the society. But, she warned, those who had visited the South, as she had, realized the inadequacies of a law that depended on the military for its enforcement. The "rebels" still had power and land, and the day was perhaps not far distant when they would regain their civil and political rights. What would happen to former slaves then? Dissolving the society would abandon blacks to their own slender resources. Even in the North, she asserted, no one except for the abolitionists really favored the black franchise. She offered a resolution in favor of continuing the society.

Charles Burleigh disagreed, saying that the society had done its work and that it could only act as its constitution allowed. Henry Wright favored dissolution but suggested setting up a human rights association. Foster then took up the argument. Was the society's mission really accomplished? Did not the society have the best machinery to do the work that needed to be done? His resolution declared that the dangers to colored citizens were such that it was "unsafe" for the AAS to adjourn.

He did not convince his opponents. Frederick Douglass said that he was ready to trust black men with the rights the laws had secured for them. When Phillips pointed to the gains of southern blacks, Tappan tartly pointed out that there were two classes of blacks in the South, and those who had made good were free blacks educated in the North. Phillips implied that the organization was on its last legs anyway since many former members of the AAS had already decided the society had done its work and were thus lost to the organization. Aaron Powell, editor of the *National Standard*, recognized the importance of having a group that was more radical than the Republicans but nonetheless supported dissolution. Powell favored establishing a new organization with better machinery, while Phillips expressed his confidence that if a crisis occurred, "a new movement would rally all the old strength of this society." A motion to disband carried. The debate was over.[13]

Those who defined the movement's goals as emancipation, the vote, and the constitutional provision for equal rights before the law had won the day. But they lost the means to lobby and pressure politicians and to draw public attention to racial issues. Those who had argued against dissolution had realized the seriousness of this loss. There was little recognition, however, of another important consequence of their decision. Without an institutional structure in which to formulate, promote, and sustain their own understanding of the history of their movement, abolitionists would have to act as individuals in countering alternative constructions of the past that undermined possibilities of creating a more equitable and inclusive society.

The conclusion of institutional life and the decision on the part of some societies to donate their records to historical societies did, however, generate reflection on the achievements and meaning of antislavery work.

RITUAL REMEMBRANCES I

Those like Wendell Phillips and Mary Grew who had supported dissolution quickly composed uplifting historical narratives that placed abolitionism as the agent of historical change, giving little credit to the impact of outside events, forces, and personalities. They avoided confronting the troubling questions raised by those opposing dissolution and perhaps their own doubts as well. These triumphant narratives would soon seem inadequate as the hopeful expectations of the future proved false.[14]

Mary Grew used the final report of the PFAS, published independently and in the *National Standard*, to provide an interpretation of its antislavery work and, by implication, the role of women in the crusade. Reviewing records of over three decades of "arduous labor," Grew acknowledged "thrilling events" in the past. But her narrative lacked excitement and drama. It depicted members quietly and successfully working to change "the Nation's heart" by providing "truth" and "facts" about slavery. She painted a conventional picture of women as steadfast laborers in God's cause, sustained by their deep sympathy for the slave, never doubtful of success, never self-interested. Consistent with these themes, Grew highlighted the ample rewards of their commitment, never its frustrations. She maintained that her efforts had entailed no "self-sacrificing": "It has brought me so rich a return of spiritual culture and strength . . . I account it one of the great blessings of my life . . . [that] I have been taught to do a work which, otherwise, I might not have been taught." This low-key narrative gave little sense of female radicalism in the abolitionist movement or of the accusations that abolitionist women had moved out of their sphere in embracing immediate emancipation. It set the stage for allowing women to drop out of the story altogether.[15]

If the history of the PFAS were ever formally written, Grew suggested that one of its most interesting chapters would focus on the yearly fundraising fairs. Her discussion highlighted just how vital institutional support had been to a poorly financed, unpopular reform movement. Fairs paid for the "books, tracts, newspapers, and lectures" that revolutionized public opinion and helped to support the Pennsylvania Anti-Slavery Society. They also helped to recruit new workers for the cause and kept the spirit of abolitionism alive by enabling abolitionist visitors "to take counsel together, to recount . . . victories won, to be refreshed by social communion, and to renew . . . pledges of fidelity to the slave." Her overview also hinted at the role that organized events could play in overcoming the discouragement that accompanied over thirty years of a difficult commitment.[16]

Like many abolitionists, Grew wanted Americans to acknowledge slavery's contamination of both church and state. The churches had suffered a moral failure, and politicians passed the Fugitive Slave Law, which became a symbol of the nation's disgrace and marked an "epoch" in the history of the antislavery cause. The law "so carefully and cunningly devised for the purpose of depriving men of liberty" had resulted in terrible scenes as fugitives were chased down and returned to the South. She was confident that these scenes, the apathy of the public, and the failure of the pulpit would be "written in our country's history, and indelibly engraved on the memory of Abolitionists."[17]

The *National Standard* praised Grew's account for its "special historical value" and pointed out that the yearly reports, deposited at the Historical Society of Pennsylvania, constituted one of the most complete and accurate documentary records of the antislavery movement. The last report, in particular, contained "an important lesson for future workers for the well-being of mankind." What that lesson actually was the newspaper did not say, nor did Grew. Perhaps the report suggested the importance of pursuing reform for its own sake rather than for worldly fame. Or perhaps it pointed out the society's reliance on moral influence rather than physical power. For editor Aaron Powell, the history of the antislavery movement as a whole illustrated the truth of the conviction that a reform movement weak in numbers but strong in righteousness could succeed.[18]

The final report also acknowledged the persistence of racial prejudice and the continuing spirit of "Rebellion" in the South. Freed people were praised as moral heroes for their spirit of forbearance and forgiveness. "The history of the world can scarcely furnish its parallel," Grew wrote. But Grew and her fellow society members were ready to move on to new fields of labor, perhaps because they had so narrowly defined the goals of abolitionism. As Grew remarked at the final meeting, "If we put off our armour here to-day, it is but for a moment's breathing-space, to be resumed for other conflicts. However much we may feel to-day, as we close this meeting and disband our Society, that we should like to depart in peace . . . we are willing to remain and work elsewhere." For Grew and others, the new field of labor was the woman suffrage movement.[19]

Writing an even more triumphant account than Grew, Wendell Phillips provided a brief history of the antislavery movement in an editorial for the *National Standard*. Given the disagreement within the AAS over the wisdom of disbanding, his glowing narrative may have been one way of defending dissolution and burying his own doubts about it. His theme was the "wonderful influence" of abolitionism. "Hardly anything in history surpasses it," he claimed. While decades of antislavery activity had provided some evidence of its influence in the break up of parties and sects, there had never been a good way to measure its power. The year 1861, however, revealed "the loyal readiness of the masses." Prepared by the abolitionists, the northern public was ready to be reeducated by war, a truth that not even Abraham Lincoln had realized at first. He hardly dared to risk emancipation, according to Phillips, but "he might have relied more on the Anti-Slavery conscience of the people." New proof of abolitionists' power and influence, he went on, was furnished by the law (perhaps he was referring to one of the amendments) that finally swept away the "odious distinction" of race.

Phillips devoted a good part of his editorial to defending the decision to continue the AAS in the crucial years after the war. The people were weary after years of conflict; racial prejudice began to reappear. In this perilous environment, abolitionists once again played a critical role. They bolstered up the radicals and pressured Republicans to provide black men the franchise, a goal that would not have been accomplished without abolitionists' efforts. And while the long crusade was not over, since former slaves still needed counsel, education, and land, abolitionists could rejoice in their gains. Political security and industrial protection were on the side of black men, and the vote provided a mighty protection for the future.[20]

While these antislavery narratives gave abolitionists the lion's share of the credit for ending slavery, they were also insisting upon the vital and historic significance of the transformation that had occurred. Emancipation and postwar amendments were a climax in the nation's history, a proud moment that should never be forgotten. This history provided evidence that the North, in the end, had detested slavery and accepted equality. As *Harper's Weekly* observed in 1872, agreeing with the implications of the abolitionist analysis, northerners "will not forget; they will diligently remember."[21]

Few, it seems, wanted to elaborate the counternarrative embedded in the debate over disbanding antislavery societies: that after decades of agitation, the abolitionists had only achieved some of their goals. Former slaves had some legal rights but were in a position of extreme vulnerability. While abolitionists acknowledged the persistence of prejudice, which they had always argued was the basis for slavery and discrimination and emphasized the importance of continuing to battle it, they provided no firm plans to eradicate it. They hoped for the best. In addition, by taking a narrow view of their mission and dissolving their societies, they eliminated a crucial base for assisting freed people. Always a minority, abolitionists had been able to survive in a hostile environment because of their organizational apparatus. Lacking what Stephen Foster had called "machinery," they would find it difficult to respond if and when they realized the extent to which the rights of black Americans were threatened. A national reform league had been formed by some abolitionists after the dissolution of antislavery societies, but it was a voluntary organization that made "no attempt" at elaborate structure. It was an inadequate replacement for the AAS. Before long, it was apparent that the end of organized antislavery did make a difference. The *National Standard*, once supported by abolitionist societies and a voice for racial justice, could not keep afloat as a weekly and, within only a few years, merged with a temperance journal.[22]

Although abolitionists did not develop such a counternarrative, other challenges to the positive historical interpretations soon appeared. The *Brooklyn Eagle*, a Democratic paper, mocked the claim that abolitionists had been responsible for ending slavery. "It would be interesting," the paper commented, "if somebody clever at figures would estimate how much agitators of the Wendell Phillips school have contributed to the accomplishment of the work on which the expiring Society felicitates itself. What is the precise amount in which the negro is indebted to P. & Co. for his emancipation?" The paper gave its own answer, observing that the black man owed organized antislavery only "small thanks." The claim that the antislavery movement had continued to do important work after emancipation was "pigheadedness." Slavery was over, and only "obstinate" people could maintain otherwise. As for the idea that abolitionists had been martyrs, "the persecutions of the New York society were little more than ill-natured remarks . . . at the meetings."[23]

When another major abolition organization, the Pennsylvania Anti-Slavery Society, disbanded that same year, the *Brooklyn Eagle* acknowledged that the society had actually experienced danger and inconvenience during its years of operation. But, the paper said, "it set up far less of a martyr's outcry" than the AAS. Nonetheless, the paper reported, there was plenty of reminiscing about the trials of an earlier day as the Pennsylvania group met for the last time.[24]

The final meeting, in 1869 anticipated as "a grand jollification," took place in June 1870. Reported on only briefly in the *National Standard*, now appearing monthly rather than weekly, the meeting does appear to have been a "jollification." There was much congratulation and some regret, stemming apparently from "the dissolution of cherished memories and associations" rather than dismay over any unfinished work. In a celebratory show and tell, John Charles Frémont's premature emancipation proclamation was displayed, and William Still, a black abolitionist, showed the wooden box in which a fugitive slave had once escaped. While some referred to the work that lay ahead, the substance of the meeting focused on the past. Many rose to give personal recollections of their participation in antislavery work or important events in the history of abolitionism that were "suggestive of the table of contents of an important unwritten history." Accounts of harrowing experiences revived the memory of the "tragic period" and highlighted "the great change that has been wrought with such marvelous quickness." With a sense of pride at the achievement, the members agreed that the Society's "mission [was] fulfilled, the Society has passed into history."[25]

When the Pennsylvania Anti-Slavery Society held its last meeting, the *Philadelphia Press* had remarked that the organization no longer had any "existence save in memory — the complacent memory of its friends and the grateful memory of the slaves." The dissolution of most of the remaining antislavery societies may have suggested complacency or perhaps confidence in what was past and faith in how abolitionism would be remembered. But a more careful examination of antislavery societies' rites of passage and the conflicts that accompanied them reveal the underlying doubts and concerns. The cheerful narrative that depicted the triumph of abolitionism was one that some abolitionists themselves were already rejecting by the late 1860s and early 1870s. It would not easily survive the events of the following decades. As abolitionists began to write and publish their life stories, they would offer a more measured assessment of the achievements of the reform they had embraced and recognize the necessity of keeping the reform spirit alive to finish their work.[26]

The First Recollections

When *Harper's* editor George W. Curtis described the 1865 debate within the American Anti-Slavery Society over the question of disbandment, he saw the success of those wishing to continue the Society as "a victory of sentiment" by a group that was out of touch with reality. What Wendell Phillips, Frederick Douglass, Samuel J. May, and the new Executive Board of the AAS "seemed to forget," Curtis affirmed, was "that the whole country is now an anti-slavery society."[1]

The easy confidence that abolitionists had achieved their goals and that the northern public had embraced them persisted for a few years, at least in the pages of northern monthly magazines, if not in the hearts and minds of all abolitionists. An article originally published in *Harper's Weekly* and reprinted in the *Living Age* in 1867 discussed how the apparent transformation of public opinion had affected the reputation of abolitionists. The recent celebration of Garrison in London prompted the author to observe, "It is not often that we see the general verdict upon a man so wholly reversed in his lifetime." Once regarded as a fanatic, Garrison now was seen as embodying "moral inspiration" and "heroic persistence," with an understanding of slavery "in the main entirely correct." And while no one man could be exclusively responsible for the great events of history, Garrison's "moral force" had inspired the emancipation of the South's slaves. That same year, *Harper's Magazine* made a similar point. At one time, the northern public had rejected abolitionism as a crazy fringe movement. Now abolitionism's significance was so obvious that some "eleventh-hour" converts to the antislavery cause were unwilling "to allow the Anti-slavery men and women of that time the sole honor of the work" and sought some of the credit for emancipation for themselves. Agreeing with the *Living Age*'s assessment of abolitionists' influence, the writer thought that it was obvious that "the pioneers" could not have achieved their goals alone. But their role in transforming northern public opinion had been crucial to realizing emancipation.[2]

The suggestion that Garrison's analysis of slavery was justified left little room for sympathy for prewar southerners, who defended their peculiar institution and way of life. Slavery had been a "sectional and revolting inhumanity," a fact that now seemed established in the historical record.[3]

The varied rituals of honoring the war dead that were emerging prompted further reflections on the past. When editor George Curtis discussed the erection of monuments to fallen Union soldiers, he suggested that some might question the practice precisely because it kept disturbing memories of a terrible conflict alive. But he insisted that northern soldiers had given their lives for a "holy cause" and deserved to be commemorated. Southerners, whose cause had been neither holy nor just, would also recall the war but would not be able to honor their dead in the same way. "The descendants of the soldiers of 'the lost cause,' however they may extol the honesty with which the political view was held, and the bravery with which the cause was defended," Curtis wrote, "will never be proud that ancestors of theirs fought heroically to perpetuate human slavery." The day would come when northerners and southerners would share common recollections of the war's meaning and agree over the righteousness of ending slavery.[4]

Yet, despite the often-stated assurances in the pages of northern monthly journals that, as one put it, "neither you, indeed, nor any other sensible man will expect that we shall forget the causes or the circumstances of the struggle," not long after the war commentators were realizing that the passage of time could alter the relationship between the past and the present. In two articles written for *Putnam's Magazine* in 1868, Van Buren Denslow praised the tremendous achievements of war and reconstruction. Emancipation and black suffrage both represented victories for freedom. But these victories were fragile and unstable. As the war became a "historic memory" rather than "an ever-present crisis," the reform momentum fueling the Republicans during the war was losing energy. Northern Democrats and Republicans alike harbored "repugnance" for "negro equality." Northern public opinion was "unsettled" on the question of universal suffrage. Rather than viewing the country as one big antislavery society, Denslow pointed out that the passage of time was playing its part in reducing any commitment to reform goals.[5]

Denslow's articles implied the important relationship between memory and political reality. Memory was both fragile and powerful. People might forget or remember only part of what had happened; they might even fabricate the past. Whatever version or versions of the past survived played a potent role in shaping people's thoughts and actions. The ways in which slavery, abolitionism, emancipation, and the causes and purposes of the recent war were recalled all had important consequences for politics, race re-

THE FIRST RECOLLECTIONS

lations, and regional refashioning. On a personal level, they also colored the ways in which those who had participated in ending slavery would make meaning of their lives.

Samuel J. May, whose book *Some Personal Recollections of Our Antislavery Conflict* appeared in 1869, was one of the first abolitionists in the postwar period to realize the vital importance of establishing an antislavery under-standing of the past. The urgent tone of his narrative sharply contrasted with the upbeat remarks made as antislavery societies disbanded. Indeed, learning that the Philadelphia Female Anti-Slavery Society was holding its last meeting, May had written to remind the women of the dire condition of southern blacks. "You must allow me to express earnestly the hope that you will renew your organization under another name," he wrote, "and labor on for the education and elevation of the Freedmen." His letter had come too late to be read at the final gathering, although it is doubtful that it would have changed anyone's mind.[6]

With memories of war and emancipation still fresh, May did not feel it necessary to detail the South's role in instigating the conflict or the funda-mental part that slavery had played in bringing it about. Nor did he repeat the traditional abolitionist condemnation of slavery as a sin and slavehold-ers as sinners. Rather, his memoirs highlighted the ways in which slavery had corrupted the North, a point that abolitionists had been making for decades but one that was easily forgotten as northerners congratulated themselves for their victory over the South. May clearly understood the dangers of forgetting northern moral complicity in slavery. On the one hand, the refusal to accept northern responsibility for the perpetuation of slavery distorted the historical record and the role abolitionists had played in ending it. Because northerners supported slavery, abolitionists had faced social ostracism, persecution, and even death. Their courage and heroism in the face of northern hostility deserved to be remembered. On the other hand, the fact that northerners had had so little concern for black slaves raised questions about their long-term commitment to African American freed people. Indeed, May did not believe that the struggle for liberty and freedom for blacks had ended and hoped that his book would inspire read-ers to continue the work that he and others had begun.

May's account focused on Garrisonians who had used persuasion as the main tool for furthering their cause. Because he only briefly discussed abo-litionists who had disagreed with Garrison's approach, his narrative em-phasized abolitionism as a unified movement. His desire to smooth over old conflicts allowed him to speak for all who wished to end slavery and to appeal to all readers who regarded themselves as abolitionists. In this way, he hoped to enlist their support in the ongoing effort to secure rights and security for black Americans.[7]

May, a Unitarian minister, had spent most of his life as a working abolitionist. He had embraced immediate emancipation in the early 1830s and was one of the original members of the AAS. Despite pastoral responsibilities to churches in Connecticut, Massachusetts, and New York, he was active in antislavery causes until the Civil War. He was a prominent lecturer on the antislavery circuit for years and was associated with some significant antislavery events. While heading a congregation in Brooklyn, Connecticut, May supported Prudence Crandall's efforts to open a biracial school for girls in nearby Canterbury. He hosted the Grimké sisters for over a week during their controversial Massachusetts speaking tour, and in Syracuse, New York, he was involved in the Underground Railroad and assisted in at least one slave rescue.[8]

May only gradually decided to publish a book of reminiscences. A few years after the war, the editor of the Boston-based Unitarian newspaper the *Christian Register* had asked May, then in his seventies, to contribute some articles about abolitionism to his paper. May agreed, and his journal for 1867, 1868, and part of 1869 is filled with references to more than forty pieces he wrote for the *Christian Register*, as well as the *Liberal Christian*. His diary reveals an unrelenting pace, as one article followed another. Refusing to take the easy route of relying on his own memory, May read and reread biographies and abolitionist speeches and articles, perused antislavery newspapers, and consulted records of the AAS and the seven scrapbooks that he had put together himself. The diary also points to the process of reflection and "musing" that preceded composition and shows that he occasionally relied on dictation and copyists to get his work done.[9]

At the same time that he was devoting days to research and writing, May was also following politics and the fortunes of southern freed people, two subjects that were intimately connected. He greeted the Republican victory of 1868 with relief, calling the results "glorious." While his attendance at the great torchlight parade celebrating Grant's victory occupied only a few minutes, his attention to the needs of former slaves was more time-consuming. As the secretary of the local Freedman's Association, he took on a variety of obligations. Not only did he help write an appeal for funds but also folded and distributed copies. He made arrangements for a teacher to go to Maryland and looked over secondhand books for southern scholars and sent his own money and barrels of clothes to the South. He submitted at least one letter to the *Anti-Slavery Standard* asking readers to support education for African Americans. When people came to Syracuse who had

THE FIRST RECOLLECTIONS

visited or worked in the South, May was eager to speak to them and find out what conditions there were really like.[10]

May's diary also shows his interest in crossing racial boundaries in his own community. He employed a black man to take dictation and wrote several letters for an illiterate former slave and received money for her from her "friends" in Virginia. Sojourner Truth, whom May regarded as "a wonderful women," was a guest in his house and sat at his table.[11]

In the preface to his book, May explained that he had never expected that his articles would ever "be put to any further use" after they appeared in the newspapers. But "so many persons" urged him to gather them into a book that he eventually complied. Such a claim was hardly unusual as a rationale for writing and publishing a personal narrative. While many people may have encouraged May to reach out to a larger audience, the only surviving evidence of encouragement is an 1867 letter from a reader that May tucked into the back pocket of his 1868 diary. The letter stated that the recollections "somehow [ought] to have a greater reaching in Book form or other wise."[12]

In his book, May discussed other responses to his articles. Some, though sympathetic to abolitionism, faulted the series, accusing May "of ingratitude and injustice." A disapproving letter from "Justice," which May reprinted in his book's appendix and saved in the back of his 1868 diary, suggests that a number of readers expected May to provide a more general and more expansive account of abolitionism and their favorite leaders. "Justice" chided May for neglecting Nathaniel Rogers, the editor of the New Hampshire abolitionist newspaper the *Herald of Freedom*, and for including abolitionists who were "quite obscure, and of very little account in this movement."[13]

Other readers, however, may not have shared "Justice's" dismay and perhaps were even pleased with May's tribute to the obscure and those of "little account." Still, May indirectly responded to Justice's criticism in his preface when he told his readers that his recollections were limited to events and people in his own "sphere of operation and observation," Massachusetts, Connecticut, and central New York.[14]

Despite the encouragement, May did not commit himself to a book project and begin to search for a publisher until March 1869. The ways in which his diary interwove references to writing his recollections for the newspapers with descriptions of working for freed people suggest that May's efforts to reach a wider audience were related to his concern for the future of black people.[15]

May first sent twenty-one of his recollections to the established New York firm of Harper & Brothers to be considered for publication. Apparently they were not interested, but, by this time, May was determined to see his work in book form. In April he wrote to the newly formed partnership of Fields & Osgood & Company with his book proposal. The Boston firm, previously known as Ticknor & Fields, enjoyed a distinguished reputation, having published not only work by some of the country's most prestigious writers but also the high-brow *North American Review* and the *Atlantic Monthly*, a journal sympathetic to abolitionist concerns. Even before he heard back from the firm, he began to prepare for republishing by cutting up articles from the *Christian Register* and pasting them onto letter paper.[16]

In May, Fields & Osgood deemed May's articles "greatly" interesting and agreed to publish the book. They told May they planned to sell his book for $1.50 and offered him 10 percent royalties on all volumes sold after the initial 1,000. Eager to get going on the project, they suggested that May send the book to their printer at once. May must have been delighted, not only because of the firm's reputation, but also because it was a good fit for his work. Ticknor & Fields had handled Lydia Maria Child's book written for freed slaves, and the same year that Fields & Osgood brought out May's book, it also issued Harriet Beecher Stowe's *Oldtown Folks* and a volume of poems by John Greenleaf Whittier.[17]

Given the proclaimed general goodwill toward abolitionism, it is not surprising that this prestigious firm was interested in May's recollections. May was a prominent man, and biographies and personal narratives were popular with nineteenth-century readers. Most autobiographies published between 1800 and 1870 charted the writer's spiritual life or his or her adventures or sufferings. May's book would offer insights into all three of these areas of his life.[18]

May approached the preparation of his material for publication with the same energy and commitment that he had exhibited in his newspaper pieces. Indeed, he spent weeks living in Cambridge so that he could work with the press and printer effectively. He cut, pasted, and arranged material from the newspapers, did research, and spent days writing new sections and rewriting parts of those that had appeared in the newspapers. As he handed over pieces of the manuscript to the printer, he was often juggling composing and proofreading. He also was sharing his work with friends. At his request, at least one abolitionist acquaintance examined part of the manuscript for him, and May read long sections aloud to others. The Alcotts in Concord must have provided good feedback during his July visit with them, for May commented on both the delightful conversation and the forty pages that he had shared with them. From Garrison, after another lengthy reading, he received "several useful hints."[19]

As May sought reactions from a friendly audience, he may also have been considering what the reading public and reviewers might expect from the kind of first-person narrative he was completing. As a reader of autobiographies and biographical sketches, as well as periodicals like the *Atlantic Monthly* and the *Nation*, May was surely familiar with critics' perspectives on the genre. In turn, critical assumptions about what made a good autobiography or memoir likely shaped the expectations readers might bring to his book and how they might respond to it.[20]

Critics agreed that the task of writing a personal narrative was not to be undertaken lightly. Anyone who embarked on a memoir or autobiography had to believe his or her life was important enough to write about. But readers might perceive the life story as an exercise in personal vanity. To write about oneself and "to avoid the appearance of egotism" was thus "perhaps one of the most difficult of literary problems." If writers treated their lives as too important, talked about themselves too much, or included too much detail about their affairs (say, 100 pages rather than 10), they gave the impression of being unpleasantly egotistical. Egotism could not be entirely avoided, of course, but critics, at least, looked for a touch of modesty. Too much attention on the self suggested character flaws and bored the reader.[21]

Some critics suggested that few people knew themselves well enough to write their own stories. Thus most first-person accounts were better when they focused more attention on other people than on the author. Still, readers wanted to get a sense of the full flavor of the writer, the "piquancy" that was lost in a biography, a "second hand" form. The issue was one of balance and appropriateness. One reviewer was scandalized when a writer chose to include in his book extracts from his private journal. "Is it not something new for a man to put in print these entries of emotional and inner experience which he is supposed to make solely for his own edification?" he asked. Apparently these personal experiences had little to say to the reader, at least while the author was still alive. While publishing private journal excerpts after death might be appropriate and instructive, offering them to the public during the author's lifetime was not. The mere thought that a journal entry might be read by other people compromised truthfulness and smacked of immodesty. "What," the reviewer queried, "shall be said of him who, while alive, parades *his* confessions before the whole world?"[22]

Reviewers agreed that autobiographies were valuable, although their understandings about what made them so differed. The traditional reason for reading biographies or first-person narratives was that they were instructive. The writers had something "to tell . . . well worth hearing," and readers could learn from perusing their texts. Thus one autobiography was praised as a "noble" book because it was "full of wholesome incentive and suggestions to young men." Horace Greeley's *Recollections of a Busy Life* struck several critics as a model autobiography. Greeley, the influential Republican editor of the *New York Tribune*, was distinguished, and according to one critic, the "lives of distinguished men have always been considered as profitable studies . . . especially when written by themselves." Fortunately, "all really great men" cultivated self-knowledge, thus avoiding one of the autobiographer's most serious pitfalls. In Greeley's case, he depicted both his personal flaws (that a biographer might well overlook) and his personal strengths. The book offered a rare "moral tonic," and was especially "suitable" for family reading. Another reviewer, also praising the book, found its utility in the story of Greeley's rise from poverty to distinction. Acknowledging the centrality of this familiar theme, the reviewer found the book "a perpetual romance" with the power to delight and touch all.

The emphasis on value and instruction did not necessarily mesh with the importance critics gave to readers' enjoyment. "Some of the pleasantest reading in the world is to be found in books which authors have written about themselves," one reviewer suggested, warning that personal narratives could also be among the dullest. Pleasant reading, in this reviewer's opinion, did not depend on the distinction of the subject or the subject's life trajectory. Rather, personal character was the key. An agreeable person was likely to write an entertaining book, while a famous person might not. Even the distinguished poet Wordsworth, "from what we know of his character and mental habits," would have written a "pompous and uninteresting" account of his life, this reviewer contended. The emphasis on an agreeable or entertaining character reveals how the culture was moving away from the prewar evangelical emphasis on virtue as the basis of character and the reason for the autobiography.[23]

Such discussions suggested that personal narratives dealing with both the life of the writer and the times in which he or she lived might be preferable to ones that focused only the writer's life. As one reviewer warned, the autobiographer should not assume "a curiosity which does not exist" about "matters . . . entirely private." But memoirists were also faced with the challenge of finding the appropriate balance in writing about his individual life and about the times in which he lived. General Winfield Scott's 1865 autobiography, the reviewer in the *North American Review* pointed out, should have been successful since the general had lived through some of the most important years in the nation's history, had been an actor in many significant events, and had known many famous people. He "must surely have something to tell us well worth hearing," the reviewer wrote, "but [alas] the book is one of the washiest we have ever read." Scott not only included every "trifle" about himself but also provided "the usual moral mush" about slavery.[24]

Critics applauded the narrative that provided glimpses of those the author encountered. In the view of one critic, "The value of memoirs depends very much upon the amount of memory which the writer devotes to other people." While sketches of "eminent men," for example, justified the autobiography because it helped readers "understand the time," there were perils lurking in the ways in which an author treated the people who moved through his or her life. Greeley's recollections hit just the right note. Although he clearly conveyed his likes and dislikes, his treatment of friends and enemies was "temperate." Harriet Martineau, in contrast, was chided for her failure to be just and generous to those she discussed in her autobiography. A personal narrative, apparently, was no place to revive old enmities and animosities, although writers often succumbed to the temptation to do so. Mused one critic, "Great lessons of charity, and mutual respect, and mutual forbearance, how slow and hard to be learned!"[25]

Samuel J. May's finished manuscript reflects the impact of contemporary views of autobiography. He chose the favored approach of life and times. It fit his understanding of how his own life had intersected with the lives of towering historic figures and great events. By shifting the focus away from himself, he was able to sidestep the problem of appearing too self-centered. He certainly avoided the problem of overemphasizing details of his personal life. References to his marriage, family life, and children were notably absent. Also missing was any discussion of his pastoral work, the churches he served, or his theological views. The absence of introspective passages protected his privacy and avoided the charge of unseemly disclosure.[26]

May subscribed to the notion that a first-person narrative had a serious purpose that went beyond amusement. The value of his life did not lie in a personal rise to prominence, which was the lesson of Greeley's autobiography. Rather, the significance of his life lay in May's steady and faithful commitment to a difficult but sacred cause. Thus, despite a career spent in the church, the turning point in the life and narrative was not a religious conversion but May's embrace of abolitionism. The religious imagery he used to describe his experience made his transformation from man to reformer a sacred event. After spending an evening talking to Garrison for the first time, May recalled that his "soul was baptized in his spirit." The moment represented "a great epoch in my own life. The impression which [Garrison's words] . . . made upon my soul has never been effaced; indeed, they moulded it anew. They gave a new direction to my thoughts, a new purpose to my ministry. I had become a convert to the doctrine of 'immediate, unconditional emancipation.'" Other significant moments were also connected to antislavery. His participation in the foundation of the AAS was one such moment. "If I ever boast of anything," he stated, "it is this: that I was a member of the Convention that instituted the American Anti-Slavery Society."[27]

A close reading of May's narrative reveals that he not only was present at significant moments in abolitionist history but often played an active role in events. Indeed, the credibility of his account stems from the fact that he had been a participant and witnessed firsthand what he related. In keeping with the avoidance of "ostentatious display," however, May frequently minimized his own importance. When May told the unhappy story of Prudence Crandall's attempt to open a biracial school, he suggested his involvement was only a matter of his geographical proximity and apologized "that, in the following account of it, allusions to myself and my acts must so often appear." He had little need to apologize. Rather than portraying himself as an energetic participant in the Crandall affair, May claimed that he had been overwhelmed by responsibilities beyond "the measure of my ability" and uncertain about the right course of action.[28]

May's narrative reflected his awareness of critical norms for autobiography, but other concerns were more important to him than simply fulfilling literary expectations. The causes for which he had spent his life were by no means resolved, and his former co-workers were at odds with one another. The division among abolitionists over the future of the AAS persisted and had become more serious. Disagreement over whether abolitionists should support the Fourteenth Amendment because it defined citizens as males further separated the abolitionists. May, along with Phillips and Douglass, believed that the AAS had important work left to do. He also favored giving both women and African Americans the vote, but the racist language that Elizabeth Cady Stanton and others were using dismayed him. While the Republicans had carried the 1868 election, events in the South remained unsettled and troubling. Blacks desperately needed help, but the Freedmen's Bureau was only a temporary organization. Furthermore, May did not share the easy confidence expressed in monthly periodicals that northerners' view of blacks had changed in any significant way. Discussions over the Fifteenth Amendment revealed that some regarded equal citizenship for freed men as entailing only the right to vote, while others believed equal citizenship included the right to hold office and to be free of discriminatory practices like segregation in public transportation. Such concerns lay in the

THE FIRST RECOLLECTIONS

background as May put together the story of his life and his history of the abolitionist movement.[29]

The title of May's work, *Some Recollections of Our Antislavery Conflict*, suggested his themes and purpose, the audience he expected, and the readers he hoped to influence. "Some recollections" made clear that this account formed part of a much larger story. By characterizing the period as one of conflict, May implicitly linked the antislavery struggle to the recent war. His description of the conflict as "ours," on the one hand, encouraged general readers to identify with the author and the struggle and, on the other, signaled to the abolitionist reader that the book contained some specific lessons to ponder.[30]

The title also hinted at the way in which May's narrative was organized. Although May had reworked his material, the book's origin as a series of newspaper articles was evident in its episodic and nonlinear format. "I have not been guided in my narrative by the order of time so much as by the relation of events and actors to one another," May informed his readers. Despite this structure, May provided much information about the movement between the 1830s and 1861. He organized his material in two sections. The first focused on the rise of abolitionism and the second on the antislavery conflict.[31]

In the preface and often thereafter, May reminded readers that his history provided only a "fragmentary" record that was intended to "whet" their appetite for a fuller and more elaborate treatment than his episodic memoir. He was well aware of the importance of a comprehensive history of the movement but considered the task so daunting that he thought that even Garrison might not be able to carry it off. The story, like the cause itself, was a cosmic one. Yet if it were impossible to capture the full dimensions of abolitionism, May still seems to have remained confident that a historian would eventually come forward to provide the nation with the "bright" and gloomy pages "of those times."[32]

Despite what May called the "sketchy" nature of his account, he staked out a clear interpretation of the movement, its leaders, its goals, its achievements, and its trials. Misinformation and ignorance were already threatening what May considered the historical record, and the passage of time was making it difficult to recover the past. Even though most of the abolitionists were still alive, May, writing about events that took place thirty years earlier, realized it was "not easy even for us to recall, and it is impossible to give those who were not Abolitionists then, a clear idea of the state of the community at the time." Furthermore, even though public opinion seemed to have shifted from antagonism to admiration of abolitionists, May knew that behind any present goodwill lay years of hostility and accusations that abolitionists were fanatics and incendiaries.[33]

May's primary assertion was that abolitionism was "the most glorious movement ever made in humanity's behalf" and the culmination of American history. This interpretation necessitated reworking the popular narrative of the nation's early history to highlight its flaws. As did abolitionist orators of the prewar period, he contrasted the promises of sacred documents like the "glorious Declaration" to the more sordid reality. Gratitude toward "the fathers of our Revolution" should not blind Americans to "the shameful facts" that could "never be effaced from the record: — the *fact* that . . . the American revolutionists did not intend the deliverance of *all* men from oppression." Far from securing the blessings of liberty for all men, the founding fathers had left in place a system that they knew was "the worst form of oppression," slavery.[34]

What the founding fathers failed to do, May asserted, the abolitionists had embraced. Seizing upon the founding fathers' sweeping statements, they sought to make them true. Squarely in the center of the nation's historical narrative, abolitionists insisted on immediate emancipation as the means of realizing "*perfect, impartial liberty.*" This second American revolution, launched by abolitionists, completed "the great work which the American revolutionists commenced." The abolitionists thus became the nation's truest patriots and perhaps its truest fathers. Their names and achievements, May implied, should be as important a part of the nation's history as George Washington's and Thomas Jefferson's.[35]

Milestones of abolitionist history were transformed into milestones of national and human history. The Declaration of Sentiments, written in 1833 at the AAS's founding, was "our Magna Charta," May declared. It would "live [as] a perpetual, impressive protest against every form of oppression, until it shall have given place to that brotherly kindness, which all the children of the common Father owe one another." In contrast to the "selfish" founding fathers, the abolitionists who created the national antislavery society "had come together for a purpose higher and better than that of any religious sect or political party." Never had there been "men so ready, so anxious to rid themselves of whatsoever was narrow, selfish, or merely denominational." Abolitionist opposition to the annexation of Texas as "a violation of the Constitution of our Union" a few years later, he insisted, was not a historical footnote but in the mainstream of the nation's history. Garrison's speech on the subject deserved to be "preserved to the latest posterity."[36]

While acknowledging that abolitionism had been the cause of a minority, May emphasized its national credentials and inclusive nature. Claiming that abolitionism's "field" of labor had not been a narrow regional concern but rather "coextensive with our vast country," he argued that it had drawn from a cross-section of the northern public, men and women, whites and blacks, members of every social class, religion, and political party. Bound together by the conviction that slavery was wrong, these men and women labored to arouse the "public conscience that slavery could not be tolerated in the land." So powerfully did abolitionism appeal to ordinary people that most would never be known by name, because their deeds and words never passed beyond their "immediate circle." Yet their "undaunted moral courage and persistent fidelity" made a vital contribution to abolitionism's success. These nameless and faceless reformers, rather than the soldiers of the recent war, had possessed the "indomitable will and heroic self-sacrifice" that decided the "fate of many a battle."[37]

Although May acknowledged the involvement of ordinary and obscure people in antislavery, like most other Americans, he saw great men as the moving forces of history. His recollections highlighted the movement's leaders, whom he knew well and with whom he had worked for decades. His great men were not "eminent" in the usual sense, for most important people would not "touch [abolitionism] with one of their fingers." But they were able and talented, and May insisted many of them could have risen to public prominence had they chosen. Their decision to reject the usual path to honors and success carried an important message about the nature of true greatness.[38]

While May provided many vignettes of prominent men and women, he considered Garrison the towering figure in the history of abolitionism, the nation, and the world, worthy of honor "through all coming time." On a universal level, May presented Garrison as an example of the rare human being who broke through the crust of tradition to condemn a long-accepted wrong. As the medium through which God's mercy flowed, Garrison upheld the "living fountain of the *free spirit*" of humanity. On the level of national history, May gave Garrison credit for being the leader of reform "from the beginning" and for persuading the majority of his fellow citizens to "take a new direction." "Holy purpose" and "fiery indignation" fueled his condemnation of slavery and its supporters. As a human being, he was determined and resolute; his demeanor, despite the "terrible severity" of his attacks, was calm and modest. Rejecting as a gross abuse the accusation that Garrison was an infidel who intended to undermine religion, May declared him to be a "profoundly religious man, one of the most so I have ever known." In short, Garrison was "among the greatest benefactors of our nation and of our race."[39]

While not of the stature of Garrison, the other male leaders in May's account were also noble and heroic, providing vivid examples of the convictions and behavior that had eventually brought about emancipation. May was interested in making readers understand, however, that this heroism had great costs. Thus he likened the leaders to Christ and the martyrs. Abolitionist men were "ready to take up the cross, to suffer loss, shame, and even death." Unlike other Americans, these promising young men did not make decisions on the basis of "worldly wisdom" or "prudential calculations." Many had sacrificed brilliant futures to pursue what was right rather than what might profit them. Devoted, zealous, and determined in the cause, many wielded the pen brilliantly. Others were powerful and fiery speakers but neither unrestrainedly passionate nor irresponsible in their language. In May's conception, reformers appeared as capable, logical, and calmly resolute.[40]

While some might find his depiction a bit old-fashioned, May placed these abolitionists firmly in a sentimental culture that valued emotion as a source of moral activism. He gave many examples. Dr. Charles Follen, an abolitionist whom May himself loved "tenderly," was "a genuine man," brave and fearless, who "never quailed." Intellectually distinguished and a tower of strength for the movement, Follen was also modest and open to emotion. He "felt as well as said, 'that whatever affected the welfare of mankind was a matter of concern to himself.'" Ellis Gray Loring likewise had "the strength and resolution of a man with the intuitive wisdom and delicacy of a woman." Emphasizing the significance of sentiment, May described one of the high points of abolitionist history, the founding of the AAS, as a moment of extreme emotion: "Every man's heart was in his hand. . . . There are moments when heart touches heart, and souls flow into one another. This was such a moment."[41]

May's conception of manhood grew out of the evangelical and benevolent culture of his own youth and influenced the ways in which he depicted himself in the recollections. He did not emphasize his intellectual strengths or draw attention to his courage and bravery, though readers might perceive these qualities. Rather, he highlighted the role emotion and sentiment had played in reinforcing his moral commitments. His rapid decision to embrace Garrison and his program underscored the power of feeling rather than reason as the basis for his commitments.[42]

Despite the emphasis on male sentiment and despite his belief that women had played an important role in the abolitionist crusade and deserved "entire equality with men," May provided a gendered account of abolitionism. "If I live to write out half of my Recollections," May told his readers, "I shall make most grateful mention of our female fellow-laborers in general, of several of them in particular, though I cannot do ample justice to any." While mention them he did, male abolitionists and their contributions played a larger role in his narrative and occupied more space than the prominent women he sketched. Perhaps he thought memoirs more appropriately highlighted the achievements of great men. But his approach emphasized men as the most critical players and minimized the contributions of women who did so much to keep antislavery alive. And while he admired the eloquence of women like Abby Kelley Foster, Angelina Grimké, and Susan B. Anthony and the literary effectiveness of Lydia Maria Child, he also resorted to gender stereotypes that diminished their achievements. Maria Chapman wielded her pen gracefully; Anna Dickinson was one of the most attractive of the popular lecturers; Lucretia Mott's voice was sweetly female and her beautiful face was "radiant" with thoughts. Acknowledging that women had been earnest and devoted in the cause, he attributed their early support of abolitionism to their gender. Like the culture at large, he believed that "women's moral instincts made them quicker to discern the right than most men were" and that "their lack of political discipline left them to the guidance of their convictions and humane feelings."[43]

May did not provide a chronological account of abolitionism or a comprehensive view of its leaders, but he nonetheless furnished readers with a sense of its character. Since abolitionists had been accused of recklessness and of inciting others to violence, May emphasized the peaceful nature of abolitionist activities: the lecturing tours, the sermons and annual meetings, and the newspapers, tracts, and petitions. All of these activities, May emphasized, depended not on "an arm of flesh, but . . . [on] the power of truth and the influence of the Holy Spirit." What abolitionists wished to do was to "change the hearts of slaveholders and their abettors." Yet, as May's treatment of the Underground Railroad and slave rescues made clear, abolitionists occasionally had the kind of adventures that lent interest and drama to his story.[44]

Among the dramatic moments were some key events of abolitionist history: the formation of the AAS; debates over the Gag Rule; the speaking tour of the Grimké sisters in the 1830s, which brought the woman question to the fore; and, in the 1840s and 1850s, the operation of the Underground Railroad in New York State, as well as spirited opposition to the Fugitive Slave Law. But as much as May wished to capture the high points of the abolitionist past, he wanted to make it clear that abolitionists had encountered persecution right up until 1861. His use of the phrase "Reign of Terror" to describe opposition to antislavery recalled the extremism of the French Revolution. Examples of "contumely, hatred, persecution" conveyed the emotional experience of abolitionism at the same time that they provided the adventure that readers sought in autobiography and taught the necessity of suffering for a cause.[45]

As the book's title indicates, the theme of conflict was central, but the conflict May had in mind was one that might have taken readers by surprise. Rather than describing northerners at odds with southerners, May described abolitionists, who used only peaceful means in their "holy" struggle to end slavery, on one side, and on the other the far more numerous defenders of slavery, who had no qualms about resorting to violence and "foul means" to crush their opponents. May filled his account with vivid depictions of outrageous assaults on the abolitionists, many of them drawn from his own experience. A 1835 lecture in Haverhill, Massachusetts, for example, was interrupted by "the most hideous outcries" and "heavy missiles," one of which broke through the glass and wooden blind of one of the windows of the Freewill Baptist Church, sending shards into the hall. A woman who was hit in the head "uttered a shriek and fell bleeding into the arms of her sister." This was hardly an isolated incident in history or reported in May's book. During his lecture tour in Vermont, he met everywhere "with contumely and insult. I was mobbed five times," he recalled. "In Rutland and Montpelier, my meetings were dispersed with violence." To show the persistence of mob sentiment, the last incident May described in his book was an outburst of violence in 1861 in Syracuse that ended with the effigies of Susan B. Anthony and May being paraded through the city's streets and burned "amid shouts, hootings, mingled with disgusting profanity and ribaldry."[46]

This climactic outrage highlighted May's point that the Civil War was linked to an ongoing struggle that had begun thirty years before. Thus the cause of the war was not disagreement over the nature of the Union, although southerners had taken the South out of the Union. Rather, the fundamental cause was slavery, an institution that violated "the God-given rights of man," as abolitionists had been saying for decades. Like most Americans, May recognized the terrible costs of the nation's "dreadful" war. But, like other abolitionists, he also saw it as ultimately unavoidable and fitting punishment for a nation that had ignored the truth for so long. Only the "terrible chastisement" of death and destruction could have saved the country. Emancipation was thus a moral, religious, and national necessity, he implied, certainly not merely a military gesture. From this perspective, the true heroes of war were not soldiers or wartime politicians, who were virtually absent in his account, but the stalwart abolitionist warriors.[47]

Although several years had passed since the war's end, May had little sympathy for the South or interest in reconciliation. As an avid reader of newspapers, he was aware of the efforts southern states had made to undermine Reconstruction and black rights and the ominous strength of the Ku Klux Klan. The negative stereotypes of the South, its institutions, and leaders, all a standard part of abolitionist rhetoric, still had relevance. In a telling shift to the present tense, May suggested that not much had changed in the character of former slave owners and warned readers to avoid complacency: "The slave-holders of our country and their partisans have been incomparably more vigilant in watching for whatever might affect the stability of their 'peculiar institution,' and far more adroit devising measures, and resolute in pressing them . . . than their opponents have been in behalf of *Liberty*."[48]

May's focus, however, was not on the South or even the horrors of slavery. He took for granted the evils of the slave system, apparently believing his audience did too. What readers might not wish to acknowledge was how slavery had "contaminated" the North. During the war, many northerners had convinced themselves that they had never compromised with the South. With victory came a sense of virtue for having ended slavery. Rejecting this smug and self-congratulatory view, May described how slavery, like a "cancer" had infected the region and made northerners "almost as contaminated as the slaveholders themselves." This familiar abolitionist point was well worth making again, for, as May was aware, it was easily forgotten. Many of the incidents in his recollections revealed "to the present generation, and to those who may come after us, the sad state of the public mind and heart in New England [and elsewhere] thirty-five years ago."[49]

The phrase "sad state" hardly captured the extent of northern guilt and moral corruption. May showed that northerners actually became the agents of southern slavery, especially when they had turned on abolitionists with such fury. The harassment, described so often by May as shameful and outrageous, caught the abolitionists by surprise (as it might a forgetful audience). "We were slow to believe that our Northern sky would ever become so surcharged with hatred for those, who were only contending for 'the inalienable rights of man,' as to break upon us in any serious harm," May told his readers. The details of persecution that he provided were meant to remind and shock.[50]

The uncomfortable truth forced readers to consider why the North had caved in to southern slaveholders. May suggested that northerners, even wise men like Unitarian minister Dr. William Channing, lost their moral footing because they were in the habit of deferring to the southern "oligarchy." Others allowed "business necessity" to cloud their judgment. But May argued that the most important reason for the state of northern public opinion and the "most serious obstacle to the progress of the anti-slavery cause was the conduct of the clergy and churches in our country." Coming from one who had spent his life as a minister, the charge had to be taken seriously.[51]

May realized that some readers might be reluctant to confront the "evil words and deeds of ministers and churches" and assured his audience that he had raised the subject regretfully. The expressed regret was merely a gesture. May was determined to expose the failure of moral and religious leadership that he believed had had such deleterious consequences. In sections on the churches newly prepared for the book, May declared that had the clergy been "fearless and faithful in declaring the impartial love of God . . . our late civil war would have been averted!" If the past carried a message for the present, it was that those seeking to eliminate evil could not wait for spiritual leaders to bless their enterprise. Spiritual leaders could be and had been corrupted. "It has seemed to me," May reflected, "that the most important lesson taught in the history of the last forty years—the influence of slavery upon the religion of our country—ought least of all to be withheld from the generations that are coming on to fill our places in the Church and in the State."[52]

May was careful to qualify his argument by pointing out that many individual ministers had embraced abolitionism and that, as a profession, the clergy had contributed more men to abolitionism than any other group. Furthermore, members of the various churches had ignored sectarian differences and cooperated in the early years. But many of the first clergy recruits joined in the work of antislavery not because they believed in it as a moral duty but for personal and institutional reasons. They wished "to maintain the ascendancy over their sects" and prevent the blurring of denominational lines. Jealous of the influence of the abolitionists and influenced by prominent lay members, church leaders turned against the cause, denounced the abolitionists, and "woefully deceived" the members of their congregations about the character of abolitionism and slavery. The result was that "the most violent conflicts we had, and the most outrageous mobs we encountered, were led on, or instigated by persons professing to be religious."[53]

Seven separate sections provided evidence justifying May's accusations. Five dealt with the two denominations enjoying a reform reputation, the Society of Friends and the Unitarians. Many saw Quakers as "'birthright' Abolitionists." But May pointed to the historical record to counter this

THE FIRST RECOLLECTIONS

view. Monthly and yearly meetings took no action on slavery. The New England Yearly Meeting even denied May an opportunity to speak to them. "Truth compels me to add," May wrote, that abolitionists had all "too many proofs" that Quakers "with all their antislavery professions" were not much more friendly to immediate emancipation than other sects. As for his fellow Unitarians, May saved his severest words for them. Because Unitarians did not have ties with southern churches or national benevolent organizations, in May's assessment, they should have been freer to embrace immediate emancipation than any other denomination. Since they did not, a failure that May, as a Unitarian clergyman, supported with many "facts," he pronounced the Unitarians as *"pre-eminently guilty"* in the sin of slavery.[54]

May believed that the "sad truth" about the Unitarians and other denominational leaders offered "a solemn warning to all coming generations." If slavery had corrupted the nation's moral leaders in the past, May's narrative suggested, prejudice could taint those who sought positions of authority in the postwar world. Leadership in the uncertain days of the late 1860s was urgent because the elimination of prejudice, the second great abolitionist goal, still eluded the country. The abolitionists had learned a hard lesson that was relevant for May's readers. Individuals could not wait for their supposed leaders but had to do what they believed was right.[55]

May was aware that some abolitionists had never focused on the goal of doing away with racial prejudice, and that many readers might not even realize that it had existed. Yet, as the unstable racial situation of the day made clear, the persistence of prejudice threatened basic black freedoms gained through war and early Reconstruction. Insisting that prejudice was "offensive to every true human heart," May rejected the increasingly popular view that it was based in natural racial differences and argued that it had social and cultural causes. In slavery, most black men and women were "ignorant and degraded," and in northern society free blacks tended to be poor, uneducated, and in "menial" jobs. Since whites routinely saw blacks in these conditions, they assumed that they were inferior. The reality was that blacks "were not permitted to rise . . . [and] were *held down* by our laws, customs, and contemptuous treatment."[56]

Just as northerners were complicit in slavery, they were tainted by the prejudice that cruelly oppressed their black "countrymen." In addition to the extended treatment of the Crandall episode early in his narrative, May gave other examples of "the contempt" that characterized northern treatment of blacks. He reminded his readers that blacks had been forced to sit in separate areas in churches, that their children had not been able to attend public schools with white children, and that they had been either barred altogether from public transport or forced to accept the most uncomfortable accommodations. By drawing attention to these shameful forms of exclusion in the past, many of which were being reimposed as he wrote, May intended to prick the consciences of readers who might hold racist views and think emancipation ended any obligation to African Americans.[57]

Attacks on the fundamental ideas that supported discriminatory treatment would hardly have been necessary had May been confident that all his readers were free of prejudice. He knew this was not true. The "insensibility" toward blacks was "not yet wholly overpast, even in Massachusetts." But change was possible if some "easily obtained" facts were known. Ignoring science altogether, he provided "a few of [his] own recollections of facts going to establish the natural equality of our colored brethren." His examples included the performance of black children in white schools and the careers of illustrious black abolitionists like Frederick Douglass and Henry H. Garnett. A section titled "Distinguished Colored Men" contained nine sketches of men who had undermined prejudice with "abundant" evidence "of their mental power and executive ability."[58]

May's "distinguished colored men" merited different treatment than the heroic, determined, godly, and self-sacrificing white abolitionists. Because many regarded blacks as lazy, stupid, and inefficient, May's short biographical sketches emphasized qualities to counter white prejudice. He described men of action, such as David Ruggles and Lewis Hayden, who found dependence "irksome." Others he showed were successful and cultivated. William Wells Brown was an effective author, while both Frederick Douglass and the Reverend J. W. Loguen had educated themselves and won public respect for their achievements. On a more modest level, May also pointed out that "with very few exceptions," the fugitives whom he had visited twice in Canada before the war were earning enough to live "comfortably."[59]

In his section on the Underground Railroad, May balanced the picture of well-known abolitionists with descriptions of little-known fugitives who came to his house at all hours and in all conditions. Some were decently clothed, but most were in rags and sometimes "too unclean and loathsome to be admitted to my house." While acknowledging how "squalid" some of the fugitives were, May included an anecdote that suggested that fleeing slaves disliked their filth just as much as May. One dirty fugitive washed himself and threw out his rags "with a hearty good will." The new clothes May gave him, "the clean white shirt, with a collar and stock, delighted him above measure." Given the opportunity, even humble black people embraced the same standards as whites.[60]

May described some of the fugitives' stories of their escapes and a few details about their conditions in slavery. But he was less interested in the past than in their intelligence, determination, and their desire for decent lives in the future. May's overarching theme was the commitment of black people to freedom.[61]

In the section titled "A Negro's Love of Liberty," May described an incident that had occurred a few years after he had removed to New York in the mid-1840s. Sanford, a black resident of Syracuse, approached May to ask for help in rescuing his mother from slavery. The former fugitive told his story of escaping from the South, and May listened with interest. "I have repeated [the story] so often that I have kept its essential parts fresh in my memory," he told his readers. But what is remarkable about the incident is not the story itself but May's response. Wishing to "test" the "truth" of Sanford's account, he grilled him, even consulting an atlas to trace Sanford's escape route. Satisfied about the accuracy of Sanford's story, May then "with all apparent want of sympathy" told the fugitive that purchasing his mother would cost far more than the sum he had saved. When he was unable to change Sanford's mind about going through with his plan, May declared, "You must not think me as unsympathizing and cold as I have appeared. I have been trying you, proving you. I am satisfied that you know the value of liberty."[62]

May included this story in his recollections to demonstrate both the value Sanford placed on freedom and his moral superiority to his master, who refused to sell the old woman to her son. But the incident served other purposes as well. The detailed examination that May forced Sanford to undergo highlighted the former slave's veracity. May himself took on the role of doubter, a role that his readers might assume and perhaps had assumed in the past when they heard tales of escape. May was thus validating the fugitive's story as white abolitionists had done in the past when they wrote testimonials for published narratives. But May also, despite his disclaimers, revealed a side of himself that was more suspicious, patronizing, and less generous than the benign egalitarian self he projected in his memoir.

In his effort to weaken the power of prejudice and establish the case for the "natural equality" of blacks and whites, May expressed the abolitionist view that, by nature, untutored blacks might possess a moral sense that whites lacked. May did not think it inconsistent to argue for natural equality at the same time that he provided examples of "the *moral* equality, if not superiority, of the colored race." In one anecdote, by taking in a "helpless" invalid, a poor black woman demonstrated "an ardor of benevolence . . . a very rare instance of self-sacrificing charity." In another, a slave woman taken by her owners north refused to take the opportunity to free herself because she had promised to return south with her mistress. Despite efforts to persuade both women to make reasonable choices, both made decisions that from a worldly standpoint appeared irrational, imprudent, and even stubborn. The point of these anecdotes seemed to be that whites, particularly those still harboring prejudice, might fail to see or even dismiss the "elevated moral sentiment and principle" that many black people possessed. The moral character of blacks was important to recognize, for it made particularly offensive the way in which "our nation has so wickedly dared to despise and oppress [blacks]."[63]

The impact that May's recollections would have depended upon readers' willingness to accept his interpretation of past and present, and he used a variety of literary strategies to create a sympathetic community of readers. He treated his readers as friends and people of goodwill, reasonably knowledgeable about and positive toward abolitionism. Thus he trusted them to "smile" at abolitionists' foibles or even have "a laugh at our expense if you like." In the role of friendly guide, May flattered his readers by suggesting they remembered the incidents and the people that appeared in his book. Naturally, May implied, most had read Frederick Douglass's narrative, while his account of women like Lucretia Mott in the early days of the movement "doubtless" reminded readers of "many other excellent women, whose names stand high among the early antislavery reformers." If readers did not know Whittier's moving poem about the evils of slavery ("Shall tongues be mute when deeds are wrought / Which well might shame extremist hell?"), surely they would follow May's advice and "at once make themselves . . . familiar" with it. Such an approach allowed May to make his "readers . . . more fully informed" without appearing overbearing. The friendly community that May created allowed him to use the convention of direct address. Thus he spoke directly to readers so that they could "appreciate fully the importance of the event I am going to narrate to you."[64]

Despite or perhaps because of the frequent moral judgments he offered, May made a point of emphasizing his fairness, accuracy, and respect for facts. As he knew, readers expected the truth. As one reviewer of another autobiography explained, when the narrative described "the active career of a much more than ordinary man, of bright intellect, quick observation, and large practical philosophy . . . the interest must be greatly enhanced. The unmistakable truth of this narrative is its chief charm." That author had succeeded in creating a "candid and unreserved tone" that did not "permit us to doubt."[65]

May sprinkled his narrative with examples of his commitment to truth (although to some readers they may have suggested naïveté). For instance, why had he not believed the accusation that a leading Unitarian divine had said he would rather send his mother into slavery than resist the Fugitive Slave Law and imperil the Union? Because, May answered, the clergyman had "often denied that he spoke thus of his 'maternal relative' and therefore I allow that he was misunderstood." His book was a recollection "of facts," and when May "looked the facts fully in the face," they guided him as they had on the question of allowing women to speak in public.[66]

While May wanted to establish the factual nature of his narrative, he also tried to heighten its drama to make readers feel as if they were participating in events that had taken place years earlier. Excerpts from speeches and sermons brought past scenes to life. Describing a meeting at Boston's Faneuil Hall after the murder of Rev. Elijah Lovejoy, May reported that one of the speakers spoke of slaves in a "really atrocious manner." "Hear him!" he directed his readers, providing them with an excerpt of the speech's "most disgusting passage."[67] May re-created conversations in a way that allowed readers to feel they were part of the dialogue, to be present at dramatic moments. The credibility of the reimagined passages came from May's position as both witness and participant.[68]

Yet, as a man in his seventies, May realized that some might question the accuracy of his memory. Defending his ability to remember, he suggested that some memories had never faded. Thus one memory "glow[ed] with the recollections of the fervor" of abolitionist hymns, "like the bugle's blast to an army ready for battle." Other memories remained strong because he often spoke of them. When he was not sure of the accuracy of a particular story, he qualified his retelling of events with a phrase like "if I remember correctly." Rather than suggesting forgetfulness, this type of comment implied his concern for accuracy and honesty.[69]

Telling the truth brought to life emotions experienced long before. The use of words like "terrible," "sad," and "disgusting" to describe the tribulations of abolitionists suggested what it had felt like to be an abolitionist and a reformer and encouraged readers to identify with those feelings. By entering into a community of sentiment, readers could learn from May's experiences. It is revealing that May chose to end the appendix to his recollections with the text of a letter written to Daniel Webster in 1850 by 800 "prominent citizens of Massachusetts." The letter that praised Webster for "the service" he had done for the Union in a recent speech on slavery, May wrote, represented "the saddest, most astounding evidence of the demoralization of our Northern citizens in respect to slavery." At the conclusion of the appendix, May wove historical and emotional truth together in what was, perhaps, a warning to his readers of the danger of "depraving" influences in the future.[70]

After May submitted the appendix and the preface to the publisher in the summer of 1869, he returned from Cambridge to Syracuse. Although he had been troubled with the pace of production, by mid-September he had received 100 copies of the book. Bound in green cloth with gold lettering on the spine, May's volume had an elegant and stylish appearance. Within, the text was unadorned, lacking any illustrations, even a picture of the author. On sale for $1.50 at booksellers, the book was advertised in publications like the *New York Times*. There May was hailed as one of the "very few persons" able to tell the antislavery story. His approach meshed with autobiographical expectations, and he had a "well-stored memory" that provided "a most graphic and valuable series of sketches of prominent persons and incidents of the great struggle." In the *American Literary Gazette and Publishers' Circular*, the book was featured in a full-page ad listing Fields & Osgood's new books for the fall, including a volume of poems by Whittier and Henry James's *The Secret of Swedenborg*.[71]

The book received, as May noted in his diary, "friendly and complimentary" reviews in newspapers. In the *National Anti-Slavery Standard*, Lydia Maria Child predictably found the book "very interesting, partly consisting of history, but mainly of the author's own memories." The *Independent* also had good things to say. The comments in the *Monthly Religious Magazine* were perhaps less positive, for May called the review a "critique."[72]

In addition to critical response, there are some hints of how a few people, sympathetic to abolitionism, read the book. One called it "charming" and said it reflected "what good and brave souls were stirred up to do battle in the righteous but most unpopular cause!" Lucretia Mott, who received the book as a present from Garrison, noted that it was an incomplete history of the antislavery movement but that she appreciated how May's "beautiful spirit marks the book throughout." Lydia Maria Child was carried back to the past when she read the book and understood some of the messages May intended. "All who took part in the great moral conflict," she wrote, "will find it pleasant to refresh their memories with this book . . . and others will find in it salutary lessons to transmit to posterity."[73]

Child's comments suggested that she hoped that those readers who had not been active abolitionists would welcome May's "salutary" lessons. But his interpretation of the nature and achievements of abolitionism, his condemnation of the failure of moral leadership in the prewar period, and his emphasis on the continuing power of prejudice could also offend those who did not share his perspective. At the same time, readers would discover some familiar themes. Benson J. Lossing's three-volume *Pictorial History of the Civil War in the United States* (1866–68), for example, confidently blamed southerners for the war that the author pictured as a conflict between right and wrong. The end of slavery still seemed to be one of the war's great achievements, and, in 1867, in recognition of such a sentiment, Congress passed a bill to erect a monument to Lincoln as the emancipator. Forceful arguments insisted that blacks had the potential to join society on equal terms with whites. Many white northerners had positive images of southern freed men and women and showed their interest in black culture by flocking to the concerts of southern black jubilee singers.[74]

Realizing that the recent past would attract readers to their periodicals, publishers of monthly magazines printed articles and stories that described the experiences of abolitionists, former slaves, and slaveholders in the recent war. As the editor of *Harper's* explained in 1868, "nothing certainly can be more interesting to people who have just emerged from a tremendous conflict than the stories of individual experience — the romances, the poems, the comedies, the tragedies which spring from such a war." An exploration of the monthlies during the late 1860s reveals perspectives that had much in common with May's understanding of the past and his hopes for African Americans. Yet even writers who sympathized with African Americans and emancipation aimed at entertaining their readers rather than giving them moral encouragement. In fact, few stories or articles exhibited May's deep interest in and commitment to freed people. Even more troubling were the signs that a more favorable view of the Old South was emerging that reached thousands of American middle-class families every month. The past was beginning its process of reconstruction.[75]

Many stories in the monthlies depicted African Americans before and after emancipation. By using the common literary convention of claiming their stories to be true, authors presented fiction as reality. "Miss Nichols," a "teacher" of freed people in Beaufort, South Carolina, posed as the author of "Too Late," a story published in *Harper's* in 1866. In actuality, Elizabeth Stuart Phelps, a young Boston writer, was the author. Phelps supported efforts to educate former slaves and appreciatively portrayed Miss Nichols and her desire "to live her life with them; to sorrow in their sorrows . . . to be glad in their joy." Her characterizations of the gravely ill quadroon washerwoman, Corinne, and her long-lost husband were so favorable that her story almost crossed the boundaries of propriety.[76] In one scene, for example, when Miss Nichols is in her schoolroom, a man who could have passed as white comes to the schoolroom and asks to be taught to read. Phelps's description of the newcomer highlights his sexual attractiveness.

HARPER'S WEEKLY.

JOURNAL OF CIVILIZATION

VOL. X.—No. 491.]   NEW YORK, SATURDAY, MAY 26, 1866.   [SINGLE COPIES TEN CENTS.
$4.00 PER YEAR IN ADVANCE.

Entered according to Act of Congress, in the Year 1866, by Harper & Brothers, in the Clerk's Office of the District Court for the Southern District of New York.

THE MEMPHIS RIOTS.

THERE was in Memphis, on the first two days of May, an excitement unequaled since the close of the war. The origin of the disturbances between the whites and negroes of that city was highly discreditable to the colored soldiers, and the riotous proceedings which followed were a disgrace to civilization. For the riot the lower class of white citizens were as responsible as were the soldiers of the Third United States Colored Infantry for the original difficulty. This regiment, whose reputation has been a bad one, had been mustered out, since which they had frequently whisky-shops in the southern part of the city, and had been guilty of excesses and disorderly conduct. On the evening of May 1 some drunken members of the regiment were on South Street, talking loudly, when in an insolent manner they were ordered by two policemen to cease their noise and disperse. Words ensued, followed by blows, throwing of missiles, and firing of revolvers.

To understand what followed it must be remembered that the police force of Memphis is composed mostly of Irishmen, whose violent prejudice against negroes was so shamefully displayed in the New York riots of 1863. The Times correspondent thus described the riot:

Word was sent to police head-quarters, and the whole force at once proceeded to the scene of the fray, being joined on the way thither by armed and excited citizens. Meanwhile the firing had brought other negroes to the spot, some armed with clubs and some with revolvers, so that by the time the police force reached the two parties were about equal in manner. The negroes held the original

position, and, upon the approach of the police, showing no determination to abandon it, were fired upon by the police and citizens who accompanied them. The fire was returned, and for a while both parties busied themselves in discharging their revolvers as rapidly as possible. Meanwhile word was sent to Gaines, a regiment, who promptly dispatched to the scene of action a company of Regulars […] when the negroes were quickly dispersed and driven in every direction.

During the evening the wildest and most exaggerated reports soon spread throughout the city. Every conceivable rumor of the intelligence of the fight took a different story, and the highest excitement prevailed. Each rumor placed a worse aspect upon the affair than the preceding one, and only served to develop the pent-up prejudice against the negro. Soon after dark this excitement and prejudice found vent. Large numbers of armed citizens repaired to the scene of the fight and commenced firing upon every negro who made himself visible. One negro upon South Street, a quiet, inoffensive laborer, was shot down almost in front of his own cabin, and after life was extinct his body was fired into, and hacked in a most horrible manner. In all parts of the city, wherever they could be seen, negroes were fired upon by policemen as well as citizens. They were shot while driving hacks, and quietly walking in the streets about their business. The police seemed to make it their special business to shoot every negro they could see, no matter where he was or what he was doing. The result was that by 9 o'clock the colored population were in-doors trembling with wild alarm. How many negroes were killed during the night it is impossible to ascertain, as figures are constantly passed during the day; the hours in all parts of the city. It is estimated that from 15 to 20 were killed. So far as I have been able to learn, not a white man was fired upon by a negro during the whole night.

After the fight of Tuesday evening the negro soldiers and most of the colored population residing in the vicinity of the fight fled to the fort for security. They were perfectly quiet—in fact, were terribly frightened for their own safety. At an early hour yesterday morning every thing

SCENES IN MEMPHIS, TENNESSEE, DURING THE RIOT—BURNING A FREEDMEN'S SCHOOL-HOUSE.

[SKETCHED BY A. R. W.]

SCENES IN MEMPHIS, TENNESSEE, DURING THE RIOT—SHOOTING DOWN NEGROES ON THE MORNING OF MAY 2, 1866.—[SKETCHED BY A. R. W.]

The man's figure is massive and manly; his smile sends "the hot blood into . . . [Miss Nichols's] cheeks." His face is "finely moulded . . . the eyes deep sunken, restless, defiant" with "not a shadow of coarseness." He is "a *man*." He is also Corinne's husband, Du Bois.[77]

Phelps's characterization of Du Bois emphasized his physical magnetism to a degree that might have shocked some readers and raised the specter of interracial sex and even marriage. Phelps made Du Bois's physical appeal more palatable for her white readers, however, by following the tradition of antislavery fiction and emphasizing that both husband and wife are light skinned. The fact that Du Bois almost appears to be a white man could make Miss Nichols's response to him seem like a natural mistake, but it is a mistake without consequences. Although Phelps could imagine a sexually attractive African American man, like other white authors, she could not visualize a romance crossing racial lines. By removing both of the black characters from the story (Corinne dies and Du Bois walks "alone into his freedom," clearly intending to seek his own death), Phelps precluded any chance of sexual or social racial mixing and neatly avoided having to address the issue of how former slaves were to live in freedom.[78]

In an 1869 review of a book about black troops during the Civil War, a writer for the *Atlantic Monthly* made it clear that "Too Late" was but one of many popular works depicting blacks in the "familiar aspects of martyr or hero, or his present 'transition state.'" The positive characterization of African Americans in popular culture probably dated back to the assault on Fort Wagner in 1863. Postwar stories featured light-skinned freed people as well as those with dark skins and even an African appearance.[79]

"The Freedman's Story," by M. Schele DeVere, a professor of linguistics at the University of Virginia, appeared in *Harper's* in 1866. It explored a slave's desire for freedom and his flight from a plantation in an area controlled by Union forces. Despite Oby's dreams of one day being free and

opposite:
The front page of the May 16, 1866, issue of *Harper's Weekly*. In the immediate postwar period, northern periodicals and newspapers often took a sympathetic view of freed people in the South. This issue of *Harper's Weekly* is somewhat ambiguous, however, in terms of its stance toward black soldiers during riots in Memphis. The illustrations highlight white violence against free blacks and show the destruction of the freedmen's school, while the text blames lower-class whites for the "riotous proceedings." But the weekly also accuses black soldiers of drunkenness and bad conduct and finds them equally responsible for "the original difficulty." (Courtesy Photographs and Prints Division, Schomburg Center for Research in Black Culture, The New York Public Library, Astor, Lenox and Tilden Foundations)

owning a little shop, he finds it difficult to leave his slave home. His mother opposes the idea, telling him it is much better to belong to "genteel folks" than to be a "poor nigger" with no one to take care of him. His "mighty good" master persuades Oby to abandon his first attempt by arguing that he is not strong enough to sleep outside and that his parents cannot bear the separation. Finally, Oby becomes a man and escapes with a group heading north. There he and his lady friend find work, proving their ability to take care of themselves, a welcome message for northern readers who worried about black dependency. The story ends with an uplifting conclusion that emphasizes the former slave's worthiness for and appreciation of freedom. "When I looked around me I saw . . . a beautiful flag flying from the top of the house," Oby declares, "and that was the first night I slept under the Stars and Stripes, a free man."[80]

While slave owners were not the evil characters so commonly depicted in antislavery propaganda, many stories provided a critical appraisal of plantation masters. In "The Freedman's Story," Oby's master is condescending, talking to his slave "as if [he] was a little baby and had not any sense at all." Robert M. Copeland's "My Man Anthony," published in 1869 in *Putnam's Magazine*, also dissected the relationship between slave owner and slave, to the slave's advantage. Billeted with a Mr. Seaver, an arrogant secessionist, the narrator is told during dinner that none of Seaver's slaves would ever leave him. The narrator, though, sees Harrison, the butler, who is standing behind Seaver's chair, raise his eyebrows and give him a "look which seemed to say he wasn't a fool; but in a second it was gone, and he was the faithful slave." That night, Harrison steals into the narrator's room and expresses his desire to be free: "Dat ole man talks 'bout our never leabn' him — d'ye s'pose we're such fools as not ter want dat?" When the narrator, like the master and Oby's mother in "The Freedman's Story" raise the question of whether Harrison is capable of supporting himself, Harrison replies with scorn: "Why, me an' my old woman hab fed, an' clo'd dese ole people, an' nussed dar chil'en, an' ef we don't run away, we'll hab to bury en." Soon after, Lucy, the housemaid, a "tall, good-looking negro woman," appears to make the same request. Like Harrison, she ridicules the notion that hers is a comfortable home. All of her children but one have been sold. "Home! . . . I call it a grabe, or wuss."[81]

The intelligent and competent Harrison and his wife escape, and like the fugitives in other stories, they thrive as free people. Harrison is reported to be the head waiter in Cincinnati's best restaurant, and his children all attend the public schools. Such endings embodied the hope and expectation of northerners that blacks could succeed on their own, that they could realize

THE FIRST RECOLLECTIONS

the promises of economic mobility held out by the American dream. Such independent black people deserved the freedom that war and their own actions had secured for them.[82]

While these stories usually envisioned freed people working in lowly jobs or serving others, and none visualized the equal rights that May espoused, the main black characters, whether slave or free, were vigorous and self-reliant. Bearing no signs of mistreatment, a familiar theme that had vanished in popular literature by 1864, they were depicted as physically attractive, and African features were neither exaggerated nor ridiculed. Old Tenah, a character in one story, for example, has an aged and wrinkled face and sad eyes, "wells of beauty which so often dwell in the face of the pure-blooded Guinea negro, and give a touch of the poetic to the blackest countenance."[83]

Characters that later would become figures of fun warranted serious treatment. In one serialized novel in *Harper's*, Uncle Simeon, a preacher during slavery days, despite his lack of education, "actively" speaks "to God on the mercy-seat. All his religion has been drawn direct from the Bible, and it brims his heart." "With the exception of the color," he reminds the story's narrator "of one of the old prophets." A white preacher visiting this mainly black congregation has a moving experience that puts into perspective his time at seminary: "Charles sees and feels more genuine human heart in the glad eyes, and smiling teeth, and hearty exclamation, and warm grasps of the hand than during a six months in the seminary." While the emphasis on eyes and teeth could seem to caricature black features, the author made no effort to mock black appearance but rather gave an admiring description of the slaves' intense religious emotion.[84]

While the black characters in these stories freed themselves by escaping from their masters, a few articles and stories also presented short, mostly positive vignettes of abolitionists. Several mentioned northern women who went south to teach former slaves. The work was described as enriching for the young women and essential for the freed people. Other stories portrayed northern soldiers as abolitionists. The narrator of "My Man Anthony" describes his Massachusetts regiment as mixed on the question of slavery, although the unit contains true-blue abolitionists "who had enlisted for freedom's sake, and nothing else." Experiences with fugitives, however, turn even the conservatives into abolitionists, and the story made clear that this transformation was a good thing. In another story, for a young soldier whose father has been "a firm anti-slavery man" but "a brutal task-master" the transformation is more conflicted. Taken in by a kindly southern cousin who is his "new father" and a "gentle master of slaves," the young man fights for the Confederacy. This experience enlightens him, however, and he develops "a freedom-loving, slavery-hating heart." In these stories hating slavery and loving freedom were synonymous.[85]

If abolitionists were scarce in stories, they were somewhat more evident in articles and obituaries. Garrison was lavishly praised, and other abolitionists and their work received brief, usually positive mentions. The cause itself was identified with progress, and the struggle was seen as one between slavery and freedom. Praising a biography of Massachusetts's war governor, John Andrew, the reviewer lauded Andrew as an example of sturdy manhood. Like the ways in which May had pictured abolitionists in his recollections, Andrew's manhood encompassed feeling as well as more typically masculine qualities: "He had a great big heart . . . an active brain, an indomitable will, an industry that never tired." Describing other abolitionists, Eugene Benson, a frequent contributor to various monthlies, emphasized aggressive qualities, recalling some of the prewar negativism toward abolitionists. Theodore Parker, Unitarian minister and abolitionist, according to Benson, used vigorous and emphatic rhetoric, while Wendell Phillips's speeches were "full of intense and alarming sentences, which are shot forth like minie balls, mortal messengers of his indignant and questioning spirit."[86]

The periodicals described actual emancipated slaves and their rights less frequently than fictional freed people. In an article summarizing the nation's history between 1854 and 1867 for *Putnam's Monthly*, Van Buren Denslow gave an abstract but glowing retrospective on the events of those years. Denslow had good antislavery credentials, having written and published a novel titled *Owned and Disowned; or, The Chattel Child of a Southern Life* before the war. In this article Reconstruction represented the apogee of freedom because it reconceived the Union on the basis of universal suffrage. "Never before in the world's history," wrote Denslow, "has there been so sublime a vindication of the power of an idea to mould parties, revolutionize governments, raise and mass armies, overthrow institutions, and change the social destinies of races." As far as the actual workings of emancipation and rights guaranteed by Reconstruction legislation, universal suffrage was working as well as "could be expected."[87]

In a less euphoric but more pragmatic article in *Harper's* a few years earlier, an observer noted approvingly that while former "chattels" indulged in the desire for showy but pretty goods, especially spring hats, they also purchased spelling books, "destined to open for them the alphabet of literature, as the arts of dress open the alphabet of society." The enthusiasm for freed people rested on the quiet way in which they had embraced their new condition. Stating what many white people believed, the writer emphasized that "the negro's status depends on what he can do."[88]

This conviction that blacks needed to help themselves pervaded articles written by J. W. De Forest, who was a novelist, short story writer, and employee of the Freedmen's Bureau after the war. Describing his Bureau work, De Forest saw plenty of problems stemming from slavery. "Oh! but that slavery was costly, with its breed of parasite whites, and its remaining dross of decrepit old Negroes!" he lamented. Still, De Forest did not favor handing out food rations either to poor whites or to indigent blacks. While he denied that freed people were as vicious or irrational as some conservative (but unnamed) journals claimed, he believed former slaves to be ignorant, unaware of the industry needed to succeed, and somewhat imprudent. They were like grown-up children.[89]

In a story drawing upon his Bureau experience, De Forest conveyed an even more negative view of blacks. The story is set on the Sea Islands of Georgia, and the main character is a lieutenant connected with the Bureau. Blacks are incidental to the plot that revolves around the lieutenant's courtship of Jennie, the daughter of a Yankee-hating, drunken plantation owner. De Forest's racism appears when he describes the servant Jim as a "dirty blackamoor," whose "greasy" laughter drives the lieutenant to violence. Although De Forest's lieutenant later decides that kicking Jim had been a mistake and inappropriate for an officer of the Bureau, this insight does not prevent him from venting his bad humor on several "negro urchins" whom he sends to jail the next day.[90]

The prejudice about which May had warned appeared in other pieces as well. It is doubtful that there were any deliberate editorial decisions involved. Rather, it seems more likely that editors freely published materials reflecting different points of view that might appeal to different segments of their audience. As George Curtis, the editor of *Harper's*, explained, "This magazine is designed for general entertainment, and its contributions are therefore upon subjects of universal interest."[91]

The same year that *Harper's* published De Forest's pieces, the magazine carried a humorous story titled "Border Reminiscences." The story features several illustrations that make fun of the characters. But the picture of "A Demoralized Negro" presents a dramatic contrast to the mildly comical depictions of the whites. Here, a black man with grossly exaggerated features—pop eyes, thick lips, and kinky hair—is shown alarmed and fearful on his horse. In the text, he introduces himself as "the wust demurralized niggar that perhaps you ever seed in all yer born'd days." It is immediately made clear that the man has deserted his master and run away in a "cowardly manner." The visual and textual characterizations of this man and the depictions of the noble blacks in other stories could not be more distant.[92]

In the northern monthlies, other subtle signs hinted that the commitment to the idea that black men deserved the rights of white men was shallow. Van Buren Denslow's discussion of the election of 1868 suggested how firmly rooted racial bias was in the North. Less hopeful than May, Denslow did not believe that the "negro question" could be solved by trying to prove that prejudice had no basis in reality. The fact was that prejudice did exist. Most Americans had little commitment to universal suffrage, and even Republicans were lukewarm to the idea. As for Grant, the presidential candidate, he had not "invested . . . a feather's weight of influence for or against colored suffrage." Public opinion on the race issue was unsettled, and the most positive implication of his article was that the intellectual and social progress of black people might one day resolve the troubling "negro question."[93]

Abolitionist and then Republican lecturer Anna Dickinson, among others, grappled with the problem of racial prejudice, which she attacked in her 1868 novel, *What Answer?* Reviews of the novel acknowledged the problem but suggested that her focus on racial intermarriage as a solution missed the point. Blacks needed, said one reviewer, fair pay and equal rights as citizens not racial intermarriage. The "solution," said another, seemed facile since the heroine did not look black and was both beautiful and brilliant. It took "no heroic effort" for the main white character to fall in love with her.[94]

The 1869 tale "Uncle Gabriel's Account of His Campaign" begins with Gabriel Edwards refusing to have a white man write his story. The narrator explains, "Even his friends at the North" did not believe "that any of his race could distinguish themselves by their literary ability; and . . . therefore, feeling in himself consciousness of a talent for narrative, he must have the credit of his own efforts." This point about his so-called friends hinted at what might become the new reality. At the end of the story, however, Gabriel has not given up hope, reiterating his point: "I wish you to believe that one of my race can tell a history if we can get a writer to put it down."[95]

While northern antipathy toward the South still remained, Denslow and others sensed that it was dissipating. In 1867, Wendell Phillips had blasted "milk and water conciliation, all this forgetting—of the lessons of 30 years." Indeed, there were hints in the northern monthlies of a more sympathetic view of the South that would shape any retelling of the story of slavery, war, and reconstruction, and, of course, the historical reputation of abolitionists. The fiction presented southern slaveholders as not knowing their

THE FIRST RECOLLECTIONS

slaves as well as they presumed they did and misunderstanding their desire for freedom. But many were described as good masters and were far more sympathetically rendered than they were in abolitionist prewar writings, where they were depicted as lustful brutes. J. W. De Forest reminded readers of *Harper's* in 1869 that while the old plantation class was dying off, this group had exhibited many fine qualities and were an example of highest humanity. It still represented the South's most powerful moral force, De Forest believed. Plantation owners had accepted emancipation, he stated, although they were angered by the way in which it had been accomplished. From his point of view, hostility served little purpose. "When will this sectional aversion end?" De Forest asked. For the nation's sake, it was important to make southerners as well as northerners feel like Americans.[96]

May would hardly have agreed with such a generous sentiment about ending sectional hostility. Events in the South were extremely troubling. While Republicans were politically dominant in the South and implementing Congress's reconstruction plan, southern Democrats condemned both the "mongrel despotism" of "carpet-bag aliens and their African confederates" and the new state constitutions containing provisions protecting black suffrage. As one Louisiana newspaper explained in 1868, "We proclaim that we are opposed to negro suffrage under any circumstances, and stand ready to use all legitimate means to prevent its present and future exercise." Others were quite willing to resort to illegitimate means to prevent blacks from voting, and during the election of 1868, members of the Ku Klux Klan as well as other southerners resorted to violence to do so. While these sorts of incidents fell off after the election, many southern Democratic leaders were determined to continue their campaign against Republicanism and its goals through politics.[97]

May's *Recollections* were infused with his understanding of this uncertain present. He saw "portents" that the conflict with "the enemies of liberty, the oppressors of humanity" had not yet ended. He noted that Union men had been driven out of Louisiana and that the franchise was "meanly withheld" from blacks in some states. In his book, May exhibited no sympathy for the increasingly popular position that blacks could lift themselves out of poverty, essentially without assistance, or that the vote by itself was adequate to protect their interests. Sympathizing with the radicals, May knew that Reconstruction policies had not gone far enough: "Our Government has been guilty of great injustice to the colored population of the South, who were all loyal throughout the war. These should not have been left . . . at the mercy of their former masters. Homes and adequate portions of the land . . . ought to have been secured," and former slaves should be entitled to education. As for the Republican Party, May hoped that it would "be guided or forced to pursue" measures that would ensure that American blacks enjoy "all the privileges and the exercise of all the prerogatives of American citizens."[98]

May's message for northern readers was clear: "The great antislavery reform . . . must be thoroughly accomplished — before our Republic can stand upon a sure foundation." Many abolitionists had believed that their reform would only succeed if people's views were transformed. As May recognized, this had not happened. Thus, the abolitionist struggle that had led to the Civil War had not yet ended, and the duty that informed his book was the duty "to rouse the people," as abolitionists had done for thirty years. When Americans had refused to listen, there had been a "fratricidal, parricidal," and nearly suicidal war. Now was another moment to listen and take action, for "our country is not surely saved." The sad experiences of the past, some of which May had recounted in his recollections, should "prompt and impel our nation, before it be too late, to do all for the colored population of our country, South and North, that righteousness demands at our hands."[99]

How did this call to arms sell? Did May's old-fashioned appeal with its faith in moral suasion and the politics of sentiment reach a large audience? Was the essential message May wished to convey embraced by those who needed to hear it?

May himself had received positive feedback and favorable reviews. He had told his story in the modest fashion critics appreciated in an autobiography; a "gentle spirit" and sense of fairness permeated the narrative. Furthermore, he provided an example of a life of "protracted usefulness." But these qualities so much admired by the literary critics and presumably appreciated by those who enjoyed autobiographies were not enough to attract the readership for which May had hoped.[100]

When he stopped in at Fields & Osgood in December 1869, the news was not good. The press had printed 2,000 copies, but May reported in his diary that he was "sorry to learn that only about 1250 of my books are sold." The publishers were not happy (their royalty arrangement suggested that they might have anticipated sales of up to 5,000 books). They tried to reassure May, telling him "that the book trade is very dull. No books sell quickly now." The book never did sell as well as the publisher had anticipated and May had hoped, and it appears as if the publisher did not even break even. By 1875, the book had sold an additional 432 copies; the publisher's accounts suggest that 654 books had left their warehouse while 318 unbound and 38 bound volumes still remained on hand. The next year, the publishers destroyed the sheets still in their possession and sold the plates in March.[101]

Years later, William Lloyd Garrison's son Frank, who worked for Houghton Mifflin, remarked that the sales of May's book had been "restricted" because there had not been much demand for the "admirable little volume." The book's lackluster performance suggests that, despite the ways in which May's recollections met autobiographical expectations and despite the fact that some people viewed blacks and abolitionists positively, even the friendly readers he expected to buy the book were not very interested in what May had to say. While James R. Osgood & Company (formerly Fields & Osgood) did not immediately abandon antislavery publications and issued Wilson's *History of the Rise and Fall of the Slave Power in America* in 1874, that book did not sell readily either. In the future, mainstream publishers would do well to avoid publishing such recollections, whether written by those who hoped to end slavery through moral suasion or those who devoted themselves to antislavery politics as a means to emancipation. Most former antislavery and abolitionist activists who wished to give their version of the past to the public would find it impossible to publish with a major house and difficult to connect with the readers who most needed to hear what they had to say.[102]

Samuel May had staked out an interpretation of abolitionism, its heroes, and its opponents at a time when he considered its work ongoing, its opponents not fully vanquished. Because the work was incomplete, his interpretation was unstable, subject to modification as circumstances shifted. Heroes and villains might change places with the passage of time. And with time, the understanding of antislavery history must also shift. But May had his eye on the longer view, beyond his own era. In late November 1870, the day after he was "beset" with black people wanting help, he looked over his antislavery books and chose about 100 to give to Cornell University. Eventually, he donated over 10,000 pamphlets and other printed materials to the library, where they became the heart of a major collection of antislavery materials. If May's own interpretation did not reach the audience for which he hoped, at some future time, the basic materials for understanding the past would be available. As a group of abolitionists including Garrison and Wendell Phillips had pointed out when they asked their English colleagues for financial help to support the collection, it was of "great importance that the literature of the Anti-Slavery movement . . . be preserved and handed down, that the purposes and the spirit, the methods and the aims of the Abolitionists should be clearly known and understood by future generations."[103]

2 *Fugitives as Part of Abolitionist History*

In 1870 and 1871, *Harper's Weekly* featured an advertisement for plaster statuary suitable for display in genteel parlors. The piece pictured, created by the popular sculptor John Rogers, was called "The Fugitive's Story" and featured a female fugitive slave recounting her adventures to several well-known abolitionists, including John G. Whittier and William Lloyd Garrison, who had posed for the artist. Rogers had proven to be very successful at producing small plaster groupings on subjects that attracted middle-class buyers. In 1859 he had appealed to antislavery sentiment with his piece "The Slave Auction." After enjoying success with many Civil War pieces during the war, he returned to an antislavery theme to capitalize on the sympathies of genteel Americans who wanted art in their homes. "The Fugitive's Story" cost $25 and could be shipped without charge to any railroad station in the country.[1]

The interest in the fugitive story had also been apparent at the final meeting of the Pennsylvania Anti-Slavery Society. William Still, an African American member of the Society, showed one of the relics of exciting days now past: the wooden box that had concealed a fugitive slave. Still had also entertained the audience by presenting a paper on Henry "Box" Brown and several other fugitives. As a member of the Philadelphia Vigilance Committee, which had helped escaped slaves who had reached the city, Still had been active in the Underground Railroad network and had firsthand knowledge of fugitives and their stories. His paper fascinated his listeners. According to the *National Standard*, "The mournful tales thus unfolded were like the thrilling fantasies of romance, but more harrowing because of their reality." In one of its last actions, the society passed a unanimous resolution asking Still to "compile and publish his personal reminiscences and experiences relating to the Underground Rail Road."[2]

The resolution seemed to call for personal recollections, perhaps along the lines of Samuel May's book. Still's own life was certainly noteworthy enough for a conventional autobiography. Born free in New Jersey, Still had migrated as a young man to Philadelphia, where he eventually found a job with the Pennsylvania Society for the Abolition of Slavery. When the Fugitive Slave Act was passed in 1850, he became a key figure in the Vigilance Committee's work. During the war he moved into the coal business, which he made into a flourishing concern. Despite his successes, particularly impressive for a free black man, Still chose not to tell his own story. His narrative thus differed both from a conventional autobiography and from May's memoirs. Perhaps the audience's enthusiasm encouraged him to highlight the tales of fugitives rather than his own experiences in the Pennsylvania Anti-Slavery Society office or as the chairman of the Acting Vigilance Committee. Certainly he believed that stories demonstrating the widespread desire of black people for freedom ought to be told.[3]

The book that resulted represented another form of historical memory about abolitionism and suggests that there was a racial divide in the construction of the past. Still's account had a different purpose, message, and cast of characters than May's book and its tone contrasted sharply with that of the effusive memorializing statements made as antislavery societies dissolved. In this narrative, white abolitionists were marginalized. Blacks became the engine of their own liberation, a theme that other black abolitionists would also highlight in their autobiographies published later in the century. Still's story made clear not only the basic humanity of black slaves but also the justice of emancipation and citizenship. Many black men and women had seized the opportunity for freedom under the most difficult of circumstances. Their actions symbolized blacks' commitments to core American values and offered proof that they deserved the fundamental political rights associated with freedom.

Still's massive book (almost 800 pages long) appeared in March 1872. Its principal title, *The Underground Rail Road*, suggested Still's strategy of receding into the background of the narrative. Clues about Still's work and character, however, appeared in letters written by and to him included in the narrative. Of the two, the letters to Still were the more revealing, showing his kindness, his thoughtful treatment of fugitives in Philadelphia and in Canada, and his involvement in Underground Railroad operations. Through the voices of others, readers might gain a faint inkling of the kind of man that Still was. John Hall, an escaped fugitive, wrote to Still in 1856, "As for your part that you done I will not attempt to tell you how thankful I am, but I hope that you can imagine what my feelings are to you. I cannot find words sufficient to express my gratitude to you. . . . No flattery, but candidly speaking, you are worthy all the praise of any person who has ever been with you." With these sorts of secondhand comments readers would have to be content.[4]

While Still remained a shadowy figure, his book provided a firsthand account of the Vigilance Committee. Scattered throughout the book were vignettes of the committee listening to and recording stories of fugitives, sympathizing with their sufferings, and gathering information and giving them advice and funds. But despite these vignettes and the inclusion of pictures of four colleagues on the Acting Committee, members remained blurry and indistinct. Still did nothing to personalize individuals or the group by revealing their positions or feelings. Still described the moments when emotions ran high in the most general terms. A comment like "Never before had they witnessed a sight more interesting, a scene more touching" was typical. Who said what was rarely clear. Not until more than three-quarters of the way through the book did Still offer basic information about the committee's organization and its original members. Like Still himself, committee members hovered at the fringes of the narrative.[5]

Although Still remained mostly in the background, he wanted no challenges to his authority. Unlike slave narratives like Frederick Douglass's that relied on validation from whites for acceptance, Still felt no need for testimonials. The title page fixed his position as observer and interpreter, noting that the book contained "Facts, Authentic Narratives, Letters &c." drawn from firsthand accounts or "witnessed by the author." Lower on the title page, in a different typeface to attract attention, Still's credentials appeared: he had "for many years" been active in the antislavery office and was "chairman" of Philadelphia's Acting Vigilance Committee. Opposite the title page a portrait of Still with his large and graceful signature appeared. His signature, of course, established his literacy, while the portrait showed him in impeccable middle-class attire, staring out, not at the reader, but into the distance, as if recollecting some of the events and people that he would include in his book. Further highlighting his credibility, the preface began with a direct quotation of the resolution unanimously passed by the Pennsylvania Anti-Slavery Society requesting him to undertake this project.[6]

Still went to some length to establish the historical nature of his work. Although he stated that he vividly remembered many of the events included in his book, he emphasized that memory alone could not make "a trustworthy history." His narrative drew upon facts known to him and records that he had created and preserved. Although initially he had not taken notes of interviews with fugitives, he eventually realized the personal and historical value of documenting information that one day might help unite family members separated by the flight north. He carefully pointed out gaps in his records and explained that his narrative kept true to the evidence. Assuring readers that he had not embellished his material, he declared that he had taken "the most scrupulous care . . . to furnish artless stories, simple facts, — to resort to no coloring to make the book seem romantic." Similarly, he vouched that the stories he included were true. The Vigilance Committee, he explained, was not easily taken in. "When charges or statements were made by fugitives against those from whom they escaped," for example, "particular pains were taken to find out if such statements could be verified; if the explanation appeared valid, the facts as given were entered on the books." Accuracy was "doubly" important because "it was barely possible" that fugitives described in the book might "still be lost to their relatives, who may be inquiring and hunting in every direction for them," and might "turn to these records with hope."[7]

At the outset, Still differentiated his work from the kind of general antislavery history that May had so recently published. As he compiled his book, he seemed to have been hopeful that later generations would be able to learn about the existence and destruction of slavery and "the deeds of the brave and invincible" men and women who had opposed it. Even though his intention was not to describe abolitionists and their accomplishments, Still courteously acknowledged the "labors" of abolitionists and honored friends of the slave, particularly "the Ladies' Anti-Slavery Societies and Sewing Circles of Philadelphia" and abolitionists like Lucretia Mott and William Lloyd Garrison. But his book did not describe antislavery meetings, lectures, pamphlets, or detail antislavery fund-raising or antislavery mobs. The persons he was introducing to his readers would hardly merit a place in a treatment of "the Anti-Slavery question proper" and held very different views from well-known abolitionists. The people who crowded his pages did not subscribe to the nonresistance embraced by Garrison and others; one, Daniel Gibbons, after reading the constitution of an antislavery society, had actually refused to join it. "He said that he could not assent" to the rejection of force, that "he had long been engaged in getting off slaves, and . . . had always advised them to use force . . . he did not see how they could always be got off without the use of some force." Nor were all of those included in Still's book disinterested reformers. Some actually received pay for their dangerous work, which was "no more than fair," considering the risks their efforts involved.[8]

At center stage in Still's history were the black fugitives themselves, while the white and black friends and "agents," like Gibbons, who sometimes assisted them, remained on the sidelines. The runaways were heroic actors who seized freedom for themselves instead of waiting for abolitionists to free them and then tell their story. They stood at the front line of the battle against slavery, a battle that was often physical, violent, and deadly. To the Vigilance Committee, the fugitive slaves who appeared in Philadel-

This dignified portrait of William Still appears at the beginning of his account of the Underground Railroad. Still's clothes and signature help to establish his authority and respectability. (Courtesy Photographs and Prints Division, Schomburg Center for Research in Black Culture, The New York Public Library, Astor, Lenox and Tilden Foundations)

phia in increasing numbers were the human evidence that freedom was making great strides among those still enslaved. The inspirational accounts fugitives gave of their trials in slavery and their flight from it had a unique power that put abolitionist rhetoric in its place. Even Senator Charles Sumner's "great and eloquent speech on the Barbarism of Slavery," Still wrote, "seemed almost cold and dead," compared to the bearing and speech of escaped slaves. "Their love of liberty, and of the determination to resist Slavery to the death, in defence of their wives and children — this was Sumner's speech enacted before our eyes."[9]

While Still's narrative differed from the more familiar story of antislavery, at its heart stood the shared emphasis on freedom that abolitionists were now insisting was so central to understanding slavery and the coming of the Civil War. Freedom was what abolitionism was really all about and what the fleeing slaves were seeking. Just as their masters did, slaves insisted they had a right to individual liberty. Even lowly field hands harbored "the spirit of Freedom, so natural to man." Furthermore, they acted upon that belief. "Where could be found in history a more noble and daring struggle for Freedom" than the efforts of Robert Brown — or many others of the fugitives whose stories Still told? Indeed, properly understood, the individual accounts of the fugitives and of their "Friends" were central to grasping the significance of abolitionism. All had helped to weaken slavery and thus contributed to the story of its abolition. From this perspective, emancipation was not the result of a military necessity but of the innate urge for freedom. It was "the grandest event in modern history." As he ended of his preface, Still expressed the hope that the "true friends of the slave" would recognize that his book was, in its way, a "tribute to the Anti-Slavery cause." Many did, for after the book was published, abolitionists praised it as part of the antislavery narrative. James McKim, a prominent Pennsylvania abolitionist, hailed the book as a contribution to both antislavery history and literature and saw one of its chief values as the characterization of those who labored to overthrow the institution of slavery.[10]

The stories Still told were important not only because these courageous men and women deserved "the applause of . . . liberty-loving citizens" but also because he believed that the personal memories that illiterate slaves passed down orally would not last more than two generations. Using committee records, Still was preserving deeds of black heroism that belonged on the pages of history that, so far, were empty of black achievements. The inclusion of supporting materials like newspaper articles, runaway slave advertisements, private letters, and copies of legislation were all part of this historic record. Still inserted the Fugitive Slave Bill in full, for example.

Without it, people would "hardly be able to believe that such atrocities were enacted in the nineteenth century" under an enlightened, Christian government.[11]

Still's desire to ignite an interest in the past took on urgency as 1871 and 1872 unfolded. The Enforcement Acts (1870–71) and the Ku Klux Klan Act (1871) helped curtail antiblack violence in the South. But as Amos T. Akerman, the attorney general who enforced these laws, realized, the situation had "revealed a perversion of moral sentiment about the Southern whites which bodes ill to that part of the country for this generation." In 1872, at the same time that Still's book was in production, a group of liberal Republicans broke from the party to form the Liberal Republican Party. They nominated Horace Greeley to run for president; their choice won the endorsement of the Democrats. During the campaign, Greeley and his supporters attacked southern Reconstruction as corrupt and pressed for reconciliation with the South. Although Greeley lost the election, the reformers' bolt from the party left the Republicans more conservative and more conscious of the political appeal of reconciliation.[12]

In 1873, Still must have understood the significance of such events as he reflected that "the future looks very dark to me for the colored man both North + South." This was a view he had held "for a long time." Faced with this dark future, Still hoped to influence public opinion by selling thousands of copies of his book. "What a grand monument this would be to the heroism of the late Slaves & what encouragement and credit to the colored men of this country," he declared. Garrison shared this goal. "I hope that the sale of your work will be widely extended," he wrote, "for the enlightenment of the rising generation as to the inherent cruelty of the defunct slave system, and to perpetuate such an abhorrence of it as to prevent all further injustice towards the colored population of our land. It is a book for every household."[13]

Still's central themes appeared at the very beginning of his narrative. In what turned out to be one of the book's longest sections, he described the heroism of Seth Concklin, a white, "Christlike" man of action, who gave his life for the cause of freedom. Having read a newspaper article describing how a slave, Peter Still, with an "undying determination to be free" bought himself, traveled north, where he was reunited with some of his relatives, but was unable to forget his wife and children still in bondage, Concklin determined to rescue the slave family living thousands of miles away in Alabama. In this bold attempt Concklin lost his life, and subsequent attempts to buy the black family failed.[14]

The story nicely paired a white northerner and a black southerner both motivated to heroic action by their love of freedom. Both white and black families suffered from the blight of slavery: the Concklins because their beloved brother, Seth, lost his life, the other because beloved family members remained enslaved. But while there was racial symmetry in the text, the inclusion of a portrait of the former slave and his mother but the absence of any picture of Concklin suggested that the book would emphasize fugitives rather than their white helpers.

As Still pointed out, the public already knew something of these events because they had appeared in print during the days of slavery. But many details had necessarily remained "hidden." Now Still was in the position to furnish the missing information since his own records contained letters and newspaper notices that were pertinent to the case. In addition, since the former slave was his brother, the author was perfectly placed as observer and narrator to provide new and interesting material.

While the book's opening suggested Still might have some overall plan in mind, it soon became clear that he did not. The nearly 800-page book was repetitive and disorganized, with a narrative that jumped around chronologically. The lack of structure prevented any dramatic buildup and made it difficult for readers to identify turning points in the antislavery struggle. Since Still submitted parts of the manuscript to the printer as he went along, he had no opportunity to correct or add to sections of the book already written. Thus people and events that should have appeared together did not. As Still explained, an account of an incident about a young fugitive had already been handed to the printer and "was in type" when the story of the fugitive's mother was "discovered . . . among the records preserved. Under changed names in many instances, [fugitives often took new names] it has been found no easy matter to cull from a great variety of letters, records and advertisements, just when wanted, all the particulars essential to complete many of these narratives." While it was impossible to put the relevant material in "its proper place, yet, since it has been found," Still decided, "it is too important and interesting to be left out."[15]

Still struggled between his need to control the length of the narrative and his inclination to include everything. On the one hand, he wanted to captivate readers with tales of thrilling adventures and escapes and keep the book to a reasonable length. As the book progressed, comments about the necessity "to economize time and space" became more frequent. On the other hand, he also considered it important to give "an account of as many of the travelers as possible." Still piled story upon story, filled with information about fugitives' original names, their new names, their ages and physical appearances, even the slave advertisements calling for their recapture. The

FUGITIVES AS PART OF ABOLITIONIST HISTORY

result was an unwieldy mélange of material, a problem he sensed but failed to correct. It is likely that, like many writers, Still had difficulty leaving out material that he had painstakingly collected. But his strong commitment to detail and inclusion also stemmed from his sense of justice, that all of those who had risked so much should receive proper notice and his hope that all the particulars might help family members long separated find one another again. He understood the tradeoffs. "Some lost ones, seeking information of relatives, may find comfort," he explained, "even if the general reader should fail to be interested." Still's interest, however, was unflagging. One senses his regret, after he had written 600 pages, about the fugitives' stories that he had to abandon to turn to the Underground Railroad agents and other friends of the slave. "With this interesting case, our narratives end," he wrote. "A large number on the record book must be omitted . . . although there are exceptional cases even among those so omitted, that would be equally as interesting as many which have been inserted, time and space will not admit of further encroachment."[16]

Unwieldy as the final product was, Still's book occupies an interesting place in the emerging field of abolitionist memorials written during Reconstruction and in the tradition of slave narratives so popular among abolitionists before the Civil War. Like the slave narrative, Still's book contained accounts of the sufferings of black men and women under slavery and their determination to escape at all costs rather than descriptions of the trials and triumphs of mostly white abolitionists. Like the slave narrative, the book was rooted in the South rather than the North, the focus of Samuel May's recollections and others that followed. And like the slave narrative, Still highlighted the flight from masters and slave hunters. But unlike the slave narrative, Still provided details that had been too dangerous to publish in the antebellum period. Even such a popular tale as that of Henry Box Brown, which had been widely reported in antislavery newspapers and by the fugitive himself, was actually "very little . . . known." Thus Still "briefly" was able to offer his readers the "facts . . . never before . . . fully published." Still's book was one that filled in the blanks.[17]

One of the reasons for the popularity of slave narratives was the claim that they offered authentic witnesses of the evils of slavery. Even though white abolitionists often surrounded the former slave's story with testimonials about its veracity, and even though the narrative itself was shaped for a white audience, the voice was supposedly that of the black slave. In Still's book, that voice did appear in letters from fugitives in Canada, in occasional passages where a slave was "allowed to speak for himself," and in excerpts from fugitives' interviews with the Vigilance Committee. Still recalled one such incident when the committee had listened to a "thrilling tale": "Wishing to get it word for word as it flowed naturally from his brave lips, at a late hour of the night a member of the Committee remarked to him, with pencil in hand, that he wanted to take down some account of his life." But while this technique provided a direct transcript, the resulting story was scripted not by the fugitive but the committee. "'Now,' said he, 'we shall have to be brief. Please answer as correctly as you can the following questions.'"[18]

For most of the book, Still himself was the medium through which the stories came to life. As the portrait at the book's beginning made clear to any reader who might not know, Still was black. In a curious way, the black author assumed the validating role that white abolitionists had played in their testimonials for prewar slave narratives. Often pointing to his role as listener and record keeper, Still established his credentials as the intermediary between slaves and readers whose judgment about the truth of what he heard could be trusted. Not only had Still been in a position to evaluate slaves' narratives, but he took his responsibility of transmitting their stories seriously. In recounting the escape of Charles Gilbert, for example, Still assured his readers of the essential truth of his account: "As to the correctness of the story, all that the writer has to say is, that he took it down from the lips of Charles, hurriedly, directly after his arrival, with no thought of magnifying a single incident. On the contrary, much that was of interest in the story had to be omitted." Still made it clear that he regretted not taking more copious notes. Had he done so, "a far more thrilling account of his adventures might have been written."[19]

While Still claimed his stories accurately reflected fugitives' experiences, as the writer, he shaped and controlled their histories. Still suggested that often fugitives were inspired as no others could be when they told their stories. He noted the pleasure the committee derived from Gilbert's "remarkable" story, "narrated so intelligently." But Still inserted Gilbert's "own language" only here and there, primarily to add drama to the story. It was Still who must have added many of the vivid touches, describing Gilbert as "drunk with joy" once he had boarded the steamer that was to carry him to freedom, praising Gilbert's "inventive intellect" that "led him to enrobe himself in female attire" when officers searching for him boarded the vessel. It was also Still, acting on his sense of propriety and regard for the readers' possible response to "harrowing" or "painful" details, who chose what material in the records should be included and what should be left out. It was also Still who made it clear to his readers what the slave might not have realized. Frequently, the important points emerging from the narrative were so obvious that Still was content to let the reader "interpret for himself" or used heavy irony to underline the point. But in other cases, he acted as a corrective. Thus when Isaac spoke kindly of his former mistress, Still made sure that readers were not deceived: "His view was a superficial one, it meant only that they had not been beaten and starved to death."[20]

One scholar has estimated that around sixty-five slave narratives were published before the Civil War. Here, Still provided hundreds of cases that reinforced and elaborated the antebellum narratives. Although the voices of slaves came primarily through Still, the repetition of stories revealing the cruel nature of slavery and slaves' desire for freedom had a power that individual slave narratives could not. The book literally overwhelmed readers with information, refusing to let anyone who took up the book dismiss slavery as unimportant, benign, or morally acceptable. As Still had made clear in the preface to *The Underground Rail Road*, his purpose was not to amuse his readers. Slavery might be over, but its cruelties and crimes should not be forgotten by Americans as they wove their historical narratives to explain the coming of war and its meaning.[21]

Nor should one forget the very real slaves themselves. Still often commented on the rewards that masters offered for the return of runaways or the prices for which slaves had been sold. By contrasting the dollar estimates of worth with the physical details that he provided for fugitives, Still suggested the insubstantiality of economic valuation as a primary way of understanding human beings. His emphasis on appearance also differentiated his account from antebellum slave narratives, which gave only indirect information about a fugitive's looks. Still drew the physical descriptions of fugitives not only from the Committee's records but also from runaway slave ads, which often provided small details: a fugitive may have had a goatee, for example, or bowed shoulders, or a certain color hair. If the ad contained inaccurate information, Still corrected it. Thus Still commented that "Theophilus is twenty-four years of age, dark, height and stature hardly medium . . . [h]is bearing is subdued and modest," while "Stepney was thirty-four years of age, tall, slender, and of a dark hue."[22]

Still almost always noted skin color. The wide range of skin tones he described revealed the common intermingling of the races and the inadequacy of bipolar racial classifications. His attention to color also highlighted the individuality of each fugitive. One might be chestnut colored or yellow, another gingerbread or dark orange, others merely light or dark.

In a dramatic departure from white abolitionist literature, Still rejected the preference for the light-skinned slave. This popular stereotype implied that white blood fostered intelligence and that beauty consisted in light skin and white features. Still directly challenged this common view by turning the scheme on its head. Far from finding light skin desirable, Still suggested that it diminished a person, revealing that he or she had been "bleached" by the patriarchal institution. At best, a fugitive might look "none the worse for having so much of his master's blood." But for Still, whose own coloring was dark, beauty consisted of a jet-black complexion with no signs of racial mixing. His descriptions made it clear how blackness added to beauty: "John was about nineteen years of age, well grown, black, and of prepossessing appearance"; Thomas was "well made, wide awake, and of a superb black complexion." While Still realized that some might still consider deep black "not . . . a fashionable color," in *The Underground Rail Road* a black "hue was perfect, no sign of white."[23]

Descriptions of fugitives provided a sense of individuality and variety, but Still assured his readers that all the fugitives shared common characteristics. Most important and emphasized over and over from the dedication and the preface through the hundreds of pages of text was the bravery of those fleeing slavery. Young heroes, men ready to throw "off the yoke, even if it cost them their lives," abounded. They were ready to suffer hardships that would daunt many a brave man or women. "If such sufferings and trials were not entitled to claim for the sufferer the honor of a hero," Still asked, "where in all Christendom would one be found" with a better claim? They were also physically courageous, ready to use firearms and other weapons if necessary. Still described four slaves who arrived together in Philadelphia with two butchers' knives, three pistols, and two other knives between them. The pluck and bravery of such men was evident in their stories. Betrayed by a man posing as an Underground Railroad conductor, Henry Predo and those who were with him found themselves not in a safe house, as they had expected, but at the Dover jailhouse. When they realized their plight, they fought their way back down the jail stairs, despite the efforts of the sheriff, who had "revolver in hand," "plunged into the sheriff's private apartment," where his family was sleeping, tossed live coals over the room, and headed for the window. "Our hero Henry, seizing a heavy andiron, smashed out the window entire" and with the others jumped out to the ground twelve feet below. Black men like Henry were examples of "determined manhood."[24]

Still explained at the outset that most of the slaves who escaped were "physically and intellectually above the average order of slaves." Most were not field hands on large plantations; they worked for small or medium farmers, or in urban areas; many hired themselves out. They were in the best position to understand their situation and the possibility of changing it. In a curious way, rather than robbing them of intelligence, slavery had made many slaves deep thinkers, capable of reasoning for themselves. One should not be misled by appearances, Still argued: "Those who would have taken this party for stupid, or for know-nothings, would have found themselves very much mistaken. Indeed they were far from being dull or sleepy on the subject of Slavery at any rate." Fugitives not only understood the risks involved in planning their escapes, but they also proved to be ingenious in plotting them out. "In very desperate straits," Still explained, "many new inventions were sought after by deep-thinking and resolute slaves determined to be free at any cost." Some escaped unaided; others succeeded in locating Underground Railroad agents to help them, despite secrecy surrounding the Underground Railroad operations. Surprisingly, even slaves kept in darkest ignorance had the mental ability to recognize their intolerable situations. Uneducated as one slave named Charles was, wrote Still, "he was too sensible" to believe his master "had any God-given right to his manhood."[25]

Still and the committee were surprised when a party arrived with more women than men. Most fugitives were male. As Still pointed out, women faced more obstacles in escaping and were more likely than men to fail in their attempts. His own mother fled with her four children, but slave-catchers discovered them in New Jersey and carried mother and children back into slavery. But "she was incurable." Having lulled her owner into a false sense of security, she bided her time and made another "bold strike for freedom." This time she determined to leave the boys behind, and this time she succeeded. Other women disguised themselves as young men, probably thinking males attracted less attention than females, and slipped away from slavery in that way. Because of the difficulties and perhaps because of his own family history, Still paid special tribute to women, deeming them worthy of "double honors."[26]

Still's mother was not the only woman who left her children behind, although the most common pattern Still noted was men who deserted their wives and families in the South. This raised a delicate but important issue. Abolitionists had condemned slave owners for ripping families apart and argued that slaves felt the same strong bonds of affection for spouses and children as middle-class northern whites. How did the pattern Still depicted square with the familiar abolitionist rhetoric about the force of family ties among slaves? How did it square with the southern claim that free black people lacked the moral values that bound white families together? What did abandonment say about those who escaped? Why did Willis Redick, one of the escaped slaves in the book, and many others leave their spouses without a word?

Still was clearly uneasy with such questions. At one point in the narrative, he acknowledged that some fugitives forgot their southern families. At another, he admitted that a number of fugitives found new wives in Canada: "It is more than likely, that there are white women in Canada to-day, who are married to some poor slave woman's fugitive husband." The range of explanations he presented suggested he was casting about for a convincing rationale for what seemed to be heartless behavior. So he insisted that men had to tear themselves from their wives and found the separation extremely painful. Though parted, husbands continue to love and pine for absent wives, hoping that they would one day follow them to freedom. Having emphasized that fugitives did not lack family feelings, Still insisted that slavery (and thus white owners), not husbands, were responsible for desertion. For example, he pointed out that the runaway slave Joe did not "let affection . . . keep him in chains." However, it was not Joe but "the slave lash" and cruel treatment that "widowed and orphaned" his family. In any case, slave husbands were powerless to do anything for their wives and children. While the decision to flee might look "exceedingly hard . . . what else could the poor fellow do? Slavery existed expressly for the purpose of crushing souls and breaking tender hearts."[27]

When Thomas Jones fled to the North, he took with him a daguerreotype of his wife and locks of her hair and of their four children. The reason for Jones's flight was his master's decision to sell "the wife of his bosom" for rejecting his sexual advances. The specter of sale was one of the most common reasons motivating slaves to escape, Still believed: "The slave auction block indirectly proved to be in some respects a very active agent in promoting travel on the U.G.R.R."[28]

Somewhat surprisingly, the first section of the book did not provide the usual abolitionist picture of savage whippings and other physical cruelties. But as the stories piled up, there were plenty of examples of violence sparking the determination of a slave to escape at any cost. While Still spared readers many of the gory details, he succeeded in highlighting the brutality of the slave system that was fundamental to explaining the Civil War. One of his favored approaches was to contrast a fugitive's testimony about a good owner, a statement for example that he or she "'had not been used very hard' as a general thing," to the gruesome details provided in the ensuing interview. Sheridan Ford, who spoke "rather kindly" of his mistress, revealed that he had been "stretched up with a rope by his hands" and "whipped unmercifully." Still did not set up these contrasts to suggest that slaves were stupid but rather to show that the system was so vicious that slaves did not always see violence as extraordinary or any cause for "special complaint." In other cases, while Still suggested some fugitive testimony was "too horrible to relate," he included enough of the fugitive's own words to convey the reality of brutality. Finally, he emphasized that these accounts were not unusual. The master who flogged his female slave naked was "the representative of thousands in the South using the same relentless sway over men and women." Such tales of violence suggested not only that violence was a constant in southern life, no matter what whites might now say, but also that constant vigilance was necessary to control it.[29]

Still's narrative raised broad questions about southern veracity as slaves revealed how their masters had duped them. In several cases, fugitives reported that their masters had promised to free them in their wills. But when these masters died, their wills were either missing or said nothing about manumission. Another fugitive thought he had an agreement with his master that he could buy himself. After paying $600 over the agreed-upon price, and then not given his freedom, that slave "concluded to bear the disappointment as patiently as possible and get out of the lion's mouth as best he could."[30]

What was most surprising and what made the condemnation of slavery so crushing was how many fugitives had found slavery intolerable even though it had not brutalized them. Many just wanted to earn their own living; like their white counterparts, they realized the value of their labor and believed they deserved its rewards. Others, like Daniel, had not "had it very rough as a general thing; nevertheless, he was fully persuaded that he had 'as good a right to his freedom' as his 'master had to his.'" Indeed, the many comments indicating that there was no special reason for flight were surprising. Luther Dorsey, for example, "was prompted to escape purely from the desire to be *free*." Such stories suggested that the love of freedom was innate and, despite any good treatment, slaves found their condition intolerable.[31]

The stories of favored slaves provided dramatic evidence that even the best of treatment did not make slaves content or compensate for the loss of freedom. When Maria Joiner arrived from Norfolk, she bore no "visible marks of ill usage." It was the attractive and fresh appearance of such slaves that had led many visiting the South to conclude that slavery was benign. But close questioning always revealed that there was no such thing as a "'comfortable' existence in a stage of bondage." Too many uncertainties lurked. A mistress might die and leave her slave to an abusive heir. Children might be sold away. While owners might never resort to using a whip, slaps and blows that left no marks were all part and parcel of slavery. Such cases made it "evident that even the mildest form of slavery was abhorrent," rendering any claim that slaves loved their owners unbelievable.[32]

Still's choice of illustrations (engravings as well as portraits painted from photographs) reinforced the messages of the text. Only three images depicted slaves in passive roles. Two showed a master, armed with a knife, attacking a young black male slave. The third exhibited a slave hanging by his wrists, his toes barely touching the floor. Most illustrations revealed slaves in action, carrying out their thrilling, dangerous, and ingenious escapes. One picture showed over twenty fugitives, men, women, and children, stalwartly marching through the driving rain toward freedom. Another placed in the foreground two horse-drawn carriages (stolen from the master) filled with escaping slaves, boldly driving through a town, with white men in the background looking quizzically on. Many focused on a battle between fugitives and their pursuers. One, titled "Desperate Conflict in a Barn," showed on one side of the picture black men armed with pitchforks, guns, and swords advancing on their white opponents, who were retreating. Text and illustrations together highlighted the driving force of the love of liberty and implicitly endorsed the necessity and importance of emancipation.[33]

The portraits included mostly white "friends of the slaves"; some were well known, like Lewis Tappan and Thomas Garrett, while others less so. The blacks whose portraits appeared were former fugitives who had attained positions of importance or respectability. One portrayed Mary Milburn, who had escaped from Norfolk in men's clothes. Milburn's picture showed a handsome, mature black woman with an elaborate hairstyle, large dangling earrings, and an opulent jacket with fringe and braid trimming. Her richly decorated but tasteful clothing and ladylike appearance demonstrated that Milburn had risen in the world. The text revealed that Milburn had an "excellent character" and had succeeded as "a fashionable dressmaker."[34]

Contemporary messages were embedded in the historical narrative. They ranged from the ability of black people like Milburn to work hard in nonslave occupations and rise in the world to the burning desire of black people for a life in freedom. The determination to grasp freedom forcibly and to resist enslavement in all its forms provided an inspiring example for free people who faced many challenges in their new lives. The messages also presented the rationale for whites to ensure that blacks continued to enjoy their rights as free citizens.

Toward the end of his book, Still included a speech by William Lloyd Garrison in which Garrison declared that he had "never deemed it neces-

"Desperate Conflict in a Barn." This illustration suggests slaves' determination to be free, the theme of William Still's account. The fugitives clearly have the best of the situation as the whites retreat from their assault. Pictures such as this one helped to sell Still's book. (Courtesy Picture Collection, The Branch Libraries, The New York Public Library, Astor, Lenox and Tilden Foundations)

sary to go down into the Southern States . . . for the purpose of taking the exact dimensions of the slave system." What Garrison and other abolitionists had failed to do in their speeches and tracts before the war, and May, as a northern abolitionist, could not do in his book, Still was now accomplishing. Centered in the South, the book offered a damning and particularized picture of southern society. As readers learned about hundreds of former slaves, they also found out about hundreds of slaveholders, furnished with names, geographic locations, and personalities. Here was the specificity, the details, and the numbers missing not only from many prewar abolitionist tracts but also from individual slave narratives that could only depict a small slice of the slave system. The volume of information was overwhelming and guided readers to the conclusions Still intended.[35]

Still introduced the South at the very beginning of the book with the story of his brother, Peter, and Seth Concklin. After Concklin's effort to free Peter's family had failed and they were returned to slavery, the owner sent Peter a letter offering to sell him his wife and children. As Still emphasized, that letter was "inserted [in his book] precisely as it was written, spelled and punctuated." After Still's fluid prose, the letter offered a shocking example of an untutored slave owner who bore little resemblance to the flattering image of the chivalrous, cultivated master beginning to emerge in literary fiction. "I will take 4000 for 4 culerd people," the letter read, "& if this will suite him & he can raise the money I will delever to him or his agent . . . said Negroes but the money must be Deposeted in the Hands of some respectable person . . . let me Know his viewes amediately." It was Peter Still's response that bore the signs of refinement: "To say that it [your letter] took me by surprise, as well as afforded me pleasure, for which I feel to be very much indebted to you, is no more than true."[36]

Slaveholders of all kinds appeared in these pages. There were examples of the genteel and supposedly noble large plantation owners, but more frequently there were vignettes of small or medium farmers with only a few slaves. At the middle or bottom of the slaveholding hierarchy, these men and women were often poorly educated, brutal, and intemperate. Their power rested neither on racial superiority nor on the affection of their slaves but on physical force. In the comparison of masters and slaves that the narrative presented, the owners were put to shame.

In several telling incidents, armed fugitives clashed with owners, slave hunters, or other defenders of the racial status quo. The possession of weapons leveled the playing field and revealed that when blacks faced whites in an equal contest, they were perfectly capable of routing their white opponents. In one such clash, six white men and a boy tried to stop a group of black men and women whom they suspected were fugitives. The blacks pulled out their pistols and dirks and cried out that they would not surrender. When one of the whites aimed his gun at one of the black women, she cried out "'Shoot! Shoot!! Shoot!!!'" while waving her own pistol in one hand and a long knife in the other. Faced with the determination of the fugitives, the cowardly whites "prudently" backed off. Still commented with heavy irony, "As chivalrous as slave-holders and slave-catchers were, they knew the value of their precious lives and the fearful risk of attempting a capture, when the numbers were equal."[37]

Especially singled out for criticism were mistresses. They belied the stereotype of the affectionate, generous, and sensitive southern lady who supposedly exhibited restraint in her personal relations. In typical accounts,

James reported that his mistress, a widow, "'upwards of eighty, [was] very passionate and ill-natured,'" while Nancy commented that her owner frequently gave "way to unbridled passions." Many were so stingy that they stinted on food. They did not hesitate to exploit their slaves so they could enjoy "leisure, comfort, and money" wrung from the "sweat" of their slave's brow. Charles delivered a common opinion: "the despotism of his mistress was much worse than that of his master, for she was all the time hard on the slaves."[38]

The vignettes of the occasional good masters or mistresses highlighted the corrupting influence of slavery. Oscar had been the "pet" of Elizabeth Gordon, a young lady who had taken care of the slave since he had been a child, even having him sleep in her bedroom. Oscar had no hard words about his mistress and described her "character as the lady would have been pleased with in the main." Nonetheless, his efforts to buy himself failed because, pet or not, she knew that she might get as much as $1,500 if she sold him. When Oscar asked her price, she initially said $800. When Oscar tried to bargain her down to $700, "after reflection," she raised the sum to $1,000.[39]

As Oscar pointed out, Elizabeth Gordon was a member of the Southern Methodist Church and "'strict in her religion.'" One of the details Still almost always included when possible was a slave owner's religious affiliation. While Still did not denounce the churches for their involvement in slavery, as did Samuel May or Mary Grew, he did not need to. The descriptions of the excesses of slaveholders' behavior combined with their religious affiliations made the point. "Outwardly they were good Christians," as Still put it, but the reality of their lives demonstrated that Christianity was dead within. The ways in which slave owners treated those in their care proved they "were strangers to practical Christianity."[40]

Southerners and most northerners believed black skin symbolized savagery and lack of civilization, a view supporting both slavery and race prejudice. Still's book inverted this conviction and challenged softening views of the prewar South by reaffirming the abolitionist characterization of white southerners as uncivilized and barbarous. The slaveholding class was composed of "perfect savage[s]," and its slave-catchers were "hyena-like." In many stories, the brutality of white southerners stood in vivid contrast to the humanity the fugitives demonstrated over and over again. Still's vivid depiction of masters and mistresses made it difficult to believe they might have a serious change of heart after losing a war and their slaves.[41]

Despite the disorganized, repetitive, and lengthy nature of his narrative, Still succeeded in hammering home his points. As he turned over early sections of the book to the publisher, he seemed to have realized that he had insufficiently dealt with some important matters. Increasingly he emphasized the ability of black men and women to flourish in freedom, the qualities they needed to succeed, and the obstacles they might face in their new lives.

Some of Still's points were basic. The four slaves who executed a daring escape in a skiff across the Chesapeake Bay were courageous examples of "the rising mind of the slaves of the South." But, like many other fugitives, they were also very dirty. The filth and the odors were not their fault, as Still pointed out. As slaves, few had had any changes of clothes, and their slave cabins had been "incentives to personal uncleanliness." Owners never encouraged their slaves to wash and were responsible for their slaves' squalid condition. Nonetheless, fugitives needed and received "practical lessons" on how to keep themselves clean. Often delivered in "a very gentle way," these lessons were obviously fundamental to flourishing in freedom then as well as in the 1870s. Do "'not forget from this time forth to try to take care of yourself,' &c., &c."⁴²

When Still praised certain fugitives, he signaled the attitudes and behaviors associated with worldly success, attitudes, and behaviors that he feared many blacks had not yet acquired. In recounting the meeting between the Vigilance Committee and Robert Jones, Still informed readers that the committee found him "among the most worthy and brave travelers" passing through Philadelphia and was confident that he "would do credit in Canada" to himself and "his race." Still added that Jones was literate and determined to "do something to lift his fellow-sufferers up to a higher plane of liberty and manhood." Jones, he explained approvingly, was convinced that black men needed to throw themselves fully into a variety of occupations and prove that they could rise in the same way as white men. Still recalled that the committee had found Jones's letters so inspiring that they had often shared them and even had some of them published.⁴³

Particularly in the second half of the book, Still sketched out "a brave, intelligent class, whom the public are ignorant of." Even with no advantages, fugitives exhibited their "smartness" that "if properly cultivated" would allow them to "fill any station within the ordinary reach of intelligent American citizens." Noting with approval those who were literate, he pointed out that, in some cases, slaves had actually taught themselves to read or had criticized their owners for preventing them from learning. Above all, he praised those bent on self-improvement. He provided success stories, describing, among others, the former fugitive who acquired a restaurant, the ambitious man who "successfully" sold kerosene and lived near Boston in "a comfortable home," and Sam, who transformed himself into Dr. Thomas Bayne by doing "just what every uncultivated man should, devoted himself assiduously to study, and even . . . hard subjects," and who eventually became a member of the New Bedford City Council.[44]

Still acknowledged that not all fugitives were as capable as these men. But few were hopeless. John, "a sturdy-looking chattel," was among the least intelligent of those whom Still encountered. But "he was not too old . . . to improve." Another, John Smith, who was "rough" in appearance and demeanor and had "deficiencies" caused by "the poorest kind" of nourishment, was bright enough to discover how he could escape. "As green as he seemed he had succeeded admirably in his undertaking."[45]

Still's discussion of the challenges of freedom were drawn not only from his long-standing concern with the possibilities of fugitives but also from his observation of contemporary events. Increasingly he pointed to obstacles facing people of color. His extended account of an unsuccessful effort to end racial discrimination on Philadelphia's railways showed the continuing power of prejudice in the North. As one of the freedmen who had worked to overturn discriminatory practices had warned, "this prejudice was akin to slavery." John William Dungy, who returned from Canada to Richmond after emancipation highlighted the pressing educational needs of freed people. Still passed along Dungy's description of the absence of educational and religious institutions for freed people in the Shenandoah Valley and pointed out, "There is still need of efficient laborers."[46]

The final 150 pages of Still's narrative contained vignettes about abolitionists, supporters of the Underground Railroad, and some of its leading figures. On the title page, the notice that the book would contain "sketches" of these individual appeared in much smaller print than the statement that the book would feature the "hardships Hair-breadth escapes and Death Struggles of the Slaves in their efforts for Freedom." The size of the print indicated that, in Still's opinion, these men and women, many of whom were white, were far less important than the slaves themselves, a point Still conceded once in the text. "Such hungering and thirsting for liberty," he wrote, "made the efforts of the most ardent friends, who were in the habit of aiding fugitives, seem feeble in the extreme." This view, of course, implicitly challenged white narratives in which white abolitionists assigned themselves a central role in the antislavery struggle.[47]

Despite the fact that these activists (most of whom were white) had engaged in daring exploits, they never came to life. In the absence of the kinds of physical details Still provided about the fugitives, these twenty-four men and women appeared generic rather than specific. Not even the inclusion of twenty pictures, four to a page, could make them real. Cast against a white background, the heads and shoulders of each man and woman floated eerily in space, disconnected from one another and their earthly exploits. The lack of pictorial drama was especially striking when compared to the illustrations earlier in the book of fugitives engaged in vigorous action scenes.[48]

That Still was less interested in this section of the book is suggested by the way in which he handled the text. When his subjects were dead, Still padded the account by including selections from newspaper articles "breathing a . . . spirit of respect," descriptions of the funeral service, and letters written in praise of the dead man or woman. These eulogistic materials established the worth of the deceased but gave little sense of their vitality. The inclusion of often hastily written letters to Still did suggest some of the character of their work and hinted at their personalities but not to the extent that they established them as forceful presences in the narrative.[49]

When he could, Still had someone else write the vignettes. He solicited submissions from former abolitionists but was often refused. However, Lewis Tappan agreed to provide a "few reminiscences," but they revealed more about fugitives he encountered in New York than they did about him. John Hunn also included some material about fugitives but not about himself. He explained that he did not deserve any credit for what he had done nor did he consider that he had made any sacrifices for following a course of action that brought him peace of mind: "Would it be well for me, entertaining such sentiments, to sit down and write an account of my sacrifices? I think not. Therefore please hold me excused." While such a response was a credit to his modesty, his reticence contributed to the lack of vigor in the book's conclusion.[50]

The appearance of this somewhat motley group did, however, convey some sense of Still's understanding of the abolitionist movement. Still set his sketches in the context of a cause that had triumphed, largely due to the efforts of the men and women whom he memorialized. In the last years before emancipation, "the force of events" had overwhelmed the leadership of abolitionists and reunited "them with their countrymen in the irresistible flood which no man's hand guided, and no man's hand could stay." While perhaps antislavery activists could not claim credit for emancipation, those who were still living had the satisfaction of knowing that their work had borne fruit. Men like Elijah Pennypacker, who had been active in his local and county antislavery society as well as the Pennsylvania State Anti-Slavery Society, could look "abroad over his beloved country" and see "millions of enfranchised men beginning to avail themselves of its pecuniary, education and political advantages, and beholds them starting on a career of material and spiritual prosperity."[51]

This upbeat assessment, however, collapsed at the end of the book. Still included a lengthy section on Frances Watkins Harper, a black poet who had been active in the abolitionist movement and the Underground Railroad before the war and was now lecturing to white and black audiences throughout the South. Still wanted to feature Harper because, aside from slave narratives, he knew of no portrayal of the contributions of women of color in any written account of the antislavery crusade.[52]

Still provided ample examples of Harper's talent, including letters and lectures as well as some of her poems. He revealed that her four "small" books had sold at least 50,000 copies, a feat that, as an author, he hoped to emulate. The fulsome treatment he accorded to Harper made clear how successfully she had spoken and written for her race. "May we not hope," Still wrote, "that the rising generation at least will take encouragement by her example and find an argument of rare force in favor of mental and moral equality, and above all be awakened to see how prejudices and difficulties may be surmounted by continual struggles, intelligence and a virtuous character?"[53]

Among the letters and lectures included were those written as recently as 1870 and 1871. While Harper refused to be discouraged about the realities of black southern life, she described incidents that did not bode well for the future of freed people: the shooting of a young black man who had married a white women, the casual beating of a black women in her own house by a group of white foxhunters, poverty, and the desire of "this old rebel element" to rob blacks of the vote. The conclusion readers might draw from such information might be Harper's hopeful one or one that saw how a still unreconstructed South threatened black people. Whatever the conclusion, the message that work remained to safeguard black freedoms was the same.[54]

Still's awareness of the realities of black life encouraged him to view the completion of his manuscript as merely one step in a larger project. The new phase of overseeing the production of his book and then in fostering its sales contributed to his goal of making black achievement more visible in society at large.

His publisher, Porter & Coates, was one of the subscription publishing houses located in Philadelphia. The firm published many popular books, including Horatio Alger's series for boys. For Still, the contract with Porter & Coates was a good arrangement. His book was long, with many illustrations, and would be expensive to produce. Regular publishers, like Ticknor

& Fields, Samuel May's publisher, were wary of taking on the costs associated with books like Still's, fearing that it would be impossible to make any profit. Subscription houses were willing to produce expensive books that would not be handled by bookstores but marketed directly to buyers. Canvassers solicited individual sales by allowing a potential buyer to examine a few pages or the entire book, if it were already in print, select a binding, and then pay for the book. Later, the canvasser would return with the book itself. This method of producing and selling books matched supply and demand and channeled cash to the publisher as books were printed or bound. The system of canvassing brought books to people who might own few or no books and have little contact with bookstores. Literary magazines considered buyers of subscription books innocents who made unsystematic and bad choices. Snobbery aside, such comments suggest that Still's book reached a humbler and more racially mixed audience than May's book, whose readers picked it up in a bookstore.[55]

As Still recalled later, the book had cost many thousands of dollars to produce, but, in preparing it for publication, he had determined to spare no pains or expense. In the arrangement worked out with Porter & Coates in January 1872, Still agreed to furnish the publisher with the electrotype plates and the woodcuts for book. The publisher agreed to produce the book "in first-class style" with a good quality of paper and several different bindings. If either side was dissatisfied, the supplemental agreement made it possible to terminate the legal agreement.[56]

After the year named in the contract was up, Still and the publisher agreed to end the arrangement. Still took over the responsibility of publishing the book as well as the sales operation. Still explained that, while Porter & Coates had valuable expertise in the subscription business, he was eager to provide a personal example of a successful black entrepreneurship. "When the great problems connected to our present and political status are being brought under constant review," he remarked, "I could not forgo the opportunity of endeavoring to add one more permanent enterprise to the few existing among us." With 10,000 copies of his book in print by 1873, he first set a very ambitious goal of selling between 50,000 and 100,000 copies over three years.[57]

One of Still's most important tasks was the recruitment of capable canvassers. Although he preferred black agents, Still was aware that he needed aggressive men and women, black or white, to sell the book. He sought canvassers who were "first-rate," energetic, willing to devote substantial time to pushing the book, and knowledgeable about "the art of selling books to all classes of people." A point in favor of black agents was Still's conviction that an agent who had personal experience of oppression could use it to advantage in persuading people to buy the book.[58]

Still corresponded with applicants, asking them about their experience, the time they expected to spend as agents, and whether they could furnish him with a reference. His "Confidential" circular offered financial arrangements that Still claimed were more generous than those of most subscription houses. "Experienced" agents were to receive 40 percent of their sales, while "persistent canvassers" would receive 50 percent. The difference between what agents paid to Still and received from their customers was their profit. Still told one canvasser that one of his very successful agents earned up to $100 a week. With these generous terms, Still hoped to encourage black men and women to improve themselves and rise in society. In a letter Still wrote to the *New National Era* in 1873, he claimed that one black man had done well enough with canvassing that he was able to attend Oberlin College.[59]

Once Still had accepted a person as canvasser, he assigned him or her a territory to cover, and sent a kit costing the agent $3.75. The kits contained free posters, circulars with the agent's name and addressed printed on them, a copy of Still's book in one of the possible bindings, and the canvassing book. Still often provided agents with two extra copies of the book to give to newspapers for review along with examples of the different bindings buyers could choose. The cheapest was English cloth, which could be ordered in green or red (or some other color if the purchaser desired) for $4.50. The paneled style (also called gilt) cost $5.00, while the sheepskin edition was priced at $5.50. No matter what the style, the books were expensive. May's *Recollections* had cost $1.50, much cheaper than any versions of this volume; many other books could be acquired for as little as fifty cents.[60]

Still was determined that his book sell and peppered his agents with advice on how to market the book most effectively. They needed to read the book, of course, and become so familiar with it that they could easily open it to "thrilling" incidents and images to dazzle a possible buyer. The first potential buyers an agent should approach in any community were influential people like ministers, to whom Still suggested offering a special discount that would be offset by increased sales. If an agent could show that well-known and respected people had signed up in the canvassing book to receive a copy, others would be impressed and place an order. It was also important to give some evidence that early subscribers had actually received the book. Still urged agents to get books to those who wanted them as fast as possible, knowing how people might change their minds about paying for the book if the delay between ordering and receiving the book was too long. Never lend the book to a potential buyer and never give credit and demand cash before handing over the book, he told his sales agents. Knowing that many could not come up with a lump sum for the book, however, Still did advise allowing people, especially blacks without much cash, to pay for the book in installments.

Arousing interest before trying to sell the book was important. Still advised his agents first to leave circulars for people to read before encouraging subscription. Getting a review in the newspaper was helpful because, even if it was negative, it got the book noticed. Still himself placed advertisements for the book, furnished with laudatory comments, in various newspapers. Securing testimonials was normal practice in the subscription trade, and Still used his antislavery contacts to get prominent antislavery figures to praise his book. Senator Charles Sumner, for example, noted approvingly that "the army of the late war has had its 'Roll of Honor.' You will give us two other rolls, worthy of equal honor . . . fugitives from slavery . . . and . . . self-sacrificing benefactors." Fifteen "prominent members of the Anti-Slavery Society" expressed their "confidence" in Still's "ability to present to the public an authentic and interesting history of this enterprise." Agents doubtless used these statements in their sales pitches. In contrast to another book that had no "high endorsement, and no illustrations," Still's agents would easily "awaken an interest" among potential buyers as they listed the words of praise for *The Underground Rail Road*.[61]

Agents wrote to Still and described how they did their jobs, but most of that correspondence seems to have disappeared. In a communication to the *New National Era*, however, Still provided excerpts from agents' letters that gave some idea of how they went about canvassing. One agent in Delaware described visiting several black communities where people remembered some of the incidents featured in the book. At one place, the recognition of the book's veracity led one person to exclaim, "'Well! Well! Well! I do think that is the greatest book I ever read in my life.'" At another place, when the agent read from the book at a religious meeting, a member of the meeting attested to the story's truth. As a result, nine people subscribed to the book. In Schenectady, New York, the female agent reported that her subscribers were "first-class whites," including the president of Union College, a Catholic priest, and even the Democratic mayor. Although the mayor ordered the book merely out of respect to her, after reading it, he said everyone in the country should read it. Such praise obviously helped generate more buyers.[62]

Still's desire to sell more than 50,000 copies of his book was not merely a matter of personal ambition but part of his larger effort to reform race relations and the realities of black life. As he told one agent, having granted emancipation and suffrage, whites now needed to see their effects on black people, "some striking proof" of black "business capacity," and of their literary, artistic, mechanical, and intellectual abilities. There were thousands of books in libraries around the country, but only a few slender volumes here and there bore the names of black authors. As the content of his book made amply clear, slavery had prevented people of color from competing in the world of arts and literature. His book's success would provide critical evidence that black men, like white men, now had the competence and drive to succeed and would open a "wedge" to allow others to try their hand at writing. As far as business went, blacks were only "meagerly" represented in "productive enterprises." Indeed, his intention to highlight black enterprise had been a major reason for taking over from Porter & Coates. By managing the book's publication and sales, Still intended to demonstrate that blacks could succeed and to inspire others to follow his example. As a publisher, he hoped to represent his race at the upcoming Centennial Exhibition, anticipating "that our black citizens of Phila[delphia] shall be found in no mean place among the publishers and merchants."[63]

Still's conviction that his efforts aided race reform explained why he preferred to engage black agents. His sales operation offered an important opportunity for young black men and women, both in the North and South, to succeed in a business occupation, to move beyond the inferior manual jobs that blacks had held in both slavery and freedom. In seeking a reference for a black man who wished to become a canvasser, Still asked whether the applicant realized the need for blacks to work their way up in order to gain respect and a proper regard for black manhood. This was the big challenge. White canvassers knew how to stick to the work of selling books and make a business of it. Blacks had to learn the same skills. If blacks did not improve as a result of their changed conditions, they would lose the public's respect.[64]

Still also believed his book could have a transformative effect on those who bought it. The history of the Underground Railroad needed to "be kept 'green' in the memory of this and coming generations for the lessons which may be learned." One lesson emphasized the crushing impact slavery had had on black life and culture. The white nation must understand that blacks recognized "the long years of hard struggles and gross wrongs that have been inflicted upon us." Implied was the message that whites should not abandon blacks because change did not come overnight. The nation should remember and honor the black drive for freedom so amply documented in fugitive stories. For black people, an awareness of the history of oppression made the vital point for "our children and posterity" that "the causes of being behind" were not black inferiority but enforced servitude. Furthermore, the heroism and bravery of the fugitives provided an inspiring example for black people as they faced the challenges of their new lives in freedom.[65]

Still anticipated reaching thousands of people with his uplifting history. He donated two copies of the book to the Library of Congress and selected his canvassers. By the summer of 1873, he had over forty agents in the field and was shipping orders to states as diverse as California, Massachusetts, Indiana, Illinois, Tennessee, Texas, Pennsylvania, and North Carolina. He encouraged agents to target whites, especially Republicans, who might be disposed to buy the book and who needed to remember the history it detailed, especially after the Liberal Reformers had urged reconciliation with the South. Agents should, of course, seek out blacks, and perhaps even a few Democrats. He anticipated healthy sales in the South, telling one of his canvassers in North Carolina that he thought it was not unreasonable to expect 5,000 purchasers over a three-year period. "Rebells" would presumably not want the book or welcome its message, as one anonymous letter to Still, seemingly written by a white southerner, attested to. "mr nigger which I can't cal you ar for you nante as good as me," the letter writer proclaimed. "Such a man as that ought to bee put back in slavery. I could drive such a nigger as that."[66]

As part of his marketing strategy, Still not only urged his canvassers to supply local papers with review copies but also, in addition to securing testimonials, solicited reviews himself. He contacted Oliver Johnson, a former abolitionist associate who worked at the *New York Tribune*, asking if he would write a book notice. While reviews were not Johnson's responsibility, he provided Still with the name of the appropriate reviewer, remarking that even a brief review was worth hundreds of dollars in sales.[67]

The fact that many newspapers and even some journals noticed Still's book in a favorable way is a credit to his tenacity and to interest in the subject of his book. In a number of ways, Still had violated some of the standards usually deemed essential for a good autobiography. It was not a "pleasant" story, nor was it well constructed or well written. But as several reviewers pointed out, the book was exciting. The *New York Tribune* spoke of its "narratives of audacious and almost hopeless enterprise, romantic adventure, and wonderful incidents," a perspective with which the *Lutheran Observer* agreed. The "thrilling personal dramas and tragedies" that caught the attention of reviewers led some to compare it to *Uncle Tom's Cabin*. Others noted that the book provided historical insights, one of the approved functions of a good autobiography. The volume gave readers a "precise knowledge . . . of a peculiar epoch that was not [even] understood by most who lived in it," and revealed details that illuminated the workings of the Underground Railroad. This information was timely, for some reviewers realized how few Americans had known much about the Underground Railroad operations, while others noticed how quickly people were forgetting the recent past. The *New York Times* considered that one of the book's contributions was its reminder of the existence of the Underground Railroad. Most people no longer associated that term with fugitives from slavery, the paper claimed, but with rapid transit.

The editor of *Harper's*, like others, commended the book's simple style and forgave its lack of literary qualities because Still had acknowledged his literary deficiencies and never attempted "fine" writing. Surprisingly, *Harper's* did not find the narrative "diffuse." Of course, Still's self-effacing posture came in for praise. "There is not the least savor of egotism in his pages," noted the reviewer approvingly. The *Philadelphia Inquirer* agreed that the narrative's "great simplicity and natural feeling . . . cannot but make a deep impression." The book should "have a place in every comprehensive library, private or public," concluded the *Friends Review*.

"It is a big book in manner, matter and spirit," said one commentator. That bulk, though, was a problem for the *Times* critic, who thought the book was too long. The narrative certainly could have been condensed. But Still himself seems to have considered the book's heft a good thing, writing one canvasser that the book was the "largest" ever from a black author. The size of the book may also have proved to be a good selling tool; more pages justified the book's high price.[68]

During the summer of 1873, reports of healthy sales made Still confident that he would meet his sales target of 50,000. By early October, however, he was beginning to realize that the financial panic that had started the previous month would probably weaken sales. By December, he had stopped placing ads in papers or encouraging canvassers to go out to sell the book. By spring he was intending, if things improved, to take up the sales operation "with renewed vigor." Despite the continuing serious economic downturn, Still began to push the book actively again the following spring, placing ads in black papers like the *Christian Recorder* and recruiting enterprising young people as canvassers. He continued to enlist agents over the course of the decade.[69]

How many copies of the book canvassers managed to sell is not known, but it is likely that Still's vigorous sales efforts got his book into far more hands than May's. The book was displayed at the Philadelphia Centennial

Exhibition, just as Still had hoped. Still continued to exploit various strategies to move the book along. In 1877, the *New York Times* reported that a consignment of Still's book would be offered the last day of the fall trade sale in the city. The next year, the *Christian Recorder*, a black newspaper, announced that it would give a copy of *The Underground Rail Road* to anyone who signed up five subscribers to the newspaper. While these two pieces of evidence could suggest that the book was no longer selling well on its own, it is more likely that Still was trying to get rid of the remaining copies of printed books before he came out with another edition. In 1883, his third edition appeared, and it was this edition of the book that Mark Twain acquired. In 1886, Still presented a copy of the book to President Grover Cleveland, perhaps thinking it would be a good influence on him. The continued sales of his book suggest that, despite their growing indifference to the actual fate of southern blacks, Americans enjoyed reading stories, conveniently set in the past, about fugitives who freed themselves.[70]

Still's effort to illuminate an important part of the struggle against slavery and to place black people, if not himself, firmly in the center of the story suggests how clearly he understood the need to get his version of the past into public consciousness. Black men and women had not just received freedom but had actively sought it. By doing their part to undermine slavery's power, they had prepared the way for its end. On the one hand, the heroic struggle of black fugitives demanded respect from the nation. On the other hand, the legacy of slavery could not be easily or quickly overturned. Thus the laudable efforts black people were making to improve themselves called for praise and patience. Still was proud to declare that the country had no other book like his.[71]

The sheer heft of Still's book and its success made it unusual, but other blacks wrote and published similar stories, hoping to contribute to the construction of a memory of the past that honored their place in history and clarified the evils of southern slavery. Two former slaves produced modest narratives of their escapes from slavery and lives in freedom at about the same time that Still's book appeared. John Quincy Adams was only twenty-seven when he published his autobiography in Harrisburg, Pennsylvania. Like authors of traditional slave narratives, he included personal testimonies from white men about his character, intelligence, and honesty. William Webb dictated his life to his wife and had it printed in Detroit. It appeared without personal testimonials. Like many authors of slave narratives, however, Webb assured readers that his book, though written down by his wife, was "composed by himself."[72]

Neither Adams nor Webb could have anticipated the large readership to which Still aspired, and certainly neither could have contemplated sending his story to a mainstream publisher. A Houghton Mifflin reader's evaluation of a manuscript titled "From Slavery to Freedom: The Story of Archer Alexander" suggests why one leading publisher had little interest in the sorts of stories Webb and Adams produced. The reader remarked that Alexander's narrative (written by a white minister) was too short to be profitable. While interesting, the account had "no such singular features as to attract any considerable audience; and . . . the form of the narrative, while personal and unaffected," had "no special felicity."[73]

Like other humble writers before them, ranging from beggars and convicted convicts to Civil War prisoners, Webb and Adams found local presses or newspapers willing to publish their work. They probably paid all the costs themselves and produced only a few copies of their books. But the fact that they decided to publish their work at all suggests a strong desire to circulate their views. Webb may have only expected a black readership, but Adams, like Still, intended to get his story into white hands. He thought that some white gentlemen and ladies would acquire his book if only to show they supported his efforts to improve himself.[74]

The narratives emphasized many of the themes central to Still's work: the oppression and inhumanity of slavery, the longing for freedom, the desire for and importance of education, and the importance of honest industry that was properly recompensed. Unlike Still, both Adams and Webb carried their stories well into their life of freedom. Adams addressed his book to "friends of progress and elevation," describing not only his life as slave and his escape but also his experience as "a citizen." "Nothing is more glorious than to know I am a free man," Adams declared. "My country is much dearer to me than my life." Webb also included his "views of the present time" and indicated that he was writing his book in order to earn money to pay for his education.[75]

Both attacked racist stereotypes, especially the view that blacks were ignorant, a perspective that justified whites' denial of social, civil, and political rights. As Adams pointed out, "They took my labor to educate their children, and then laughed at me for being ignorant and poor, and had not sense enough to know they were the cause of it." Webb said much the same thing: "If they look at it right, [they] will see that we never had a chance." Both suggested their determination to rise in the careful way in which they listed their jobs. "I am one of those that is trying to rise up," Adams stated simply.[76]

In his preface, Adams claimed that his book was not "published to create any excitement or accuse any one wrongfully." Despite the disclaimer,

Adams provided a scathing view of the slave-owning class. In the past, blacks had provided "that class all their pleasure" — the handsome parties and the splendor and style. "Since the Negroes are all free," Adams said, "that style is broken up," and former masters and mistresses lamented its disappearance. "How the aristocracy of the South has fallen since slavery has ceased. I say let them go to work." Toward the end of his autobiography, Adams described returning to visit his former owners in Virginia. Things did not look so good as they had under slavery, and neither did his master's family. He had little sympathy for their situation. "It was negro ancestors that kept them up," Adams exclaimed. Recording the death of his former master, Adams assured readers that he had forgiven him for his actions during slavery as Scripture taught. "But believe I cannot forget," he confessed, and neither should his readers.[77]

Both men were sensitive to the perils of freedom. Adams warned about false friends, and Webb discussed in detail the politics of the postwar period, Andrew Johnson's perfidy, and the government's failure to provide slaves with any help "to make a living." But both reminded readers of the legal protections with which they had been furnished. Adams included the preambles to the Constitution and the Declaration of Independence as well as the postwar amendments at the conclusion of his narrative to highlight the promises made, and he asserted his confidence (or perhaps just his hope) that the government would continue to protect blacks. Webb praised the Republicans as wise men for giving blacks "all the privileges of other men," encouraged the second election of Grant, and dismissed the Democrats as having no "good feeling for the colored people." He looked forward to the day when the party "would grow weaker, and . . . finally die out and be forgotten." If black men "are only faithful, they will reap the benefit of that law" that gave them equality. On paper, at least, Webb was as hopeful as Adams.[78]

In these two life stories, Adams and Webb documented their transformation from individual slaves to free men by escaping during the Civil War. As Adams pointed out with some pride, "I stole John Q. Adams . . . they valued me at $2,000. At that rate I stole $2,000." But they did not attribute the larger change, the emancipation of a race, to human agency. Unlike white abolitionists and Still, they had little if any awareness of abolitionism's lengthy struggle for immediate emancipation. Webb did meet some abolitionists during his wanderings and reported that he had "a great liking to talk to them. I found that they all talked the one thing, I found they had no proud heart for themselves but had kindly feelings for other people." But Webb had little sense that abolitionists did anything beyond talking.

Politicians, in Webb's view, were vehicles though which God acted. Adams agreed that "God . . . made us free men and free women." These narratives placed emancipation and freedom into a sacred framework that minimized human agency in favor of the divine, an interpretation that increasingly was confined to the black community.[79]

The appearance of Still's massive book and these two slender ones suggest the attraction of the fugitive theme. The 1873 publication of a novel titled *John and Mary*, first serialized in the *Lancaster (Pa.) Inquirer*, points to the appeal of local fugitive stories. But the white author, Ellwood Griest, brought a very different perspective to his subject than black writers publishing in the same decade. In Griest's novel, white abolitionists are the main characters, and blacks play subsidiary roles. Although the author acknowledges the bad treatment of freed people during Reconstruction and hopes his readers will find both "pleasure and profit" in his story, he gives little sense of the necessity for urgent action on behalf of former slaves.[80]

Griest portrays whites and abolitionism in a flattering light. Members of the Brown family are simple Pennsylvania Quakers who unexpectedly find themselves sheltering two escaping slaves and their infant. This experience introduces the Browns to "the righteousness of the[ir] act and its probable consequences." Years later, the recollection of the fugitive mother encourages the Browns' son, Frank, to oppose slavery. At least one other member of their community who assisted in helping the fugitive mother becomes a brave and stalwart defender of abolitionism in the days when "the vials of pro-slavery wrath were emptied on the heads of all who countenanced 'abolitionism.'" After the account of the fugitive family's escape concludes, the story jumps thirty-five years to postwar Florida, where the noble Frank Brown, now an army captain, is stationed. Brown and the author are highly critical of the unrepentant southerners who have not improved since the days of slavery. Whites are lazy and complaining. They "hated the negro because he had obtained his freedom" and "the same legal rights with themselves." The situation is a bad one, and some northerners are part of the problem. Brown bravely opposes antiblack violence that a few federal officers, who have more in common with rebels than with northern abolitionists, shamefully tolerate. The author notes approvingly that Brown's blood boiled as he contemplated the injustice: "His education had been anti-slavery, and his sympathies were all with the oppressed race. Besides, he thought this action on the part of a Federal officer was an outrage."[81]

In the course of the story, Brown rescues Sergeant Evans, a black former soldier who has been casually shot by a member of a white gang composed of "as worthless a set of fellows as there is upon the face of the earth."

Brown's ability to sympathize with Evans is a credit to both of them. Brown's attachment to Evans is one "a man will form . . . regardless of rank, color, or caste" for one "who shows in his daily acts those true qualities of manliness that are as rare as they are valuable." Unfortunately Evans's wound proves serious, and his mother, Mary, is summoned from Pennsylvania to be with her son. When the mother tells her story, Brown realizes that she was the fugitive who had appeared at his home so many years before. This amazing discovery does nothing to reverse her son's decline. Before long, he dies and is buried "with the flag of his country wrapped around him." Shortly afterward, his mother follows him to the grave. Rather than returning to the unpunished perpetrators of the crime or the venality of northern army officers and offering some resolution to this part of the story, Griest ends his novel with a burst of sentimentality and two dead blacks: "Through turmoil and trouble, through perils and dangers, with hearts untainted, happy rather as the victims than the doers of wrong, they have reached HOME AT LAST."[82]

The portrayal of mother and son as victims dovetails with Mary's characterization early in the book. Far from being the brave and courageous fugitive of Still's narrative, Mary is timid and fearful, concerned only with her child. When outsiders approach the Brown's house, Mary grabs her baby and runs down into the cellar, "a picture of absolute, perfect terror," of "dumb, speechless agony." Later, after almost being retaken by slave-catchers, Mary runs back to the Brown homestead with her son in her arms. She totters feebly in the door "with eyes distended, great clusters of foam gathered about her mouth, and blood streaming from her nostrils." Although the abolitionist doctor declares her a heroine, her heroism consists primarily of mother love.[83]

While some of the black characters have a certain nobility, many are scoundrels. Mary's husband, John, is a lazy sort, declared "'wuthless'" by one of the other black characters in the book. The pair is almost caught by slave-catchers due to the inability of one black character to stay sober and keep a secret and the treachery of another. Davy Jones, a mulatto man of around seventy, is one of the few black men in the book positively depicted. Davy helps fugitives because he hates slavery. He is "shrewd, quick-witted and cool headed . . . equal to any emergency." The black miller is also an admirable character, but it is apparent that Griest, unlike Still, was ambivalent about the miller's blackness. Griest explains that the miller has a full-blooded African appearance, thick lips, kinky hair, and a large head. The narrator is amazed and puzzled that whites treat a man with these physical characteristics as if he is white, "but such is the undeniable fact."[84]

This novel was unusual in its selection of abolitionists as admirable central characters. Its condemnation of unrepentant southerners certainly conveyed dismay at the continuing hostility of southerners to Reconstruction, but the book demonstrated little commitment to changing the status quo. The way in which the story fizzles out at the end suggests that any commitment Griest might have had to black Americans and Reconstruction was fizzling out too. Further, his failure to conceive of blacks as active agents in their struggle for freedom and to portray blacks in freedom primarily as victims gives the impression that blacks had only minor roles in their own liberation or were never even part of the story. The novel, of course, was fiction, but fictional views of the past have a way of shaping collective memory just as much as historical accounts.

In 1872, after the Liberal Republicans had nominated Greeley and Democrats had decided to support that nomination, *Harper's Weekly* criticized the call for reconciliation: "The earnestness of its appeal to forget the past should arouse the suspicion of all thoughtful men. For history cannot safely be forgotten." With this general sentiment, Still, Webb, Adams, Rogers, Griest, and former members of antislavery societies would all have agreed. All had attempted to ensure that their version of history should inform the present. As the *New National Era* observed about Still's book, the incidents appearing there "become historical when thus placed on the record."[85]

Still, Adams, and Webb had insisted upon the centrality of black people's role in their own liberation, and this perspective would survive in autobiographies written by African Americans. In accounts by Still, Adams, and Webb, flight offered the most powerful example of slaves' resistance to servitude. This theme of resistance was one that was less powerfully expressed in reminiscences penned by white abolitionists, who, not surprisingly, tended to focus on their own activism. Indeed, before long, the idea of resistance disappeared altogether from the formal historical record, only to be rediscovered by historians during the second half of the twentieth century.[86]

In 1872 with the call for reconciliation, *Harper's Weekly* was concerned about the pertinence and power of the historical record that Still and others were trying to preserve. "Instead of forgetting, this is the very moment to remember," the paper insisted. "Why is the past to be forgotten? Has it no lessons?" While the specific lessons that the writers and abolitionist speakers had provided were not all the same, all had accepted the necessity of emancipation and saw it as a central and defining moment in the nation's history.[87]

II

Reunions

Soon after the antislavery societies disbanded, abolitionists began to gather to commemorate their long years in the antislavery struggle, to regain the sense of camaraderie that reform commitments had once provided, and to ensure that their memories lived on in the hearts and minds of a new generation. In 1874, western abolitionists held what they hoped would be the first of many reunions in Chicago. A year later, members of the Pennsylvania Society for the Abolition of Slavery, an organization that had resisted the rush to dissolution, held a meeting to commemorate 100 years of activism. At both meetings, speakers laid out their understandings of the abolitionist achievements. Abolitionists also revealed a keen interest in contemporary events, understanding that they could help to realize or undermine the accomplishments they celebrated.[1]

Not all approved of such gatherings. In June 1874, abolitionists appeared before the Massachusetts legislature to hear George Curtis deliver a eulogy for the late Charles Sumner. The pro-Democratic paper, the *Brooklyn Eagle*, labeled the event as a national antislavery reunion, although it was no such thing. The paper ruminated on the value of meetings of former activists and pronounced them nuisances. "The work being done, of what avail these meetings, save to remind others of the conflict that attended it?" it asked. These assemblies stirred up bitter feelings that impeded reviving the "old feelings of American brotherhood." As for the idea that abolitionism still had a purpose, the paper was dismissive: "In the direction in which it worked there remains no more to do." While the remarks had a hostile tone, they eerily echoed some of the comments uttered by abolitionists during the debates over dissolution.[2]

The *Chicago Tribune* disagreed, hailing the Chicago reunion as the most important assembly of abolitionists held since the war's end. The gathering was the brainchild of some Chicago abolitionists who had determined in early 1874 to call together those who had been active "at any time the cause of the slave needed friends." Sending the announcement of the upcoming meeting to 400 newspapers, planners hoped to attract to Chicago a cross section of antislavery workers, from those who had assisted fugitive slaves to political abolitionists. Like the members of antislavery societies who had created historical narratives of their organizations and achievements, the Chicago group realized the need to influence the historical record. Thus they urged the public, especially young people, to attend the reunion along with the abolitionists.

The planners of the proceedings visualized a review of the past, starting with the period of "self-sacrifice" and culminating with its success in influencing public opinion and "its final triumph." The format would provide ordinary abolitionists with a chance to reminisce and offer prominent abolitionists the opportunity to read to the audience biographical sketches of important leaders. Zebina Eastman, secretary of the planning committee, hoped the reunion proceedings would provide "chapters . . . more important than have yet appeared in writing or print" for the historical record and suggested that "the subject matter which this reunion will intensify will occupy the attention of philosophers and historians in future ages." He also believed that the events of antislavery history might have a positive impact on present events. As he told those who came to the convention, "It seems to many of us . . . that this nation cannot afford to have this chapter blotted out, and the valuable lessons lost upon our children." The *Chicago Tribune* agreed with such an assessment, telling its readers on June 10, the first day of the reunion, that the meeting "appertains at once to the past and the future, to tradition and to history."[3]

The *Tribune* was enthusiastic about the reunion, which promised stories, abolitionist songs, and a festive atmosphere filled with well-deserved congratulations for the "enormous success" crowning abolitionist efforts. Nine years had passed since the war's conclusion, leading the paper to assert confidently that the meeting would not run the risk of arousing sectional hatred or southern jealousy. The "passions and hatreds" of the war had diminished, the enemy was dead, and "the negro is as free as the air he breathes." As it turned out, however, many of those attending the convention vehemently rejected such a view.[4]

The "veterans of the great moral war," as the *Tribune's* headline labeled them, who crowded into the Second Baptist Church during a torrential rainstorm, came primarily from the midwestern states of Wisconsin, Nebraska, Iowa, Michigan, Indiana, Ohio, and from Kentucky. Eastern abolitionists had been invited, and they came from New York, Pennsylvania, and Massachusetts. Most of the most prominent eastern abolitionists declined to attend, but Wendell Phillips, John Whittier, Thomas Wentworth Higginson, and William Lloyd Garrison, among others, sent letters that were read to the audience. The majority of attendees were white men "well along in years. Gray beards, bald heads, and spectacles, were the rule among the men, and sober, Quakerish garbs among the women." Few black abolitionists were in attendance.[5]

As the speakers addressed the audience, the outlines of the "RECORD FOR HISTORY" emerged. Slavery was an inhumane and barbarous institution, as those with intelligent consciences had always grasped. Most Americans, however, had tolerated it, and eventually the North lay in thrall to southern power. Church and state both catered to southern views. Abolitionists, however, embraced both the Declaration of Independence and the Gospel and publicized the truth tirelessly. "But for the alarm and rallying cry of the Abolitionists, the servile slumbers of the nation would have deepened into the sleep of death." As the abolitionists were increasingly successful in persuading the North of the horrors of slavery, the South "in desperation" went to war. Bitter as the conflict was, it embodied great principles: freedom and good versus slavery and evil. The bloodshed cleansed the country from the sin of slavery in which the North as well as the South had been implicated.

While such a narrative repeated points abolitionists had been making for years, the argument about the sinful nature of slavery and the disinterested motives of abolitionists needed forceful restatement. Many had taken the moral reprehensibility of slavery almost for granted and argued vigorously that abolitionists had sacrificed brilliant careers for the reform. Now, the *Brooklyn Eagle* mocked the motives of abolitionists, accusing them of being as ambitious and self-interested as any other reformers. Their movement, it charged, was "principally compounded of four very mischievous elements, misinformation, false pretense, prejudice and interference. Slavery was not what they painted it."[6]

Speakers extended the narrative well beyond the outbreak of war. If abolitionists had been instrumental in awakening the country to the evil of slavery, they played an equally important role during the war by refusing to let the North forget the real cause of the conflict. One speaker credited abolitionists with persuading an uncertain Lincoln to issue the Emancipation Proclamation. Meeting with him in the White House the evening before, they supposedly informed Lincoln that emancipation was a divine command, "an argument for which the President had no answer." After the war, their continuing moral pressure brought about the legal end of slavery. Illinois's governor, in his introductory address, highlighted the most recent accomplishment: racial equality before the law.[7]

Several speakers likened abolitionists to Civil War soldiers and the reunion to the new rituals honoring the war dead. While not questioning the heroism of Union combatants, they suggested abolitionists were especially worthy of the nation's respect. Their war had lasted thirty years, and abolitionists had enlisted not for a bounty or because of the noisy clamor of trumpets but because of the silent call of duty. The war they had waged was not just for the slave but for humanity.[8]

The *New York Times* saw the event as newsworthy and covered the Chicago reunion. The *Times* provided far fewer details than the *Tribune*, and it is not clear whether it had its own reporter at the meeting. Nonetheless, the *Times* noted "much good feeling" on the first day of reunion and gave the gist of Eastman's remarks on the purpose of the meeting. "It will be seen that we are here making 'a record for history,' and the world must accept it as such," Eastman said. The gathering "had been already termed a mutual admiration society. Well, what of it, he [Eastman] asked. They have never been overpraised by the world, and now at this time of age they stood in no danger of being spoiled by flattery."[9]

As the reunion proceeded, however, it did not go entirely according to the organizers' plan. While there was plenty of good feeling, there was also less mutual admiration than Eastman had anticipated, and less willingness to observe the planning committee's rules. Members of the audience had a strong desire to tell their stories, "some of them very funny, others touching, and a few common-place." Organizers, however, had set a limit of ten minutes for ordinary speakers, but as the meeting progressed reduced it to seven, and finally whittled it down to five minutes. Yet prominent men like Dr. Jonathan Blanchard, president of Wheaton College, and Edward Beecher, Harriet Beecher Stowe's brother, were allowed to present long, "exhaustive," and sometimes "tiresome" prepared papers on abolitionist worthies. In a letter written to the *Chicago Tribune* after the event, James Brisbin condemned the planning committee for allowing "a few to do all the talking." "I do not believe in turning a convention into a literary society to eulogize the dead," he asserted. A number of participants also disliked the emphasis on the famous in a reform movement that drew in many ordinary people, including themselves. Those wishing to have more time for their own stories complained angrily that the papers gobbled up time that would be better spent on personal reminiscences. One, a Mr. Grover, who was reading the names of antislavery men and women who had not been mentioned at the meeting, refused to stop speaking when told his time was up. As the newspapers reported, "Mr. Grover said he (Blanchard) was not the proper person to call him to order, and he concluded his speech."[10]

Others had different ideas about the purpose of the reunion and pressed an activist agenda. A few years earlier, when several important antislavery societies had disbanded, some members had argued that they had accomplished their goals. Others had remained hopeful that prejudice would wither away. A number of participants at the reunion disagreed with both positions. On the first day, a letter from a Massachusetts abolitionist, J. W. Alden, was read. Alden urged those attending the reunion to report for further duty and to do whatever remained to be done to ensure that freed people were granted their civil rights. As for the proposals to reconcile the blue and gray, Alden stated harshly that if southerners repented, they would be forgiven. As for the dead, "We would leave their memory to rot." To compare the southern soldiers who had lost their lives with fallen Union soldiers, according to Alden, was "to offer a premium on another rebellion." That same day, the audience heard Garrison's letter that warned of "the siren-cry of 'conciliation' when it means humoring the old dragon spirit of slavery, and perpetuating caste distinctions by law." The truest friends of the South, Garrison argued, were those who refused to compromise.[11]

During the evening session of June 12, not long after Mr. Grover had refused to give over the floor, another man diverged from organizers' plans for the meeting. Mr. Sinclair did not think that the gathering should focus exclusively on the past. In his short address, he argued that the abolitionists' duty was not done until blacks enjoyed the same social and political rights as whites. He offered two resolutions. The first stated "that so long as the freedmen are excluded from the public schools, equal seats on the railroad cars and churches . . . and places of amusement and hotels, our work is not done." The audience applauded Sinclair's suggestion. In the second, Sinclair called on the meeting, temporary though it was, to revive abolitionists' long tradition of lobbying Congress. He suggested a resolution that urged Congress to "step to the very verge of its power to remove these disabilities, and to secure to the freedmen the rights and privileges which we claim for ourselves."[12]

The call to political action caused what the *Times* described as "wrangling." While one attendee remarked that Sinclair's resolutions contained nothing that was not already in the Bill of Rights and should be passed immediately, a point greeted by applause, another did not want to vote on the resolutions too hastily, without discussion. Eastman tartly noted that Sinclair (and those who supported him) had misunderstood the purpose of the reunion. Dr. Brisbain agreed that the resolutions seemed out of place, but he "did not want it to go out that the old-time Abolitionists had any fear about passing them." In the end, the resolutions were sent to the Committee on Resolutions with the understanding that it would report back to the assemblage.[13]

The final day of the reunion demonstrated lingering discontent over time restraints on speakers and anxiety about the situation facing freed people. The Committee on Resolutions acknowledged this feeling and presented two resolutions for approval. One suggested that it was the duty of those present to battle prejudice that so severely affected black life and that it was necessary "to secure" for black people "by all proper legal as well as moral means, the complete possession and enjoyment of all their civil and social rights." The audience applauded this resolution, although it was far less specific than Sinclair's original proposal of launching a petition campaign. The second resolution pointed out the need to work harder to educate and elevate former slaves. Both resolutions passed, but they did not eliminate the concern some felt about the status of blacks. Individuals rose to point out the perils facing black Americans and to urge greater efforts on their behalf. Amasa Walker, a Massachusetts abolitionist, warned that the work was only half over. He had just returned from the South, he said, and his "mind is fearfully impressed with the great necessity of continued efforts in [blacks'] behalf. Emancipation without enlightenment, without elevation and Christian civilization . . . is a terrible calamity to the nation." If abolitionists did not continue their work, he added, "Anti-Slavery had better have done nothing." He challenged the audience to re-embrace a life of activism: "Should we not feel the deep responsibilities of the present hour and gird ourselves for the great struggle?"[14]

On the afternoon of June 12, several women also disrupted the plans of the organizers by introducing the woman question and urging the convention to embrace it. Whether the disruption was planned or spontaneous is not clear. The *New York Times* disapproved, reporting that "women laid violent hands upon the Convention and were near taking complete control with their women's rights and demands."[15]

Men outnumbered women at the reunion, but the reasons for women's absence was not discussed. Perhaps women did not think that their stories of feeding and clothing fugitives were dramatic enough to be told to the audience. Or perhaps, as Rebecca Mott, in her brief remarks to the meeting, may have been hinting, organizers had not made enough of an effort to encourage women to attend the convention. Mott confessed that "sadness mingled with her joy because she felt that the meeting, like thousands of others[,] was a man's meeting particularly." She went on to advocate the liberation of women, arguing that in the future women should take their rightful place beside men on every public platform. Her comments prompted other women to take the floor. Sadie Bailey established her antislavery credentials by pointing out that she had been born in an Underground Railroad depot, then urged the audience to support the enfranchisement of women. Another woman set this goal as well, pointing out that abolitionists had been the first to bring their wives and daughters to political meetings. Supporters applauded the proposed agenda, but others clearly did not like the direction in which the meeting was moving. One man accused these speakers of injecting "extraneous" matters into the proceedings and argued that female enfranchisement had nothing to do with the purpose of reunion. Despite the applause that his remarks elicited, the audience welcomed abolitionist writer Jane Swisshelm even more warmly. Her thirty-minute speech contained antislavery anecdotes but was sprinkled with comments about the wrongs afflicting women. Swisshelm obviously gave a lively address, so spirited that the *Times* called it "a violent harangue."[16]

While the *Tribune* noted approvingly that the reunion got back on track that afternoon, the issue did not disappear. Some women were obviously concerned that their contributions would not be part of the historical record. If they had read Samuel May's or William Still's books or the historical overviews delivered as antislavery societies folded, they could well think that women's contributions had been insufficiently recognized. When Laura Haviland, an activist in Michigan's Underground Railroad, spoke on the final day, she said she "regretted that her sisters had so poorly responded to the call for the convention" and reminded listeners of the energetic role women had taken early in the history of abolitionism. She stated that women had followed their own course in the past and "they intended to go on paddling it as long as there was any necessity." A Chicago man clearly thought that the role of women in abolitionist history had been minimized during the three-day meeting and urged the passage of a resolution supporting the efforts of antislavery women, "which he thought had been overlooked."[17]

If not all members of the convention were sympathetic to efforts to encourage support for changing the position of women or felt that the participation of women in the antislavery movement had been neglected, it was clear that many agreed that the reunion should inspire political and moral activism. When an abolitionist from Brooklyn asked the assembly if their work was done, some in the audience cried out, "No." Several resolutions promoted support for temperance, closely connected with abolitionism and now seen as critical to improving the status of blacks. Other resolutions urged abolitionists to work more forcefully to improve the situation of blacks and to continue to labor for them until "the proscription of the colored man was removed." As one advocate of change explained, abolitionists had learned lessons during their many years of opposing slavery, and it was time to apply these lessons to pressing problems. Political abolition-ist George Julian had developed this theme at length on the conference's second day. In a speech the newspapers called "somewhat sensational," he called upon abolitionists as natural leaders to use their knowledge, exper-tise, and moral insights to confront political parties when they abandoned principles and neglected the pressing questions of the day like the tariff, poverty, the growth of giant corporations, and the vote for women.[18]

When Eastman spoke to the "veterans" of the antislavery movement on the reunion's opening day, he encouraged them to see the reunion as a useful gathering. He and other members of the planning committee an-ticipated that the reminiscences and papers would contribute to the cre-ation of a lively and rich memorial to the abolitionist movement. At the conference's conclusion, Eastman and two others formed a committee to try to find a publisher for the proceedings, an effort they deemed especially important since the young audience they had hoped to attract apparently never materialized. The volume was to be sold through subscription and to cost no more that $2.50. Additionally, the Committee on Resolutions rec-ommended constructing monuments to two early abolitionist publishers: Elijah Lovejoy, who was murdered by a Cincinnati mob in 1837, and Benja-min Lundy, publisher of the *Genius of Universal Emancipation*.[19]

As George Julian's speech, which the *Times* called a treatise on political economy rather than antislavery, and the remarks and resolutions of other attendees suggested, the purpose of the reunion went beyond commemo-ration of past achievements. Participants sought to remind the audience that their obligation to freed people had not ended with emancipation and that they were uniquely positioned to work to improve the situation of blacks and to support other reforms. Perhaps this understanding of the pos-sible purpose of reunion is what led one New York man to offer a resolution encouraging abolitionists all over the country to hold local reunions. The resolution passed.[20]

Almost a year later, the Pennsylvania Abolition Society held its centen-nial anniversary in Philadelphia. The only antislavery society still in opera-tion, it also was the oldest American antislavery organization. William Still, chair of the Committee of Arrangements, extended special invitations to abolitionists whom the committee especially wanted to come, taking the opportunity, in at least one case, to include his book along with the invita-tion. Notice also appeared in newspapers, urging "as many old workers and advocates for freedom as can possibly make it convenient to be present."[21]

The meeting on April 14 was held at Philadelphia's Concert Hall in the afternoon and in the Bethel AME Church in the evening. Both blacks and women were more in evidence than they had been in Chicago, doubtless because the Committee of Arrangements had included them on the program, placed notices in African American newspapers, and scheduled the evening program in a black church. The seating arrangements for the key guests on the Concert Hall stage highlighted the diversity of abolitionist workers in the Northeast. Seated on the platform, which was garnished with "bouquets of tasteful flowers" and the American flag, were white men and women, including Lucretia Mott, Abby Kelley Foster, Charles Burleigh, and Vice President Henry Wilson, and black abolitionists Francis Harper and Robert Purvis, along with Frederick Douglass and John Langston. Still opened the meeting and was followed by the Rev. William Furness, a white Unitarian clergyman, who gave the invocation.[22]

The gathering was quite different from the Chicago meeting. There was no time spent on personal reminiscences, but rather invited speakers addressed the audience in both the afternoon and evening. The two reunions did share a common goal of ensuring that abolitionist efforts were properly recognized. As the published proceedings of the Philadelphia meeting pointed out, the Pennsylvania society was the nation's oldest and most "efficient" antislavery society, but it had "received less recognition than others that accomplished no tithe of its work."[23]

Dr. William Elder provided the official overview of the organization's long campaign against slavery, one that had first pursued gradual emancipation and then rejected that flawed approach for immediatism. Elder's historical perspective of the previous century made it clear how entrenched slavery was and how northerners bore as much responsibility for it as the southern slaveholders. "Everything that malice and fear could suggest, the monster [slavery] practiced," Elder asserted. "It bribed and bullied our politicians; it dominated the press; it profaned the pulpit."[24]

Elder's narrative divided the history of antislavery into four periods, with the last phase lasting from around 1840 to the beginning of war. He depicted these years as "a war under the forms of peace . . . a battle to the death." The weapons were "arguments" that finally woke up the nation to the evils of slavery. While Elder credited Lincoln as the person who "officially gave the foe the *coup de grace*," his analysis made it clear that the real force behind the end of slavery was the steadfast work of abolitionists. Carrying his story to more recent days, he assessed the "purity of the principle and the righteousness of the policy" by the lack of violence that accompanied freeing the slaves. "These people have passed from bondage into freedom more safely than have any other people in the world's wide history."[25]

This uplifting tale of success, however, constituted only a minor theme of the conference. As the published proceedings stated, the first objective of the society had been achieved with the elimination of slavery. "The Society," read the proceedings, "is now remitted to its second purpose—the improvement of the condition of the African race; a labor as great perhaps as its predecessor,—certainly as important to the nation, the race and the world." Abolitionists could not retire from labor "until the whole end of the early organization has been fulfilled in every detail and to the spirit as well as to the letter." Most speakers discussed what the society's remaining objective meant in a cultural and political climate they characterized as increasingly hostile.[26]

Reverend Furness's invocation established an anxious and urgent tone for the meeting. Although it contained the necessary thanks for abolitionists' successes, the invocation suggested broad forces threatened antislavery achievements. "Worldly prosperity" had the capacity to dull the nation's moral sense, while just and equal institutions might not have the power to change the hearts of the American people. Unless people learned basic human respect, "the fetters of pride and prejudice" would remain intact. Subsequent speakers fleshed out Furness's sense of the perils facing the gains reform had made. As Frederick Douglass insisted, "No man of anti-slavery instincts can now look out upon the moral and political situation of this country without seeing danger to the results" of years of effort and bloodshed. "Every effort should now be made to save the results of this stupendous moral and physical contest," he declared.[27]

Vice President Wilson took the floor after Furness and delivered the first of several addresses that bluntly set out the challenges facing those who had worked for emancipation. He emphasized a point that was increasingly obvious: slavery had been ended by war, not by a shift in public opinion. The stubborn persistence of prejudice meant that the black man's rights as a citizen were uncertain. Indeed, Wilson warned that a crisis was at hand: "I fear ladies and gentlemen, that there is in this country to-day, a counter-revolution against the colored man." Like the pioneers of abolitionism, "the men whose hearts are bathed in anti-slavery sentiment" now must confront the counterrevolution head on, until prejudice was dead and all men, black as well as white, enjoyed their rights as citizens. Specifically, "we must animate, vitalize and enforce all that we have added to the Constitution."[28]

The letter from Garrison, read not long after Wilson's speech, attacked the call for historical amnesia and friendly relations with the South. Garrison had been moving further and further away from the confidence that he had felt at the war's end. While it was true that there were no longer slaves, he wrote, the argument that conciliation and goodwill were "the duties of

the hour" and that memories of the past only stimulated feelings of alien-
ation and bitterness was wrong. "Suggestions like these," Garrison insisted,
"have a plausible sound, but they are illusory." When all Americans enjoyed
their rights and none suffered from intolerance, then there might be some
progress toward unity. But abolitionists must never rest. Sounding the call
that had long energized abolitionists and that May had forcefully restated,
he warned that "the price of liberty is eternal vigilance."[29]

When Frederick Douglass spoke, he identified himself both as a man
of the present and as a man who valued history. Douglass argued that the
story of the antislavery movement and celebrations like the centennial held
contemporary meaning. They were "serviceable," for they offered evidence
of human progress (and, by implication, of human agency), a position that
some Americans were now denying. Others shared Douglass's concern that
a cultural shift away from the belief in moral progress that had underpinned
the abolitionist crusade against slavery and racism was occurring. In his letter from Charleston, South Carolina, Reuben Tomlinson decried those who
would back away from working for positive change. He derided the "sham
intelligence which seeks to justify its own apathy and indifference by assertions of the hopelessness of attempting to remove the ignorance and vice
bequeathed to us by slavery."[30]

Frederick Douglass made a similar point when he referred to those who
now were saying that enough had been done for freed people. What, in
fact, had been done for former slaves? True, they had been given their freedom and the vote, but they had been turned free to starve and to face the
anger of their former masters. They had been given freedom and famine at
the same time. Despite the dire economic picture Douglass painted, however, he emphasized that what black people wanted was education and the
protection of their legal rights. As he and surely everyone in the audience
knew, education and legal rights and often life itself were under assault in
the South. Schoolhouses were torched, and armed white gangs killed more
than 100 blacks in Colfax, Louisiana, and shot down many former slaves in
Vicksburg, Mississippi. Blacks in some parts of Alabama and Louisiana (and
many places Douglass did not mention) were too frightened to go to the
polls. Black people, Douglass insisted, "want your voices again; we want
disinterested laborers as of old." They wanted more radical women like
Abby Kelley Foster and more people, outside of the Republican Party, willing to hold up the standards of what was right.[31]

At Bethel Church that evening, Frances Harper delivered a major address that complemented Douglass's remarks. While she acknowledged the
need for freed people to help themselves, she asserted that white people

had the responsibility to make black political rights secure and to destroy prejudice by embodying the idea of human brotherhood. "It may not seem ... a gracious thing to mingle complaint in a season of general rejoicing," she acknowledged, but "I do not believe there is another civilized nation ... where there are half so many people who have been brutally and shamefully murdered ... as in this republic." She went directly to the heart of the problem with her pointed question, "And who cares? Where is the public opinion that has scorched with red-hot indignation?"[32]

Harper realized the central problem was the disinterest on the part of the public in what was happening in the South and elsewhere. From her perspective, there were two major reasons why the nation should confront the deteriorating racial situation. One drew on the old abolitionist argument that if the nation failed to respect men, they were failing in their obligation to God. Harper seems to have realized that this straightforward appeal lacked some of the power it once had, and she attempted to modernize it by referring to new views about the origin of the human race. Whether one agreed with Darwin, Huxley, or another ethnologist, she argued that the central truth remained that all human beings came from one common heavenly Father. Harper's second point left aside "humanitarian" views for political economy: surely the nation would be in better political and economic shape if blacks progressed rather than stagnated.[33]

Like many other speakers, Harper insisted that the work was not yet done. In her final minutes, she gave an eloquent appeal to young men and women, telling them that a noble battle awaited them. For young men, she suggested that a moral war against ignorance and poverty would "give power and significance to your own life." She appealed to young women, urging them not to allow refinement or fortune to prevent them from doing work among the least favored. Elizur Wright struck the same note, saying that the duty facing the younger generation was to complete the task of elevating blacks and ensuring their freedom.[34]

At the Chicago meeting, observers noted that the attendees were well along in years. The same was probably true in Philadelphia. Given the advanced age of the audiences, there was a deep sense of the importance of persuading young people of their version of the past and encouraging them to carry on the work. In schools, many history textbooks referred to abolitionists as "demagogues" and extremists and argued that they were partially responsible for the outbreak of war. Reunions and commemorations provided a means of countering such views and transferring abolitionist perspectives from one generation to another. It made sense that participants wanted to publish accounts of what had happened during their meetings. Although Chicago organizers never succeeded in publishing their proceedings, newspapers provided adequate coverage of each day's events to inform readers of all ages. In Philadelphia, the planning committee had the funds to pay for publication of the proceedings.[35]

The effort to inspire young men and women to devote their lives to reform by offering a stirring picture of the past and its unfinished business faced significant obstacles. Occasional reunions and printed proceedings could not compensate for the lack of an organizational base from which to make the case. The national antislavery society in Great Britain continued its work after the abolition of slavery in the British West Indies and acted as an informational and lobbying group with funds to support its newspaper and publish material for the public. It provided continuity even as individual members died or pursued other interests.[36]

In the absence of an ongoing framework in the United States, the loss of well-known abolitionists, many of whom had spent most of their life agitating for the end of slavery, was especially damaging to the effort to keep memories and commitments alive. As the *Christian Recorder*, an African American newspaper that knew well the importance of old abolitionist allies, observed sadly, "One by one, are the men who formed the advance guard of Liberty [are] falling from the ranks." By 1875, Samuel J. May, Thomas Garrett, Jermain Loguen, Joshua Leavitt, Lewis Tappan, Beriah Green, and Charles Sumner had all passed from the scene. The *Recorder* had rejoiced that Gerritt Smith, Wendell Phillips, and Garrison, who was "still the mightiest preacher of righteousness in the land," were still alive. But by the end of the decade Smith, Garrison, Henry Wilson, and Charles Burleigh were dead. An 1878 article in the *New York Times* listed some of the prominent living abolitionists; the youngest ones mentioned by age were sixty-two.[37]

Obituaries, even in papers that were critical of abolitionists, tended to be respectful. The *Brooklyn Eagle*, for example, praised Burleigh for his zeal and earnestness and commended Lewis Tappan for his calm and judicious approach. Even Garrison, never a favorite, was remembered as a radical who "always had the courage of his opinions."[38]

For some commentators, the passing of well-known antislavery agitators afforded an opportunity to reflect on their importance and relevance to contemporary life. In 1878, the *New York Times* wrote about antislavery leaders, whom they called "heroes" seemingly "engaged in a hopeless contest." While once they had seemed "almost like demi-gods," with time, one could see their "personal foibles . . . errors, and . . . lapses." While the *Times* was at least willing to wager that history would look kindly on these human weakness, it was reluctant to give them credit for emancipation: "It is easy now to see how a multitude of unexpected events conspired to hasten the day when emancipation . . . should come at last." These men and their achievements, the writer reflected, seemed "to belong to a distant period in our history." "Slavery in the United States," he concluded, "has long since been destroyed, [and] even the acerbities excited by a civil war have almost wholly disappeared."[39]

"Nigger Thieves"

WHITES AND THE UNDERGROUND RAILROAD

As William Still was completing *The Underground Rail Road*, he received a letter inquiring whether his book would include accounts of Underground Railroad activities in Illinois and Missouri, stories the writer believed were among the most "thrilling" fugitive tales.[1] Still was in no position to provide information on the workings of the midwestern network so far from his own base in Philadelphia and had "deemed it best . . . to confine himself to facts coming within his personal knowledge, and to the records of his own preserving." Even with this limited focus, however, Still found himself having to omit many interesting narratives told by slaves passing through Philadelphia. Elsewhere, as the letter writer had suggested, were many more stories worth preserving.[2]

The sales of Still's book suggested the popularity of exciting adventures connected with the Underground Railroad. Many of those who had aided fugitives in some capacity were eager to describe their experiences. One of the attractions of the abolitionist reunion held in Chicago in 1874 was the opportunity it provided for participants to hear and share Underground Railroad reminiscences. Rev. George Thompson told the audience of spending five months in a Missouri prison for "stealing" slaves. Mr. Turner related the dangers he had faced during his Underground Railroad career, and Mr. McBride shared his story of his efforts in Ohio. The well-known midwestern abolitionists Levi Coffin and his wife and Laura Haviland were especially well-received. Levi Coffin, a Quaker born in North Carolina who moved to Indiana in 1826 and to Cincinnati in 1847, was a businessman so active in helping fugitives that he was known for many years as the president of the Underground Railroad. He and "Aunt Katy" Coffin, his wife and helpmate, were "greeted with the warmest applause." Coffin made some remarks about his activities, estimating that he and his wife had helped over 3,000 escaping slaves. Laura Haviland, dubbed "an ancient Quakeress of Adrian, Michigan" by the *New York Times* (although she was only in her midsixties), created "a good deal of feeling by her graphic portrayal of the way in which she and other good old souls used to aid the 'niggers' in their onward flight to freedom." Within a few years of the gathering, both Coffin and Haviland published accounts of their careers as abolitionists, finding that the Underground Railroad themes so popular with the public also lent themselves nicely to the purposes that encouraged them to tell their life stories. While each would emphasize his or her own role in orchestrating fugitives' flight from slavery, they also highlighted the intrinsic worth of black people and the continuing obligations of white Americans to those so recently emancipated. In addition, because the media was increasingly publishing material that cast slave owners in a favorable light and was dismissive of slaves, material that could easily pass into the realm of history and memory and affect understanding of the abolitionists and their cause, both writers recognized the necessity of reminding readers of the true character of slavery and of the elite who had profited so mightily from the sinful institution. Aware of the changing tides of public opinion, both took pains to clarify the character and purpose of abolitionism and those who pursued its goals.[3]

Several months after attending the Chicago reunion, the Coffins celebrated their fiftieth wedding anniversary and Levi's seventy-sixth birthday. The couple renewed their marriage vows at the Friends Meeting House in Cincinnati before friends and well-wishers, and then Coffin spent some time reviewing half a century of labor for "the colored people." A *New York Times* correspondent reported that, as he concluded his remarks, he observed that "abolitionists used to be called . . . persons of one idea, which he did not think was strictly true. They had many and various experiences, but time would fail him to go into particulars."[4]

While Coffin did not consider himself a public speaker or an author, audiences clearly wanted to hear the particulars of his life. In a letter to the *Chicago Tribune* after the 1874 reunion, a reader expressed his regret that Coffin had not given a complete account of his interesting and instructive activities in the Underground Railroad. Such enthusiasm suggested that there was a market for his reminiscences, should he decide to write them. Indeed, as he recalled in the preface to his book, published in 1876, he had "been solicited for many years" to record his antislavery labors. But, lacking any desire for literary fame, he had resisted writing about a life devoted to doing his "Christian duty." Friends and acquaintances had kept up the pressure, and their arguments apparently grew more convincing as time passed. Although he had initially disregarded the plea that the "rising generation" needed to learn about his past, the death of many co-laborers in the antislavery movement and his own increasing age began to persuade him that "a part of the history of our country . . . should not be lost." The shifting political climate, signified by the Democrats' congressional victory in 1874, the election of nineteen Democratic governors, and pronouncements like that delivered by the *New York Times* that the issues connected to antislavery had "utterly . . . faded" may also have encouraged him to undertake the task. Whereas, for some writers, autobiographies may serve a personal purpose, for Coffin, a public purpose seems to have been most important in shaping the character of his reminiscences. But there was a private concern as well. Coffin had few financial resources, and he apparently hoped that the publication of his recollections would help to support his wife after his death.[5]

The realization that his recollections had historical value led Coffin to emphasize the historical sources he had used, including diaries and other "documents" he had "preserved." In the main, he assured his audience that he told his story "without any exaggeration," resisting the temptation to treat true incidents like fiction by adding happy endings. "This is a narrative of facts," he emphasized later in the book, in which apparent victories might be followed by "fresh scenes of danger and distress" and even distressing conclusions. Despite his insistence on veracity and accuracy, Coffin's autobiography expressed not the literal truth but what one scholar has called his "own moral vision of the past."[6]

Coffin asked his friend Rev. William Henry Brisbane to write some introductory words for the preface. Brisbane praised Coffin as "the placid, the benevolent, the kind-hearted friend of the slave, and of all mankind," and described the book as "a legacy to his thousands of friends, white and black, in this our beloved country, redeemed from the curse of slavery." Coffin followed these effusive comments with a short statement that may well reveal his primary motive for taking on the burden of writing his reminiscences. While Brisbane had emphasized the glorious end of slavery, Coffin addressed contemporary racial problems, so recently exposed by the passage of a Civil Rights bill in 1875. Racial justice was still elusive because the power of prejudice was still strong. Coffin's hope was that his life story would furnish an important lesson and "accomplish something toward the eradication of the spirit of caste which still exists in our land—though, in the providence of God, slavery itself has been removed."[7]

As a prominent midwestern abolitionist, Coffin must also have been aware of the questions being raised about the achievements and character of abolitionism as the war receded into the past. While Democratic newspapers like the *Brooklyn Eagle* directly attacked abolitionists' reputation, claiming that there was "no evidence" that abolitionists "were really desirous of emancipation at all," more subtle challenges appeared in other forms of popular media. Coffin was a reader of fiction, although it is not known whether he read the popular monthly *Scribner's*. There, a short story by Constance Woolson, appearing just about the time Coffin was working on his book, exemplified shifting views about antislavery adherents. Woolson was a frequent contributor to literary magazines. Although she was born in New England, she lived for years in the South and had traveled there extensively since the war's end. Her portrayal of the abolitionist character was more insidious than newspaper diatribes because her assertions were slipped into an intriguing story where a reader might absorb them almost unconsciously.[8]

The story, set during the war, describes how an abolitionist surgeon from Boston falls in love with Jeanette, a fisherman's daughter of racially mixed ancestry. Although Jeanette is actually part Indian, rumors circulate that some of the young woman's ancestors were black. This gossip quickly cures the surgeon of his affection. He declares to the narrator, "'That taint I could not pardon.'" As the narrator makes clear, the surgeon's racism is typical: "And here, even as the surgeon spoke, I noticed this as the peculiarity of the New England abolitionist. Theoretically he believed in the equality of the enslaved race, and stood ready to maintain the belief with his life, but practically he held himself entirely aloof from them; the Southern creed and practice were the exact reverse."[9]

Woolson's tale was fiction. As Coffin's narrative made clear, however, as much his stories might at first glance appear to be fiction, they were true. False abolitionists did appear in his book, but they were not men who failed to live up to their ideals but impostors claiming antislavery credentials to further their "schemes of deception." The man who visited Coffin pretending to be "a friend of the oppressed slaves" and interested in liberating them was, Coffin concluded, "a spy" intent on entrapping him.[10]

Like Samuel J. May a few years earlier, Levi Coffin rejected the negative characterization of abolitionism suggested by Woolson and others. But while the two abolitionist writers may have agreed on many points, they described very different kinds of reform careers and presented very different pictures of abolitionism. May confined his book to his adult life and his experiences as a Garrisonian in the Northeast. Coffin began his book with his childhood years in North Carolina and then described his experiences living in the Midwest. His own antislavery work suggested how abolitionism had moved from gradualism to immediatism, from individual acts undermining slavery to organized efforts to eliminate it. While Coffin knew and respected Garrisonians, referring to men like May and Wendell Phillips as his "old co-laborers in the anti-slavery cause," these men and the antislavery societies to which they belonged stood far from the center of his narrative. Coffin's account highlighted Midwestern reform activities, especially the Underground Railroad and the Free Produce Movement. Abolitionism did not end with the outbreak of war, and neither did Coffin's book. He included descriptions of his work with contrabands and freed people during the war years and then his role as general agent of the Western Freedman's Aid Commission after the war was over. He closed his narrative with the passage of the Fifteenth Amendment. The conclusion did not suggest, however, that Coffin considered the work of abolitionists complete. However different his picture of abolitionism was from May's, both agreed that emancipation did not represent the victory of the abolitionist agenda but was merely one step along the way.[11]

Coffin devoted many pages to the operation of the Underground Railroad, as had William Still, although Still's experiences were confined to Pennsylvania. Despite the common focus, the two books were very different. Still's book emphasized the stories of fugitives, while the thrust of Coffin's book was to provide "a brief history of the labors of a lifetime in behalf of the slave," and the fugitives who would appear in the book would be those "who gained their freedom through his instrumentality."[12]

Coffin's book was thus a true autobiography that took its shape from his journey from childhood to old age. Although he omitted much about family life, he was more revealing about himself and his personal circumstances than either May or Still. His wife, whom he described at the time of his wedding in 1824 as "an amiable and attractive young woman of lively, buoyant spirits," became an "able and efficient helper" in his life's work. Coffin described his early career as a schoolteacher and his youthful adventures. Business ventures and temperance work helped round out the picture of his busy life. Provided it was given with restraint, such information added to a life story's appeal, or so critics believed.[13]

Coffin had had a variety of opportunities to tell stories about the past, but writing an autobiography demanded making sense of many events and his choices over time. Now, looking back over his seventy-eight years, he reflected upon a multitude of experiences, the person he once had been, and the person he had become. He saw the meaning of his life in one dominant moral commitment: abolitionism. This emphasis on a central moral purpose situated his narrative within the evangelical tradition of the useful exemplary memoir, even though Coffin himself did not belong to an evangelical denomination. The approach he adopted had the possibility of attracting the support of an evangelical publisher that, in turn, was capable of getting the book into the hands of evangelical readers in particular and religious readers in general.[14]

In the first chapter of his book, Coffin described the crucial incident that triggered his "conversion to Abolitionism," in retrospect, a life-changing event that he could hardly have recognized as such at the time. Coffin's family was living in North Carolina, and, at the age of seven, the boy saw a gang of chained slaves coming down the road followed by their driver. Coffin's father, who had been chopping wood, asked the men why they were restrained in this fashion. One of the slaves replied that the chains were to prevent them from escaping and returning to their families. Coffin's "childish sympathy and interest were aroused" when his father explained in simple terms what slavery meant. What the young boy did not realize, the elderly Coffin made clear. His "sympathy with the oppressed . . . together with a strong hatred of oppression and injustice in every form . . . influenced my whole after-life." Reiterating his early commitment to a loose form of abolitionism, Coffin related another boyhood incident also "indelibly engraved" in his memory. Coffin credited these early exposures to slavery with intensifying "my hatred of slavery." They "inspired me to devote myself to the cause of the helpless and oppressed, and enter upon that line of human effort, which I pursued for more than fifty years." Coffin's words suggested that he visualized himself as a person whose essential moral identity remained constant throughout his long life.[15]

Coffin described his first informal efforts to assist fugitives and freed blacks who had been kidnapped and carried south and the feelings of intense excitement and stress that he experienced. His other antislavery work in North Carolina included teaching in a Sabbath school for slaves until neighboring slaveholders forced its closure. When Coffin and his family moved north in 1826, Coffin and his wife became involved in the Underground Railroad. Reminding readers that the Bible never mentioned color, Coffin asserted that he and his family were "willing to receive and aid as many fugitives as were disposed to come to my house." The commitment entailed work, worry, and excitement, but in Coffin's story, there was no room for discouragement. We "bore it cheerfully."[16]

Coffin's reference to the Bible as a guide for moral conduct pointed to ways in which religious belief fed abolitionist commitment. Like so many abolitionists, however, Coffin found that organized religion interfered with the performance of Christian duty. Because many denominations had ultimately accepted the necessity of emancipation during the war, people might forget about the churches' moral failure in the decades before the war. As a Quaker, Coffin was all too aware that the popular belief in the antislavery credentials of the Society of Friends was wrong, "strange as it may seem to the rising generation who read the part of Friend's Discipline relating to slavery." The Society of Friends, like other Christian denominations, had thrown "the weight of their influence against the few true abolitionists who advocated immediate and unconditional emancipation." When the Indiana Yearly Meeting forbade its members to join antislavery societies, Coffin and others withdrew. The point was obvious: one should listen to the voice of the Bible and one's inner moral voice as a guide to Christian duty rather than to the voice of organized religion.[17]

Coffin's abolitionism included crossing racial boundaries, and he gave many examples to show that he did so. As part of the Underground Railroad network, he and his wife harbored fugitives. But his life story pointedly made clear that white responsibilities for black people went beyond briefly sheltering and feeding them. As his career demonstrated, blacks needed help establishing themselves as free people. Coffin supported fugitive communities in Canada. He advised and oversaw children emancipated by their slaveholder fathers and settled in the North. He worked to improve the situation of local Cincinnati blacks and hired black people to work for him. During and after the war he focused on newly freed people, even making a trip to England to raise money and supplies for them. Emancipation did not end obligations to black people, and the work of making a just society remained.[18]

Coffin admitted that being an abolitionist "tried a man's soul." His description of his wife's nephew having his two front teeth knocked out during an antislavery meeting acknowledged that northern mob violence had played a part in his life. But although he included a chapter on mob activity in Cincinnati, he did not suggest, as had May, that he or other abolitionists had been martyrs or victims of a northern reign of terror. Despite the unpopularity of the cause of immediate emancipation and the trials associated with it, he stressed slow but steady progress. "Quiet, well disposed citizens" gradually became sympathetic to the abolitionists, and the passage of the Fugitive Slave Law stimulated the hatred of slavery among "the better class of citizens." By the time of the war, the "odium" against abolitionists began to disappear. This picture of steady progress encouraged readers to identify with abolitionists and their goals. The insistence that human efforts could bring about change also countered the growing popularity of Social Darwinism during the Gilded Age. The idea that it was futile to attempt to reform social or economic arrangements constituted what George Julian would call a "sickly moral fatalism."[19]

In an article in *Harper's* appearing a few years before Coffin began his book, the editor recalled the early history of antislavery and its "most desperate and ridiculous" advocates. Many men and women, he observed wryly, thought that the cause of liberty demanded long hair and uncooked food. This critique was a good-natured one, but many were not. Coffin's narrative countered accusations that abolitionists were merely rabble-rousers and extremists and therefore to be disregarded. While he included in his book a sketch of John Fairfield, a daring young man who not only accepted money for helping fugitives escape but also was willing to use violence if necessary, Coffin made it clear in the section's heading that Fairfield was a *southern* abolitionist, and an exception. Coffin admired the man's commitment and daring, but he "could have no sympathy with his mode of action . . . [nor] indorse the principles he acted upon." His own moderation was far more exemplary than Fairfield's "wicked . . . daring and reckless[ness]." Even southern slaveholders listened carefully to his antislavery views, according to Coffin, because he used "mild and respectful language" and "endeavored to speak with moderation."[20]

But the abolitionists pictured here were not dour, humorless extremists, either. Abolitionists actually displayed a healthy sense of humor in this book. Coffin recounted one incident in which a druggist, "a staunch abolitionist," planned to "have some fun" with a marshal pursuing an escaped slave. His idea was to substitute a free woman for the female slave, pretend to escape with her when the marshal approached, and then allow himself and the girl to be taken. Then the "farce" would come to a satisfying climax when the marshal and his posse were arrested for kidnapping a free woman. Coffin himself was not above a little mischief. When a female slave disguised as a boy appeared at the Coffins' house, Coffin insisted that his hired girl take the "boy" in her bed. The girl was disconcerted; she "glanced at us wildly, then covered her head," resisting Coffin's instructions until the practical joke was revealed.[21]

Abolitionists who had a sense of humor and played practical jokes did not fit the negative stereotypes that were undermining respect for their achievements and point of view. In Coffin's account, midwestern abolitionists, at least, were not fanatics but "a few unarmed, inoffensive men, who felt it right to plead the cause of the oppressed, and to endeavor, by moral suasion, to convince the people of the evils of slavery." Included in his definition, if not in his language, were women like his wife who not only fed and clothed fugitives but also developed ingenious plans to spirit them away from their pursuers.[22]

Coffin's autobiography provided a compelling example of the committed reformer who was willing to risk everything, "life, property and reputation," for a just cause. The lesson was simple. Principles without moral courage were useless. Principles without action were equally problematic. All too often Coffin waited for someone to step forward, and all too often no one did. As he wryly observed, time and time again, "the duty seemed to devolve on me," which highlighted not only Coffin's willingness to take on the burden of action but also the necessity of taking on what others refused to do. At a time when many had given up on freed people, Coffin's example was a powerful indication of what must be done.[23]

Coffin's autobiography defended the importance of sympathy and emotion rather than scientific reason as the wellspring of reform action and encouraged readers to share the feelings he described and valued. Throughout the book, sentiment prompted the manly tears and empathy that spurred his determination to work for the oppressed. The sight of a gang of chained slaves awoke his "childish sympathy and interest." But when his father explained what slavery was, it struck the young boy "'how terribly we should feel if father were taken away from us.'" The ability to empathize with others prompted Coffin's youthful conversion to abolitionism. In a similar fashion, his response to a slave auction he witnessed during one of his later trips to the South reinforced his will. The sight and sounds of a mother being separated from her child moved Coffin's "heart to its depths; I could endure it no longer." For weeks he heard her anguished cries, cries that fed his hatred of slavery and strengthened his resolve to work for emancipation "until the end of my days." Despite the burdens of "care" and "troublesome" responsibilities, heightened feelings spurred him to take on additional duties and labors over the years.[24]

Some emotions, Coffin insisted, had played no part in his life. While his heart might throb with "intense excitement" and "anxiety," he had never felt frightened in dangerous, even potentially deadly situations. "Men often threatened to kill me," he recalled, "and at various times offered a reward for my head. I often received anonymous letters warning me that my store, pork-house, and dwelling would be burned to the ground." But, Coffin said, these threats "made no impression upon me—struck no terror in my heart." Coffin knew that his prominence in the business community and his many friends offered him some protection from enemies, and he acknowledged that often threats against him never materialized. Still, it is difficult to believe that he never felt any fear in his risky work. But in the context of a life that exemplified how the reformer acts in the world, it was important to insist that he or she must never "run from danger." Bravery (or perhaps the appearance of bravery) was useful, Coffin pointed out. It motivated others to overcome their hesitations and even might intimidate opponents.[25]

The only fear that Coffin discussed was his "fear" of speaking in public. Convinced that he lacked the skills to address an audience effectively, he "had always avoided public speaking—or prominence." During the war, he overcame his misgivings and agreed to visit Great Britain to inform antislavery friends about the situation of freed people and to raise money for them. Once in London, however, he experienced bouts of discouragement and depression.[26]

The space that Coffin devoted to this subject suggests its importance to him and to the purpose of his book. Acknowledgment of rare weaknesses, of course, humanized his self-portrait and made it more "truthful" or believable. But conscious of the need to inform the "rising generation" of the lessons of the past, Coffin was also suggesting that commitment to a great moral cause demanded overcoming personal misgivings and weaknesses that limited one's effectiveness. While his discomfort in speaking before audiences had not hampered his rescue work, Coffin realized that the ability to communicate was crucial to the cause of freed people. Thus he took on an assignment seemingly incompatible with his talents. The key to conquering his "diffidence" demanded a role reversal. The confident giver of advice became the humble seeker of help and counsel from others. Furthermore, prayer proved useful, for it allowed the "self" to "be entirely subdued," leaving "nothing but the cause of Christ and his poor" in his mind. With "calm and quiet" in his mind, "the fear of man was taken away." Then it "an easy matter to talk on the subject of the freedmen; I was never at a loss for words to express myself. The subject lay near my heart and I could talk, concerning it, to any class of people."[27]

Coffin's recollections included ample examples of other qualities that he possessed that furthered the cause of reform and, perhaps, seemed in increasingly limited supply in others in the postwar years. Scrupulous honesty, even when dishonesty would seem prudent, a sense of fairness, and moderation all were central to his success. So too was his disinterest in the rewards of money and fame that were increasingly valued in the postwar world.

When Coffin first began to work with fugitives, friends warned him that his efforts would threaten not only his life but his business as well. The possibility that his reform commitment might affect his livelihood did not deter Coffin from following "the injunctions of the Bible." He was not interested in riches but stuck to the old-fashioned conviction that "if I was faithful to duty, and honest and industrious . . . I could make enough to support my family." Although he had modest material goals, he actually achieved considerable business success. As he pointed out, however, he valued prosperity not for what it provided for his family but for its utility in his work. "[Underground] Railroad business . . . was attended with heavy expenses," he told readers, "which I could not have borne had not my affairs been prosperous."[28]

Eventually, Coffin accepted the difficult job of running a free produce commissary in Cincinnati, and, as a result, he retired from business with "very limited means." But the rewards from antislavery work far outweighed the lack of money. On the one hand, Coffin insisted that the true reward was the work itself and the feelings that it generated. "The approval of conscience" was the "most unalloyed joy of life," a point well worth making during the Gilded Age. On the other hand, woven through the narrative were the scenes that revealed that Coffin also prized the effusive thanks he received from former fugitives. In 1822, Coffin encountered Jack, a slave he had helped escape from North Carolina. Jack recognized Coffin and "clasped [him] in his arms, uttering exclamations of joy and gratitude." Now employed and earning good money, Jack was eager to pay Coffin for the assistance he had provided. "I told him," Coffin recalled, "that I was amply repaid and would not receive a cent." During later visits to Canada, fugitives thronged around Coffin and his wife. Over the years, the couple had helped so many fugitives that they often "did not recognize or remember [them] until they related some incident that recalled them to mind. . . . The gratitude they expressed was quite affecting...very gratifying to us."[29]

The runaways who furnished the stories for Still's book on the Underground Railroad provided a grim picture of the South that raised questions about whether that region would support the drastic changes that Reconstruction had introduced. Coffin's depiction of the past was more nuanced, although he shared Still's concern about the future.

One of the sources of Coffin's credibility as a witness to the character of the South was the fact that he was southern. Coffin did not leave North Carolina until he was twenty-eight, and he included material to show how familiar he was with the region and its people. He made several trips back to the South, not only to areas he had once known, but also to new places like New Orleans. Coffin attributed his courteous treatment to the fact that he "was a Southern man and understood Southern character."[30]

As a former southerner, Coffin presented a more complex picture of southern society which differed from the hostile abolitionist views of the South circulating before the Civil War or Still's negative depiction. The poor white farmers, some from "principle," others from poverty, from whom he bought his cotton had no slaves. Community members of more substantial means, like an English family in Kentucky, were "kind-hearted . . . [and] opposed to slavery." Coffin wrote of a man in Louisville who, like some other southerners, was actually "a strong abolitionist" who "aided runaway slaves whenever it was in his power." And not all slave owners were necessarily brutal masters, either. Coffin described good owners and even masters who were "very civil and gentlemanly." At least one slaveholder agreed with Coffin's analysis of the evils of the system. "The gentleman from Alabama," Coffin wrote, "said that he believed slavery was a curse to the South, and that he would be willing to give up his slaves at any time if they could be properly provided for."[31]

Coffin's historical depiction of a South not solidly wedded to slavery offered some hope that the contemporary South could be reconstructed as the basis for a positive sectional reunion and that some southerners might learn to cooperate across racial and political lines. But in no way did his narrative suggest that slavery had been a benign institution. Indeed, the objectivity that allowed Coffin to acknowledge that some slave owners were good masters heightened the credibility of his condemnation of the system. The fugitives who arrived at Coffin's house told the usual stories of owners who mismanaged their financial affairs and sold slaves' family members to raise cash or who were "cruel task-master[s]" and whipped their slaves "unmercifully." While Coffin included far fewer condemnations of individual owners than Still, his examples of the horrors of slavery were powerful because he had not only heard about them from fugitives but also witnessed them firsthand during his youth in North Carolina and during later trips to the South. Thus he could describe with authority the slave auction he witnessed in Virginia where buyers inspected slaves as they might "examine a horse" and then dragged their screaming purchases away.[32]

Like Still, Coffin stressed that slavery was a system that not only oppressed black people but also corrupted whites. Still had emphasized that male and female slave owners had been prone to violent behavior and drunkenness. Coffin focused on sexual licentiousness and moral turpitude. One Mississippi planter who came north to emancipate over thirty slaves turned out to be the father of most of them. He had kept a "slave wife on each of his plantations. Yet Thompson was a professor of religion . . . and a member of the Baptist Church." Not only did Coffin make it clear how often slave owners had abused slave women, he also challenged the notion expressed in *Scribner's* and elsewhere that blacks "move[d] on a far lower moral plane than whites as a class." In fact, some victims possessed a superior morality to their exploiters. Jane, for example, had been the mistress of her owner who heartlessly determined to sell her and their son because Jane had experienced conversion. "She felt keenly the degradation of her position," wrote Coffin, "and longed to be free that she might live a purer life." Rose, another slave, was even more determined to avoid becoming "the property of some sensual wretch, and she would choose death rather than such a lot."[33]

Despite acknowledging that some slave owners had cared for their slaves, Coffin suggested that they were the exception. The callous treatment of slaves during the Civil War offered the most convincing proof of owners' heartlessness. When masters fled south to escape Union troops, they took the healthy male slaves with them but abandoned slaves who were old or sick, as well as all the women and children. Coffin grimly observed that "in many cases there was nothing for this helpless class to live upon." Slave owners' treatment of male slaves who tried to escape to Union lines was equally despicable: "They were pursued and fired upon by their masters, who had rather shoot them down than let them go free."[34]

Coffin saved his most searing condemnation for slave hunters. These "bloodhounds in human shape" had invaded northern territory in an attempt to force their values on those who did not share them and to drag fugitives back to a life of miserable enslavement. Coffin emphasized how routinely slave hunters had resorted to violence and trickery to achieve their goals. They employed black and white spies to ferret out information that would assist them in recapturing fugitives and hired the worst northern roughnecks to help them in their work. Often heavily armed, they hoped to "intimidate" anyone assisting fugitives by threatening them with death and destruction of property. As Coffin made clear, the slave hunters were bullies whose bravado sometimes masked cowardice. He recounted, for example, an incident in which slave hunters were "completely cowed" by a northern posse that was "commanded . . . to charge [and] . . . not to leave a kidnapper alive."[35]

Such characterizations of slave hunters could well have resonated with contemporary cultural rhetoric that drew connections between the past and present. In 1872, during Horace Greeley's campaign for the presidency, *Harper's Weekly* accused supporters of the new party and its program of reconciliation of being former slave hunters. In 1875, the weekly called members of the White League slave hunters and "depraved and profligate young men" living in a "land of ignorance and brutality."[36]

On one of his last trips to the South before the war, Coffin visited Yazoo City, Mississippi. Coffin was depressed by the place and horrified by the slave mistresses supported in luxury by elite men. Coffin was further disgusted when he was told that passengers and crew on the packet on which he was traveling wanted to witness a slave being whipped just for the "fun" of it. Calling Yazoo City the "Sodom of debauchery" for its moral laxity, Coffin said that he had "never before been so sensible of the Egyptian darkness that overhung the land" and became more convinced than ever that soon slavery would be destroyed.[37]

Such an analysis left no question about what Coffin believed to be the cause of the Civil War. Coffin also emphasized northerners' initial attempt to avoid facing up to the truth and their own complicity in perpetuating slavery, points many northerners had conveniently forgotten. When southern states first seceded, Coffin pointed out, various denominations in Cincinnati, "still under the influence of that pro-slavery power," held prayer meetings to ask that the rebellion be suppressed without war. Many confessed to sins like drinking and misusing the Sabbath, but "the sin of slavery was not mentioned, not a prayer for the poor suffering slaves was heard." As Coffin told an associate, "The real cause of the war is not alluded to; . . . the sin of slavery is not mentioned. . . . This war has been permitted by the Almighty to come upon us as a judgment and the North must suffer as well as the South, for we are partners in the national sin."[38]

Coffin presented this familiar abolitionist analysis at a time when some northerners were once again denying the sin that was "the real cause of the war." A few years earlier, for example, the editor of *Scribner's* asserted that the war had merely sought to reestablish "the old relations" of union. He avoided the whole moral issue. "We have nothing to do with the question whether [southerners] . . . sinned, and deserved punishment," he concluded.[39]

Coffin's discussion of the war established the connections between the conflict and the goal of black freedom. Vignettes of antislavery fervor indicated that others shared his view of the war's objective: the Oberlin students singing antislavery songs in Cincinnati when the city was threatened by a southern army; the "Abolitionist" regiment from Wisconsin, filled with "true-hearted men," who rescued a slave girl whose master had intended to put her in a brothel; the religious groups assisting with contraband work; and the white soldiers who taught black soldiers to read all helped make the purpose of the war obvious. Abraham Lincoln's role in emancipation received only passing mention, however. Perhaps because he and other abolitionists had spent their lives working to end slavery, Lincoln's action seemed merely the final conclusion of a long campaign that had engaged the president only briefly.[40]

Just as blacks had claimed their freedom through flight before 1861, Coffin reminded readers that they had also earned their freedom through loyal military service. During the defense of Cincinnati and long before blacks were formally accepted in the Union army, a black regiment had been established. It helped construct fortifications and "was said to be the most orderly and faithful regiment that crossed the Ohio River to do the work." Coffin described other black troops that he encountered later in the war, men who had eagerly proved their manhood and proved they were worthy of the rights of men.[41]

Like most of his contemporaries, Coffin was shocked by the brutal nature of the conflict. "I never before so fully realized the horrors of war," he confessed when he recounted his visit to some of the wounded. The fact that the war dragged on for years certainly could not be blamed on abolitionists. It was the fault of a "troublesome element" among Democrats that refused to acknowledge slavery as the basic cause of the war either because of their business interests in the South or because of their southern sympathies.[42]

For Coffin, emancipation and the conclusion of warfare hardly signaled the end of the nation's responsibility for black people. Coffin went to England to raise money and supplies for them, telling English audiences that the work with freed people had "no parallel in history." At one meeting, attended by many prominent men and women, a London bishop raised the critical issue of what sort of participation blacks could expect to enjoy in their new state of freedom. The bishop said he had heard that blacks were not allowed to ride with whites on public transportation or to eat with them and that frequently hotels turned them away. Coffin replied that social prejudice still existed in the United States but "had lessened since the war commenced." By the time he composed his book, however, Coffin was persuaded that prejudice was not disappearing because the necessary moral transformation had not occurred. Whites had ignored the plain message in the Bible that loving one's neighbor was a religious duty.[43]

Throughout his reminiscences, Coffin emphasized that attempts to establish firm divisions between the races were futile, a position that challenged the system of racial separation emerging in the South. With the end of slavery, one way of distinguishing race had disappeared. Color remained, but color was a misleading marker. Coffin filled his book with examples of men and women who appeared to be members of one race but were actually members of the other. Coffin related the story of one former slave, nearly white, who had "none of the negro features" and was "very gentlemanly in his appearance." This man married a white woman, arousing the anger of some Newport, Indiana, residents, many of whom, Coffin remarked, had darker complexions than the "black" man. Similarly, a young fugitive woman who was staying at the Coffins' house was so light that when she accompanied Coffin and his wife on a visit, his acquaintances were hard-pressed to decide which woman was Coffin's wife. Other fugitives disguised themselves as whites to escape their pursuers. One, when suitably clothed, "presented the appearance of an elegant Southern lady." Others merely powdered their faces and put on wigs and "passed for white people." Another slave was so light that slave dealers stained his face and curled his hair with a curling iron so that he would be "black enough to sell without question." Reversing the pattern, Laura Haviland, on one of her rescue efforts in Kentucky, passed herself off as a member of a light-skinned black family. The slave mistress accepted Haviland's racial identification without question. Such examples highlighted the folly of discrimination based on color.[44]

Coffin's recollections of the heartlessness and irrationality of racism in public places were perhaps triggered by the recent passage of the Civil Rights Bill. He recounted that while on a trip to Virginia years earlier with a free light-skinned mulatto, his companion fell ill. The local tavern keeper would not allow the man to be cared for in a comfortable room but put him in a slave cabin. When Coffin protested, the owner assured him that he would be "'made comfortable.'" That "comfort" consisted of "some ragged and dirty blankets" and "poor coffee and corn bread, . . . yet when we came to settle our accounts, his bill was the same as mine." Coffin was "much disturbed" by such treatment, the reaction he hoped his readers would share. A more difficult subject was interracial marriage, which even Coffin did not favor. But the fury felt by a local "mob" when a "quiet, orderly and industrious" freed man married a white woman slightly lighter in color than he Coffin pronounced as "foolish." Even more ridiculous, many of the city's women "were as much afraid of him [the groom] as if he were a murderer." Despite his personal views, Coffin considered marriage decisions private. "We were in favor of justice and right-dealing with all colors," he proclaimed.[45]

Coffin's own behavior provided a model for a life lived without the taint of caste feeling, a model particularly relevant for the uncertain racial climate of the 1870s. "I was no respecter of color or race," Coffin explained. "The negroes had souls equally as precious as ours . . . we were all alike in the divine sight." Specific examples demonstrated his attempts to treat black people as he did whites. When a proslavery merchant came into Coffin's store, they fell into conversation about a fugitive who had arrived at

Coffin's house the night before. The merchant asked Coffin where he kept such people, assuming that they were housed in the cellar. Coffin replied, "'We don't put people in the cellar; we take them into the parlor or sitting-room,'" the social heart of the house. Fugitives ate in his dining room, their meals prepared by Coffin's wife and the hired help. Coffin frequently employed fugitives as well as free blacks and paid them a good wage. In fact, Coffin "often gave" poor and destitute blacks "employment in preference to whites, not that I felt any greater attachment to them on account of their color, but because I knew that they were often unjustly refused and neglected." Coffin rejected the view that blacks were poor workers, a point that people sometimes used to justify not employing them. Just the opposite was true, Coffin, said. His experience had shown that they had been the best workers, although it was not surprising to him that they did not labor effectively for those who despised them.[46]

Coffin believed his duty also included helping "the poor and destitute" blacks since they were not "looked after as such classes were among the whites." If that had been true before the war, it was even truer after the war. Coffin's narrative set an ambitious standard for readers. In one case, he had actually purchased a house for a fugitive who faithfully repaid the purchase through work. But Coffin's life called for more than acts of charity and providing employment. It called for reciprocal affection. At least one fugitive who lived with the Coffins for a period addressed them as Uncle Levy and Aunt Katy and wept when she left them. When Coffin traveled to Canada, he was fond of visiting those whom he had sheltered in his house, and he even shared a meal with them. In turn, fugitives called upon the Coffins when they came to Cincinnati.[47]

These visits were gratifying to Coffin because many worthy blacks succeeded in making a life for themselves in freedom. Coffin often noted their snug and cozy homes and his "pleasure" at seeing former fugitives in good circumstances. He pointedly praised those who "by industry and thrift managed to live very comfortably." In his belief in the potential of black people Coffin stood in sharp contrast to the abolitionists in the 1870s who were beginning to doubt the ability of blacks to thrive as free people. Moreover, the examples of success in Canada highlighted the importance of providing blacks with a material basis for progress. The ease with which blacks obtained land in Canada also highlighted the American government's failure to help freed people become property owners after the war.[48]

Coffin was realistic about what could be expected from former slaves. Even in Canada, not all had managed to succeed. The "evil influences" of slavery had created great obstacles for fugitives who needed material assistance and especially education. Those who argued that blacks could become self-reliant without any assistance were mistaken. As Coffin's postwar career pointed out, freed black people had pressing needs that whites had to meet.[49]

Enlightened about the situation of former slaves and dismissive of rigid lines based on race, Coffin was not entirely free of the common racist views of the time. Still had embraced blackness and identified black with beauty. To him, pale skin indicated forcible racial mixing and the power of white southern men. But Coffin, like many abolitionists before him, was fascinated with light-skinned slaves and featured a disproportionate number of them in his book. The closer to white the slave, the more likely he or she was deemed attractive. Female quadroons and octoroons, Coffin declared, had a "peculiar style of beauty . . . rich olive tint of the complexion . . . large bright eyes . . . perfect features, and the long wavy black hair." Rose, so "nearly white that a stranger would never suspect that there was a drop of African blood in her veins," was striking, "tall and graceful" with a beautiful face, intelligent expression, long, straight hair, and hands "as delicate as those of any lady." Charley "possessed none of the negro features, [and] was very gentlemanly in his appearance and manners."[50]

People with dark skin, of course, could not look like ladies or gentleman and were never described as beautiful. Robert Burrel received the highest praise, for "his sober and intelligent appearance," while another admirable group was composed of "able-bodied, good looking men and women." Stereotypes popped up here and there. Aunt Rachel was "one of those good old darkey aunties whom we have all known or heard of," while a group "of darkies . . . in a good humor" sported "white teeth in broad grins." A particularly revealing vignette of Margaret Garner, whose trial for killing one of her children gained national attention, disclosed Coffin's standards. Garner was a mulatto. She owed her "high forehead," "finely arched eyebrows," and "bright and intelligent eyes" to her white forebears. "But the African appeared in the lower part of her face," Coffin explained, in her less attractive features, "her broad nose and thick lips." Two of her dark-skinned sons were "bright-eyed, woolly-headed little fellows." The murdered child, on the other hand, had been "almost white, a little girl of rare beauty."[51]

Because Coffin conceived of his book as the story of his own life and experiences, it was natural that he became the interpreter for the lives of others. Although he sometimes included slaves' actual words (or more likely what he remembered them to be), Coffin usually conveyed their experiences in his own language, with his own understanding of what had happened. While he reassured readers that he heard the accounts he wrote about from slaves' "own lip[s]," he made the critical selections and choices. Of the "many interesting stories of individual adventures and trials" he had heard about, he would provide only "a few," he explained. Coffin devoted several pages to Aunt Rachel's story. Aunt Rachel had told her story "in simple but thrilling language." But Coffin's voice replaced Aunt Rachel's, describing her escape and adding dramatic excitement to the sketch with rhetorical questions and insight into Rachel's emotions. "How could she ever make her way to freedom and safety?" he asked. "Must she not perish of hunger? . . . As she reflected on these questions, distress filled her mind."[52]

In Still's book on the Underground Railroad, heroic slaves emancipated themselves through flight. Likewise, Coffin included plenty of descriptions of brave and clever slaves who orchestrated their own escapes from the South. Aunt Rachel managed to slip away from her master, destroy most of her chains with a rock, and escape with one ankle still manacled. Jim, who was both shrewd and intelligent, fled his master successfully but then returned to rescue his family. Understanding his master's character, Jim appeared before him with the look of a "whipped dog." He told his master that he had tired of taking care of himself and was "sick of being free." Claiming that he had been cheated of his wages and disillusioned by abolitionists, "a mean set of rascals," Jim declared that he had wished return to "the old plantation" and "live with massa again." Of course, the master was delighted and welcomed Jim back. Before long, Jim had pulled off a second escape, this time with a group of fourteen other slaves.[53]

Although it had been given to him by others, Coffin's "title" of president of the Underground Railroad captured his self-conception. Coffin probably never thought of himself in heroic terms, but he was nonetheless the capable white hero of his story. When he first became involved in Underground Railroad activities, in Newport, Indiana, he remarked that operations were frequently unsuccessful. Fugitives often stayed with free blacks who were not "very skillful in concealing them, or shrewd in making arrangements to forward them to Canada." He also leveled this charge against Cincinnati blacks. In contrast, Coffin depicted himself as a brilliant if cautious manager. He gave advice to fugitives who did not know what to do. In the case of one fugitive, he recounted, "I told her that she had no time to cry, she must dry her tears and act with promptness." He devised ingenious plans to help them elude pursuers. When a large group of fugitives lingered on the outskirts of the city "in great danger of being discovered and recaptured by the police, who were always on the alert for runaway slaves," Coffin came up with the idea of arranging a fake funeral procession that would allow the "mourners" to move out of their hiding places to safe houses. Coffin was the one to make "arrangements" for concealing fugitives and sending them on, and he often raised the necessary money to pay for the teams to spirit fugitives away to the next "conductor."[54]

The fugitives who appeared in Coffin's book ranged from the competent and intelligent to the exhausted, sick, and bedraggled. Some of these "poor hunted creatures" had lived outdoors so long that they were "almost wild" and "so fearful of being betrayed, that it was some time before their confidence could be gained." By depicting most slaves as dependent on his expertise, Coffin credited whites for the success of the Underground Railroad rather than to blacks, as Still had done. Yet the sheer volume of material on black people in his reminiscences kept the centrality of race clear.[55]

When Coffin wrote his book, the Underground Railroad was a thing of the past. But the last large section of his book focusing on his work for contrabands suggested the ongoing needs of former slaves. He described their suffering, their joy at being free, their desire for learning, their eagerness to cultivate land but also the importance of basic necessities like tools and supplies. His narrative ended abruptly with the celebration held by Cincinnati blacks to mark the passage of the Fifteenth Amendment. The brief conclusion may merely have signified Coffin's fatigue with his narrative. But the lack of closure also pointed to unfinished work. The Fifteenth Amendment had not resolved the issue of race, as Coffin himself made clear at the end of his preface.[56]

Whatever lay behind Coffin's decision to end the book as he did, the length of his narrative, more than 700 pages, certainly discouraged Coffin from carrying his story any further. He had already exceeded the page limit that he had agreed upon with his publisher. The book was going to be both bigger and more expensive to publish than originally anticipated.[57]

Coffin's publisher, the Western Tract and Book Society of Cincinnati, was a successful Methodist publisher of books and pamphlets and a natural choice for Coffin. Coffin had ties with the society, having been a member of it "for many years." When he made his trip to England to raise money and supplies for newly freed slaves, the board of directors had written a supporting letter for him. Coffin's book was also a natural choice for the Western Tract and Book Society. During the first half of the nineteenth century, Methodists had become leaders in the field of evangelical publishing, printing and distributing denominational materials as well as works with a useful Christian message. Coffin's book provided an example of a life inspired by religious belief and duty, engaged readers' imagination, and, like missionaries' memoirs, provided out-of-the-ordinary adventures. The publisher was in the process of expanding its business and had erected a new six-story building only a few years earlier. Coffin's work meshed with their economic and religious interests.[58]

The book appeared in 1876 without illustrations. How many copies were printed or sold initially is not known. Coffin's death the following year may possibly have increased interest in his life story. But in 1879, the Quaker periodical the *British Friend* reported, "There are 280 copies in America, for which there is no demand; so that when those in England are all bought up, there will still remain a heavy debt in America, which the subscriptions of sympathising Friends could soon cancel." Whether Friends came through or not, something about Coffin's story encouraged the Cincinnati publishing house of Robert Clarke, which had a long-standing interest in books of local history and biographies and autobiographies, to issue a second edition of Coffin's *Reminiscences* in 1880. The second edition, which was more elaborately designed than the first, sported the house's distinctive green cloth binding as well as portraits of both Coffin and his wife. There are hints that this edition did better than the first. The obituary of Coffin's wife in 1881, for example, noted that "many copies" of the book had been sold, which had helped to support the widow. In 1899, the publisher issued a third edition that included accounts of Coffin's death and funeral.[59]

The second edition of Coffin's *Reminiscences* was one sign of the potential appeal of adventurous tales of escapes and rescues. Laura Haviland, the "ancient Quakeress" who, like Coffin, had been warmly received at the 1874 reunion in Chicago, apparently believed there was still enough interest in the Underground Railroad to merit writing and publishing her life experiences a few years later. Haviland had occasionally collaborated with Coffin, and some stories appeared in both books. *A Woman's Life-Work; Labors and Experiences of Laura S. Haviland* was issued in 1881 when Haviland was seventy-three. Subsequent editions, containing updated material on her recent activities, were issued in 1882, 1884, 1887, 1897, and 1902.[60]

Laura Smith Haviland had a long career as a reformer, as the title of her book suggested. Born in 1808 in Canada, Haviland became interested in antislavery as a child. A book of her father's on the slave trade "often affected" her "to tears," and she recalled in her reminiscences that her "sympathies became too deeply enlisted for the poor negroes who were thus enslaved for time to efface." The cruel treatment of "that crushed and neglected race" stimulated her "indignation."[61]

In 1825, located in western New York, Laura married Charles Haviland.

She was only sixteen. A few years later, the young couple emigrated to Michigan, where Laura's family had moved. There Laura helped organize the first antislavery society in the state, a step that created problems with the Society of Friends, to which she belonged. Like Coffin, she and her family eventually withdrew from their Quaker meeting and joined the Wesleyan Methodists, who had separated from the Methodist Church in 1841 over the issue of slavery.[62]

Despite having a large family to care for, Charles and Laura Haviland worked energetically to live up to their abolitionist ideals. They established Raisin Institute, a biracial school modeled after Oberlin College, on their Michigan farm. Most of the students intended to be teachers, and, Haviland explained, most "came to us with their prejudices against colored people . . . but [the prejudices] soon melted away." The Havilands also harbored fugitives on the farm, so many, in fact, that Haviland observed, "We richly earned the cognomen of 'nigger den.'" In the midst of this busy life, when Laura Haviland was only thirty-seven, an epidemic disease swept through the community. Within the space of six weeks, she lost her husband, both her parents, her sister, and her youngest child to the epidemic. She later claimed to have foreseen this personal devastation in a dream.[63]

Despite her early travails as a widow, she devoted much of her time before the Civil War to helping fugitives elude their pursuers and reach Canada safely. She made several trips to the South to facilitate escapes or to carry out other antislavery work. During the war, she worked with freed people and wounded soldiers behind the lines in the South. After the war, she assisted refugees and orphans and, in the 1870s, she helped blacks fleeing from southern oppression to Kansas. She worked for the Women's Christian Temperance Union (WCTU) in her later years and died in 1898 at the age of ninety.

Haviland recounted her long and busy life in a narrative of over 500 pages. In her preface she explained that she had "hesitated" to write her life story because she recognized her "inability to compete with writers of the nineteenth century." Yet she asked "an indulgent public" to understand that her "deep and abiding sympathies for the oppressed and sorrowing of every nation, class, or color" provided the impetus for her "simple, and unvarnished" account. She was candid about her goal: to inspire readers with a desire "for the active doing, instead of saying what ought to be done," and to prevent them from "excusing" themselves from a life of moral action by claiming that they lacked ability.[64]

Many aspects of Haviland's life story likely struck readers as contrary to gender norms. She traveled alone, outwitted slave hunters, and undertook numerous daring assignments. She was courageous and cool in the face of adversity. On one occasion she faced down with a "steady gaze" three bloodhounds, one as large as "a yearling calf." On another, in a confrontation with a group of slave hunters waving guns at her, shouting that she was a "'nigger stealer,'" she bravely replied, "'Man, I fear neither your weapons nor your threats; they are powerless. You are not at home—you are not in Tennessee. And as for your property, I have none of it about me or on my premises. We also know what we are about; we also understand, not only ourselves but you.'" She subsequently recounted this adventure to the whole community in the schoolhouse and then at the Adrian, Michigan, courthouse.[65]

Haviland's autobiography contained many examples of bold missionary work. She converted the dying and prayed with the sick, even Irish Catholics. "It would seem to many like casting pearls before swine to turn aside to present the truth to such ignorant and disliking people," she reflected, "but it is ours to obey these little impressions." She played such a prominent part in religious exercises that several freed people living in Canada asked her to marry them. She attributed their request to their ignorance rather than to the fact that, to them, she appeared far more important than an ordained minister. She also organized a nondenominational union church in one Canadian community. "I exhorted them to attend to their own religious impressions," she explained, "as I was not there to present particular religious tenets, but to present the crucified, risen, and glorified Savior."[66]

During the war, she decided to undertake "tender nursing," without an organizational sponsor. As "a self-constituted agent" she collected her own supplies and acquired her own free-travel pass. She counseled the contrabands she met during her trips about living in freedom and delivered sermonlike addresses encouraging them to accept Christ. Eventually she established a Freedmen's Relief Association in Detroit and continued her war work under its auspices.[67]

Haviland was aware of the need to head off accusations of improper and unladylike behavior. In her portrait at the beginning of her book, Haviland, dressed soberly with a black cap tied under her chin, looks straight out at the reader. In her flowing penmanship, she had written, "Thine for the oppressed," and signed her name. Her words established her connection with the familiar conception of women as selfless and altruistic. This idea was reinforced in the narrative. Not until she was appointed an agent for the Freedmen's Aid Commission in 1864 did she receive a salary, she revealed. For years the labor itself had provided her reward; it provided more "satisfaction" than any sum of money could. To counter the depictions of

"Mrs. Haviland and the Blood-hounds." The fact that this illustration from Laura Haviland's *A Woman's Life-Work* shows Haviland rather than fugitives facing down bloodhounds reveals that, despite the rich materials about escaping slaves she included in her book, she is very much at the center of her narrative.

unfeminine boldness in her book, she admitted to fear and encouraged her readers to picture her as just a harmless "little old lady," "a little, insignificant looking woman." Her emphasis on her frailty and age obscured the truth of the narrative and of her life. When Haviland began the more public part of her career, she was only in her late thirties. Even after her book was published, friends spoke of how lightly time had touched her. As late as her eighty-fourth year, a newspaper commented on her "erect" posture and her "light and active" step.[68]

The preface to her narrative also offered a forceful rationale for her unorthodox life and autobiography. Borrowing language from the Bible, she described herself as a toiler "in the great field so white to harvest" and prayed that the "Lord of the harvest . . . arm and send forth more laborers, because they are so few." What success she had enjoyed in the work of reform came not from her own individual strength but from Christian weakness. For she had only followed "Him who is saying, 'My grace is sufficient for thee, for my strength is in perfect weakness.'" The posture of humility and weakness may not have been entirely convincing, however.

Rev. F. A. Hardin's insistence in the preface to the fourth edition that Haviland's aim "was not prominence" or "self-glorification" but the praise of "the abounding grace of God" hints that some may have read her story in another way.[69]

Haviland began her autobiography with a conversion story, one of the most familiar and acceptable forms of first-person narratives in American culture. The predictable story of her religious doubts, anxieties, despair, and ultimate conversion was compressed into thirty-two pages. As Haviland described her spiritual journey, she identified a serious misunderstanding of what the Lord required: "I yielded to my timidity, and the conclusion was reached to live a quiet Christian life, with my Bible and secret communing with my dear Lord." She soon learned, however, that "the greatest source of retrograding in the divine life is unfaithfulness in the performance of known duty. . . . The talent committed to our charge is to be occupied." Such an overview established religious duty as the rationale for the activism she described in the next 500 pages. Accounts of dreams and prayerful reflections scattered throughout the book emphasized continuing connections with the divine that provided further direction and confidence. Thus in the midst of one of her emphatically unfeminine adventures, she recalled praying "for a guiding hand to direct our actions in case we should find ourselves in the camp of the enemy, face to face with traffickers inhuman souls and bodies." Even deathbed scenes served a similar purpose. When one of the trustees of Raisin Institute was dying, he told Haviland, "'Your anti-slavery mission is not yet finished. . . . Greater dangers are for you to pass through — I see it. O, may the Lord prepare you for the work he has for you to accomplish! . . . He will grant you his protecting arm. I know it.'"[70]

While only a few years separated the publication of Coffin's and Haviland's books, the shifting political and cultural landscape profoundly influenced the way in which Haviland handled her autobiography. Of course, the changes had been under way for some time, and Coffin himself had confronted some of them. But the transformations were becoming increasingly evident. In 1876, the year in which Coffin's book appeared, for example, the *New York Times* proclaimed that abolitionists like William Lloyd Garrison and Wendell Phillips espoused "ideas in regard to the South which the great majority of the Republican Party have outgrown." These ideas included a commitment to civil and political rights for blacks. The *Brooklyn Eagle* had never supported these commitments and continued to attack Reconstruction and "its plundering" carpetbaggers and invented "outrages" foisted upon the public just before elections. In a "dialogue" published in the paper, a supposed former abolitionist declared, "I was as rank an Abolitionist as ever lived years before the Republican party was organized. . . . I want to see white slavery abolished now, and I am just as much opposed to the enslaving of the white man, as he is now enslaved by government in the South, as ever I was opposed to the enslaving of the Negro." The view that southern whites, not southern blacks, were oppressed did not go unchallenged. *Harper's Weekly* predicted that if "national authority were wholly withdrawn from the Southern States," Democrats would "annihilate the political rights of the negroes."[71]

Although political Reconstruction came to an end in 1877, the full implications of the government's retreat from the South were not immediately apparent. Worried blacks visited President Rutherford Hayes in the White House, hoping to confirm that his assertions that he would not desert former slaves were true. The next year, the black newspaper the *Christian Recorder* rejoiced that Thomas Higginson, the "war horse of the younger Abolitionists," had visited the South and proclaimed his belief in southern good intentions. By November, after elections were marred by violence in the South, the paper proclaimed Hayes's policy a failure and that "intimidation reigns." Grace Greenwood, an occasional correspondent for the *Times*, was skeptical from the beginning. As she ironically commented, "Martyred Presidents and emancipation proclamations have gone out of fashion." But, she insisted, many found "it impossible to turn their thoughts away from the perils that menace . . . the great principles" that the Republican Party seemed to have abandoned. In 1879, the exodus of black people from the South to Kansas offered tangible evidence of the fragility of black civil and political rights in the South.[72]

In one of her articles, Greenwood commented that Confederate graves in the North were decorated on Memorial Day but Union graves went unadorned in Florida. There was "a large, magnanimous, munificent lopsidedness about this conciliation business," she proclaimed. As another example of the flawed nature of the "conciliation business," Greenwood noted that a northern journal was paying Stonewall Jackson's widow for her personal recollections of her husband, "the saint militant of Virginia."[73]

The fact that a northern periodical was paying Jackson's widow for reminiscences highlights the cultural and financial role northern middle-class journals played in spurring increasingly sympathetic views of the white South and in reinterpreting the recent history of the nation and region. The decades following the Civil War have been called the great age of American magazines both in terms of numbers of different periodicals published (from 700 in 1865 to 3,300 in 1885) and their steadily expanding middle-class audience. The most prominent journals, the *Atlantic Monthly*, published in Boston, and *Scribner's* (renamed the *Century* in 1881) and *Harper's Monthly Magazine*, both published in New York City, along with a host of lesser magazines, vied for the attention of American readers. Each sold thousands and thousands of copies every month. The new cultural environment created by the magazines colored the ways in which abolitionists like Haviland would write their autobiographies and the ways in which readers would understand them. The material presented in literary monthlies also offered a robust challenge to the narratives that abolitionists had been presenting.[74]

While each journal had its own character, all carried poetry, short stories, biographies, and essays. They frequently included historical articles, perhaps responding to the interest in history sparked by the country's centennial. *Scribner's* and *Harper's Monthly* also featured lavish illustrations. These materials helped to influence public opinion but were in turn affected by what readers, and northern readers in particular, wanted to read about. By the 1870s northern readers seemed interested in knowing more about the postwar South and eventually in looking again at prewar southern life and culture.[75]

Some journal articles seemed relatively unbiased. In the 1880s, *Century* ran a series on military leaders and battles of the Civil War that was so popular that it doubled the journal's circulation. The series was balanced in that it featured accounts from northern and southern combatants, but editor Richard Watson Gilder was consciously moving beyond narratives that highlighted slavery and southern sin as the war's cause. "We rightly judged," he commented, "that articles celebrating the skill and valor of both sides would hasten the elimination of sectional prejudices and contribute toward reuniting the country by cultivation of mutual respect." In other genres, like short stories, comic pieces, and travel articles, changing ideas and views about the war, the South, and blacks were embedded so deeply that they seemed to be true. While some pieces published in the monthlies were written by northerners, as Greenwood's reference to Stonewall Jackson's widow suggests, southerners' work was accepted on generous monetary terms as well. *Scribner's*, the most widely read of the monthlies, noted the trend in 1881. "Attention has recently been called to the large number of southern contributions to the magazines," the editor remarked. "No less than seven articles contributed by southern writers appeared in a recent number of *Scribner's*, and we are glad to recognize the fact of a permanent productive force in literature in the southern states." In fact, most southern writers who achieved prominence late in the century got their start in northern magazines.[76]

At the time that Samuel May was writing *Some Recollections of Our Anti-slavery Conflict*, there was little interest in romanticizing southern whites or the prewar South. Positive depictions of freed people like the stately Linda, in "Linda's Young Lady," who was glad to be in the North and free, or the black preacher in "The New Timothy," who, "with the exception of color," resembled "one of the old prophets" appeared in *Harper's*. In the early 1870s, these noble figures who had deserved their freedom and justified a war to liberate them were disappearing, and a new cultural reality was emerging with which Haviland would have to contend. A wide variety of materials in magazines demeaned and ridiculed blacks, particularly in *Scribner's* and *Harper's*. William H. Ruffner, the superintendent of the Virginia Board of Public Instruction, was the author of a critical article appearing in *Scribner's* in 1874. Ruffner had been active in establishing Virginia's segregated school system and was determined to turn back the part of the proposed Civil Rights Bill that would integrate public schools. Now he pronounced Africans as the "lowest in the scale of races," stating that the history of American blacks was "unrelieved by a single heroic passage, or even by an average degree of virtue, ability, or attainment of any sort."[77]

Edward King, a northern newspaperman who had once worked for the Springfield, Massachusetts, *Daily Union* and the *Republican*, wrote a highly praised and influential series of articles titled "The Great South" for *Scribner's*. The project was the brainchild of Roswell Smith, the company's president, and the magazine spared no expense or effort on the series. King and the artist who accompanied him traveled more than 24,000 miles at a cost to the magazine of $30,000. Appearing in 1873 and 1874, the articles totaled more than 400 pages and featured almost as many engravings. On the one hand, the articles were intended to "enlighten our country . . . [about] the wonderful resources, the social condition, and the political complications of a region which needs but just, wise, and generous legislation, with responding good will and industry, to make it a garden of happiness and prosperity." On the other hand, as one of *Scribner's* editors recalled, the series "was conceived in magnanimity and sympathy," so much so that "we were accused of 'catering to a Southern audience.'" The success of "The Great South" was such that the articles were collected and issued as a "beautiful" book.[78]

Scribner's editors were persuaded that "The Great South" had "given great satisfaction to the region represented," and it is not difficult to see why. While King reported on each southern state's economic potential and its relation to the political situation, he also provided many vignettes of free blacks. In some cases, he praised them as industrious workers. More

WHITES AND THE UNDERGROUND RAILROAD

often he characterized them as "recklessly improvident." In New Orleans, beggars were too lazy to close their hands over the coins offered to them. Richmond blacks, all dressed up for a day excursion, preferred bad food and housing, so that they could frolic on outings. In Tennessee, black children rolled in the dust, with no thought of school, and their parents had no idea of thrift or progress. Travel articles in other magazines made similar points, helping to establish the themes taken up in fiction, poetry, and comic pieces.[79]

A strategy that writers employed to lend credibility to increasingly negative views of black people was to portray black characters themselves uttering the criticism of freedmen and freedwomen. In one story modeled on a travelogue, "A Glimpse of Modern Dixie," the narrator describes taking a train in the South where a freedman named Abraham tells him the "real" truth about the South. The narrator asks Abraham why black people on the train eagerly spend money on the goods hawkers are selling but whites are not. Abraham replied, "'I spect it's because de niggers is all dam fools!'" If they had money in their pockets, it would not stay there long. There was black trash just as there was white trash. Later in the day, the white narrator has another opportunity to see the foolishness of black people. Accompanying Abraham to a country store, the narrator witnesses a "huge . . . innocent-looking lout," a "bewildered darkey," being snookered by the black store owner and his wife. Not only do they press all kind of "finery" on him, but they also sell the gullible fellow a pair of shoes that are too small.[80]

Black religion came in for pointed criticism. Blacks were shown as ignorant of the fundamentals of true religion. The behavior of Uncle Zeke, the main black character of one story, was supposedly typical of black piety: despite his surface religiosity, he is a scoundrel and a thief. That blacks misunderstood Scripture was reinforced by black's themselves, who were depicted uttering phrases from the Bible like "'de good book says *dar* shall be snortin' an' smashin' ob teef.'" As Josiah Holland, *Scribner's* editor, summarized, it was no slander to say that black religion was purely emotional and that blacks did not understand the connections between religion and morality.[81]

Commentaries, stories, and dialect poems highlighted wild religious ceremonies and targeted preachers who were, in fact, playing an important political role in the South. In "Six Weeks in Florida," by George Ward Nichols, a former Union soldier, the white narrator claims to have witnessed at a Protestant church "shocking mummeries which belonged to the fetish worship of savage Central Africa." In another sketch, the white main character tells her black maid that she wants to go to a black religious service.

The amazed maid remarks, "'I go no use for such preacher work as dat! An' dere's so much of 'em too!'" Undeterred, the employer goes to the service, where author is met with its predictable "wild, unearthly din." The preacher's "wild gestures" work the crowd up to a pitch of hysteria, and a "mad dance" precedes the communion service. The ill-educated preacher proudly shows off his "knowledge." Ridiculing efforts at black education, this author and others mocked the way supposedly educated blacks, like preachers, misused words. Here, the preacher talks of the "puffections" of King David and shows off his half-digested knowledge with his references to "metzfores" and "Universalers." In another magazine, a comic piece ridiculing black dialect describes a congregation that cannot understand anything that their minister says to them. But one member assures their bishop that he preaches "'so like a niggah dat we un'stan ebbry word you say, suah!'"[82]

The attempt of blacks to exercise citizen rights came in for its share of humorous commentary, often placed in a magazine by the editor. "Editor's Drawer," a *Harper's* feature, contained the following anecdotes: In Jacksonville, Florida, where three blacks were to serve as jurors, they were asked if they had any objection to capital punishment. When they replied no, they were asked to define capital punishment, and they had not the slightest idea of what it was. During a South Carolina election, two blacks supposedly discussed whether to vote for a candidate who claimed to support reform. "'Well, I dunno,'" said one. "'Dat Whipper say he go in for reform. Now reform bin runnin' in dis country eber since de wa', an' he neber bin 'lected yet. Time he stop funning.'" A more extended treatment of a "yellow" former slave who enters political life was equally damning. The author of the anecdote that appeared in *Scribner's*, William Baker, had grown up in the South and was nostalgic for the old ways. In this story, Milton sells his soul and masters the art of lying to voters, newspapers, and congressional committee. "There are aspects of evolution in the man which would astonish and, possibly, terrify Darwin himself," the author says, identifying Milton as "the problem of the day!" The cumulative effect of fictional depictions and seemingly innocent snippets of information, some sent in by the magazine's readers, was to undermine belief in the political capacity of blacks and the wisdom of making them citizens.[83]

The use of black dialect, popular from the 1870s on, was part of a larger cultural interest in ethnic and regional speech patterns, but it also suggested black ignorance and was meant to elicit laughter. As *Harper's* editor explained, "Our Irish friends fill a large placed in the [Editor's] Drawer, and not unjustly, for there seems no end to their blunders and their wit." Since blacks were featured far more frequently than Irish, it would seem that their blunders were funnier than those committed by other groups.[84]

As Edward King's series "The Great South" made apparent, sympathy for the plight of white southerners was rising. In Louisiana, King found planters who had once offered such generous hospitality now eating corn and pork. Ladies of culture and refinement were taking in washing to earn enough money for food. Despair was etched on white faces; a generation had "been doomed." While these men and woman had not been bitter opponents of the Union, they were paying the price for its preservation. Those whom abolitionists had called victimizers had become victims.[85]

King's depiction of Louisiana's former elite was an early indication of the rehabilitation of the slave-owning class. Even *Atlantic Monthly*, which during the 1870s avoided demeaning material about freed people, published articles that began to modify harsh views of the South and its decision for war. In 1874, along with a piece by Whittier focusing on the antislavery convention of 1834 and one about John Brown's son's escape from Harpers Ferry, the magazine published the first installment of a series of articles written by former Confederate soldier George Eggleston, titled "A Rebel's Recollections." Eggleston believed that his writing might "change some people's view of the South and Southerners," and he hoped that northern readers would be able to see things through southern eyes. Eggleston insisted that southerners had "honestly" believed in the right of secession and believed they were doing their patriotic duty in leaving the Union. "You, reader, who shouldered your musket and fought like the hero you are, for the Union and the old flag," Eggleston suggested, would have fought for secession had the reader lived in the South. Eggleston recalled the prewar period a "dreamy" time when whites were "loved almost reverentially" by a "faithful and affectionate people."[86]

"The Gentle Fire-Eater," a story that appeared in the *Atlantic* in 1878, indicated just how far the magazine was straying from its abolitionist origins. The author, Clarence Gordon, was a New Yorker who had spent several years living in Georgia and his sympathies here lay with the southern point of view. At the story's opening, Roelff Damrell, the main character, has just returned from Harpers Ferry where he has seen John Brown executed. The trip, Damrell explains, was a sort of "religious pilgrimage" that allowed him to witness "the vindication of the law on the arch-personification of abolitionism." Later in the narrative, Damrell pronounces slavery a blessing for Africans for it has taught them the agricultural and mechanical arts. Despite the narrator's supposed distaste for some of Damrell's views, he regards Damrell as one of those "superbly virile type of players" of the prewar period who has held fast to an "old knightly creed." He repeats a Union soldier's supposed remark that called into question the necessity for the Civil War. The narrator muses, "I sometimes feel that he was worth keeping at the expense of slavery." Of the slave-owning class, he asks, "Was it not with all its imperfections a heroic group?"[87]

In "Uncle Gabe's White Folks," published in 1876 in *Scribner's*, and in many other stories and poems, slaves and former slaves love their masters beyond measure. Uncle Gabe greets his master's son return to the plantation with an outpouring of thanksgiving to "de Lord for all his grace!" Another former slave had often heard people talking of Washington and Franklin and acknowledges they were "might fine," but, he adds, "dere wuzn't nar a one ob 'em come up to Mahsr John." Blacks also had plenty of affection for the great former military leader of the Confederacy Robert E. Lee. One ditty described a freedman's cabin and the "man uncouth" who had "pictures twenty-three! / Cheap prints and small / Save one, are all . . . of Lee." "Real" plantation negroes loved their white folks. As an 1879 story in *Lippincott* that revealed the supposed depth of affection slaves had harbored for their white family concluded, "we Yankees have but a meager conception of the negro character, the real plantation negro — a fact [that the writer] did not admit forty years ago."[88]

Life under slavery had been a good one, not the miserable existence that abolitionists had claimed. "The darkeys" had joyful jamborees in the quarters at holidays. "How unrestrained their mirth — how hearty!" In fact, some of this popular literature suggested that for former slaves, freedom didn't measure up to slavery. In the poem "Dis Ole' 'Oman an' Me," the freedman would trade his steak, wheat cake, tea, coffee, and broadcloth coat for his slave diet of ashcake, pone, and buttermilk and his old jeans. He dismisses his wife's desire to read: "'Tis no consarn o' hearn.'" The problem is freedom: "It seems ter me / We's done gone changed our natrel selves / From what we used ter be." A supposedly true anecdote carried in *Harper's* described a slave who had bought his freedom before the war. But the jobs he found in freedom all turned out to be dangerous, and "with wings lent him by fear," he returned to his master and begged him to return his money in exchange for his former "nigger property." In another story, a former slave dies of a broken heart when he discovers he cannot remain as his master's property after the war. Emancipation, it turned out, according to popular literature, was not even valued by those who supposedly had benefited from it.[89]

Haviland could not help but be aware of the views being promulgated at the time she was writing her autobiography. As a reader of the literary monthlies and as a reader and contributor to newspapers, Haviland was familiar with changing cultural currents, and her book represented a vigorous effort to challenge them and the historical narrative of slavery, war, and Reconstruction they implied. Her reminiscences refuted the emerging new stereotypes of blacks and their desire for happy servitude. In the first half of her book Haviland establishes the "thirst for liberty" among blacks with account after account of fugitives and their daring escapes. George Taylor, Willis Hamilton, John White, William Allen and family, nine slaves, two young men: readers could hardly help losing track of how many slaves were striking out for liberty as the incidents accumulated. The arrangement was hardly artful but made the point. These slave narratives of escape, once familiar inside and outside antislavery circles, now needed emphatic restatement and they found it in this book.[90]

The fugitives' stories were varied but highlighted their determination to leave slavery behind no matter what the consequences. Some had attempted flight more than once. Many had been punished. Some even had been tortured and put in irons. Some had successfully fled but would do anything to recover family members still enslaved. The unusual escapes and clever ruses attested to black intelligence and persistence, although Haviland, like Coffin, described herself as playing a key role in orchestrating flight from the North to Canada.

The actions of the fugitives belied any notion of the affectionate slave. Several anecdotes seem almost to be a direct reply to emerging fictional views. For example, after working for several months in Ohio, Tom returned home to Kentucky in order to rescue his wife. He led his master to believe that he had found freedom a great mistake and even gave him the $80 he had earned as a free laborer. The abolitionists, Tom said, were "the greates' rascals I ever seen. . . . Massa Carpenter, all I wants is one good stiddy home." Tom "was never more trusty, diligent, and faithful in all that pertained to his master's interest" and eventually even won the confidence of the neighboring planters. The assumed affection lasted right up to the moment he and his wife fled. This and other incidents Haviland related sharply exposed the nature of slavery and the determination of slaves to free themselves.[91]

Haviland assured her readers that she had more material than she could include in her book. But she made sure that they got a good picture of the southern slaveholder, and it was a far less charitable characterization than Coffin had provided, perhaps because of the ongoing rehabilitation of the plantation class. Haviland begins chapter 3 by introducing "to the reader the representatives of a large proportion of slave-owners of the Southern states, who were perverted by a system well-named 'the sum of all villain-ies.'" As this generalization suggested, very few good owners played a part in this narrative. One, deemed "remarkably kind," fed his slaves on corn dodgers, sour milk, and a saucer of greens mixed with a tiny amount of pork. This "best of slave holders" also told one of his female slaves untruth-fully that her husband had married again and "was riding around with his new wife mighty happy." If these were the best, then the worst were bad indeed. One furious representative of what Haviland ironically called the "land of chivalry" appeared after another. "Rage" was the adjective Havi-land repeatedly associated with slaveholders in contrast to the increasingly sympathetic portraits featured in the pages of northern monthlies.[92]

The blacks depicted in periodicals ranged from the foolish and gullible to the affectionate and simpleminded. But some pieces highlighted blacks' supposed propensity to dishonesty. Despite his "sage and dignified" appear-ance in the story in *Harper's*, Uncle Zeke was a thief and liar. As a coun-terpoint to such views, Haviland's narrative established that it was white owners in search of their slaves who were tricky, deceitful, and not to be believed. A man who claimed to be an Ohio schoolteacher and agent of an abolitionist newspaper turned out to be a "counterfeit" as Haviland sus-pected. Some slaveholders hatched far more elaborate plots to recover their slaves than that of the fake schoolteacher. One, a Dr. John Chester, claimed to be one of his own neighbors, Deacon Bayliss, who had emancipated his slaves, including Willis Hamilton. Pretending to be on his deathbed, Ches-ter, passing for Bayliss, expressed his desire to see Hamilton and his family. Hamilton's wife, Elsie, had fled from Chester, and he intended to recover her and her children and to kidnap her free husband. Largely because of Haviland's cautious nature and quick thinking, the complicated plot failed and the "villainous scoundrels" fled. "The last we saw of these tall and val-iant representatives of the land of chivalry," Haviland recalled, "were their heels fast receding in the thicket."[93]

"Avaricious and unprincipled men" like Chester were coldly indifferent to the well-being of their property. Haviland reinforced her analysis of the heartless slave hunter with portraits of masters and mistresses drawn from her own trips to the South. As she told readers, abolitionists had been ac-cused of exaggerating the evils of slavery and making assertions based on "the few unprincipled men we had seen." Determined to "see . . . the sys-tem of slavery in its own territory," Haviland was able to provide evidence that was trustworthy. In Kentucky, she described a white owner shedding tears as she told Haviland the sad tale of a slave woman being separated from her children. Then the women "cheerfully" entered her own kitchen to see her "nigger baby." "There," she told Haviland. "Isn't that a fine boy? He's worth $100. I could get that to-day for him, and he's only eight months old." When Haviland glanced at the mother, she saw "a downcast look" and heard the woman's sigh.[94]

Haviland challenged other emerging racial stereotypes. The scenes of black religious life appearing in her book, for example, acknowledged the heightened emotional character of black worship, and even the occasional "wild excitement" it elicited. Yet these expressions of feeling did not suggest barbaric exuberance but thanksgiving for freedom long awaited. At one of the services, "a half-hour was spent in these outbursts of long pent-up feelings," and then, "they settled down into comparative quiet."[95]

The black preachers she encountered were deeply spiritual men. Uncle Dodson, a plantation preacher, "had some queer Scripture quotations and believed Eve received her name because she 'was the mother of all evil.'" Such misunderstandings, said Haviland, needed to be corrected, not ridiculed. It was "no wonder these poor people should misquote Scripture, as a few months ago many . . . were not allowed to read," she observed. Uncle Phil was an "aged saint" with a noble tale. Converted while still a slave, he suffered fierce beatings because he refused his master's order to give up prayer. When his master saw that violence had no effect, he decided to humiliate his slave by inviting all the black and white people in the vicinity to come and hear him preach. On the appointed day, Uncle Phil "trimbled an' sweat all over. But once I was up my strength cum to me." The Lord preached through him, Uncle Phil said, and twenty-three attendees were converted. Haviland remarked, "That poor ignorant man could not read the written Word, but God took his own way to lead and instruct him, to fit him for an instrument in his hand of turning many souls to the knowledge that is the truth."[96]

Haviland told Uncle Phil's tale, as she put it, "in his own language as I took it down in my note-book at the time of my interviews with him." Although some of the fugitives and freed people who appeared in her book spoke excellent English, many spoke in dialect. Yet her speakers did not make themselves ridiculous by misusing words or relying on pompous expression. Instead, they told harrowing tales in a moving and authentic voice.

Haviland extended her analysis through the Civil War, to which she devoted many energetic pages, refuting the argument that Eggleston and others were developing about southern patriotism and the sincere belief in secession as the fundamental reason for war. Haviland did not even bother to discuss secession. Her treatment of the war made slavery central to the conflict. The army's understanding of the conflict changed, she explained, when northern soldiers witnessed slavery's cruelties and realized what the war was really all about. They "saw that man's inhumanity to man was the outgrowth of slavery. They clearly perceived that the iron rod of oppression must be broken, or the unholy rebellion would succeed."[97]

This section of her book contained her harshest condemnation of southerners and slavery. The man who took an oath of loyalty to the Union in an attempt to save his property, and the woman who, when Union troops approached her plantation, begged her slaves to pretend to own silver bought with the proceeds of sales of their own children exemplified the slave-owning class. The poor whites in a refugee camp Haviland visited, "Clay-eaters," as she referred to them, were "the most ignorant, listless, and degraded of any people I had ever met." Unlike the blacks in the camp, who would "do anything," these filthy and degenerate whites were unwilling to make the slightest effort to fend for themselves.[98]

Haviland's work gave her many opportunities to interview slaves who had fled from their masters. Some were homeless slaves heartlessly forced off their plantations. The owners of one old woman told her to go to the Yankees because she was of no account. Her master threatened to shoot her if she didn't go, while her mistress announced she would burn down the old slave's cabin. Other "truly revolting" examples revealed horrific aspects of slavery that Haviland learned about firsthand: the three generations of slave women, grandmother, mother, and grandchild, for example, all children of their master, and the various instruments of slave torture, the cuffs, the chains, and the shackles, and the irons with special barbs. A picture of a solemn looking Haviland showing the slave irons she had collected accompanied this part of her narrative. Some, like heavy neck irons that could not be removed, were especially gruesome. She learned that Uncle Tim had worn a neck iron for two years. When he died, his master "'had his head cut off to get de iron off,'" a former slave woman told Haviland. "'Is it possible for a human being to become so brutal as to cut a man's head off when he is dead?'" Haviland asked. Her anecdotes, the pictures of devices to torture slaves, and her question all rendered impossible any southern attempts to evade guilt for their defense of slavery and raised doubts about trusting them with the future of southern blacks.[99]

So extreme was some of the material in her book that Haviland took great pains to establish its veracity. "I put in my diary only such as I found were proven to be facts," she asserted. Northerners had not known then (and certainly not at the moment when Haviland was composing her book) "the perfect hell on earth" that was the South. The sadistic nature of what whites did to their slaves was often "too shocking for the public eye or ear." By refusing to reveal all she knew, Haviland allowed readers to imagine "persecution and outrage" even more horrible than she described.[100]

Bringing her story right up through the 1870s (and in subsequent editions even later), Haviland forcefully argued that emancipation had failed to bring "the glorious light of freedom" to blacks. After more than a decade of patiently waiting for things to change in the South, freed people realized they faced "submissive vassalage, a war of the races, or emigration." Acting less as the autobiographer and more as an advocate for free people, Haviland justified her continued activism. "Surely we have a right, and it is our duty to ventilate these facts, though we may be deemed sensational," she asserted. Stressing how carefully she had collected her evidence and the time she had spent interviewing former slaves in Kansas in 1879, she emphasized that nothing had changed in the South, "that poisoned land." Whoever claimed that southerners had accepted the changes that the war had brought was wrong. She pointed to a recent article in a Mississippi newspaper that had proclaimed that black people would either become slaves again or cease to be. Many places in the South exhibited a "re-enlivened treason." Atrocities abounded, and she provided plenty of examples. "The following incidents," she wrote, "will serve as data, for which we have a right to judge of the manners used to bring the colored people into what they [white southerners] deem their proper place."[101]

The exodus to Kansas represented yet another example of the black desire for freedom and the dire realities of southern life, and Haviland urged her "dear reader" to do everything possible to help blacks who had reached Kansas: "Let every man, woman, and child arise and work for the refugees, who are suffering for food, fuel, and clothing. . . . It is a debt we owe these people." The debt was not just a charitable obligation but something blacks had earned. Haviland reminded her readers of the bravery of black troops during the war and the willingness of slaves to help Union soldiers. She also reminded readers that the government's primary duty was to protect former slaves. But if the government was too weak to carry out its first duty (as it was with the end of Reconstruction), there were still obligations that it could fulfill: "Welcome the fleeing refugee and point him to work, or to the thousands of acres of good government land, and help him where he needs to keep body and soul together during the few months it may require to make himself self-sustaining."[102]

Haviland's book made a powerful connection between past and present, emphasizing the continuity between the Old South and the New, between atrocities against blacks in the past and those in the present, between fugitives seeking freedom at any cost before the war and those pursuing their dream in the present. She rejected the view expressed in the *New York Times* that the concerns of antislavery belonged "to a distant period in our history." The message of her autobiography was that this was no time to forget history and no time for reconciliation. Her book did not end in quiet contemplation of a life well spent but in judgment and a call to action.[103]

Haviland's call to action, like Coffin's, was published by the Western Methodist Book Concern, appearing under the name of Walden & Stowe, agents for the house. Her book, like Coffin's, suited the publisher's religious and economic interests. Haviland even had Methodist credentials since she had joined the Wesleyan Methodists when she abandoned Quakerism over the slavery issue. Haviland may also have been attractive for monetary reasons: she appears to have taken on financial obligations for the first printing of 1,000 books, for she wrote in 1882 that she wanted to "be square with the Concern before the second Edition comes out" and asked for terms for the second, particularly when payments would be due. While southern writers were being paid by financially powerful monthlies for their work, Haviland was risking her own resources to get her own interpretation of past and present into the public's hands.[104]

It is doubtful that Haviland ever considered submitting her work to a trade publisher. It was unsuitable on many levels. It had a local rather than general appeal and it contained the kind of detail on subjects that many "ordinary" readers might not find "attractive" in the 1880s. Sophisticated or secular readers might find the religious theme dated and the style lacking in grace. But, as Haviland must have realized, the character of her reminiscences suited a denominational publisher and fit neatly into the niche of subscription books. Although literary commentators self-consciously dismissed subscription books as lacking enough serious history "to have value" and rejected the focus on the "exploits" of an author who might be unknown to potential readers, her adventures were daring and unusual, and her story was laced with religious feeling. The visuals, though they might strike the aesthetic observer as "cheap illustrations," were prized in subscription books and conveyed the activism of the author.

The fact that Haviland was preparing her second edition within a year of the first suggests that the first edition sold well. Certainly, she paid meticulous attention to its production and sale. By 1883, if not before, canvassers were helping to sell her book, and she actively promoted it herself. She sent her editor glowing testimonials to include with promotional materials. And she encouraged the placement of her book in stores. "I hope to meet my *nice* book at my Friend Hallecks Clothing store on Woodward Ave Detroit,

Chicago, 5 mo 9 1889

Laura S Haviland

In a/c with Pub Assn of Friends

To PUBLISHING ASSOCIATION OF FRIENDS, Dr.

416 DEARBORN STREET.

PLEASE RETURN THIS BILL WITH REMITTANCE.

	960 Womans Life Work @ 45¢	$432 00	
	Steel Engravings $17. -5.00 off	12 00	
8	Electrotype plates	8 75	
	Correction on "	75	
	Dies from Fees	1 60	
	Marbling 960 books @ 1¾¢ Ea $16.80		
	Binding backs 960 " " ⅓¢ " 3.20		
	8pp aditional paper binding + press work 7½ 4.80	24 80	
4/26/89	Cash Drayage	70	
	Correction on page 555 .37		
	" " 235 .43		
	" " Title .30		
	" " page 362 .32		
	" " " 7 bad folios .75		
	" 15¢, 30¢, 20¢, ? 17¢ = .82		
	Composition + Type for Cor. 1,07		
	" + 2 New Illustrated pp 1,50	5 56	
	New Signature on plates	2 91	
			489 12

Cr

4/21/89	Cash	300,00	
4/22/89	"	140,00	
"	Note for	43,23	483 23
	Bal due		5 89

This bill from the Publishing Association of Friends itemizes the various expenses associated with publishing Laura Haviland's book. She was involved in many aspects of her book, wanting it to be as perfect as possible. (Courtesy Lenawee Historical Society Museum, Adrian, Mich.)

as I expect to be there on the 31st inst," she wrote her agent in 1883. A week later she reported that the twelve copies she brought with her to a WCTU meeting in Detroit sold readily and that she could have sold more copies had she had them with her.[105]

Haviland was also concerned with the physical appearance of the book. In 1882, she explained she wanted "the electrotype *perfect*" so that the resulting book would be perfect. "I should regret the least misplaced or sentence," she said, although she knew she was perhaps "too sensitive." She particularly wanted to present a copy to John Greenleaf Whittier, but she felt that she could not send him a book that did not meet her standards. (When she did send him a copy, she received a testimonial from him that appeared in a later edition). She also made decisions about bindings and edgings, but, since her goal was to have her book read, she was always careful not to make it too expensive. But she realized the appeal of an attractive volume. Having asked her publisher for a particular binding's cost, Haviland said that "a few friends have indicated a [desire for a] richer binding for their center table, combining the ornamental with the useful they say, sufficient to pay 50 cts. more on a book. I can tell better when I get your figures, whether it will pay for the calf." She furnished her publisher with a wood engraving of one of her most exciting adventures, "Author's Encounter with Bloodhounds," to include in future editions. She asked for twenty-five copies so that she could send them to people who had already purchased the book.[106]

The excerpts from the "voice of the press" and testimonials included in later editions suggest that some readers grasped Haviland's purpose. Whittier wrote that "thy beautiful and saintly example will be followed by others who read thy story," while the *Inter Ocean*, a newspaper to which Haviland had contributed articles, commended the book "not only for its historical facts, but because the beautiful life is WORTHY OF STUDY and IMITATION." The special correspondent for the *Chicago Tribune* observed another important theme of Haviland's autobiography: "This work gives us an inside view of what sufferings the blacks endured, and of what risks they ran to secure their freedom, which was little dreamed of in this northern land of freedom, and were it not from such a high source of authority, could hardly be credited even at this day."

Other comments pointed to some likely reasons for the book's success. A writer for the *Christian Cynosure* noted, "The pursuits, the exciting attempts to recapture, the hair-breadth escapes, the coolness, bravery, intrepidity and success of our quiet Quaker heroine—O! I can't tell you, you must read the book to know." Other reviewers agreed with the assessment of one, that "the book is as full of thrilling incidents as a romance." Some found it as vivid and exciting as *Uncle Tom's Cabin* or "Prof. Finney's Autobiography . . . A wonderful book!" Because some critics might claim such an amazing narrative was fiction, Haviland included letters attesting to her "pure character" and "the perfect truthfulness" of her account.[107]

A Woman's Life-Work went unnoticed by the major journals, since it had neither the literary and aesthetic qualities that would attract attention nor the credentials that its publication with a major publishing house would have provided. In fact, it is likely that the sensational character of Haviland's book would not recommend it to critics who valued understated realism. But she enjoyed a continuing readership nonetheless. Five editions had been published by the end of the century, and, in 1902, a special memorial edition, bound in blue with silver trim, was issued to celebrate her life. But her sales, only 2,500 by 1887, paled in comparison to the numbers of monthly magazines sold. The most successful, the *Century*, reached a circulation of nearly 200,000 by 1885.[108]

Despite the popularity of Underground Railroad stories, some never appeared in print, either because writers could not bear the costs of publication or because their perspective might offend potential readers. Others, some written by black men and women, reached small audiences because their authors could afford to have only a limited number of copies published. Like Still, the stories they told were black-centered in theme and tone. While Haviland scrupulously emphasized the burning desire for liberty that led so many fugitives and freed people to flee from the South, her white voice and presence dominated her book and made it appealing to white readers. Haviland, as did Coffin, told most of the stories and supplied details and invented dialogue for scenes that she had not witnessed herself. She presented herself as the key to many rescues, revealing how she provided plans for escape and subsequently advised former slaves how to live successfully in freedom. None of the pictures in the book showed black people, and Haviland, not a black fugitive, was shown facing down bloodhounds and carrying the chains and restraints that signified the cruelty of the system.[109]

There were, of course, many black people who could still remember the courage and independence that flight and life in freedom had demanded. John Malvin, a free black southerner who had moved to Ohio in 1827, had assisted fugitives, explaining in his recollections, published in 1879, that, "so great was my abhorrence of slavery, that I was willing to run any risk." In the pages of his account, neither he nor other blacks seemed to have any need of white oversight or assistance in helping slaves escape, and it was black people who fought to desegregate churches and public schools in the North. Although Malvin was a member of the Cleveland Anti-Slavery Society and became its vice president in 1858, he never mentioned his connection to the organized abolitionist movement. His depiction of the Republican Party as God's instrument "for the miracle of ending slavery" at the book's conclusion was a rare acknowledgement of the role white people played in bringing about emancipation.[110]

Malvin ended his narrative on a hopeful note. Although he condemned events in the South that were making "the life of the colored man a thousand times more miserable than the worst condition of bondage," he believed that "right will sooner or later prevail." The day would come, he warned, "when another nemesis will overtake and destroy the evil at the South."[111]

Malvin had his short reminiscence printed by the Cleveland *Leader*, and, since he was doubtless paying for the job, it is likely that only a few copies were printed. While thousands read stories of happy slaves, it is likely that only a few people acquired or read his story, especially since Malvin died the year after his pamphlet's publication. Even far more famous black men and women found a smaller audience than they wished.[112]

John Parker, a former slave and operator on the Underground Railroad, told his adventurous tale to a white newspaperman in the 1880s, but it was not even published until 1996. Given Parker's black-centered and somewhat aggressive perspective, it is hardly surprising that his story did not appear at the time of the interviews. While a white reader of the 1880s might have understood Parker's colossal hatred of slavery, the violence his hatred inspired was disturbing. He actually attacked a white woman who was striking a female slave. "I seized the whip and gave the white woman a sound beating," Parker revealed. His self-assurance would not sit easily with whites, either. Even Garrison had characterized black people as "docile, patient, and grateful." These qualities were remarkably absent from Parker's personality. He felt a sense of "confidence in myself, in my ability to meet any and all situations which might arise to confront me." Thinking, Parker concluded, was the key to success, and it was something he could do better than many whites: "For ten months I educated myself how to outwit men and combinations. . . . I worked out a method which gave me a great advantage in meeting situations. . . . Mind you, I was dealing with ignorant men. I soon saw that they were slow thinkers." Parker made other unflattering references to white men. "If I do say it myself," he stated, for example, "I was very much better dressed and more intelligent-looking than the white men."[113]

Eventually Parker bought his freedom, but before leaving the South, he soundly beat a white superintendent who had stolen Parker's model for a new farm tool. His "fight to the finish" contained a violence exuberantly expressed: "I hit him again with every ounce of vengeance I could muster. This time he went down for good. I gloated over his bruised face, discolored eyes. As free man, I had met him fairly and asserted my superiority . . . [over] a contemptible foe."[114]

Parker viewed his twenty years of Underground Railroad work in Ohio as part of his "own little personal war on slavery." He armed himself with knives and guns and proved willing to use them. In an effort to foil the attempt of several slave owners to capture Parker and take him to Kentucky, where there was a reward for his capture, Parker "opened the encounter by firing point-black at one, who fell . . . , then exchanged shots with the other." While white conductors appeared in the background of his story, Parker was clearly in command of his operations and had no need of white assistance. Although some of the fugitives he helped were "riff-raff" from areas bordering the Ohio River, where escape was easy, others came from long distances and were "resourceful" and "people of character." They were capable of "heroism and self-sacrifice" that made Parker "proud of my race."[115]

In 1879, John T. Butler, a former slaveholder from South Carolina, came north with the intention of changing northerner's minds about the cruelty of pursuing fugitives with hounds and making some money by capitalizing on the fugitive story. His demonstration, held at a race track, featured his hounds chasing a black man named Sam who simulated escaping on foot and on horseback. *Harper's Weekly* proclaimed the whole event absurd "as an illustration of a real slave-hunt." Apparently northerners could agree that Butler's claim that using hounds to track down fugitives had been merely a means of "detain[ing them] . . . without injuring" them was false.[116]

But the same year as Butler's demonstration, Lydia Maria Child was thinking more deeply about northern public opinion. As she wrote to a friend, "All our troubles originate in the fact that the American people, North or South, never really felt the enormous wickedness of slavery." Because Americans had not been persuaded of the character of slavery, they showed little commitment to any cause beyond emancipation itself. Both Coffin and Haviland used their life stories to highlight the wickedness of slavery and the moral necessity of racial equality, and their books did attract a moderate but limited readership. But as one literary critic pointed out, some readers were "not over-anxious to be instructed." The tales told by Coffin and Haviland were devoured more likely for the excitement they provided rather than for their moral messages and lessons. Indeed, Underground Railroad stories continued to be popular, but many accounts lacked the reformist zeal that Coffin and Haviland demonstrated. Offering only the most general condemnation of slavery and showing more interest in white "conductors" than in the supposedly timid fugitives who needed white assistance, these tales encouraged complacency and disregard for black freedom in the contemporary world.[117]

THE 1880s

In 1887, a story titled "Mrs. Stowe's 'Uncle Tom' at Home in Kentucky" appeared in *Century* magazine. An illustration showing a slave owner reaching into his pocket for coins for three black boys captured the spirit of the piece. The author, James Lane Allen, had grown up in Kentucky and suffered through the years of war and Reconstruction. Now he looked back fondly on the past, depicting slavery in Kentucky as a benign institution. "Tenderly associated" from infancy with black slaves, kindly masters sought to transform their blacks into capable and contented workers all the while caring for those who were too old to labor. "How unjust," then, to declare that such masters "did not feel affection for . . . [their] slaves," Allen asserted. He lavished special praise on slave mistresses as "the real practical philanthropists of the negro race." And northern women had never given southern plantation mistresses any credit for furnishing the guidance and training necessary to mold their slaves' "superstitious, indolent . . . most impressionable nature."[1]

Sometimes these admirable slave owners, Allen continued, emancipated their slaves, and the slaves, in turn, headed to Canada only to return voluntarily to serve their former masters. The slaves remaining on Kentucky farms never "felt any burning desire for freedom." In fact, the author proclaimed, some of them actually resented "agitators of forcible and immediate emancipation." Now free, Kentucky blacks remained "content with their inferiority, and lazily drift[ed] though life."[2]

Such a view of Kentucky slavery and the slaves' disinterest in freedom sharply contrasted with the picture Laura Haviland and Levi Coffin painted of Kentucky fugitives desperate to leave servitude behind. Allen's article was but one sign of the diffusion of historical and racial perspectives in middle-class magazines during the 1880s that contested the meaning and achievements of abolitionism, its connection to the Civil War, and the need to remain committed to free black rights. Abolitionists writing their reminiscences in the 1880s thus faced formidable obstacles in correcting what they saw as false interpretations of their work and the meaning of their cause. Jane Swisshelm's autobiography, published in 1880, insisted upon the evils of slavery and praised the achievements of political abolitionism, as did Frederick Douglass's 1881 autobiography and George Julian's 1884 *Political Recollections*. Parker Pillsbury's angry volume, published the year before Julian's, insisted upon the heroism of Garrisonian reformers and fumed that they were being denied credit for emancipating the slaves. President Ulysses Grant published his autobiography in 1885, and while he was not an abolitionist, his book lent the prestige of his former office to the view that the South must be reconstructed on northern terms. "The cause of the great War of the Rebellion," he stated baldly, "will have to be attributed to slavery."[3]

Despite the popularity of Grant's memoirs, which sold over 300,000 copies, abolitionist authors of the 1880s must have felt that their perspective was increasingly regarded as irrelevant. True, the monthly magazines did not entirely neglect the abolitionist point of view. The same year *Century* published James Allen's story, it also continued its serialized biography of Abraham Lincoln, published a piece on black troops at the battle of Petersburg, and editorialized that southerners were content with the outcome of their failed struggle for secession. The magazine, one of *Century*'s editors claimed, was "national and antislavery in its views." But even essays that acknowledged the necessity of eliminating slavery and black contributions to the war expressed reservations. While the authors of Lincoln's biography praised Charles Sumner's "moral fearlessness," they characterized John Brown as a fanatic, completely unsuited for the heroic role that he fancied for himself. The "little coterie of radical [Boston] abolitionists" supporting Brown were "extravagant in demonstrations of approval and admiration" for a man who was warped and an act that "was reprehensible and fraught with evil result." The colored troops at Petersburg, stereotypically characterized as "dark men, [with] white eyes and teeth and red lips," were inappropriately described as "picturesque" just before the carnage that followed their charge was recounted.[4]

Some articles published in the 1880s reinterpreted the past, while others discussed contemporary conditions in the South. Many were sympathetic to the southern point of view. Indeed, as *Century*'s editor Richard Watson Gilder explained in 1886, he wanted the magazine to "be so hospitable to Southern writers and Southern opinion" that it "should insist upon giving a fair show to Southern views, even when they are not altogether palatable to our Northern readers, among whom, of course, is our greatest audience." Stories and poems about the prewar era portrayed simple-minded slaves and loving masters in the spirit of Allen's piece. The point was that the past had been not only a happy time for both loving masters and affectionate slaves but also better than the present, especially for the slaves.

In "My Life as a Slave," supposedly a true tale recorded "from the lips of its hero," a trusted former slave described his happy years as a servant. He concluded, "We jes' went on peaceful an' happy till de war come and rooted ebery blessed thing up by de roots." Far from being noble or necessary, war had destroyed a valued way of life, and freedom was fraught with difficulties. As Walter B. Hill, a Georgia lawyer, pointed out correctly, freedom for former slaves often meant a marginal economic existence. Those too old to work depended on their children for their livelihoods or faced old age alone because family members had been sold away years before. Neither of these situations, Hill pointed out, had occurred in slavery, when masters took care of their slaves. The jollity of the past disappeared also, and black voices, rendered by white authors like Thomas Nelson Page, proclaimed their longing for the old days: "Dese heah free issue niggers don' know what Christmas is. Hit tecks ole times to meck a sho-'nough . . . Christmas." Authentic black voices with contrasting views of the past were rarely heard by whites, the majority of whom did not read black papers, journals, or novels.[5]

The literary monthlies vied with one another to supply the richest mix of information to northern readers eager to learn about the conditions of freedmen and freedwomen. There were occasional positive assessments of black progress. "A Georgia Plantation," for example, praised blacks for their successful adjustment to freedom and their continued improvement. But the response to Albion Tourgée's novel, *Bricks without Straw*, was revealing. Tourgée was an abolitionist, former carpetbagger, and novelist who vehemently rejected the fashionable sentimental views of the Old South and held true to the goal of refashioning the South into a more equitable society. Yet a reviewer found the novel's presentation of virtuous blacks and oppressive whites objectionable and untrue. The aim of such positive characterizations of blacks was presumed to be inflammatory: to create "and perpetuate" passions. Most writers contributing to the periodicals during the 1880s avoided such unpopular interpretations. Fiction presented simple black folk with "diverting traits" and kindly whites. As the main character of one story explained, "We always treat the negroes, even now, as so many children, and dislike to disappoint them." Articles that purported to provide a realistic picture of former slaves gave harsh, unsentimental evaluations. Blacks might be striving to be educated, but their "grotesque, illogical mind[s]" made progress difficult. The *Atlantic Monthly*, once the mouthpiece for abolitionism, featured a series early in the decade titled "Studies in the South." *Harper's* followed suit with Charles Dudley Warner's "Impressions of the South" and "The South Revisited" and Rebecca Harding Davis's "Here and There in the South" several years later. Collectively, they presented a dismal picture of the situation of southern blacks and established the folly of emancipation.[6]

Portraying himself during the war as "an enthusiastic young abolitionist," the unnamed author of "Studies in the South" explained that he had joined the army because he hoped that the conflict would end slavery. During his service in the South, he had planned one day to return and to study southern character. Now, dissatisfied by what he had read about the South since the war had ended, he determined to visit the region and see its peoples and prospects for himself. While he acknowledged the complexity of southern social, racial, political, and economic conditions, he admitted that he had been unable to find substantial evidence of black improvement in most of the places he toured. Even an industrious black planter in Louisiana who had had some success in training other black men to work for him explained to the author that what former slaves needed was not education but good work habits. "Not many of our race can work and read too," he remarked. In the author's view, "this man seemed to have a firm grasp upon reality" and was pursuing the kind of reconstruction that the South really needed. All too often, however, blacks were lazy spendthrifts. If they could only grasp the fact that they could improve their lives by working and saving, they would be able to acquire land that was so cheap in the South. "For quiet, solitary, constant toil a first-rate white laborer is, I think, superior to almost any negro," the author concluded.[7]

Other aspects of black life were equally disheartening to this author. The natural leaders, the clergy, were failing their race. Old-style ministers were "ignorant, fat, lazy, and licentious." The younger and better educated men were poorly prepared to reach "the tropical and impulsive nature of the colored people," whose lives were more "a matter of instinct than of thought." Not surprisingly, the moral state of ordinary blacks was regrettable. Young women, especially, were criticized for their almost "universal" failure to honor female chastity.[8]

The journals carried many articles addressing the question of black political rights. That these articles appeared during a period of interracial political cooperation in several southern states that was alarming to racial conservatives could hardly be a coincidence. Opinion on black suffrage was mixed. Editor Gilder provided a familiar abolitionist point of view when he declared, "The extinction of negro slavery and the conferring of the right of suffrage on the emancipated slaves were the final steps, so far as we are concerned, in the long-continued struggle for freedom and human rights." He confidently expected that "the ground thus won" would never be lost. Yet articles also emphatically stated that white southerners were determined to retain political supremacy. Reconstruction had forced educated white men to bend to the will of ignorant black voters, and this experiment would not continue. But while Gilder might proclaim that violence was immoral, and "because the blacks are still restrained in the free exercise of their legal rights, the situation at the South is to-day morally unsound," he could still agree with "every well-wisher of the blacks" in counseling "them to accept the foot of the political ladder . . . and work up" as "the last to be apprenticed to citizenship."[9]

Charles Dudley Warner, a travel writer and member of *Harper's* staff, pointed out that suffrage without the provision of education had been a "hazardous experiment." As "Studies in the South" explained, blacks, no more than sheep (an analogy that was more than a little reminiscent of slavery), had the knowledge needed to vote. Fiction rounded out the picture established in Warner's firsthand reporting. In "Politics at the Log-Pulling," for example, a black voter exclaims, "I goes in on de side dat gibs *de biggest bobby-kews!*" And in another story, Uncle Elijah, who left his owners after the war, was so delighted to care for their horses again that he forgot all about having a vote or serving on a jury. In a third, damning statements from a "black" voice denounced "rot'en lazy" "free niggers" who "flops 'round arter politicks and sech trash." This "informant" cast a responsible vote, however, for "my own white folks."[10]

Some writers expressed concern at the southern racial violence or supported black civil rights, but they also argued that it was time to let southerners solve their own problems. White southerners understood how to manage their blacks, and the region was more peaceful, prosperous, and tolerant without federal involvement. Passionate denunciations of the South were no longer appropriate. Rather, white southerners deserved sympathy for their experiences during and after the war. Warner declared that the lack of bitterness in the South was amazing considering how much southerners had actually suffered. Now true Americans, white southerners were loyal to the Union and apparently, unlike black southerners depicted in fiction, relieved that slavery had ended.[11]

A writer for *Atlantic Monthly* in 1880 rejected such tolerant assessments. He berated the South for justifying "the rebellion in the pages of history," attempting to eliminate in the public mind the difference between loyalty and disloyalty during the war, and curbing black suffrage in order to achieve its political goals. Yet only a year later, Theodore Bacon, writing in the same journal, rejected the argument that former rebels were winning the contest over memory and politics. At the beginning of the war, he reminded his readers, Union leaders had not even contemplated eliminating slavery. How remarkable the results of the war actually were when compared to the realities of 1861. While it was true that former rebels had reemerged politically, surely no American would have accepted disenfranchising white southerners permanently. Even the black exodus to Kansas was striking, for, unlike the night flights of prewar fugitives, it had taken place in the light of day. Furthermore, blacks left the South because they were dissatisfied with their wages and share of the crops. The fact that blacks were receiving wages at all indicated a "stupendous" revolution that had "gone beyond the most radical abolitionist's subversive fancy."[12]

One way in which writers undermined criticism of the southern situation was by reminding northern readers of their limitations. Often blinded by prejudice and political propaganda that was whipped up to win elections, northerners could not see what was actually happening in the South. Moreover, they were guilty of many of the same practices that they condemned. How could northerners find fault with southern racial arrangements when racial prejudice still flourished in the North? Was it not common to exclude Jews from some public places like hotels? Why should northerners be surprised when the same sort of thing happened in the South? Why should northerners be astonished that white southerners wanted to ban ignorant black men from politics when they did not want political control to rest in the hands of ignorant immigrants in northern cities? As for any northerner who thought he would be able to deal with freed people more successfully than white southerners, the evidence showed otherwise. The author of "Studies in the South" noted that the realities of living in the South could transform even a philanthropic abolitionist into "a tyrant of merciless severity." He gave as an example the Mississippi planter, the son of "a red-hot abolitionist" originally from Minnesota, who proclaimed, "I tell you a nigger has no affection, no gratitude, no heart" and, according to the author, whipped his "free" workers.[13]

Rebecca Harding Davis's picture of the South in "Here and There in the South" was so idyllic that she did not believe that any one could have resisted its influence. Twenty years earlier, Davis's novel dealing with interracial marriage condemned racial prejudice. Now, she suggested that if "Sumner or Garrison had been born on one of these sleepy plantations, with a thousand darkies to earn his living and wait on him, breathing this bay air loaded with the scent of magnolias all his life," they would have been as conservative as the best of southerners.[14]

Such comments were part of a reevaluation taking place in the 1880s of abolitionists, the historical significance of their contributions before and after the Civil War, and, by implication, the meaning of that war and Reconstruction. Theodore Roosevelt weighed in on the subject with his assessment in an 1887 biography published in Houghton Mifflin's series on American statesmen. "Owing to a variety of causes," Roosevelt wrote, "the Abolitionists have received an immense amount of hysterical praise which they do not deserve, and have been credited with deeds done by other men whom, in reality, they hampered." Henry Cabot Lodge suggested that great social and political movements produced two different sorts of leaders. The first group was composed of fanatical agitators, able to penetrate the consciousness of the public but entirely incapable of "leadership, or, in other words, of dealing with . . . fellow-men." If they lived long enough, they were apt to claim credit for the transformations that, in fact, they had not brought about. There had been too much eagerness, Lodge suggested, "to treat the original and extreme abolitionists as if they were the men who not only began the great movement, but who finally carried [it] . . . to a successful termination." Lodge himself was certain that the second group of leaders, who had established a political organization as a means of bringing about for change, was responsible for the "far greater work of saving the Union and carrying the civil war to a triumphant conclusion."[15]

Nasty attacks on abolitionists who had believed in moral suasion appeared in monthlies with some regularity. Congregational clergyman Leonard Woolsey Bacon accused the "indignant philanthropists" of New York and the "malignant philanthropists" of Boston of "false positions, bad logic, and in some cases malignant passions." Their insistence that all slaveholders were wicked was "mischievously and suicidally wrong" and undermined southern abolitionists who were often slaveholders themselves. Bacon, whose father had opposed Garrison, was determined that the "ingenious youth of American should know the truth of the matter—that Mr. Garrison and his society never succeeded in anything."[16]

When Garrison died in 1879, Lydia Maria Child wrote a respectful obituary. Here was a man "honored by the wise and the good, and blessed with the grateful benediction of the poor." While she acknowledged that some found his language harsh, she suggested his fierce tone came partly from his intimate acquaintance with the Bible and the influence of Puritanism. As those who knew him were aware, Child explained, he had cherished a deep tenderness and love for his fellow men.[17]

Reviews in 1886 of the two-volume biography of Garrison written by his sons, however, revealed the rapid decline of Garrison's reputation. One reviewer encouraged readers who might be willing to honor Garrison but were reluctant to "give him exclusive laurels" to take advantage of the "ample opportunity" the book provided to "investigate" the man further. Inadvertently, the reviewer pointed out, the "sturdy" sons had provided evidence to support the charges that Garrison had been egotistical, domineering, and harsh. In particular, Garrison was guilty of wild exaggeration about southern slaveholders. "Draconian inflexibility . . . [was] a very common code upon the antislavery platform," read the review. "It was part of its power, but it brought also a certain weakness, as being really based upon an untruth." Now it was certainly time for even "the most ardent abolitionist" to recognize the false position adopted by Garrison and his followers.[18]

Bacon's review for the *New Englander and Yale Review* was even more scornful of the "paradoxical but filially pious portraiture" provided by Garrison's sons. Bacon declared that Garrisons' scurrilous language had been adopted "in cold blood." Unable to attract attention through the power of his character or the nobility of his language, Garrison had chosen to use insult as a "cheap substitute for eloquence." This language, once seen as an effective instrument for quickening moral sensibilities and recruiting for abolitionism, now was blamed for blighting the cause. His venomous attacks on slaveholders, Bacon argued, actually killed the southern antislavery movement. The story of Garrison's life, according to Bacon, was "the story of the failure and wreck of what could hardly . . . have been a great career, but might have been a wholly honorable and useful one."[19]

Other abolitionists came in for their share of debunking. The lesson of Wendell Phillips's life was not his lifelong devotion to a moral cause but the fact that one could be honored without being an officeholder or conformist. While many acknowledged Phillips as "a knight without fear and without reproach," they also said he indulged in "vivid overstatement of his point" and personal invective. During the war, his schemes to confiscate southern land were "full of vehement unreason." John Brown, of course, was crazy. And John Charles Frémont's unwise emancipation proclamation in the early days of the war became a "rallying cry for men holding extreme anti-slavery opinions."[20]

The only abolitionists to escape unscathed were those who had believed change would come through political action. Instead of resorting to "the wild cries of the abolitionists," they had been willing to work slowly, surely, and steadily to fight and triumph "under the Constitution."[21]

The singling out of political abolitionists as practical reformers implicitly acknowledged slavery's contribution to the coming of the Civil War.

Century's series on the life of Abraham Lincoln also emphasized that the southerners had begun their rebellion to defend slavery, although the editors had encouraged its authors to soften their characterization of secessionists. But increasingly, the sense that slavery had played a central role in the coming of the conflict or that emancipation was its objective was fading in the culture at large. In an article on the Grimké sisters, the author reflected that "it was long claimed by those who believed that they thought and wrote with authority that not only was slavery the main cause of the civil war . . . but that the abolition of slavery was its chiefest object." Now "a more sober criticism of the motives and deeds of those who were its prime actors" had "somewhat" altered that view. The original intent of the war, another writer insisted, was not emancipation, although a "little cluster of reformers" may have wished it was. A letter writer to *Century*, identifying himself as a southern Democrat, declared that the question of the cause of the Civil War was still open but that it would be resolved in a way that would eliminate controversy. "Well, History will settle this matter to her own satisfaction," he suggested, "and we may be sure that few will dispute the justice of the verdict." While both northerners and southerners were going to have to moderate their views, he asserted, the greatest changes would occur in northern public opinion. The time was coming when no northerner would deny the gallant fight southerners made for what they believed was right. "Moreover," he concluded, "there is not a thinking man at the North who will not admit that American slavery seems to have been a provision of providence for the advancement of a large part of the negro race."[22]

As the most popular magazine in the country, *Century* played a leading role in reevaluating the meaning of the war. Between 1884 and 1887, the magazine published scores of articles about the war, many of them written by veterans. These reminiscences overlooked slavery and even secession as causes of the conflict and studiously avoided any discussion of the war's specific results. As associate editor Robert Underwood Johnson explained, the series was intended to "soften controversy" by excluding "political questions." In this way, the materials appearing in the magazine would foster "intersectional reconciliation" as both sides contemplated the "sacrifice, resourcefulness and bravery in [former] foes."[23]

As *Century*'s policy suggested, reminiscences and recollections were popular with the reading public and with critics as well. First-person accounts fulfilled "a universal and instinctive desire to know under what outward conditions the events that interest us occurred, and the persons who are historic moved." They made history compelling either by providing details about the past or by giving insight into "the affairs and men of the past." "Who are to give us the authentic accounts of events if not the chief actors?"[24]

Yet the cultural trends of the 1880s did not make it easy for former abolitionists to write or publish their life stories. While autobiography was held in high regard, the kinds of texts former abolitionists offered had fallen out of favor, and their message was increasingly seen as irrelevant. In addition, as reviewers and publishers realized, tastes in reading had changed. Critics rarely praised an autobiography because it provided an inspiring example of a life well lived or of a success achieved through earnest effort and hard work. Rather, they recommended recollections that were charming, delightful, entertaining, or even funny. The major function of an autobiography was to give its readers pleasure.[25]

Although *Harper's* editor, George Curtis, suggested that "no canons can be prescribed for writing autobiography, because its essential charm is its individuality," there was remarkable consistency in the types of autobiographies that publishers thought worthy of publication and that critics applauded. The life story that gave pleasure might be a valuable eye-witness report providing insight into important events, the recollections of a famous person, or an account of a varied and interesting life. The successful autobiography must avoid many tedious facts (the reader should not have to work too hard or lapse into boredom) and should be clearly and straightforwardly organized. In recounting a history of the events and people the author had known, he or she was well advised to strive for a moderate tone and to avoid nasty or disagreeable comments about friends, acquaintances, or even enemies. In praising the second half of William Cullen Bryant's narrative, the critic noted approvingly the "judgment and charity" exhibited by "a man whose years had mellowed him."[26]

Readers for the Houghton Mifflin press revealed the rationale for accepting or rejecting an autobiographical manuscript. Fully aware of public taste, readers and editors agreed that there was little interest in subjects that had been "reaped and gleaned again and again." A new autobiography covering ground already addressed in other memoirs and recollections "would never prove a business success." Publishers wanted material that was "good, new and interesting" and that would attract a broad rather than a local audience. Length was also a consideration; from a business point of view, too long a book was "fatal to its success." They also favored narratives written by famous people who had reputations and a circle of friends likely to buy their autobiographies. A mainstream publisher did not want to handle a book dealing "with the exploits of a man who needs to be accounted for to every one who buys the book," although such a work might well be handled as a subscription book.[27]

It was possible that an obscure person might also have a lively and interesting tale to tell, although often enough autobiographers included trivial anecdotes and burdened the narrative with insignificant details. A key consideration was how the story was told. The pleasant and amusing autobiographies that critics appreciated owed their character partly to style. Especially if the subject was not well known, "literary grace" and "charm" were "essential."[28]

The *American Missionary*, a monthly that detailed work with freed people and tried to keep old ideals alive, noted the silence on the part of abolitionists but attributed it to a partial misunderstanding of abolitionism's goals. Why, the paper wondered, were there "not more frequently heard in the land such trumpet blasts as used to break with startling power upon the national conscience from the lips of a Garrison and a Phillips. The fact is, even many of the old abolitionists have come to think their mission in behalf of freedom ended when slavery was abolished in the South." The explanation was clearly more complicated than complacency about the completion of the antislavery mission. Changing literary taste and a preference for personal narratives that were amusing to read as well as a general disinterest in abolitionism stood in the way of both the composition and publication of abolitionists' life stories. Moreover, many of the abolitionists still living were old and not ready to reenter public debate, whatever their private views. Some prominent abolitionists like Garrison, Phillips, and Mott died without leaving accounts of the past. Yet even the towering figures were not always deemed of interest. When Lucretia Mott's granddaughter submitted a biography of her grandmother to Houghton Mifflin in 1884, the reader thought that although Mott had been "a remarkable" woman, "the very minuteness of the work and the details upon subjects not attractive to the ordinary reader must limit circulation." While the subjects not considered "attractive" were not itemized, antislavery was doubtless one.[29]

The obstacles did not deter all abolitionists from composing their personal recollections of the antislavery movement during the 1880s. Frederick Douglass, Jane Swisshelm, George Julian, Henry Stanton, and Parker Pillsbury joined Laura Haviland in publishing accounts of their antislavery exploits. While the hostile cultural climate sharpened their focus and purpose and their selection of autobiographical material, with the exception of Douglass, they did not follow Haviland's example of vigorously attacking the pervasive negative stereotypes of blacks and denouncing the limitations on African American political and civil rights. The reluctance to deal directly with contemporary assessments of black potential suggests that the white writers may have been troubled by the slow progress of southern blacks and shared some of the misgivings about their future as citizens. Certainly, the desire to fashion the story of a successful life and the achievement of important goals made it difficult to acknowledge how impermanent some of their accomplishments seemed to be in the 1880s. Even Douglass seemed more interested in his autobiography in defending his own reputation than discussing contemporary events in the South. But none was willing to overlook the evils of slavery or its centrality in their era's history.[30]

When May had written his autobiography in the late 1860s, he had confined his story to Garrisonians. He did not discuss Garrison's opponents or reveal the infighting among abolitionists. These omissions suggested that abolitionism represented a unified effort to emancipate the slaves. Likewise, the authors of various recollections of the Underground Railroad revealed an activism that contrasted with the Garrisonian commitment to moral suasion, but they viewed their efforts as complementing other strategies. Now, in the 1880s, abolitionist autobiographers stressed divisions and insisted that their own approach had been correct and effective in ending slavery. It may be that they were reacting to dismissive comments in the media or even saw their old enemies' hand in criticism. And while it is probably true that abolitionists would not have had any more influence on public views of their historic importance had they all told the same story and remained silent about old differences, their fractured picture of the past made it easy to dismiss them altogether.

Of all the abolitionist narratives published in the 1880s, Frederick Douglass's *Life and Times of Frederick Douglass* may have had the best chance of commercial and cultural success. His book satisfied many of the criteria for a good, salable autobiography and presented an effective, moderate view of the abolitionist movement and his place in it. The depiction of his early years as a slave had appeared in the two previous versions of his autobiography and had had a powerful impact as an exposé of the evils of the slave system. Douglass had achieved prominence as an abolitionist orator and newspaper editor before the war, played an active role in Republican politics, and held a variety of significant posts after the war. No one would have to be told who Douglass was. Moreover, his acquaintances, who ranged from well-known British politicians and literary figures to influential Americans, provided him with many interesting anecdotes to include in his life story. The writing was lively and clear, if not up to the literary standards of a

Houghton Mifflin editor. Perhaps readers for Houghton Mifflin would have found it, as they did one autobiography they reviewed, "pleasantly written" in a way that "would do" for a newspaper. The tone of the narrative was judicious and avoided censorious comments about others in the movement. And as a subject, there was much about Douglass that was attractive. He had that "singular force of character" and the "manliness" that commentators appreciated in an autobiographical writer and provided a picture of self-development that readers presumably found interesting.[31]

Douglass started out the new installment of his autobiography by revealing the details of his escape from slavery. *Century* considered the story of such broad appeal that it published it as an article in 1881, the year that the entire autobiography appeared. Douglass also spiced up his narrative with a detailed description of his connections with John Brown and his disapproval of the raid on Harpers Ferry. Another intriguing aspect of the new volume was the disclosure of his meetings with various members of the Auld family, his former owners, and his visit to the places where he had spent his early years as a slave. Readers would learn something new in these chapters.[32]

In the new sections of Douglass's autobiography, much of the story followed the lines established by May. Recounting his career as an antislavery lecturer for the "holy cause," Douglass emphasized the violence that attended his work and the many ways in which the North was implicated in slavery. As May had done, Douglass condemned northern prejudice, but Douglass, of course, could provide vivid examples drawn from painful personal experience. Both men depicted the abolitionists as a noble band of men (neither spent much time or energy on women), although they disagreed on abolitionists' role in bringing about the Civil War. While each saw slavery as the fundamental cause of war and emancipation as a central moment in that conflict, Douglass attributed the growing interest in antislavery to southern intransigence and the tumultuous events of the 1850s rather than to the moral arguments of abolitionists. For Douglass, Abraham Lincoln, whom May had scarcely mentioned, was the great emancipator. Perhaps responding to contemporary criticisms of black suffrage, Douglass emphasized the necessity of allowing African American men to vote no matter what the problems with it might be.[33]

But unlike May, Douglass did not gloss over the conflicts that beset the abolitionist movement. And unlike some abolitionist autobiographers in the 1880s who lashed out against their old opponents, and while there had, in fact, been much bitterness between Douglass and Garrison in the 1850s, Douglass adopted a measured tone in describing disagreements among abolitionists. On the one hand, in reflecting on those who had embraced political action rather than moral suasion, Douglass commented that it was "surprising how small the difference appears as I look back on it, over the space of 40 years." On the other hand, indulging in harsh denunciations would undermine the picture he was presenting of himself as deliberate and reasonable. Emphasizing the pain of breaking with the Garrisonians, "good people" for whom he had something like "a slavish adoration," he made it clear that each step he had taken had been necessary and rational. Publishing his newspaper, for example, played an essential role in undermining the low opinion whites (and some blacks) held of black abilities. "Careful consideration" and the perception of new truths ultimately convinced him that moral abolitionism was incapable of ending slavery. Douglass welcomed the emergence of abolitionist political parties and ultimately the resort to violence. "I confess," he wrote, to having felt satisfaction "at the prospect of a conflict." For all the differences he had with the Garrisonians, however, Douglass devoted an entire chapter to his "special friends" to honor and applaud them for the help they had generously given him early in his career.[34]

In other respects, Douglass's narrative was similar to Still's *Underground Railroad*. As Douglass pointed out, he had lived several lives, starting with the life of a slave, followed by the life of a fugitive. Anyone who had read Still's book would find familiar themes in the sections of Douglass's autobiography dealing with the evils of the slave system and his escape. Like Still, Douglass regarded his life as proof of black ability and as an inspiration to his own race. He shared Still's commitment to the social, economic, and moral improvement of black people, especially through education and the adoption of middle-class habits and values. Writing almost a decade after Still and keenly aware of the criticism of the former slaves' lack of progress, Douglass emphasized that in his "communication with the colored people I have endeavored to deliver them from the power of superstition, bigotry, and priestcraft . . . [and] have urged upon them self-reliance, self-respect, industry, perseverance, and economy." While he acknowledged that his "views at this point receive but limited endorsement among my people," he ended his text with a resounding dedication to his work and presumably its ultimate success: "Forty years of my life have been given to the cause of my people, and if I had forty years more they should all be sacredly given to the same great cause."[35]

In one important respect, Douglass's narrative differed from both May's and Still's autobiographies. Both men had been adept at keeping themselves in the background of their stories. Douglass, however, placed himself at the center of his narrative. As he explained, when he had established the *North Star* in Rochester, he had discovered how "to be a principal and not an agent." Actually, many incidents already described in the book highlighted his willingness to act alone and his belief that he was usually right. Time did little to alter his point of view.[36]

Somewhat surprisingly, even the freed people receded from the text after Douglass's account of the passage of the Fifteenth Amendment. They briefly reappeared when Douglass discussed their exodus to Kansas, a movement that he opposed. The last few chapters were filled with Douglass's "strange if not wonderful" appointments and honors, mingled with justifications for his connection with the Freedmen's Bank, his visit to his former owners, and some of the issues surrounding his tenure as the U.S. Marshall in Washington.[37]

Douglass seemed to sense that he was perhaps crossing far beyond what one critic called the "borderline between native modesty and an innocent love of approbation." Scattered throughout the autobiography were phrases that served to minimize his exploits as well as acknowledgments of "a little of vanity at my part." The chapter near the end of the book titled "Honor to Whom Honor" may have been prompted by Douglass's desire to ensure that he gave others some of the credit for his success. Still, as he concluded the book, he seems to have sensed that such efforts had not entirely established the proper balance between egotism and modesty. "If I have pushed my example too prominently for the good taste of my Caucasian readers," he wrote, "I beg them to remember that I have written in part for the encouragement of a class whose aspirations need the stimulus of success."[38]

Douglass entered an agreement with the Park Publishing Company of Hartford to publish and distribute his book. Park was a subscription house with many canvassers in their employ. The company had high expectations for the book's success, as its initial agreement with Douglass suggested. The royalty rate it offered was twenty-five cents a copy for the first 20,000 copies sold and twenty cents a copy thereafter. The agreed-upon book was to be handsome and expensive: good paper, a steel engraving of the author, and two possible edgings. The speckled-edged book would sell for $2.50, and gilt edging would cost $3.00.[39]

Without consulting Douglass, Park decided to add illustrations that it believed would help the canvassers sell the book. Douglass was furious, writing that the contract did not allow the publisher to "load the book with all manner of coarse and shocking wood cuts, such as may be found in the news papers of the day." Park had "marred and spoiled my work entirely," Douglass fumed. "I have no pleasure what ever in the book." He

This advertisement was intended to persuade people to subscribe to Frederick Douglass's autobiography. The text extols Douglass and asserts that the book will "impress on a younger generation" the significance of Douglass and the other great men of the abolitionist movement. The advertisement also makes clear the physical character of the book and the fact that the buyer could choose gilt edges for $3.00 or speckled edges for fifty cents less. (Courtesy Library of Congress) insisted that some copies without illustrations be published for circulation in the North, but he remained unreconciled to the book's appearance. He thought his own portrait looked like a "caricature." He made such a fuss that the publisher begged him to "say nothing disparaging to the illustrations" when its Washington agent visited him. "It will dishearten our Gen agent there, and do no good."[40]

Park undertook a vigorous sales effort, requesting that Douglass inform it of when and where he was making a speech so that its agents could "push" the book in the vicinity and asking for a list of his prominent friends for canvassers to visit. The firm advertised extensively; by April 1882, it had spent about $600 on advertising, spending aggressively in various parts of the country like New England and even in Canada. Fifty thousand circulars had been distributed, and 500 agents were in the field trying to sell the book. In July, however, there were signs of problems. The firm informed Douglass that expensive new electroplates were needed and complained about all the heavy costs the publisher had been bearing. By that time, the firm had produced over 200,000 circulars. But, it explained, "Your book does not sell quite as well as we expected, for the simple reason that the interest in the old days of slavery is not as great as we expected." The firm persuaded Douglass to accept a five-cent reduction in royalties for every volume sold and decided to put some of that money into a more attractive binding.[41]

Douglass proclaimed himself satisfied with the sales. Surviving records suggest that the book had sold about 2,500 copies by April 1882, and it would sell at least another 900 in Great Britain, where Douglass, without consulting Park, had given a British publisher the right to issue the book. The British publisher told Douglass that "extensive" advertising and a larger than usual discount for booksellers had been necessary to sell that many books.[42]

If Douglass was content, the publisher was not. Given the effort put into sales, the results were not very good. At the end of the decade, another 463 volumes had been sold. Park told Douglass they had "pushed and re-pushed the book constantly" without the success originally anticipated. Beyond the statement that readers were no longer much interested in slavery (or at least the picture of slavery Douglass provided), the publisher did not analyze the book's disappointing sales. But lackluster results may well have been due to reasons other than Douglass's views on slavery. One significant factor must have been the critical silence that greeted the new book. Douglass's British publisher reported that many strong reviews had appeared in Great Britain, but Park only mentioned one American review, which appeared in a Troy, New York, Republican paper. The *New York Times* ignored it, as did

Although this illustration created for Douglass's book shows him at an important moment in his life, as marshal at President Garfield's inauguration, the crude quality of this and other images infuriated him. He felt that Park Publishing Company had cheapened his book by including images of this quality. (Courtesy Library of Congress)

the literary monthlies, although several of them actually published articles by Douglass during the 1880s. Even when *Century* published Douglass's account of his escape from slavery, it neglected to include the notice about Douglass's forthcoming book and a lengthy advertisement for it, both sent by the publisher. Since two versions of his book had been in circulation for years, the new autobiography may not have offered enough new to justify a review or acquisition. Then, too, the book's appearance, with its crude illustrations, may have put it in a class of books that were not considered worthy of attention from the literary establishment, a possibility Douglass must have sensed when he became so angry at Park. Perhaps the ways in which Douglass dominated the book smacked too much of egotism, an "ill-concealed enthusiasm about himself" that was the "common bane" of autobiographies. Finally, Douglass's attempt to use his own life as proof of black ability ran counter to conscious or unconscious racism. The fact that other autobiographies written by white abolitionists during the decade received some critical notice (although not necessarily positive) strongly points to the possibility of racism.[43]

Jane Swisshelm was not as prominent as Douglass, although she had been well known as an activist and editor in antislavery circles in the years before the war. Her autobiography, *Half a Century*, appeared in 1880, but, unlike Douglass, she gave almost no details of her life after 1866, when her antislavery career ended. Like the Coffins and Haviland, she had attended the 1874 reunion in Chicago, where she was enthusiastically received. Her thirty-minute speech on the "wrongs" of women, however, was judged a "violent harangue" by the *New York Times*. She also traveled extensively between 1866 and 1880, but the conclusion of her reminiscences suggested she had passed the time quietly in Pennsylvania. The final sentence of her reminiscences depicted the author living in the old house she had rescued "from the tooth of decay, . . . sit[ting] . . . and recall[ing] those passages of life with which it is so intimately connected." If the description was factually misleading, it did suggest a psychic distance from the recent past. But the body of her narrative belied the ending, for it demonstrated her awareness of contemporary perceptions of abolitionism and slavery and their relationship to the Civil War and emancipation.[44]

In her preface, Swisshelm stated her intention "to correct" misguided views of the past that had crept into contemporary discourse. Accepting as indisputably true that the antislavery struggle had culminated in the Emancipation Proclamation, she sought to counter the charge that antislavery had "originated in Infidelity, and was a triumph of Skepticism over Christianity." The best way to do this was to provide a "personal" or "inside" history of the movement, an especially important duty, she believed, since so many of the old warriors had died without leaving a record of the "motives that underlay their action." Related to this primary purpose was her sense that it was important to restate the real character of slavery. Faced with renewed interest in the war and the claims for the nobility of participants and leaders on both sides, she planned to remind readers of the war's cost and its mismanagement. She also intended to provide an explanation of the emergence of the woman's rights movement.[45]

Her final purpose was personal. She proposed to trace her development from a retiring, private woman, who would never have been considered out of her place, to a public woman, who cared little about what the newspapers might say about her and who, in 1862, ably and without embarrassment, addressed the Minnesota state senate. She would tell her story in a way that would not only explain this transformation but also persuade readers of its necessity. What she did not say in her preface is that she also planned to present her version of a failed marriage and to justify a contentious career as a political journalist. Her intentions challenged both gender norms and female autobiographical practice.[46]

Of course, the general expectations about autobiographies published in the 1880s also applied to those authored by women. Women's life stories should be lively and reveal the writer's personality without "a heavy or tedious page." But, like women themselves, female autobiographies should be candid, "graceful" and "light," providing a "charming side entrance into historical fields." While both men and women were encouraged to be tasteful and reticent "about passages" of life "well adapted to arouse a vulgar curiosity," this expectation had special relevance to the story penned by a woman. Moreover, as critical appraisals of Harriet Martineau's autobiography published in the late 1870s suggested, women writers who made negative comments about others (as Swisshelm would do) ran a special risk: "The reader is rather disposed to judge sharply one who is so free with her strictures upon the character and the behavior of others."[47]

Harper's discussion of Elizabeth Custer's autobiographical work, *Boots and Saddle*, reveals that critics prized female authors whose self-presentation expressed traditional gender norms. While Custer lacked a "trained literary hand," she had created a charming work because of her "entire self-forgetfulness, her unusual absorption in another, her singular lack of self-consciousness." Custer had not only a "genuine" modesty but also a higher purpose. At the center of her story, the critic pointed out approvingly, was not the writer herself but the "hero." In contrast to Swisshelm' story, this autobiography expressed the author's "perfect and utterly unselfish devotion" to her husband. Swisshelm's story dramatically differed from such an autobiography. She would violate many expectations, especially those concerning the sort of life story a woman should tell.[48]

Like Laura Haviland, Swisshelm began with memories of childhood. She recalled apple blossoms falling on her face and hands, an "indelible imprint" that signified the "inner something I call me." Her second memory, also from early childhood, was of her first conversion, her discovery of sin and her "lost and undone condition." The experience established the importance and power of the religious impulse as a guiding force in her life. For her, as for Haviland, religion initially involved anxiety and grief as she struggled to "submit to God's will." After much anguish, Swisshelm experienced another conversion that brought personal peace and a sense of mission. Her pastor instructed her "to follow the Lamb, through good and through evil report . . . even if he should lead you out of the church." This advice reinforced Swisshelm's own understanding that her conversion would lead her to "tasks from which other laborers shrank." This was a key moment in the autobiography since it legitimated much that was to follow. "No other act of my life has been so solemn or far-reaching in its consequences," she explained, "and it is the one I have least cause to repent." For Swisshelm, as for Haviland, the divine imperative served to justify behavior that departed from female norms and allowed her to occupy the solid center of her narrative.[49]

Swisshelm devoted a substantial part of her autobiography to her unhappy marriage. Although she assured readers that she omitted much material about her marriage because "it was neither possible nor necessary to describe," the depictions of her husband, "livid with rage," pouring out "such a torrent of accusation as I had not dreamed possible," went far beyond the boundaries of female good taste and reticence. No doubt she wanted to include enough personal information to justify her ultimate decision to abandon her husband and their subsequent divorce. Moreover, one of her autobiographical goals was to explain the emergence of woman's rights activism. When she described her husband coming to take "possession of [her,] his prospective property with the air of a man who understood his business" or the fact that in twenty years of marriage she had no legal right to privacy, she was outlining fundamental social and legal realities that drove her own decisions and feminist protest.

While she could not avoid including examples of the couple's basic incompatibilities, she was conscious of the potential dangers of alienating her readers with unsavory details. Thus she omitted her struggles with her husband's family over land and money and appealed to her readers' sympathies by casting her marriage conflicts as "all spiritual." The initial problem was that her husband and his family tried to convert her to Methodism, and, in the spirit of her English forbears who had died at the stake for their religious beliefs, Swisshelm resisted their attempts to force her to change her religion. Not quite so easy to explain in religious terms was her decision to nurse her dying mother against her husband's wishes, which could well be seen as an expression of defiance and independence. Rather unconvincingly, Swisshelm wrote that she had realized that the injunction that wives obey their husbands was not part of divine law that demanded "allegiance to God." Rather than heed Scripture, she listened to "God, in nature" who "spoke with no uncertain sound."[50]

Swisshelm was on stronger ground when she credited religion as the source of her antislavery convictions and activism. The Covenanter Church, to which Swisshelm's parents belonged, rejected slavery as incompatible with its basic beliefs. Swisshelm had grown up as an abolitionist, carried around abolitionist petitions in her neighborhood, and argued with orthodox Presbyterians who claimed that blacks had no souls. Later experience solidified her antislavery views. In 1838, Swisshelm's husband decided to leave Pittsburgh and join his brother who had a business in Louisville. Swisshelm devoted two chapters in her autobiography to her sojourn in the South. The firsthand picture she provided of slavery and southern owners sharply contradicted the sentimental views becoming so popular in the monthlies and the vigorous effort of southern writers during the 1880s to heroize southern culture.[51]

The chapters titled "Habitations of Horrid Cruelty" and "Kentucky Contempt for Labor" mocked the supposedly mild character of Kentucky slavery. With short, well-chosen, and powerful examples, she conveyed what she had "learned" about the institution of slavery. Whether she was as conscious of the lessons at the time as she was in her autobiography is uncertain since she had destroyed her diary and all other personal material before she wrote the autobiography. But in the autobiography, she strove for dramatic effect. Her first impressions set the tone. On the way to the boardinghouse where the Swisshelms were to live, she was surprised by the number of well-dressed men standing around in the middle of a working day. Later she discovered that they were "the advance guard of a great army of woman-whippers" that stretched throughout the entire South. These men did not work but supported themselves by the sale of children conceived with their own slaves and "the labor of their mothers extorted by the lash." There were no affectionate ties here: children were callously sold away for the money they brought in, women were beaten until they would accept sexual advances, and "the old mammys from whose bosoms they had drawn life in infancy" were horsewhipped. And if female readers had any trouble sympathizing with black women and children, they could readily do so with white women who were accosted by men Swisshelm described as the "staring brigade." They were insulted by "a stare so lascivious as could not be imagined on American free soil."[52]

Other examples of southern manhood included young men who saw an old family slave whipped to death over a wager that it was possible to "lick the religion out of any nigger," and the preacher who told this story, not to protest the death of an innocent man, but to show that the power of religion. To highlight the complicity of male religious leaders with slavery, Swisshelm also included anecdotes that covered the major dominations: the Methodist preacher who complained that the cries of a cook nailed to a fence by a member of his church might injure the reputation of his congregation, the Presbyterian Elder who punished a ten-year old slave who had tried to run away by forcing him to wear an iron collar, and the Baptist clergyman who owned and hired out 100 slaves. She concluded her section on the South with a rejection of southern masculinity. "I wanted to be . . . out of an atmosphere which killed all manhood, and furnished women-whippers as a substitute for men."[53]

Swisshelm did not spare southern mistresses, and two examples sufficed to make the point about the inhumanity of southern women. Far from civilizing their slaves, as James Lane Allen's story had suggested, they abused them cruelly. One of the mistresses was the "Kentucky lady" who ran the boardinghouse. This "hostess," as Swisshelm ironically called her, shed tears when she told Swisshelm the story of some young slave boys sold down South. But when Martha, the old slave whom she hired as a cook, refused to work because an acute inflammation of her eyelids temporarily blinded her, the woman summoned Martha's owner to determine what to do. Swisshelm was called in as an abolitionist "that I might learn to pity the sorrows of mistresses and understand the deceitfulness of slaves." Rather than the lesson the slave mistresses expected Swisshelm to learn, what she and the reader discovered was the sorrow of slaves and the self-deception of mistresses. The self-pitying language that Swisshelm attributed to the white women was perhaps fictional, but it dramatically drove home her point.[54]

The owner, a "bedizzoned martyr" dressed lavishly in "costly attire" that Swisshelm declared "odious," was filled with complaints. Martha was one of nine women whose wages furnished her with a personal allowance, and while they were all "ungrateful," Martha was the worst. She had "took on" every time one of her children had been sold, and the owner had had to send Martha to the public whipping-post. "One hated so to send a servant to the public whipping-post; it looked like cruelty," she remarked. Swisshelm's hostess agreed that Martha was ungrateful for she even sent her a cup of tea each day since she had "complained" of being sick, but "the old wretch had not gone to work."

After this introduction, Swisshelm described Martha, who had only been briefly characterized at the beginning of the anecdote as old, rheumatic, and religious. The contrast between the selfish and heartless boarding-house owner and Martha's mistress and the old slave woman could hardly have been more dramatic. There was the old slave, "clutching the table . . . trembling in every limb, her eyelids swollen out like puff-balls, and offensive from neglect, her curls making a border to her red turban, receiving her sentence without a word," struck dumb "by a cruelty perfectly incomprehensible in its unconscious debasement." Although Martha was a powerless victim, like all the slaves in Swisshelm's account, she was also virtuous. Swisshelm remembered this incident as a climactic moment in her life. Despite her early sense of mission and her abolitionist activity, it was at this moment she promised "the Lord then and there, that for life, it should be my work" to toil for the end of slavery. As for Martha, Swisshelm could only provide her with medical care that would cure her ailment and save her from punishment.[55]

Swisshelm claimed that this experience with Martha transformed slavery for her from an abstraction to a reality, and, in turn, inspired her to take the unconventional step of writing for the newspapers. When the first antislavery political party emerged in the 1840s, Swisshelm contributed articles to one of its papers, *The Spirit of Liberty*. Fearful of bringing up the divisive issue of gender and attracting publicity, she signed her pieces with only her initials. Ultimately she explained that the biblical directive "open thy voice for the dumb" demanded that she engage in public debate under her own name. Religious duty justified each stage of an increasingly unorthodox career as a political journalist. She entered into the "long conflict with the southern tiger" by contributing to a variety of newspapers. Eventually she started her own political newspaper. She was the first woman to do so, and the step, she told her readers, represented her "Red Sea." "Duty lies on the other side, and I am going over."[56]

Swisshelm's journalism provided an antislavery perspective on local and national events. Legal actions against fugitive slaves and those harboring them, the dereliction of the American churches on the slavery issue,

Washington's slave markets and pens, and the infamy of the Fugitive Slave Law all brought forth biting commentary. When she moved to St. Cloud, Minnesota, she led a campaign in the *St. Cloud Visiter* against the local Democratic boss who also managed the town's Democratic newspaper. While her struggle with the local boss was actually more complex than she made it out to be, Swisshelm depicted the boss as a representative of the slave system's "brute force, pious pretenses, plausibility, chivalry, all the good and bad of the Southern character." In her account, Minnesota was an outpost of slavery and she was the courageous warrior who took on the institution and its powerful minions. It was "God and I against that little clique."[57]

Although Swisshelm reassured her readers that she had not formally affiliated with any political party, her autobiography revealed that she plunged into antislavery politics. In 1844, she wrote for the Liberty Party. "It seemed good unto me to support James G. Birney, for President, and to promulgate the principles of the platform," she explained. "This I would do, and no man had the right or power to stop me." Four years later, she threw her paper's influence behind the Free-Soil candidate, Martin Van Buren. Although her stand attracted the criticism of Democratic and Liberty Parties, as well as Garrisonian newspapers, she believed that her advocacy would either end in the destruction of one of the two major parties, both of which she deemed proslavery, or win over enough voters to force one of the parties into an antislavery position. Acknowledging the limitations of the Free-Soil Party's program, she still saw "checking the advance of an enemy" as one stage in driving him from the field. As the editor of the *Visiter*, Swisshelm embraced the Republican Party. Dismissing any criticism of the limitations of the party's views on slavery, she depicted it as the culmination of political abolitionism. Reflecting the enthusiasm of the 1850s and perhaps hindsight, she declared that there was "no doubt of its final triumph."[58]

Swisshelm emphasized the influential role she played in the struggle for emancipation, writing that "men of good judgment" believed that her journalism won thousands of votes for the party. This was her objective: "votes! votes!" Conscious that some readers might question such a role for a woman, Swisshelm cast her efforts in gendered terms. She sought "votes for the women sold on the auction block, scourged for chastity, [and] robbed of their children." Furthermore, no less a lofty figure than Charles Sumner had encouraged her activism. On her visit to Washington, Sumner informed Swisshelm that "'the slave never had more need'" of the newspaper or "'had more need of you.'" His blessing, she suggested, represented "almost a divine call."[59]

While Swisshelm never presented herself as one of the martyrs of the antislavery struggle, she revealed the dangers she faced in Minnesota. Ruffians destroyed her press, threatening her with death if she dared to publish another paper in St. Cloud. When some of the town's citizens planned a public meeting to support freedom of the press, Swisshelm agreed to describe the events that resulted in an attack on her paper, which she considered the climax of her publishing career. Mobs were so threatening that she arranged with her nephew to shoot her if she fell into the hands of the angry crowd. The dire situation drove her decision to speak in public. "At length the time had come when I could not longer skulk behind a printing press," she wrote. ". . . Now I must literally open my mouth for the dumb, or be one of those dogs spoken of in Scripture who would not bark." Public speech came "as a command not to be questioned."[60]

Swisshelm described the triumph of the Republican Party in Minnesota, a triumph to which she contributed by lecturing around the state. She ingenuously claimed that she had not really been campaigning because "I never spoke in public during an election excitement, never advocated on the platform the claims of any particular man, but urged principles." She gave a spirited defense of the Republican Party, using arguments she had used to persuade abolitionists critical of the party's antislavery credentials to vote Republican. Even here, religion served its purpose. Election day was the Lord's day, "for no creed, no form of worship, no act of his life, is a man more directly responsible to God, than for casting his vote." Insisting that the Constitution was an antislavery document, she argued that it was better to support "an imperfect means of reaching a great end" than to wait for the perfect solution. When she revealed that the Democrats had burnt her in effigy as "'the mother of the Republican party,'" it was a description she did not bother to deny.[61]

The structure of Swisshelm's autobiography and the description of her work made an extended discussion of the causes of the Civil War unnecessary. Slavery had mounted a "great conspiracy against the nation's life." Swisshelm, herself, was not opposed to secession; indeed she claimed that she wanted to drive the South out of the Union and then to do all that was possible to encourage slaves to escape. But when the South fired on Fort Sumter, "the actual flame of freedom" was lit.[62]

Swisshelm had only briefly discussed Lincoln, declaring him "an obstructionist instead of an abolitionist." While she softened her opinion when she met the Lincolns, finding Mary Lincoln "a loyal, liberty-loving woman, more staunch even than her husband in opposition to the Rebellion and its cause," Lincoln did not emerge from her account as a commanding figure or great war leader. His failure to support Frémont's order emancipating slaves "damned" the "great rushing stream of popular enthusiasm" and replaced it with "the dismal swamp of constitutional quibbles and statutory inventions." Lincoln had missed a moment for true historic greatness. When he issued his Emancipation Proclamation, Swisshelm felt he had drained it of all nobility, replacing nobility with "meanness of . . . motive." Lincoln failed to provide a moral foundation for the nation, and, during the conflict, Swisshelm had doubted the North could claim to be "Freedom's standard-bearer!"[63]

As a nurse, Swisshelm witnessed the great struggle firsthand. The picture of war that she gave belied the contemporary emphasis on heroism and glory rather than bloodshed and destruction. "May none of my readers ever see such darkness made visible — such rows of haggard faces looking at them from out such cavernous gloom!" Swisshelm declared. She revealed shocking mismanagement, disorganization, red tape, and great suffering and exposed the dismal conditions, like in the hospital where patients had never been washed since leaving the battlefield and where vermin were their bed companions.[64]

Swisshelm portrayed herself as a loving, competent nurse who saved lives and limbs by her good sense and careful, imaginative ministrations. Despite what others might do or expect, she "set about doing that which was right in my own eyes." She ran the risk of alienating some female readers in her comments about other women who worked with the wounded. She criticized their refusal to abandon their hoops and said that most women would more readily kiss a wounded soldier than give him "solid" help. Miss Dix's "totally unsympathetic manner," for example, "chilled" Swisshelm.[65]

Swisshelm concluded her autobiography with two brief chapters that carried her story to 1866. One chapter focused on Washington's near escape from Confederate occupation in early 1864. Expecting that the city would be taken, Swisshelm experienced another revelation. Observing the "pitiful" contrabands, some "gray with terror," Swisshelm's "eyes were opened, like those of the prophet's servant." She realized, despite the doubts she had had about the government and the people, that northerners "had developed a sublime patriotism . . . an almost miraculous growth in good." She felt certain that God had imposed the duty of wiping out slavery and that "'the prayers of centuries are to be answered now!'" In the final chapter, Swisshelm reported that President Andrew Johnson had her dismissed from her position at the War Department for her disrespectful comments about him. She gave no particulars. Secretary of War Edwin Stanton, on the other hand, helped her secure ownership of the family property near

Pittsburgh not long before he barricaded himself in the War Department to protest Johnson's "policy of making the South triumphant."[66]

The abrupt conclusion of Swisshelm's autobiography provided little sense of closure or resolution. Swisshelm showed her readers a life successfully spent in promoting the antislavery cause and shared personal details of her activities and views. Her title, *Half a Century*, emphasized her many decades of labor. Yet the book ended with an account of ragged and frightened contrabands, her conviction they would be rescued from slavery, and the first step taken by President Johnson toward sectional reconciliation and forgetfulness. Of her own thoughts about Reconstruction, the fate of those contrabands "so pitiful to see," or subsequent events in the South she said nothing. The rushed and unrevealing ending that omitted any reference to her support for land and political rights for former slaves, or her hostility toward the defeated South, and little information about her attacks on Andrew Johnson, suggest the difficulty she was having evaluating her life's work. To discuss these efforts and the changing fortunes of southern blacks would call into question the picture of a successful life. Yet ending the book as she did with the image of herself sitting and brooding over the past in her "old log block house" had the same effect.[67]

Whatever Swisshelm's private reflections, she was determined to see that her autobiography reached the public. She had the book printed in Chicago, an important publishing center by the 1880s. The first edition appeared under her name, but other print runs that same year noted the flourishing firm of Jansen, McClurg & Co. as publisher. Jansen, McClurg & Co. was less interested in publishing books than selling them, a position that must have been attractive to Swisshelm. The books were probably priced differently according to the bindings. Among the surviving books are one bound in dark brown cloth embossed with gilt letters and decorations, and another bound in green cloth and leather.[68]

There is little evidence to show how readers responded to Swisshelm's autobiography. No resident of Earlville, Illinois, ever checked out the library's copy of *Half a Century*, although the book stood on the library shelves for 100 years. But, unlike Douglass's *Life and Times*, Swisshelm's autobiography received a long review from the *New York Times* the year it came out.[69]

The reviewer praised the autobiography for being so "cleverly done" that the reader was "impressed at once with its reality." Declining to comment on the book's "political complexion," the reviewer mostly summarized the major events of Swisshelm's life. He was struck, however, with the "romantic warmth" of certain sections and singled out Swisshelm's evocation of her early childhood as modern in spirit and a riveting beginning for her life story. Surely, Swisshelm was pleased with his reaction to her account of slavery but perhaps not so pleased that he saw no connections between past and present brutalities: "The horrors of slavery we have never seen written in such dramatic form. Mrs. Swisshelm's words bit into one's brain and make one thank God that such brutality is of a past age." Her criticism stemming from her Civil War work he deemed "truthful," practical, and sensible.

Swisshelm herself did not come out so well. The characterization of her as having the "tenderness of her sex" but also "the iron will of a headstrong man" was not flattering in its suggestion of an unruly nature and was indicative of how far she had strayed from conventional female autobiographical standards. Several references to her "pluck" rather than her courage and the comment that "true to her nature" she often "got into hot water" diminished her bravery and accomplishments. Her interest in reform was labeled "her hobby." But the most damaging aspect of the review was its refusal to discuss her political career, a topic the reviewer deemed "beyond the pale of literary criticism." Having excluded "higher political fields in which Mrs. Swisshelm has played the part of minor earthquake," the reviewer chose to emphasize Swisshelm's somewhat ridiculous diatribe against New England cooking as one example of her reform activism. But in her wartime hospital work, the reviewer pointedly noted, Swisshelm "found a sphere she was admirably fitted for." The implication was that, as a woman, she had not been so fitted for her work as a political journalist.[70]

———•———

The critic who reviewed George Julian's *Political Recollections* for *Atlantic Monthly* in 1884 certainly did not think that Julian had been out of his sphere because, as a man active in abolitionist politics, first as a Free-Soiler and then as a Republican, he had rightfully been involved in public life. Nor did he confine himself to a discussion of the autobiography's literary qualities rather than its political content. As a "chief actor," Julian was providing what a good autobiographer did: "authentic accounts of events" and "sincere testimonies to actual character and significance of famous people." The reviewer singled out for approval the book's vivid account of the rise and triumph of political abolitionism that stirred "the blood like the shouts of battle." Unlike Swisshelm, Julian had succeeded in finding the proper autobiographical balance: "sufficient infusion of the personal element, and not too much." In fact, Julian carefully omitted most personal material. The reader would discover nothing about his family background beyond the reference to his "Quaker training" or learn anything about his two marriages or home life. The beginning of Julian's narrative said much about his approach. He plunged right into politics with a chapter on the 1840 presidential campaign.[71]

In his preface, Julian outlined his plan to describe the major events and actors of antislavery politics and his own attitudes and actions connected with these events. Determined that nothing about the "world-famous movement" would be lost to history, he set out his interpretation at once. "An orderly progression of anti-slavery opinions" led to "organized [political] action" and ultimately the legal emancipation of the slaves. The passage of the Thirteenth Amendment, he wrote later, represented a "glorious" page of the nation's history.[72]

Julian's historical perspective owed much to the "party despotism and political corruption" that he believed "disgraced" the politics of the 1880s, as they had prewar politics. He declared that both Whigs and Democrats had been entirely unprincipled, interested only in office and "plunder." Neither faced the fundamental issue of slavery. When forced to deal with it, the parties were all too willing to make cowardly compromises that had no chance of succeeding in the long run.[73]

Swisshelm had depicted slavery in its human guise, as an institution that promoted rape and violence against black people, especially black women. Julian stressed slavery as a political threat to the Union and republican government. Southern politicians and congressmen who intended to make slavery supreme in the federal government were leading the assaults on the country's integrity. Julian described the milestones in this dark history: the cunning, audacious, perfidious "plot" to annex Texas, "one of the blackest pages" in history; the southern determination to spread slavery to the territories; the "most atrocious" Fugitive Slave Law; and the "supposed compromise" of 1850. The cause of the war was clear, and the blame lay entirely on southern hands. Despite efforts to conciliate southerners after Lincoln's election, the "slave oligarchy . . . hurried . . . into the bloody conspiracy which was to close forever its career of besotted lawlessness and crime."[74]

Neither the corrupt Whigs or their equally corrupt opponents, the Democrats, opposed the South's attempt to undermine the Republic, of course. Nor did abolitionists like Garrison or Phillips deserve much credit. Julian did not embrace the position of abolitionists' fiercest critics who dismissed moral abolitionism altogether. He agreed that these abolitionists had done useful work by appealing to the nation's conscience. "Their moral appeals" provided "a well-spring of life to the nation in its final struggle for self-preservation." But Julian did not regard the program of moral suasion as any program at all. Without a "plan of action" against the slave power

THE 1880S

that operated to successfully in Congress, the antislavery cause was power-less. Only when the Liberty Party embraced both "a great dominating idea" and the political organization that "was absolutely necessary" to "make this idea paramount" did abolitionism begin to make substantial progress.[75]

Julian's interpretation stressed the orderly and ideologically consistent progress of political abolitionism. The Liberty Party's "political creed was substantially identical with that of the Free Soilers of 1848 and the Republicans of 1856 and 1860." While many abolitionists in the 1840s and 1850s as well as Republicans of 1860 would have disputed his claim, perhaps so many years later, it was easier to see the similarities than the differences. Certainly, this ideological consistency provided a useful contrast to Julian's unflattering characterization of the Whigs and Democrats. He could hardly be too complimentary about the antislavery parties and the positions they had taken over time.[76]

Many years before Samuel May had declared the moral abolitionists the movement's heroes. Now, Julian claimed heroism for third-party activists. Though they were derided as fanatics, Julian defended the first political abolitionists as guilty only of being in advance of public opinion. The small abolitionist contingent in Congress, whom he joined in 1849, "sportively" bore the label of the "immortal nine." But, in all seriousness, they obviously deserved the epithet. While the majority of voters were "debauched," according to Julian, supporters of third-party candidates and platforms had the virtues of morality, enthusiasm, and nobility. And Republican support-ers of 1856 came in for special praise: "No political campaign had ever been . . . cheered by such a following of orderly, intelligent, conscientious and thoroughly devoted men and women."[77]

Julian sketched his own involvement in and contributions to political antislavery. His initial commitment took only a few sentences to describe. Here, there was no mention of a religious conversion or even of a con-versionlike moment. Like the movement Julian described, his decision was rational and principled. He mentioned his Quaker "training," but the major influences behind his abolitionism were speeches, newspapers, and other publications. "With truth" on his side, a "singleness of . . . purpose," and a good set of lungs, he stumped for the Free-Soil Party. Elected to Congress, he became part of the little band of political abolitionists, made his maiden antislavery speech, and gained confidence from its reception in antislavery circles. As political abolitionism moved forward, Julian pictured himself in the center of developments. He was nominated as vice president for the Free-Soil Party and was instrumental in bringing the Republican Party into existence. Looking back over his career, he credited himself for having won over the public in his district to his "earnest" antislavery opinions. "I believe no Congressional district in the Union was ever the theatre of so much hard toil by a single man," he wrote. Julian described his transcendent moment as the passage of the Thirteenth Amendment freeing the slaves. It was at that moment that he felt "born into a new life."[78]

Julian, like Swisshelm, painted a critical picture of the war years. Having aided in the formation of the Republican Party and served in Congress during the war, Julian found Lincoln personally agreeable but a lackluster leader. During the war, Lincoln had dragged his feet and made serious errors of judgment, including his decision to rescind Frémont's emancipation decree. Like Swisshelm, Julian felt that Lincoln's action had dashed antislavery sentiment. Just as important, Lincoln's desire to be a conciliator led to a longer war and the revitalization of slavery itself. As a member of the Committee on the Conduct of the War, Julian portrayed himself as continually pressing the president to pursue the war more vigorously. Neglecting to mention the commentary to the contrary, Julian asserted that his committee, not Lincoln, was responsible for the energetic war policy that "saved the country." Such a view, he insisted, would "scarcely be questioned by any man sufficiently well-informed and fair-minded to give an opinion." As for the Emancipation Proclamation, Lincoln had issued it only after intense lobbying.[79]

At the end of his autobiography, Julian declared that slavery was over and that reconciliation with the South was appropriate, now that old issues had disappeared and new ones had taken their place. But his vehemence regarding the mistakes made during the war and Reconstruction suggested at least some lingering uneasiness about the postwar situation. Julian believed that Lincoln's failure to confiscate rebel lands had dire consequences. Not only did the president miss a chance to shorten the war by undercutting the position of the slaveowning class, but he also left intact the property of the very men who had led the South out of the Union. After the war, these men would still own their lands while poor whites and blacks would be left with nothing. (Julian himself worked on a Southern Homestead bill to encourage poor southerners to take up federal lands that passed Congress in 1866 and was repealed in 1877.) This failure to furnish poor blacks and whites with property, according to Julian, explained much of what had happened or failed to happen in the South after 1865.[80]

Julian's fervent account of his involvement in securing black suffrage and the reasons for its necessity also suggest that at some level, he must have been anxious over the uncertain but by no means determined status of black voting in the 1880s. Certainly his readers found a strong defense of a practice that had come under much criticism by the time Julian wrote his recollections. Not even all his "anti-slavery friends" (and perhaps some of his readers) had been prepared to go so far as to accept the vote for former slaves. But Julian explained that suffrage was both morally and logically necessary, and, certain that he was right, he had vigorously worked to garner support for it. The provision of suffrage was a question of "national honor and gratitude" to blacks who had suffered and served during the conflict. Just as important, Julian clearly saw what would happen if southern blacks did not get the vote (or, by extension, keep it.) "To leave the ballot in the hands of the ex-rebels, and withhold it from these helpless millions," he declared, "would be to turn them over to the unhindered tyranny and misrule of their enemies, who were then smarting under the humiliation of their failure, and making the condition of the freedmen more intolerable than slavery itself, through local laws and police regulations."[81]

And yet Julian studiously avoided any direct discussion of the postwar South. His silence had much to do with his overriding desire to justify his own political choices after the war and to prove that his shifting party loyalties were ideologically consistent. Like the prewar Whigs and Democrats, the Republican Party had lost its integrity and purpose and was only interested in holding onto power. Julian saw the Fifteenth Amendment as the culmination of the party's original mission. The challenge then facing the party was to identify the pressing problems of the postwar era and address party corruption. Its failure to do either undermined any claim to moral leadership. Republicans whipped up hostile feelings against southerners, not because there was anything real to protest, but because it was the only way to unite the party and win office. This partisanship further prevented the party from recognizing the very real issues of the present.[82]

Julian argued that slavery was gone forever. Perhaps because he had focused on slavery as an institution and its impact on the political realm, and because at this point in his narrative he was justifying new political allegiances, he chose to ignore the many ways that southern blacks did not find themselves free. Slavery had disappeared, the war was over, and southerners were no longer rebels.[83]

Had Julian only been interested in "selfish ambition" and the many political "prizes" within his reach, he assured readers, he would have remained in the Republican Party. But honor, self-respect, and decency (and, by implication, ideological integrity) drove him from the party. Drawn to the Liberal Republicans because of their principled positions on land reform, the tariff, civil service reform, and the threat of big business, Julian attended the 1872 convention and campaigned for Greeley. Now the former heroes of

Julian's account turned against him with a vengeance, labeling him a rebel and an apostate. Julian was perhaps not prepared for the nature of the assaults against him, which were "unrelieved by a single element of honor or fair play." In a bizarre incident, armed black men appeared at one of Julian's meetings, having heard that Greeley and the Liberal Republicans were planning to reenslave them.[84]

It was not surprising that the black men had come to Julian's meeting, since the Liberal Republicans were promoting reconciliation with the South. Having described the Liberal Republicans as the principled offshoot of the Republicans, Julian argued that the new party had not abandoned any principles related to slavery and the war. Slavery and the tensions it caused had disappeared. Now Liberals "gladly exchanged the key-note of hate and war for that of fraternity and reunion." Although Julian presumably supported this exchange, his narrative at this point took on an impersonal tone. It is not hard to imagine why he removed himself from the discussion of former political and regional enemies suddenly transformed into colleagues. Democrats were now declared to be little different from Republicans, who had "only espoused the cause of the negro under the whip and spur of military necessity." Southerners, whom many northern politicians (including Julian) had denounced for years, "were, after all, very much like other people." Indeed, "very many of them had undoubtedly espoused the cause of slavery under a mistaken view of their constitutional obligations, and as a phase of patriotism, while sincerely condemning it on principle." It would be hard to find a passage that conflicted more dramatically with what Julian had related about his own activities and beliefs than these few sentences.[85]

Julian concluded his narrative in 1872, thus avoiding further discussion of his political affiliations. In fact, he supported the Democrats in the election of 1876 and incurred the wrath of Jane Swisshelm for doing so. She attacked him vehemently, rejecting his suggestion that Louisiana held elections that were as peaceful as those in his home state of Indiana. "The Southern people . . . never had a peaceful or orderly election," she fumed. "You are so far out of sympathy with the brutal affairs of the South that you cannot comprehend their plans. . . . You are their dupe."[86]

These were harsh words. But as Julian pointed out at the end of his recollections, he believed that a new political period with new problems had replaced the era dominated by the slavery question. He was correct, of course, although he might have added that not all the issues of the previous era had been resolved. Now a new generation had to grapple with the compelling questions that faced them. The past was useful but not because the concerns were still relevant but because it provided general political lessons. As Julian observed, young people could "scarcely fail to find both instruction and warning in the story of the anti-slavery conflict."[87]

Julian's book was published in 1884 by Jansen, McClurg & Co., the same house that had handled *Half a Century*, and sold for $1.50. His prominence ensured some critical attention. The *Chicago Tribune* hailed the book as "better than any memoirs . . . which we ever read" on "the story of Free-Soil and Anti-Slavery movement" and praised Julian's candid comments on his contemporaries. The book was also reviewed in the prestigious *Atlantic Monthly*. The reviewer also approved of the book's account of the rise of political antislavery as well as Julian's ability to convey "depth of feeling and intense conviction." The critic agreed with Julian's depiction of the Republicans' eagerness to make concessions on slavery immediately after secession and felt that the book clarified the "crime" of southern leaders who rushed into war. If anyone doubted who caused the Civil War, according to the review, he or she should read this book.[88]

But the *Atlantic Monthly's* reviewer also had substantial problems with parts of Julian's book, and his comments highlighted how far Julian's narrative departed from current wisdom. He rejected Julian's characterization of Lincoln as a conservative and insisted, contrary to Julian's assessment, that Lincoln's delay in issuing the Emancipation Proclamation had been wise. The nation had not been ready to embrace antislavery, as both Julian and Swisshelm had implied when they faulted Lincoln's decision to rescind Frémont's emancipation decree. More significant was the reviewer's rejection of Julian's argument that political abolitionists were rational and logical rather than fanatics. Julian was an extremist and radical. His fanaticism had been a necessary quality for his work, but it did not prepare him for peacetime. He and men like him were irrelevant because they believed that it was always necessary to be agitated about fundamental questions of right and wrong. Only occasionally was it necessary to confront great moral issues. Those periods were tumultuous and destructive for the body political. In normal times, like the present, there was no need for fierce conflict.[89]

———•———

The year after Julian's *Political Recollections* appeared, another political abolitionist and former Garrisonian, Henry Stanton, husband of Elizabeth Cady Stanton, had his book of recollections printed. Viewing his production as neither history, biography, nor autobiography, he stressed the somewhat haphazard nature of his offering by titling it *Random Recollections*. He did not intend to have the book sold but rather given to an audience of friends.

He either had more friends than he realized or received more requests for the book than he had anticipated, for in 1886, he enlarged the book and almost doubled the number of copies printed by the New York printers MacGowan & Slipper. While not a particularly successful lawyer, Stanton had many influential colleagues and acquaintances. One of the recipients of an inscribed volume of the second edition was Supreme Court Chief Justice Morrison R. Waite. In the preface to the third edition, again enlarged, Stanton explained that the second edition had not satisfied the demand and that he was being asked to make some arrangements that would put the book on the market. He decided to find a publisher that would take on the task of issuing the revised book and selling it. The prestigious house of Harper & Brothers published the third edition in 1887 shortly after the author's death.[90]

Given the struggles that other abolitionists faced in getting their autobiographies to the public, Stanton's success in securing a major New York publisher stands out. Stanton, of course, had more social standing than abolitionists like Laura Haviland or William Still, and he had a famous wife. He also wrote a book that seemed less problematic in its message when compared to Douglass's, Julian's or Swisshelm's recollections. Although one reviewer noted that there were few heroes in Stanton's story and that he was hardly a dispassionate observer, he appreciated the lively picture he provided of "noteworthy men and events of half a century." In fact, the recollections were superficial and could hardly have offended any readers seriously. Perhaps these qualities made them attractive to Harper's.[91]

The editor of *Harper's* knew enough about Stanton's life to comment that, while he had courageously borne "his part . . . it was not a leading part" in the world of prewar reform and politics. This was not the impression Stanton tried to give to his readers, who he hoped would see him as playing a significant role in both moral and political abolitionism. Whether he also believed that he deserved the thanks and appreciation due the "martyrs" of the cause is not clear. "The tears of an enfranchised race will bedew their graves," he wrote, "and an appreciative posterity will erect monuments to their memory."[92]

Despite lengthy sections about his legal career that detracted from the picture of the steadfast laborer for emancipation, Stanton stated that his youthful decision to "be the champion of the oppressed colored races" shaped his life's course until the passage of the postwar amendments and Greeley's run for the presidency in 1872. He gave details of his early activism and his work as an antislavery lecturer and its dangers. His life was often at risk, he assured his readers, for supporting freedom for the slaves. "I have a right to say this," he declared, "because, in this turbulent epoch, I was voluntarily pleading for a humble race which, by no possibility, could reward me or ever hear of my existence." Such a comment suggested not selfless activism in which the work was its own reward but rather his desire to be praised and remembered.[93]

Stanton gave a disjointed account of his participation in antislavery politics but showed himself at its center. He helped to draft the Free-Soil platform in 1848 and assisted New Hampshire Free-Soil senator John Hale, who was "a novice in the Anti-slavery literature" and "an indifferent reasoner," with several of his initial speeches in Congress. Stanton, by implication, was neither. As a New York State senator, Stanton offered a prescient and radical amendment dealing with the power of the federal government to control slavery and prevent its extension in the territories. "It cost a high price to utter" such ideas in 1850, Stanton assured his readers, even though they might seem quite "commonplace to-day." Stanton also claimed credit as one of the founders of the Republican Party and discussed his widely circulated speech in Rochester. "Of course, I was quite at home on the slavery topic," he boasted.[94]

In one of his chapters, Stanton paid tribute to the "constellation of leaders in the Anti-slavery cause" located in Boston, to others in New York State and the Midwest. He also noted the great contributions of women and freed black men to the cause of emancipation. Although his praise seemed sincere, he commented that the Boston abolitionists were often "indiscriminate in their censures" and charged with fanaticism in the years before the war and that the New Yorkers "became somewhat loose in their doctrines and fanatical in their operations." While declining to take sides or "disparage Abolitionists of any type," Stanton's description of one of the last American Anti-Slavery Society conventions before 1855 gave mixed messages. Garrison called to mind the prophet Isaiah and Phillips, a Roman coin. But along with these men were others who were unable to deal with "the terrible strain put upon the human intellect in those old Anti-slavery days": Father Lampson was "a crazy loon," Abigail Folsom was "another lunatic," George Mellon died in an insane asylum, Stephen Foster thought "he was a second George Fox," and Charles Burleigh "dressed like a tramp."[95]

Stanton's view of the taint of eccentricity and extremism touching the old abolitionists was benign compared to Swisshelm's evaluation of Garrison in her autobiography. Garrison's view of the Constitution as a proslavery document was "fallacious," Swisshelm declared, and his decision to stay out of politics was "moral *dilettantism.*" "It is doubtful," she wrote, "whether he labored harder for the overthrow of slavery or political anti-slavery." Julian apparently found the Garrisonians irrelevant to the serious antislavery struggle, and Garrison came in for only the briefest reference. As Julian explained, "That slavery was to be put down without political action in a government carried on by the ballot was never a tenable proposition."[96]

While Douglass, Swisshelm, Julian, and Stanton all reflected the position of political abolitionists before the war, their commentaries reinforced the contemporary views of the irrelevancy of the moral abolitionists. The irony was that their reviewers often suggested that the political world and the people they described were also irrelevant, "as extinct as if it had perished very much more than ten years ago."[97]

Stanton was eager to make another accusation against the moral abolitionists. "To state the case exactly," he charged, "some abolitionists hated ministers more than they hated slave-holders." While it was true that some of the major religious journals and urban clergy had fulminated against the abolitionists, the small journals and the clergy in rural areas had striven mightily for the Union and for freedom. "There were no firmer champions of the slave," Stanton declared, "than the mass of the Northern clergy."[98]

Stanton's comments supported the arguments of the prominent Connecticut minister Leonard Bacon and others who defended the record of the northern churches on the antislavery question. Bacon had originally been a staunch supporter of the colonization movement and had only moved gradually toward an acceptance of emancipation. Yet, in an exchange with Oliver Johnson published in *Century* in 1883, Bacon claimed that "sober, conscientious, church-going, voting, union-loving, sedition-and-secession hating" Christians ended slavery. Two years before, prominent Methodist clergymen had commissioned Dr. Lucius Matlack to write a book detailing the record of the Methodist Church on the issue. The reviewer reported the findings: "A great part of the so-called pro-slavery sentiment in the northern churches was not the expression of any advocacy of slavery or lack of earnest opposition to it; but only of doubt of the wisdom of particular methods of opposing it." Calling for a reexamination of the entire subject, the reviewer concluded that "great injustice has been done in the prevalence of indiscriminate and sweeping charges which falsely imply that their influence was for the most part in favor of the perpetuation of slavery or at least in antagonism to all anti-slavery effort."[99]

It was just these sorts of interpretations and claims that drove Parker Pillsbury to write *Acts of Anti-Slavery Apostles* in 1883. Like other abolitionists who recorded their recollections of the movement, he claimed to have been reluctant to begin such a daunting task. His "very few surviving associates in the conflict, and their friends," however, had earnestly encouraged him to proceed. At seventy-four, he did not think "much can be expected, at my head or hand." Aware that most of his "*earliest* comrades" were dead, however, he regarded his task as a "divine appointment."[100]

While previous writers had wanted to present their interpretation of abolitionism for the upcoming generation, the climate of the 1880s added urgency to the task. Pillsbury regarded his times as a "cheap age . . . [that] manufactures sham and shoddy at too many of its mills, political, literary, social, moral and religious." The exaggerated language with which Pillsbury described slavery and antislavery suggested the pressure he felt to make a compelling case in an unsympathetic and uninformed environment. "The present generation knows little of the terrible mysteries and meanings of slavery or anti-slavery," he wrote; "the outrages and horrors of the former, or the desperate and deadly encounters with the monster by the latter." If he did not describe the "'Thirty years war' before one shot was fired," he asked, who would do so? He had already started his book when the articles from Bacon and others began to appear. The claims they made about Garrison's irrelevance and their own contributions to emancipation infuriated Pillsbury. "Everybody now is an abolitionist, so son, or grandson of an anti-slavery parentage, and so all seem to claim equal honor," Pillsbury fulminated. So offensive did Pillsbury find Bacon's depiction of Garrison in *Century* that he quoted passages from the article in the book in order to expose Bacon's limitations.[101]

The assertions of "our old opponents or their children" also caused Pillsbury to alter the scope of his book. He decided to omit material detailing the work of some abolitionists he had originally intended to discuss and stood firm against the pressure of old friends who urged him to discuss others insufficiently recognized. More important to Pillsbury now was freeing space for chapters on the "*pro*-slavery apostles." By demonstrating the churches' bitter opposition to abolitionism "beyond all question or contradiction," Pillsbury hoped to expose the "misrepresentations" the clergy of his own day were busy circulating.[102]

Pillsbury's title highlighted both the sacred nature of moral abolitionism and the lofty aspirations he harbored for his account. As he explained, most of his antislavery work as well as the antislavery work of others he discussed in his book "was of the missionary character, as was that of the first Christian apostles. . . . And the purpose of this Scripture is to present a true record, as far as practicable, of what passed under my own immediate observation, and in which it was my honor to bear some humble part."

While Pillsbury did provide a firsthand account of several abolitionists' work in the movement and of his own participation, he failed to give his book the noble character that the biblical references suggested. The book was disorganized, episodic, and repetitious. He was not a good writer and knew it. "Readers doubtless have seen, if not deplored, some repetition in previous chapters," he began one chapter. But he claimed the repetitions were necessary so that readers understood "the persons and the principles" the book presented. The book also was too long, and Pillsbury was unable to control the material or to finish the book, though he acknowledged that its length might be a problem for readers. "The foregoing [discussion] may seem to young readers a narrative too long drawn out," he wrote. As the book progressed he commented frequently on its excessive length. By page 364 he announced, "It is time to draw this work to a close." Nevertheless, there were over 100 pages to go![103]

The length, the repetition, and Pillsbury's extreme vocabulary hinted at his growing frustration at serving "the cause of truth and the demands of history." The need to convey his point of view (the truth) to an uninformed audience also may explain the directive posture he adopted with his readers. After providing several revealing anecdotes about "incorrigible" and "unscrupulous" Congregational clergy who tried to prevent antislavery lecturers from speaking in their communities, Pillsbury still found it necessary to instruct readers "that every individual clergyman or separate church described in these records is only as representative of large numbers, and by no means as exceptions to general rules." Readers "whose fathers and mothers had no active, friendly hand in the mighty moral upheavals of that period," who, upon brief reflection, "were almost the whole nation then, whatever may be the boast of to-day" were provided with a "few special explanatory remarks" so that they would understand Pillsbury's point. Readers were instructed that an article included in the book was "well worth reading and even study."[104]

"This generation seems to know little of what slavery was, any more than what was genuine, uncompromising anti-slavery," Pillsbury wrote more than once in *Acts of Anti-Slavery Apostles*. His effort to capture the essence of abolitionism and to persuade readers of its nobility frequently necessitated the use of superlatives. Antislavery represented "the sublimest movement in behalf of liberty and humanity of many generations," a "divine ministry of freedom, humanity and holiness," and a "moral, peaceful and religious agitation for the rights of humanity." Pillsbury also included descriptions of antislavery conventions and lectures, the resolutions debated and passed, and the arguments presented to persuade the public that slavery was "the foulest" of crimes and a sin. Pillsbury called these sections "word pictures, [often] taken on the spot, and by actors in or witnesses of, the scenes and encounters." While these word pictures may have allowed readers to experience the past, they did not always make exciting reading.[105]

Pillsbury's account left no doubt that moral agitators had done the real work of emancipation, although exactly how they had done so was unclear, especially since Pillsbury did not organize his book chronologically or discuss the coming of the war in any coherent fashion. Perhaps prompted by the positive evaluations being given of political abolitionism, Pillsbury devoted a substantial amount of attention to the mistaken positions of the "New Organization," "such as the sacredness of human governments, and church organizations, and their machinery; Sabbath, ministry, and the like, woman's inferiority, [and] necessity of litigation." He detailed the arguments of newspaper editor Nathaniel Rogers against political action. "Legislation was force" while antislavery "was a strictly moral and religious movement, a work of repentance and reformation." The legal abolition of slavery, Rogers had said presciently, would of necessity be at "the point of the sword" and therefore immoral. Pillsbury also reminded readers of the character of the Republican Party and twice reproduced a revealing passage from Lincoln's inaugural address that readers might well have forgotten. By supporting a proposed amendment that would bar the federal government from interfering with "domestic institutions" in the states, Lincoln had "declared for slave-holding and slave-hunting."[106]

In contrast to the flawed men who supported abolitionist political action, the leaders of moral agitation were great men, "the like of whom the world has seldom seen—[and] may not soon see again." Pillsbury included sketches of those he had known and considered to be most influential. He devoted his first chapter to Garrison, hoping to restore the increasingly maligned reformer to his rightful place as hero. Here was a man who believed that moral power could be effective without physical force, who embodied all "the Christian virtues and graces," and, most important, who had completed and surpassed the work of the Revolution. His newspaper, the *Liberator*, had been responsible for changing "the destiny of a race."[107]

Nathaniel Rogers, editor of the New Hampshire newspaper *Herald of Freedom*, also merited extended treatment. Like Garrison, Rogers espoused the moral and spiritual power of persuasion rather than politics. Pillsbury, himself, had brought "pilgrims" to Rogers's grave, which lacked a headstone. They routinely asked why there was no physical monument to such an important figure. "Such as was Rogers, never die," was his response. "They need no monuments reared by other hands than their own. Time mows down all marble and granite, tramples out all inscriptions in bronze or brass." While such faith was touching, at the heart of Pillsbury's work was the threat of national forgetfulness. In fact, as he pointed out, most of the readers of Rogers's newspapers were dead, and the only volume of his editorials that had ever appeared in print had "long ago disappeared from the market."[108]

Pillsbury provided several sketches of the true apostles, the antislavery lecturers of whom he was one. The radical Stephen Foster received the most coverage. Foster was a good subject because he focused on the church's complicity with slavery. He also routinely provoked hostile reactions and thus provided evidence of the persecution abolitionists endured. One of Foster's tactics was to attend a Sunday church service and, at the time of the sermon, to rise "respectfully" and claim "the right to be heard then and there, on the duties and obligations of the church" to the enslaved. Pillsbury stressed Foster's "solemn and devout" manner and the angry responses his request elicited. In Pillsbury's narrative, Foster suffered persecution for trying to speak the truth. He neglected to mention, however, that Foster, though personally nonviolent, frequently precipitated violence, although a careful reader might well reach this conclusion.[109]

Pillsbury also described his own "apostleship." In contrast to his glowing picture of Foster as "Brave hero," the portrait of himself was subdued. "From the beginning it has been my constant care to be myself as little obtrusive as the nature of my work would warrant consistently with exact truth and right," he wrote near the conclusion of his autobiography. Uncomfortable with detailing his own accomplishments, he included, "with deep humility, and only at the earnest solicitation of his few surviving friends," several articles about him written by Rogers. Rogers's comments about Pillsbury reinforced Pillsbury's claim to modesty while also drawing attention to his talents. "He has overlooked himself. . . . He has undervalued his inestimable services," Rogers wrote, and it was "a shame that such a man as Parker Pillsbury should be unappreciated." Pillsbury's lack of egotism was one the few features in this stormy autobiography that might meet with a critic's approval.[110]

Pillsbury gave his personal story in a disjointed fashion, beginning it with his first meeting with Garrison in 1839. At the time, he was beginning a stint as an antislavery lecturer and resolved "to see the overthrow of the Southern slave system or perish in the conflict." He took pains to contradict the contemporary charge of fanaticism. Like Garrison and Rogers, Pillsbury insisted that he "relied only on truth, reason and argument for success." But his own preference for extreme language and sweeping denunciations provided an important, if unintended insight, into his temperament and supported accusations of fanaticism being hurled at moral abolitionists.[111]

Pillsbury gave a good sense of what it meant to be an apostle: "cold and most inhospitable receptions," mobs, inclement weather, and skipped meals. "But," he pointed out, "we were young and tolerably vigorous, and cared little for such trifles, well warmed within with an earnest purpose." Yet he did infer that the commitment had its costs. He described the day when there was no money for food and his wife wept. He admitted his fear of mobs and his "constitutional cowardice." Pillsbury described attempts to suspend his license to preach, which, he wrote, might seem "trivial" to the modern reader but "to myself and wife, and other near and dear friends, there was mighty meaning in every step."[112]

In their recollections, May, Coffin, Haviland, and others had denounced the Protestant denominations for their failure to condemn slavery as a sin. But their accusations were mild compared to those in *Acts of the Anti-Slavery Apostles*. Pillsbury was angry not just because the churches had supported slavery but also because they now claimed that they had actually opposed it. While he and others had embraced immediate emancipation early and suffered for their commitment, latecomers now sought credit for ending slavery. The recent spate of articles that caused him to change the character of his book apparently also revived all the fury that Pillsbury had felt during the 1840s and 1850s. He may also have been incensed by the prominent role that some clergymen were taking in promoting reconciliation. Now, he accused the ministry of arrogance, insolence, and fraud, calling the pulpit a coward's castle and a despot's throne. He provided detailed accounts of lectures in which he, Foster, and others attacked the church, showing that it not only supported but also "sanctified" slavery. "The exceptions to this charge were too few to change the results," Pillsbury concluded. In a shocking accusation, he also stated that some ministers had actually instigated mobs that attacked abolitionists.[113]

Pillsbury devoted the next to last chapter of almost 100 pages to hammer home his interpretation once more, although by this point no reader could have been unaware of his argument. Having relied heretofore on personal anecdote and materials written by abolitionists like Rogers, Pillsbury determined to prove his "sweeping and severe" charges that the major denominations supported slavery by furnishing "their own recorded, printed, published testimony." He began with the Presbyterians, progressed to the American Board of Commissioners for Foreign Missions, which represented both Presbyterians and Congregationalists, then to the Baptists, the Methodists, and the Tract and the American Bible Society, and ended with the Fugitive Slave Law and ecclesiastical responses to it. The denominations credited with antislavery positions, such as the Quakers and Free Will Baptists, also came in for condemnation. The weight of the testimony may have been persuasive, but the chapter failed to achieve the fresh and lively tone critics admired.[114]

Of course, Pillsbury had no interest in creating a lively book. The necessity of providing "strict truth and exact justice" resulted in what Pillsbury referred to as "these fearful chronicles." His chapter, "Slavery — As It Was," aimed to shock and inform, not to entertain readers who were ignorant of the institution's character. Lacking personal acquaintance with southern slavery, Pillsbury accumulated primary sources as evidence of the horror of the slave system. Black voices were absent, but he did present advertisements, judicial decisions, laws, newspaper articles, and, of course, a statement from an association of Baptist ministers that revealed its support of slavery. Pillsbury used his evidence to emphasize what abolitionists had long argued: that slavery was a sin. Pillsbury saved for last the evidence that he thought most powerful, "none other than Thomas Jefferson himself." Pillsbury included selections from Jefferson's "Notes on Virginia" that pointed out the baleful results of slavery and expressed hope for its elimination. "Happy for the nation, had it heeded his wise and timely counsels," Pillsbury concluded.[115]

But the nation had not listened to Jefferson or to the "warnings, entreaties and expostulations of the faithful abolitionists . . . [whose] terrible predictions were . . . [ultimately] fulfilled" through a bloody and costly war. Pillsbury resorted to biblical and apocalyptic language to suggest that the conflict's ultimate meaning had nothing to do with the Union but with guilt, punishment, and retribution. While southerners were guilty of "Rebellion," the North, because it had maintained slavery politically and religiously, experienced just "Retribution." At Fort Sumter, "the trump of the avenging angel first sounded . . . summoning north and south to their judgment day." An avenging justice dashed men on both sides to their death, "their last sacrament." Finally, as the "crowning, sealing sacrifice, an idolized president [was] massacred, murdered."[116]

Pillsbury ended his book with a description of the nation in mourning for Lincoln's death. He included the text of the speech he had given to the antislavery society when it was considering dissolution, in which he declared, "Our work is not yet quite done; at least mine is not done, nor will it be done till the blackest man has every right which I, myself enjoy."[117]

At the beginning of 1883, as Pillsbury was completing his book, the Supreme Court dealt a heavy blow to black rights in the decision of *United*

States v. Stanley. The decision overturned the Civil Rights Act of 1875 and undermined the Fourteenth and Fifteenth Amendments by ruling that the equal protection clause of the Fourteenth Amendment only applied to the states. Thus the only recourse available to an individual whose civil or political rights were violated lay in state rather than federal action. In a letter to Frederick Douglass in November 1883 Pillsbury commented, "Since the late decision of the Supreme Court, it has seemed to me we may have our Anti Slavery battles to fight over again." Without an organization to direct those battles, Pillsbury added, he was left to do his best as an individual to scatter "light and truth as fast and far as lies in my power." Getting his book into the hands of the public was part of fulfilling his mission.[118]

Pillsbury first approached Houghton Mifflin, where Garrison's son Frank worked. Garrison wrote to Pillsbury to "throw all the light" he could on "the mysteries of the publishing business," claiming that he was most interested in seeing Pillsbury's book in print and before the public. But he was not very encouraging. His letter reveals the obstacles facing abolitionists who were running counter to the currents of taste and interests. There was no ready market for the book. "The generation that was cognizant of those times," Garrison wrote, "is passing away; & that born since the war has no comprehension of them, & is still too young & too near to them to care to study them as history." Moreover, even the books published while people remembered the events of the years leading up to the war had not succeeded. The leading historical studies like Samuel May's "admirable little volume," Henry Wilson's book on the rise and fall of slave power, and Oliver Johnson's volume on William Lloyd Garrison and the antislavery movement all had "restricted" sales due to weak demand.[119]

At one time, antislavery societies had been able to raise funds to publish work that needed to reach the public. Now the situation was quite different. Garrison thought that Houghton Mifflin would publish the book only if Pillsbury guaranteed that the firm would not lose money. Such an arrangement would mean that Pillsbury would have to cover the cost of printing and advertising the book and pay Houghton Mifflin a commission on all retail copies sold. Garrison provided some figures for Pillsbury to study. If about 1,000 copies of the book were published and sold for $1.50 apiece, Pillsbury would have to pay out $975 and stood to recoup $675—if all copies actually sold. By selling the book for more than $1.50, Pillsbury might make money, but this price might also put the book beyond the reach of those who might want to buy it. If Pillsbury knew of those who lived in "out of the way places, where they seldom see a bookstore or read a book advertisement" and wanted to take some of the copies and sell them for what he could get, he would save the discount given to booksellers and some of the publisher's commission.[120]

Garrison was not entirely candid with Pillsbury. The firm had actually evaluated the manuscript and had considered it entirely unworthy of publication. The book was "too charged with prejudice and narrowness to give it any value as a historical work; too dull to attract readers who might wish to hear Mr. Pillsbury's side of the story, and too verbose and ill-written to rank as good literature." Garrison had, in fact, withdrawn the manuscript from consideration.[121]

Pillsbury decided to have 2,000 copies of the book printed privately. Garrison continued to act as an informal adviser and urged him to secure a publisher's imprint. Without such an imprint, he told Pillsbury, it would be hard for booksellers and interested readers to find out where to buy the books. He also urged Pillsbury not to bind all of the copies of the book at once but to do them gradually to meet demand. He also suggested that Pillsbury take out a copyright. Pillsbury, however, did not feel any great need for a copyright, and Garrison ultimately agreed: "The public is not yet so eager to read about the A.S. days" so that "books on the subject are in [no] danger of being pirated."[122]

Pillsbury sent complimentary copies of the book to Frederick Douglass, Abby Kelley Foster, and other old friends from antislavery work, as well as to prominent antislavery figures like John and Jesse Frémont. Pillsbury sold at least some of the copies himself, keeping a small supply of books on hand to fill orders that came to him. John Brown's son was one such buyer. He sent Pillsbury $1.63 only after he had received the book, explaining that he had been short of cash because his grape crop had been ruined. He told Pillsbury that he was disappointed that he had included so little about himself. He believed that Pillsbury's "journeyings and preachings . . . were of greater importance than all others." "Blessings on you," Brown wrote, "and upon all who aid in furnishing to this new generation a true record of those momentous times."[123]

Friends praised Pillsbury's efforts and appreciated his purpose. Wendell Phillips told Pillsbury "how gratified" he was with the book, in which "old scenes [were] freshened & half forgotten points brought out & set in fitting light." Abby Kelley Foster, whose fiery rhetoric had both inspired and infuriated men and women before the Civil War, was one of Pillsbury's most enthusiastic supporters. Although she proclaimed herself "no critic," she praised his "simple, unaffected, unstrained language." She found his presentation of slavery "strong" and "horrible," declaring, "You have gone down into hell to find material." "In the far future," she predicted, historians would "longest linger" over this account, yet at the present time she feared that the book would not attract a wide audience. Elizur Wright agreed with this evaluation. Although he also praised the book, he anticipated that Pillsbury would lose money on it. Perhaps responding to a request from Pillsbury that he endorse the book, Wright refused, saying that his endorsement would further burden the book. "But," he added, "if you are, or are likely to be, in a tight place on want of it, please let me know, for I will help you as far as I can."[124]

Acts of the Anti-Slavery Apostles did receive some reviews in journals like the *Free Thought Magazine*, but the prestigious monthlies ignored it. As Pillsbury told Sidney Gay, the book sold very few copies and "I shall lose some hundreds of dollars, besides the severest year's work of my life." Given the character of the book, though, it was not very surprising that it did not sell well. It is doubtful, however, that Swisshelm, Julian, or Stanton sold a significant number of books, although their books were more temperate than Pillsbury's. Douglass may well have been the most successful of all, yet his publisher was unhappy with the numbers. None of these authors, with perhaps the exception of Douglass, thought about making money, but they all must have been disappointed that it was so difficult to present their view of the past to a generation that clearly needed to know it. They were at a great disadvantage trying to counter views reaching thousands and thousands of readers, dispersed by powerful publishing firms who supported reconciliation and the construction of memory that clashed in most particulars with what abolitionists believed had happened. But it seems unlikely that even knowing all this, abolitionist authors would have kept silent. As Pillsbury explained, "I printed, as well as wrote the Acts of the Anti Slavery Apostles for History, for Humanity, and for Posterity, regardless of cost and loss."[125]

The Last Gatherings

December held a special place in the prewar antislavery calendar. It was during this month in 1833 that the American Anti-Slavery Society (AAS) was founded, a milestone event in the movement for immediate emancipation. December was also the month during which the Philadelphia and Boston female antislavery societies hosted their great annual fairs. These festive bazaars had raised money for antislavery work, but just as important, they had provided opportunities for abolitionists to assess their progress toward emancipation, to renew friendships, and to see and hear from leading men and women of the movement. They helped to create a sense of commitment, community, and continuity among those who sought to end slavery. By coincidence, John Brown had been executed in December, another reason to consider the end of the year as an evocative time for abolitionists.

Despite increasing age, abolitionists of various stripes still came together to talk about the past and to comment on the pressing issues that remained unresolved. Each man and woman must have wondered, however, if this meeting would be the last he or she would attend. At each gathering, speakers expressed their keen sense of how much time had passed since their active work in the antislavery movement.

In December 1879, on the twentieth anniversary of the death of John Brown, a commemoration was held at the Shiloh Presbyterian Colored Church in New York. It had been the hope that the memorial would attract "a grand gathering of old abolitionists," but the exercises seemed mainly to have drawn African American members of the church. Letters came from white abolitionists who, for one reason or another, could not come. But everyone was conscious of those who had no choice in the matter. As one of the speakers observed, John Brown "is gone. Abraham Lincoln is gone. Charles Sumner is gone. William Lloyd Garrison is gone. Few of the old band of brothers remain."[1]

The decoration of the church highlighted one of the themes of the day. The reading desk of Henry Garnett, the church's pastor, was covered with the American flag, and a photograph of Brown, encircled by myrtle leaves, was displayed. The gathering heaped praise on Brown and expressed their thanks for the other prophets, leaders, and martyrs who had come forward during the nation's days of trial. Speakers emphasized the situation of southern blacks who needed education and, as one man put it, the same privileges to move freely, or "get up and git," as whites. After eulogizing John Brown, white abolitionist Aaron Powell denounced the "present disgraceful persecution" and the spirit of slavery that lay behind it. His sobering comments raised implicit questions about what Brown and the crowd of martyrs had actually accomplished.[2]

Several years after the John Brown exercises, the fiftieth anniversary of the establishment of the American Anti-Slavery Society approached. Some abolitionists hoped to recall the advent of the AAS and perhaps to recapture a sense of fellowship provided by associational life by holding a commemorative meeting in Philadelphia on December 4, 1883. Only four of the original founders were still alive, but that reality did not deter those planning the celebration. The call, issued by African American Robert Purvis, one of the original members of the 1833 convention, and Daniel Neall, suggested that the organizers also felt a keen need to expose young people to a particular and increasingly unacknowledged vision of the past. "A new generation has arisen, to whom the record of the brave struggle of the American Abolitionists may well be commended as a historic treasure, and an inspiring lesson," their invitation proclaimed.[3]

Compared to the original convention that had lasted three days, the commemoration was brief, with meetings during the day and evening of December 4 held in Philadelphia's Horticultural Hall. The length of the proceedings was yet another reminder of the frailty of the remaining antislavery warriors; many "familiar faces" from the old days were missing. Wendell Phillips, Abby Kelley Foster, and Parker Pillsbury were unable to attend. Nor could Garrison's sons, Frank and Wendell Phillips Garrison, be at the reunion. Despite the brevity of the occasion and the absence of key figures, planners were determined to make the occasion memorable and accessible to a wider audience by publishing the proceedings. The preface set out the purpose of the gathering. The occasion provided an opportunity both for "devout" thanksgiving for the end of slavery for "historic" reminiscences of the "great enterprise" that formed part of the nation's historical record. The references to the historical record reflected the desire to inform the present generation about a crucial chapter of history. By engaging the sympathy and imagination of young people, organizers and speakers hoped to encourage them to embrace meaningful reform activities. Woman suffrage and temperance won special mention.[4]

Robert Purvis was chosen to chair the meeting as an acknowledgment of his long role in antislavery activities and his part in organizing the reunion. The selection of a black man as presiding officer over what was most likely a predominantly white audience also had a high symbolic value. It recalled abolitionists' commitment to abolish slavery and to ensure equal rights for free blacks, their efforts for freed people during Reconstruction, and their rejection of the emerging new racial status quo.

As it turned out, cultural, social, and political realities tempered the celebration and thanksgiving for the end of slavery. Rev. William Furness offered a brief prayer that acknowledged God's hand in eliminating the country's greatest curse and hailed the "triumph of those principles for which the fathers lived and died." Purvis "exultantly" referred to five million former slaves who had become freemen and citizens. But the jubilation and hopefulness that emancipation had inspired had long ago disappeared.[5]

As was fitting for the occasion, the first order of business was to sketch the birth of the AAS and to highlight its founding document, the Declaration of Sentiments. John Greenleaf Whittier, one of the four surviving abolitionist leaders, did not come to Philadelphia, so his article on the convention, originally published in *Atlantic Monthly* in 1874, was read aloud. Whittier's emphasis on the youthfulness of the men and women, most of whom were now dead, created a sense of the vast distance between the present and the past, as did his own absence due to age. It was a distance that some of the speakers also felt. Mary Grew remarked that for those still living "how far away seem the scenes which we recall of persecution," and James Buffum, the evening's principal speaker, said, "It is so long since I have spoken on this subject that I don't know whether I can interest you." The challenge of making the past real enough to make an impression on the audience, especially the younger members of the audience, was a daunting one.[6]

While Mary Grew felt the impossibility of conveying to the younger generation what it was like to be an abolitionist in "the country's 'Martyr Age,'" she provided an uncomplicated overview of the abolitionist movement that highlighted the central and uncompromising role abolitionists had played in ending slavery. Grew acknowledged that the work had been arduous and that many laborers had never expected to live long enough to see their cause triumph. But what stood out for her so many years later was not the northern hostility to abolitionism that so many earlier writers had emphasized but the basic "sense of justice in the heart of the American people." By appealing to this sense of justice, she asserted, the moral abolitionists had initiated a process that ultimately ended slavery. The "Anti-Slavery host grew in numbers and power until neither churches nor legislatures could afford to ignore it." Political parties emerged, John Brown's raid took place, and finally the South rose up and sealed its doom. "The brightness of emancipation morning" followed, and the "specific" work of the American Anti-slavery Society was done.

In the years since the dissolution of the antislavery societies, Grew had not changed her position that the goal of the antislavery movement had been limited to the destruction of slavery. But the version of history she now offered was far simpler than the analysis she had presented in 1870 when the Philadelphia Female Anti-Slavery Society had disbanded. At that time, she had acknowledged the power of racial prejudice in the South. But now she said nothing, despite her private views about the southern racial situation. Only a few years earlier in a letter to Garrison, she had criticized President Hayes for caving in to "those southern white aristocrats" and thanked the antislavery leader for his "protest against the miserable policy of 'conciliation & compromise' with the oppression of the colored race in the South." The situation in 1883 was hardly more hopeful than it had been in 1877. But she said nothing of her misgivings. Perhaps she was most interested in encouraging the younger generation to believe in the possibilities of moral reform. Or perhaps, on a celebratory occasion, she was unwilling to look back at such a significant part of her life's work and acknowledge publicly that its success was less glorious than she and others had anticipated.[7]

Unitarian minister Charles Gordon Ames, who spoke after Grew, painted a similar picture of abolitionism but hinted that the revolution that gave blacks the same privileges and rights as whites might be more theoretical than real. Nonetheless, emancipation represented a chapter in "the best history of the world's progress." His insistence that moral action brought progress, reiterated by at least one other speaker, was most likely aimed at younger members of the audience. The picture of successful activism challenged the prevailing belief that it was pointless to interfere with social evolution. Ames also implicitly questioned the claims of science by arguing for the importance of conviction and feeling. "Let us never be ashamed that we have hearts as well as heads," he declared. When sentiment and belief became the foundation for reform, there was less room for individual self-interest to corrupt the process of change.[8]

When Susan B. Anthony took the floor, she specifically addressed "young people." She explained that antislavery had provided her with the education necessary for a public career as a reformer. But if abolitionism was to provide the "inspiring lesson" for which the convention organizers and speakers hoped, other means were necessary to help those born since the Civil War make an imaginative connection with the antislavery past.[9]

Antislavery relics played an important role in helping close the gap between past and present. After the Declaration of Sentiments was read, Rev. Charles Spear directed the audience's eyes to the very table on which the Declaration and the signers' inkstand had rested. And, later, during the evening meeting, William Still exhibited the box in which a young Baltimore women had escaped to freedom. The box, also displayed during the final meeting of the Pennsylvania Anti-Slavery Society in 1870, still had the power to recall "the days of slavery pretty vividly," Still thought. His brief comments on the Underground Railroad and the escape of Henry Brown further brought to life the exciting days of the fugitive slaves. Another member of the Philadelphia Vigilance Committee showed an equally evocative relic to the audience, a slave auction block from Alexandria, whose story he told. At the close of the evening meeting, many members of the audience and their children came forward to examine the relics more closely.[10]

Not only the desire to influence the present generation but also the need to address contemporary problems inspired speakers. Whereas Grew avoided and Ames merely hinted at present realities, Aaron Powell, the final speaker, insisted that "the one lesson of the hour is that there must be no retrograde step; that no party shall be permitted to give license to the spirit of oppression and race prejudice." He urged the audience to keep the principles of the AAS alive and to keep "public opinion . . . up to a high moral level." A letter from Wendell Phillips, also read during the evening meeting, was equally urgent. Freedmen, Phillips asserted, still needed the protection of "a vigilant public opinion, and will need it for the rest of this generation." Both men suggested that race prejudice affected not only American blacks but also Chinese immigrants. Immigration from China had been curtailed with the Chinese Exclusion Act only the year before the commemoration.[11]

In many respects, the celebration of the founding of the AAS attempted to renew and to mobilize reform belief and to claim for moral reform its rightful historical place. Both goals were difficult given that the meeting was brief and there was no institutional base that could sustain its goals and visions after the meeting ended.[12]

While speakers rejected many of the cultural and intellectual shifts that had occurred since the war, they were not immune to their influence. In his letter to the meeting, Whittier remarked that bitterness between North and South was disappearing and that people in both sections were beginning to feel that they had "no really clashing interests." Certainly bitter denunciations of southerners were absent from this meeting. Indeed, Reverend Ames absolved most southerners of guilt for the war when he described them as

"those honestly-misguided multitudes who died for the 'Lost Cause.'" And
while to Ames abolitionists were the heroes and heroines of the hour, the
criticism of antislavery supporters apparently had had an effect. Ames explained that abolitionists were not "infallible." They were often extreme in
their language, and some were even fanatical. But, he concluded, they had
pursued what was right and violently opposed what was wrong.[13]

Those attending the commemoration clearly were pleased with it. Before the meeting ended, they passed a resolution to hold another gathering the following year. That reunion never took place, but abolitionists did
manage to come together on other occasions. In 1886, Lucy Stone invited
several old friends to an "anti-slavery reception" at her home near Boston.
Abby Kelley Foster, Samuel May (nephew of Samuel J. May), and Sarah
Southwick were among those who "met and talked of the stirring days
of the past." Garrison's four sons and Foster's daughter were also in attendance. In the photograph taken of the group on Stone's porch, despite
the presence of the younger generation, white hair and beards dominated.
Even "young" George Garrison's beard was turning gray.[14]

As Stone's small and private party attested, the abolitionists were fast disappearing. And as one woman who attended a commemorative antislavery
meeting observed in 1893, she herself had become "a relic of the anti-slavery
times." A review of Rev. Austin Willey's *History of the Anti-Slavery Cause in
State and Nation* in the *New York Times* suggested many might find such
human relics irrelevant. It was doubtful, the reviewer thought, that the new
generation would be interested in Willey's history: "Dead issues can rarely
be resurrected to any profit, and men seldom get enthusiastic over matters
which are most buried out of sight." Anyone reading his book would have
to take into account Willey's bias, which stemmed from his "strong feelings" and "intense conviction[s]."[15]

In New England, however, the interest in local history helped keep the
abolitionist heritage alive. In Boston, subscribers raised $14,000 to erect a
statue of William Lloyd Garrison. The work of sculptor Olin L. Warner, the
statue took its place on the mall on Commonwealth Avenue in 1886. Garrison was shown seated, holding a manuscript in one hand with a newspaper
at his feet. At the base of the statue were the words "I am in earnest—I will
not equivocate—I will not excuse—I will not retreat a single inch—AND
I WILL BE HEARD." But unless the viewer already knew something of Garrison's antislavery career and his insistence on immediate emancipation of
the slaves, he or she would not learn much about Garrison except that he
was important.[16]

There was no monument to Wendell Phillips, who died in 1884, although

Edwin Mead, writing in *New England Magazine*, thought that Faneuil Hall, where Phillips had made so many memorable speeches, should be renamed the Wendell Phillips Hall. Mead went on to fault a monument honoring Civil War combatants erected on the Boston Common as a "towering piece of commonplace" that failed to credit the antislavery struggle. The monument should have memorialized heroes like Charles Sumner, Garrison, and Phillips who had played such a distinctive role in Boston's opposition to slavery, Mead believed. And the work for blacks was still unfinished. If Phillips had still been alive, Mead suggested, he would say that the position of blacks was a "mockery of freedom."[17]

New England Magazine played an important role in reminding readers of their local connections with antislavery. In 1890, it published a profusely illustrated article by Archibald Grimké, the half brother of Angelina and Sarah Grimké. Grimké's purpose was to make readers aware of the "holy ground" on which abolitionists had "stood and struggled and achieved." As he guided readers to different sites, often reproduced in illustrations, Grimké told stories of local white and black activists. The magazine also featured articles about fugitive slaves and a piece on George Luther Stearns, a Massachusetts manufacturer and abolitionist. Dubbed an "anti-slavery hero," Stearns had a long history of activism behind the scenes, including efforts to persuade Abraham Lincoln to declare emancipation and to ensure equal pay for blacks in the Union army.[18]

New England Magazine's interest in keeping the memory of abolitionism alive as a significant part of local history contrasted with the perspective offered in *Atlantic Monthly*, once a mouthpiece for New England abolitionism. In a lengthy 1893 book review titled "Anti-Slavery History and Biography," the reviewer made his view of Lincoln as *the* central figure in antislavery history evident in his call for a "classical" biography of Lincoln. He was dismissive of old-time abolitionists like senator Charles Sumner. It was true that Sumner had had an eventful life, but his "moral temperament" was "fervid" and contributed to his limitations as a practical politician. When he should have acted like a statesman, he spoke like an apostle. Turning away from biography and memoirs to history, the reviewer discussed the first two volumes of James Ford Rhodes's *History of the United States from the Compromise of 1850*. "We have not been very fortunate in our later historians of the anti-slavery struggle," he declared. Rhodes had intended to be even-handed in his account of the coming of the Civil War, believing that "all the right is never on one side and all the wrong on the other." The reviewer, however, regarded Rhodes's work as one-sided, "a superior sort of anti-slavery pamphlet" with "the features of the story . . . thrown hopelessly, almost grotesquely, out of proportion." In contrast, Woodrow Wilson's *Division and Reunion* came in for praise for its interpretation of the war that undermined the historical apparatus abolitionists authors had been laboring to construct for decades. Wilson's acknowledgement of the validity of the South's constitutional position for secession, a position strenuously rejected by abolitionists and most northerners after the war, was singled out as one of the book's major contributions.[19]

With quite a different understanding of the past, abolitionists gathered in 1893 for another reunion in Danvers, Massachusetts, north of Boston. The Danvers Historical Society's decision to hold the meeting stemmed from its conviction that "it is plainly the duty of our societies . . . to do what they can . . . to procure and put on record facts or memories of the conflict which are more or less likely to be forgotten or neglected." Writers of history had not paid antislavery the attention it deserved even though abolitionism was "one of the grandest moral movements in centuries" and had played an important part in the nation's past. The historical society also felt a special obligation to collect historical materials while the "actors" were still alive.[20]

The meeting realized the society's historical objectives, eliciting much "fresh" and "new" material on antislavery and presenting "so vivid a *life-picture* of what it sought to recall." The history that was shared that day was no "formal and labored historical or philosophical disquisition" but a living and popular account that "abounded so much in personal allusions and remembrances." The society hoped to publish the proceedings of the commemoration and sent out a circular in July to see if there was sufficient support to pay for printing a complete account of "the remarkable meeting." Enough subscribers responded to allow publication of the proceedings in two forms: paper bound for $1 and cloth bound for $1.25.[21]

Initially, organizers had conceived of this event as a local one that presumably would reveal much about Danvers in the abolitionist period. Danvers had been an early center of antislavery activity and had enthusiastically supported the Free-Soil and Republican Parties. During a lecture series sponsored by the society, however, substantial interest in holding a reunion that would cast its nets beyond Danvers emerged, and plans for the commemoration became more ambitious. The society sent out hundreds of invitations to abolitionists of all persuasions as well as abolitionist sympathizers both in and outside of New England. A "surprisingly" large throng, including a "most impressive assemblage of the veterans," attended the reunion. The veterans' advanced age suggested that this would be their last such meeting. Indeed, it was too late for some veterans to participate in the gathering at all. Mrs. Putnam and Mrs. Endicott were still alive but senile, "unable, by reason of the infirmities of age, to recall, at the time of the Commemoration, the old anti-slavery days."[22]

Like the AAS reunion planners, organizers of the Danvers meeting believed that abolitionist history could teach significant moral lessons that were particularly relevant to young people. Specifically, they hoped to inspire those born since the Civil War to embrace the cause of human rights and universal brotherhood and to hold fast to high ideals. In contrast to contemporary reforms focusing on issues like the tariff or civil service, the emancipation of the slaves and the conferral of citizenship had represented the highest form of service to humankind and God. Now it was vital to continue efforts to "assuage the hurt of the people of whatever race or color." With abolitionists' work as an example, the younger generation would discover the nobility of devoting ones life to a worthy cause. Publication of the proceedings would hopefully extend the reach of the reunion.[23]

Despite the gathering's forward-looking agenda and the presence of many young people in the audience, many participants felt a powerful sense of nostalgia for a time when they were vigorous and engaged in meaningful work. One of the speakers, George W. Putnam, described himself and the other veterans as "gray-haired and bent with age." "We who still linger on earth," he said, had come to Danvers to exchange their "last greetings." The old voices and familiar language heard during the commemoration so moved the author of the preface to the published proceedings that he could almost imagine himself back in abolitionist meetings "so full of purpose, eloquence and life as to make well nigh all others seem tame and meaningless." The emphasis on persecution was muted by the recollection of youthful activism. Abby Diaz shared with the audience how "delightful" antislavery work had been for a young girl, recalling that she and her friends looked forward to antislavery conventions in the same way that other girls looked forward to balls. "We were so absorbed in anti-slavery work that we had no wish for anything else," she commented. Letters from those unable to come to the commemoration echoed the nostalgia. Wrote Elizabeth Chace, "There is no portion of my life, to which now, in my eighty-seventh year, I revert with more satisfaction." Emily Taylor, a resident of Germantown, Pennsylvania, agreed: "Oh, those were the days to which I look back with enthusiasm—days which were worth living in."[24]

The stage of the town hall was adorned with various reminders of those days. During his speech, Parker Pillsbury pointed to the picture of Samuel J. May and other relics that recalled a distant past that might still have the power to excite the imagination of newcomers. He held up a daguerreo-

The Danvers Historical Society at a meeting in 1893, one of the last gatherings of abolitionists. The advanced age of those pictured shows how much time had passed since these men and women had worked for the emancipation of slavery. The presence of children at the front of the audience is silent testimony to the abolitionists' desire to acquaint the younger generation with the importance of their reform in the nation's history. Parker Pillsbury stands to the right of the central gas lamp shaft, and Lucy Stone is directly above the portrait, right of center. (Courtesy Danvers Archival Center, Danvers, Mass.)

type of British abolitionist George Thompson and a picture of the fugitive Ellen Craft, so light-skinned and beautiful that she escaped by posing as a young white southern master. He called attention to the link of the chain that had manacled the fugitive slave Jerry, whose rescue in Syracuse in 1851 became famous in antislavery circles. The chain signified both the cruelty of slavery and the role of abolitionists in assisting fugitive slaves.[25]

The chain was one of the few specific reminders of the South's involvement in slavery that appeared in the printed proceedings. Speakers whose comments were not recorded may have reminded the audience about the character of the prewar South. The preface suggested as much in its statement that the meeting had clarified for many in the audience the nature of slavery and the slave power. Still, the passage of time seems to have moderated negative evaluations of the South; at least they did not merit publication. The admonition at the end of the preface to "cultivate friendly and harmonious relations between all sections and classes of a once distracted . . . country" also suggested some were willing to let go of some aspects of the past. But not all the veterans agreed.[26]

The Historical Society's desire to compile a suitable historical record shaped the spirit of the meeting and prompted at least one speech that specifically dealt with history. Garrison's son attacked historical works that characterized abolitionists as zealots. He lamented the short memories that assigned all the credit for emancipation to the Republican Party, which had only embraced it because of military necessity. The author of the preface took a broader view, crediting the moral abolitionists for inspiring those who actually freed the slaves: "The great work of the Abolitionists is seen, not alone in their immediate labors, but also . . . in the service of those who finally struck off the chains of the enslaved and made them free." Another speaker acknowledged the divisions between abolitionists. But whatever the perspective, all agreed that the abolitionists had held the dagger to the heart of slavery.[27]

As reform veterans, as so many of the meeting's attendees were, they were aware of and concerned about present political and racial realities. Several speakers pointed to the problematic politics of the day. Parker Pillsbury declared, to somewhat surprising laughter and applause, that there was "no moral conscience in this country in any political party. . . . I believe we have lost all knowledge of what is right and wrong . . . our politics . . . are the . . . matters of convenience." African American George T. Downing made it clear that the Republicans had abandoned the moral high ground. But he had not lost hope. He believed that the grown children of abolitionists who were moving into the Democratic Party, which was once "deeply dyed in wrong," might transform it into the party of reform ready to defend equality before the law and become the main support for other "just reforms."[28]

Downing, a free black man, took on the responsibility of speaking for former slaves. While he expressed their gratitude, he reminded the audience that their work had not ended with the elimination of slavery. He read the constitution of the AAS, recalling not the society's beginnings but its unrealized goals. In accepting the constitution, Downing charged, abolitionists had pledged themselves to end slavery and "to aid in passing the Freedmen along and upward on the line of manhood and elevated citizenship without which attainment he is not in reality free." These ends had not yet been achieved, as many abolitionists who had not attended the meeting agreed in their letters written to be shared with the audience. The Rev. Thomas Stone, for example, argued that the violence and fraud that had robbed southern freedmen of their political rights showed that the spirit of slavery was alive and well in the South, and he urged the audience to gird for a new conflict. Moral agitation to arouse the public conscience was as necessary in 1893 as ever. Everyone had a duty to do as much to deepen "indignation" so that it would ultimately reach the conscience of the "oppressor." Ednah Cheyney characterized the prejudice against blacks as inhuman, a judgment with which Dr. James C. Jackson agreed. "We have not yet paid our debt" to former slaves, Cheyney observed.[29]

Charles Whipple wrote a blistering letter that highlighted not only ongoing racial brutality in the South but also the misrepresentation of abolitionists and blacks in contemporary culture. He identified periodical literature as the site for fabrications about the past and present. Calling the *North American Review* a proslavery journal, he singled out an article that defended lynching by claiming that black assaults on white women were increasing. Whipple rejected the claim and urged the audience to read "The Burning of Negroes in the South," an article that appeared in *Arena*. Abolitionists could not sit back and let racist propaganda pass unchallenged. "It is still needful to keep an eye on those manifestations and to answer such of them as are worth answering," he wrote. But Whipple's own efforts suggested how hard it was to contest the views appearing in influential monthly magazines. Whipple had written a letter to the *North American Review* refuting the offending article, but the journal's editor had refused to publish Whipple's letter.[30]

At one time, Whipple wrote, Oliver Johnson and Samuel May had acted as watchdogs for the claims made in the periodicals. But Johnson was dead and May was elderly. "The field is large," Whipple stated, "and many more reapers are needed." Ednah Cheyney agreed, reminding her audience that the day had not yet arrived when abolitionists could sit back and relax. The permanence of their achievements was threatened, but too many of those in Danvers were too old to heed the calls to action.[31]

The documents that detail these anniversary meetings provide poignant insights into the minds and hearts of the old abolitionists. They attest to the power of collective ties and ritual events and to the desire to experience them again even for a few brief hours. They reveal the tension between the belief that the accomplishments of the movement had been important, not just to abolitionists but to the nation, and a terrible recognition that achievements had been undercut by subsequent events and by the persistence of race prejudice. But they also suggest that abolitionists refused to move to the margins of culture or memory while any of them were still alive.

CHAPTER 5

The Remembrance
Is Like a Dream

REMINISCENCES OF THE 1890S

Surviving abolitionists who had hoped to eliminate both slavery and racial prejudice and also to provide free blacks with civil rights must have found the 1890s a depressing decade.[1] Even the words that once signified deep moral and racial commitments were losing old meanings. *Century*'s editor hailed civil service reformers as modern abolitionists who had created a new emancipation proclamation freeing "political slaves." The comparison diminished the meaning and achievements of emancipation.[2]

Black slavery was gone, it was true. But without land, many black sharecroppers were trapped in a cycle of debt and poverty that made a mockery of their freedom. Starting with Mississippi in 1890, southern states ended any possibility of interracial political coalitions by systematically stripping African American men of the political rights that some abolitionists had once argued could never be taken from them. Charles Levermore, writing for *New England Magazine*, found "infractions" of black voting rights "immoral" but could only wonder what "we, the kinsmen and friends of John Brown, Wendell Phillips, and William Lloyd Garrison" could "say to those who spurn such laws." With the blessing of the Supreme Court's 1896 decision *Plessy v. Ferguson*, a system of legal segregation was being put in place throughout the South. Although violence against freed people was nothing new, it reached a new level of ferociousness. In 1892 alone, 155 blacks were lynched. Protesting against racial violence that year, the *American Missionary* argued that every man deserved a fair trial and legal protection against the rage of a vindictive mob. The outrages in the South were "a disgrace to our civilization and a crime against nineteenth century enlightenment." The entire nation should be concerned, the magazine suggested, especially since newspapers had provided the public with ample information about the problem.[3]

Some northerners clearly were distressed. In 1894, Faneuil Hall, once the scene of so many abolitionist gatherings, now hosted a large meeting with William Lloyd Garrison Jr. as one of the principal speakers. It resulted in the founding of the Massachusetts Anti-Lynching Society. A few years later, a particularly gruesome Georgia lynching witnessed by thousands of people sparked other mass protest meetings in the North. But these efforts had little impact on the South. As the editor of *Century* observed, southern lawlessness demonstrated that southern law gave way to southern public opinion.[4]

While many northerners denounced the violence, they were hardly prepared to intervene once again in southern racial affairs. Of course, abolitionists had always argued that race prejudice was a northern as well as a southern phenomenon. In 1892, the proposed bill that would have used federal power to protect black voting rights failed, and the discussion of black political rights at the level of national politics would not be resumed for decades. As the article "When Slavery Went out of Politics," published in *Scribner's* in 1895, pointed out, the period of intense political debate over the treatment of freed people had ended, and these concerns had "gradually faded from the view of the politicians." The Republican Party platform the following year neglected to include its usual support for the use of military force to defend black suffrage, thus clarifying the point that the party had little interest in southern blacks. Determined to defeat William Jennings Bryan, the presidential candidate of both the Populists and the Democrats, Republicans appealed to the South by embracing reconciliation and depicting the Civil War as a disaster. In the last years of the decade, the debate over imperialism revealed widespread racist assumptions with both imperialists and anti-imperialists indulging in antiblack rhetoric to justify their positions.[5]

Taking advantage of favorable postage rates and the expansion of advertising, the monthly magazines, especially *Century*, *Harper's*, and *Scribner's*, played an important role in reinforcing views of black inferiority and in justifying southern racial policy in the 1890s. *Century*, defining its mission as leading public opinion rather than reflecting it, took pride in presenting a national rather than a sectional perspective. Its fiction and nonfiction pieces presented a range of views about black people and the southern question. The editor, Richard Watson Gilder (or his chosen essayists), attacked lynching in several "Topics of the Times" columns, while a number of letter writers praised blacks' progress and their interest in education and supported higher education for blacks. Thomas Wentworth Higginson's account of his black troops during the Civil War portrayed them as intensely human and eager for freedom. Articles on Union generals and the "cause" for which Lincoln fought supposedly contributed to a balanced content.[6]

But the volume of material appearing in *Century* that presented a southern point of view diminished the impact of such articles. The editors valued

REMINISCENCES OF THE 1890S

the "brilliant" group of New South writers who contributed stories to the magazine that emphasized black inferiority, whereas they informed the African American writer Charles Chesnutt that his black characters were too brutal and serious to interest readers. The pages of *Century* were filled with fictional blacks whose eagerness to take care of former masters and mistresses implicitly challenged abolitionists' view of slavery and the necessity for emancipation. Accepting their subordinate status in southern society, these loyal blacks had little interest in freedom and none in equality. In what represented the height of wishful thinking, one story depicted a former slave, Travis, paying off all the debts of the old plantation. "I had been witness, even a recipient, of the old affectionateness of slaves continuing unhurt by the war and emancipation," concludes the narrator; "but now . . . I felt I had been in the presence of a majesty." The main character in another story is more pitiful than majestic, but she also proves her moral worth by caring for frail white women, suffering "aches . . . frets . . . and nervousness" in the postwar South.[7]

As one letter writer noted regretfully, however, "the negro of the antebellum days, with all of his picturesque characteristics . . . is rapidly becoming a thing of the past." The modern black certainly lacked "picturesque" qualities, at least as depicted in *Century*'s pages. "'Er nigger's boun'ter be er nigger,'" a woman points out in one tale. "'You kin whitewash him . . . an'put broad clorf an'er b'iled shirt on him, but . . . he's boun'ter be er nigger.'" Such a perspective provided the dramatic power behind an 1891 story titled "Was It an Exceptional Case?" The main female character, Madeline, grew up in postwar Georgia, and, like most southern heroines is refined, pure, and tender. She is also strongly prejudiced against freed blacks. Despite her racial views, Madeline falls in love with a visiting northern abolitionist. Shortly before their marriage, she discovers that her birth mother had been a slave and that she is not the southern white lady she had thought herself to be. Her foster mother, fearful that the birth "mother's blood would betray itself in some coarse or degraded taste," had taught Madeline to regard blacks as inferior and to view social separation as essential. Madeline's discovery of her heritage fills her with shame and brings on "strange visions" of African jungles and slaves. Although discovering the truth of his fiancée's background makes no difference to her lover, who is ready to marry her at once and to return to the North, Madeline feels too unworthy to accept his offer. In striking contrast to an antislavery novella with a similar plot that appeared in the *National Anti-Slavery Standard* in 1860 that ends with the marriage of the abolitionist and the racially mixed heroine, this story suggested that no matter how white the skin, any black ancestry demanded social separation. Thus Madeline disappears, and the union is averted. Years later, after Madeline's death, her abolitionist lover discovers that she had become a Catholic nun and had devoted her life to teaching in a black school in New Orleans. For this decision to cast her lot with her own race she could be admired.[8]

Stories also ridiculed the notion of black progress, showing that the fruits of freedom actually dragged black men and women down. In one story, the more the former slave Rory masters reading and writing, the more his "barbaric" nature comes to the surface. Eventually literacy turns him not into an educated man but a morose reticent savage. In his story "Captain Jerry," Harry Stillwell Edward, editor of the *Macon (Georgia) Telegraph*, deflated the notion that blacks possessed the military capabilities or courage of their white counterparts, North or South, and, by implication, questioned blacks' wartime service. Captain Jerry, who wants to prove that white people are wrong to believe that blacks could not fight, is given a chance to demonstrate his courage in battle, but he turns out to be a colossal coward. While other journals devoted less space to negative characterizations of freed people, their material often complemented the perspectives presented in *Century*. As a writer for the *New Englander and Yale Review* acidly observed in 1892, the black man had been thrust into "the miserable fiction of liberty which he has to-day, in which he has neither the intelligence to prize, nor the power to use, a freeman's ballot."[9]

The possibility that blacks appreciated or understood the meaning of emancipation was ridiculed in "The Gum Swamp Debate." The debate focused on the question of whether "de pen" was more powerful than "de powder." The dialect, always a feature in these stories and the source of much of their humor, reinforced the idea of black inferiority. Here, one of the characters, Ike Peterson, a man with a little schooling, announces that he wants "all you niggers what never read nuthin' to git dese facts fum me." His "facts" about emancipation are comical: "Mr. Linkum tuk er pen an' writ down dese two lines" on the back page of a spelling book. "'Nigges es free from terday.'" Then, according to Ike, Lincoln nailed the paper to the courthouse. His debating opponent successfully refutes that view, saying that freedom had not come for eleven years and that it had been necessary to kill Yanks and have Yanks kill all the black folk's whites first.[10]

The journals also featured articles about Africa that complemented such characterizations of American blacks. In a piece for *Century* titled "The Story of the Development of Africa," the explorer, Henry B. Stanley, described African history in these terms: "Murder in every conceivable shape rioted throughout these territories. Naked and bestial [blacks] had lived from prehistoric times." Writing for *Scribner's*, Stanley pointed out that one of the great positive results of the imperial partition of Africa was the damage done to the internal slave trade. The control of the superior European powers, like that of the white American slaveholder, represented for black people a step along the road to civilization, a step that apparently blacks were unable to make without white guidance.[11]

While editors did denounce southern lynching, the sentimental pictures of the old southern elite more than counterbalanced the criticism. It was hard to imagine any of these harmless figures indulging in violence. If the stories were to be believed, slaveholders had been paragons of virtue and fond of and helpful to their slaves. In fact, one article, written by an author of many religious books, accused English and New England merchants for introducing slavery and then credited southern mistresses indirectly for black citizenship. The women had so successfully encouraged the moral and intellectual development of their black slaves that the U.S. government determined that they were ready for citizenship![12]

The postwar world brought many changes but apparently little white resentment. Despite the new and heavy burden of domestic work, six southern women interviewed for an article in *Century* expressed the New South position that their region was better off without slavery. Emancipation represented a necessary and positive alteration in southern life, especially for whites. Rather than spurning labor, white men now embraced industrial and intellectual work. These vigorous men of the New South, however, were curiously absent from the stories published in other monthlies. Instead, short fiction depicted southern gentlemen who remained relatively aloof from the world of work. For example, although the main character of "A Helping Hand" assists former slaves in getting started on his land, other white men are less industrious. Major Wilby confides to the reader, "I walk about the plantation, and I sit and read much of my time, mainly about the war." In another story, Colonel Carter proves unable to navigate postwar New York.[13]

One of Major Wilby's favorite Civil War figures is Robert E. Lee whom he regards as a "splendid" fellow. He claims to have read everything on the war from both northern and southern perspectives. Like so many fictional and real southerners, Wilby concludes that southerners had given northerners "a good tussle, but they were too many for us."[14]

Century's Civil War series that began in the mid-1880s explored the military character of that "tussle," demonstrating that all combatants had been exemplary warriors. The general editor, Richard Watson Gilder, intended the series to undermine any remaining sectional animosity. Like the authors of fiction and articles appearing in the 1890s, Gilder believed that presenting nonjudgmental and positive depictions of both regions would have beneficial effects. "If the North can see the heart of the South, and the South of the North's," he declared, "they will love each other as never before!" Those who refused the reconciliation *Century* promoted were symbolized by the repulsive, fat, cigar-smoking politician in "A Decoration Day Revery." Wearing a Grand Army of the Republic button, although he had never seen combat, this piece of "scum" is "untiring" in his attacks on the South and on the soldiers who had fought for the Confederacy.[15]

The work of university-trained historians supported the conciliatory mood of the monthlies. The "scientific" analyses of the coming of the Civil War, produced by a new generation of historians, were rejecting the old theories that slavery was the sole cause of war or that the South was solely responsible for the conflict. While journals only addressed the question of causation indirectly, John Coleman Adams, a Universalist minister and the author of "Lincoln's Place in History," was not hesitant to tackle the issue head-on. Despite what many had argued over the years, he suggested that neither states' rights nor the call for emancipation had precipitated the conflict. Rather, the South had placed the Union in peril by revolting against it, and Lincoln's genius lay in realizing that the preservation of the Union was the war's main issue. "The abolition of slavery," which would have happened eventually, "was only an incident of war," the author concluded, "and not the main one." While he conceded that readers might be shocked to learn that Lincoln's greatest achievement was saving the Union rather than emancipation, he was confident that time would prove his interpretation correct.[16]

Such a revision was evident in the rehabilitation of figures like Daniel Webster, who had been villainized for his role in the Compromise of 1850. Webster's famous speech supporting the compromise "was exactly on the line of his life-work for union and nationality," one article declared. While Webster's reputation had suffered for his stand, "in clearness and consistency of purpose he stood alone."[17]

Like fiction, these explanations of the past challenged the narrative abolitionist authors had been constructing for decades. They had insisted that southern slavery had caused the war and that emancipation had been the war's most noble triumph. Both ideas were now rejected. No longer could abolitionists appear as central figures in a historical explanation of the coming of the war. At best they were irrelevant; at worst they had had a disastrous impact on events. Reconstruction, given the true nature of black people, had proven to be a ghastly mistake. Here were the outlines of what

Americans were coming to accept as the truth of the great events of war and peace. The new national memory smoothed over any lingering guilt about slavery and allowed Americans to avoid acknowledging its horrors. As one historian has noted, slavery "is an historical evil that the United States has never properly acknowledged or atoned for."[18]

Abolitionists still had their defenders in the monthlies, with New England–based magazines most willing to carry articles about regional worthies. *New England Magazine*, recognizing that, with time, a "certain indifference" to antebellum events and actors had arisen, published pieces on Lydia Maria Child, Samuel May, and John Whittier. Without these "staunch, indomitable characters," the author of one article suggested, "we might still hear the groan of the slave." The magazine also covered the activities of Boston's Old South Historical Society, which had devoted its winter and summer lecture series to the antislavery struggle. It also reported that the historical society had organized a remarkably successful "pilgrimage" to Whittier's home and "haunts" north of Boston in 1898. More than 600 young people had made the trip. Tourism and abolitionist landmarks were clearly compatible.[19]

Atlantic Monthly, a magazine that spoke to a broader northern audience than *New England Magazine*, also published numerous articles that touched upon the abolitionists. As one *Atlantic* article pointed out, it was now possible to discuss abolitionism without succumbing to the tendency to vilify abolitionists, as had been the case before the war, or idolizing them, as had been common when emancipation was so "suddenly accomplished" (the perspective *New England Magazine* writers usually adopted). The magazine presented a mixed picture of the reformers. One author admired the positive accomplishments of political abolitionists, whom he believed had not received adequate recognition. He suggested that the "typical" abolitionist was not "the agitator" like Garrison, who believed that the Constitution was a compact with hell, but the "practical" abolitionist who worked through politics. For another writer contrasting antislavery idealism with the materialism of the present age, the Garrisonians were heroes. Another author more ambiguously described abolitionists as driven by "the primary and unreasoning passion of pity" that "afforded the purest indulgence in human feeling that was ever offered to men." The author J. T. Trowbridge, who discussed his two antislavery novels in an article for the *Atlantic*, reflected the view that abolitionists had transgressed boundaries by calling himself an antislavery fanatic. He described the motivation for his first book as "a burning desire to pour out in some channel the feelings which, long suppressed had been roused to a high pitch."[20]

Abolitionists also appeared in fiction. A story serialized in *Scribner's* in 1893 by the well-known novelist Harold Frederic cast Farmer Beech, a Copperhead, as its main character. Starting before the war, the narrative emphasizes Beech's understanding of abolitionists as wicked "men, who desired to establish negro sovereignty . . . and to compel each white girl to marry a black man." The story gives no reason to fault Beech's original assessment, and while events taking place during the war do not support Beech's characterization, they do prove him generally right. The neighborhood abolitionists shun Beech, assault his Irish farmhand, try to prevent him from voting, and eventually set his house on fire. The leading local abolitionist, "the tiresome fanatic of the 'fifties," is so busy being "the inspired prophet of the '6os" that he allows his own farm to run down. As the story concludes, the local squire deplores the "thoughtless elements of the community," while the leading abolitionist's daughter suggests that something is wrong when neighbors act so violently. All of them know that Farmer Beech is actually the best man among them. As Beach affirms his belief in the Republic, the sun shining on the melting snow makes "his face to shine as if from an inner radiance."[21]

"Abolitionists and Prohibitionists; or, Moral Reform Embarrassed by Ultra-ism," published in an 1892 issue of the *New Englander and Yale Review*, criticized abolitionists in no uncertain terms. The abolitionists' single-minded insistence that slavery was a sin had taken the question out of the realm of practical statesmanship, where it could have eventually been settled amicably, and into the realm of "passion" and "fury." "The so-called abolitionists . . . pushed their schemes with a destructive violence," attracting an assortment of cranks and "infidels" to their cause. While the author's emphasis on passion and venom was characteristic of many earlier attacks on Garrisonians, he did not spare political abolitionists. While some had praised political abolitionists for their pragmatism, he condemned them for generating sectional strife by forcing the question of slavery into politics. The author found it astounding that the abolitionists, having helped precipitate a bloody war, had had the temerity to pose as "martyr-champions."

Saddling the abolitionists and southern fire-eaters with the responsibility for war, the article made the amazing claim that the conflict had been entirely unnecessary. The vast majority of northerners had opposed slavery, according to the author, and the northern clergy, united in their commitment to resolving the problem peacefully, would eventually have terminated slavery through the exercise of its moral power. In the end, although emancipation had been only an incidental result of the war, the credit for it lay with Lincoln and the genuine reformers, not with the abolitionists.

The sins of the abolitionists did not end with emancipation. The author asked what abolitionists had done after emancipation to educate and Christianize the freed people. He concluded not only that the northern churches had been responsible for working with the former slaves but also that if the abolitionists had played a more active role in the South, the condition of the freed people would have actually been worse than it had been under slavery.[22]

While the surviving abolitionists may not have scoured the monthlies for such articles, they had to have been aware of the general indifference to their cause and the extreme statements that were being made about the character of slavery, the necessity for the war, and the country's moral obligation to black people. Nor could they ignore the impact of time. In fact, the fear that time would erase the memory of their reform and their own contributions to it had long motivated abolitionists to write and publish their recollections. By the 1890s, even once-potent abolitionist symbols and rallying cries seemed to have lost their power, as the fiction in the monthlies attested. The relics of the past, like the slave auction block, one short story declared, no longer aroused emotions. Another tale about an illegal slaver picking up captives from Africa was an adventure story with no hint of moral disapproval of the slave trade. Those who came across James Russell Lowell's poem "The Present Crisis," the "battle hymn" of emancipation that once had appealed "to deepest, more fervent sentiment," escaped its spell. "So crowded is the interval with engrossing events," one writer observed, that the present generation could scarcely understand how the poem "dwelt in the heart of hearts of the reading men of the time" and how it had inspired bravery in battle.[23]

In an article discussing the "curiously sharp line" separating Civil War veterans from younger men, the editor of *Scribner's* focused on the difficulties former soldiers faced when they tried to communicate the reality of their experiences to those who had not fought in the war. Drawing a distinction between "the historic and the reminiscent point of view," he suggested that veterans' desire to convey the reality of the war years encouraged a sense of excess. "There will always seem to [be] . . . something fanatical in your way of looking at the past," the editor believed. If this were true for Civil War veterans, how much truer it was for veteran abolitionists.[24]

Still, a few abolitionists struggled against the tides of cultural indifference, forgetfulness, and even hostility. Several composed and published their recollections in the 1890s. Frederick Douglass concluded his autobiography, now less interested in his own exploits than in exposing the changing racial climate in the country. Calvin Fairbank, revisiting the days of fugitive slaves, insisted that northerners had had the moral duty to assist those escaping slavery and now should not forget the former slaves. Elizabeth Buffum Chace, Sarah Southwick, and Lucy Colman remembered what it had been like as women laboring for the cause, and like Calvin Fairbank and Aaron Powell, who also wrote during that decade, Chace and Colman used their narratives to suggest the need to confront the racial prejudice that flourished so malignantly. While the reach of these reminiscences was quite limited, their authors challenged the view that their reform had been unimportant or that it was desirable to bow to the racism of their day. They also moved away from the quarrelsome stance of the previous decade and smoothed over the divisions among abolitionists that writers in the previous decade had highlighted.

Of all the antislavery reminiscences appearing during the 1890s, Frederick Douglass's final installment of *Life and Times of Frederick Douglass* most directly confronted the changing cultural climate and the deteriorating situation of southern blacks. Although he explained that he had continued his narrative because "friends and publisher" thought it best that he should finish the story of his own life, he actually had approached the publishers in the summer of 1891 to see if a new edition was planned. If there was one planned, he wanted to add additional material. The new text came to just over 100 printed pages.[25]

While Douglass devoted some of the autobiography to the offices he had held in the decade since he published *Life and Times* and the European trip he and his new wife had made, the dominating theme of the reminiscences was that "the free, are yet oppressed and are in as much need of an advocate as before they were set free." The fundamental problem was American racism, although time and forgetfulness had also played a role in the deteriorating position of former slaves. As the Civil War receded into the past, people forgot the contributions blacks had made to victory: "The fading effects of time upon the national mind, and the growing affection of the loyal nation for the late rebels, will, on the page of our national history, obscure the Negro's part."[26]

Douglass detailed how southerners, whom he pointedly characterized as rebels, terrorized southern blacks, returned to Congress as conquerors, and moved toward political "ascendancy." The language Douglass used and the pattern of southern power he sketched out surely were meant to remind readers of past history. Once again, the "language of a sickly conciliation" permeated national politics. The standard-bearer of morality, the Republican Party, had decayed. Although Douglass explained that he had not shifted his political allegiances (as Julian and Swisshelm had done), he argued that the party's loss of moral focus lay at the basis of its electoral defeats. Implicitly, he was calling upon the party to return to its roots.[27]

Douglass also reflected upon the ways in which abolitionists had depicted themselves and their movement during the previous decade. His own discussion of differences among abolitionists in the second part of his autobiography had been muted, although other writers had been fiery in their rejection of alternative approaches to ending slavery. Douglass must have been concerned that in a time when few acknowledged the antislavery struggle as the "truly great moral conflict" of the century, abolitionists themselves seemed guilty of "prejudice, bigotry, and partiality." He attempted to explain the bitterness and to smooth over differences. Suggesting that the antislavery movement was too recent to allow an "impartial" history, Douglass claimed that it was not surprising that the old "warriors" sometimes lost perspective. Regional efforts also prevented abolitionists from understanding the utility of strategies popular elsewhere. Such squabbling obscured the larger point that both political and moral abolitionism had played a vital part in bringing the end to slavery. "As one of those whose bonds have been broken," Douglass wrote, "I cannot see without pain an attempt to disparage and undervalue any man's work in this cause."[28]

Douglass had a Boston publisher to handle the final version of his autobiography. Although the sales of his book had been lackluster during the 1880s, De Wolfe, Fiske and Company thought that Douglass's appointment as minister to Haiti might revive public interest in his life story. They bought the plates as well as the remaining unsold copies of *Life and Times* from Parks Publishing Company in a trade sale and agreed to enlarge the book for a new edition. Once again, Douglass was unhappy with the results. When he received his first copy, he wrote that he was "sorry to have to say that I have looked into it with less satisfaction than I had hoped. It is not such a work as I had hoped for from a Boston Publishing House." In fact, he found it inferior to the Parks edition. The paper was not of good quality, the binding "slovenly" and unattractive. He hoped that the publisher would correct such errors, but it may be that De Wolfe, Fiske and Company did not want to spend too much money on the book.[29]

The publishers did send out review copies of the book, which received some "flattering" notices. But, as had been true the previous decade, sales were mediocre; only 399 copies were sold by January 1895. "We must confess that we were very much disappointed," the publishers revealed to Douglass's widow that year. It is likely that Douglass himself was not satisfied with the reaction to the book. One newspaper reviewer thought the book presented a strong argument for the "manhood and the capacity of the col-

ored man." But Douglass's emphasis on persistent racism and the system-
atic denial of southern blacks' civil rights elicited only a tepid response. "It
is true they have not yet reached the enjoyment of all the rights guaranteed
them by the Constitution," wrote the reviewer; "but this will come."[30]

Like Douglass, other abolitionists also updated their life stories in the
1890s. Fugitive tales in particular still had a certain attraction. Laura Haviland, described by an attendee of the Centennial as "still full of zeal for
righteousness and liberty," reissued her book with new material on her reform commitments in the 1890s, while Coffin's *Reminiscences* was reprinted
in 1899. These new editions of Haviland's and Coffin's recollections were
one indication that midwesterners had embraced the history of the Underground Railroad. Many accounts of participation in the underground network were appearing in midwestern newspapers and county histories, and
interest in the subject was evident in the enthusiastic response to Professor
Wilbur Siebert's project of collecting Underground Railroad materials. But
the lukewarm response to Calvin Fairbank's *During Slavery Times*, published
in Chicago in 1890, suggests that the topic did not automatically attract
readers. Fairbank's perspective challenged the self-satisfied popular reminiscences that implied that the problems of racism had disappeared.[31]

Fairbank's own history was exciting enough. Fairbank was a Methodist
minister who had discovered early in life that slavery was the "vilest evil
. . . [that] ever existed." Having concluded that the Constitution was an
antislavery document and that slavery was against the law, he embarked on
a career of helping fugitives escape from the Upper South. He carried off
some thrilling rescues and was twice jailed in Kentucky for a total of seven-
teen years. Freed during the war, he traveled extensively to speak about his
prison experiences, apparently to great acclaim. When he visited Washington D.C., he even preached to Lincoln and members of his cabinet.[32]

Why had he not written his reminiscences when interest in his story was
high? As Fairbank explained apologetically in his preface, prison had ruined
his health and, although it apparently had not interfered with his speaking
tour, it had prevented him from making a timely start on recording his
story. Then books about the war "flooded" the market. Inability to pay for
the costs of publication further delayed him. And like other antislavery authors (and many writers during the Gilded Age), he just did not know when
to stop writing. The first draft of his book reached 1,200 handwritten pages,
the equivalent of 500 printed pages. "Every one considered it too long,"
and he cut the manuscript to the length that he believed "could be safely
published." But, as was the experience of other writers during this period,
"men of experience, in order to avoid the risk of financial failure, advised

condensation." It seems as if a New York clergyman took the project in hand, ending up with a book of 207 pages.[33]

Fairbank hoped to increase the attractiveness of his book by asking Laura Haviland to provide her account of his "martyrdom." She had helped him out a few years earlier when he found himself stranded in Ohio without enough money to return home to New York State. In her usual vigorous fashion, she had solved his problem by raising $84 from black residents of Chicago to get him home. Her contribution concluded the narrative. She clearly realized both the financial and ideological imperatives that had spurred Fairbank to offer his life story to the public. "I hope and trust this little sketch of Rev. Calvin Fairbank's thrilling life will find an abundant sale," she wrote, "to aid him now in his broken-down, destitute, infirm old age of seventy-four years." Oddly enough, Fairbank chose to end his book with Haviland's reference to infirmity and destitution rather than his own final sentences assuring readers that "my life, so far, has been a success. . . . 'I have fought a good fight. . . . I have kept the faith. Henceforth there is laid up for me a crown of righteousness.'" Perhaps he was reluctant to modify this triumphant interpretation of his own life and work, or perhaps he did not want to seem to be begging for readers' sympathies and dollars. But Haviland's words, hinting at the general disinterest in former antislavery heroes and their descent into poverty and old age, introduced a dose of reality into his story.[34]

Because *During Slavery Times* was relatively short, its points were clear and unequivocal. Fairbank's reference to the "AFRICO-AMERICAN's War" rather than the Civil War neatly made his point about the causes and goal of the conflict. His dedication, "To the Liberty Guard, and Their Successors, Who Recognize 'The Fatherhood of God, and the Brotherhood of Men,'" captured his characterization of abolitionism. At a time when abolitionists' efforts were being repudiated as irrelevant or destructive, Fairbank insisted on the righteousness and patriotism of his endeavors to help slaves escape from the South. Others engaged in the same activity appeared as heroes, apostles of liberty, and holy laborers "for humanity against oppression." Admiring thumbnail sketches of abolitionists like William Lloyd Garrison, Gerritt Smith, Wendell Phillips, Frederick Douglass, and Parker Pillsbury made it clear that these eastern abolitionists "all acted in harmony against the pro-slavery idea." Their arguments against the institution revealed them as "the strongest, most learned and thoroughly-read men and women in the land."[35]

Fairbank's dedication, with its reference to the successors of the original Liberty Guard, also communicated Fairbank's conviction of the necessity of a continued commitment to former slaves. At one point in the evolution of his book, Fairbank had ended his story in 1865 with the statement that "there is no need to dwell upon my continued work for the good of the Africo-American people." He apparently had changed his mind about the need to highlight a steady commitment to freed people. His appendix contained scattered information about his later life and his labor "for the good of the Africo-American people" and their ongoing and pressing needs. He also included his poem, "The Soldier's Award," that posed the critical questions facing Americans: Should "liberty be left but a name?" Should "the [southern] foeman" enter where "the patriot waited of yore?" The last stanzas of the poem rejected reconciliation and called for a defense of an inclusive freedom: "God forbid that the miscreant arm / That periled our flag on that day— / Nor a traitor's hand / Of the rebel band / Shall guard the doors of this sacred land, / Or bear her glory away. / But the hero—the citizen leal / Keeps vigils from sun to the sea; / . . . And our aegis of power be borne by the hand / Of loyalty, faithful and free."[36]

Fairbank's depiction of former foes and their relations with their slaves in his autobiography were, from one perspective, nothing new. But Fairbank seems to have been responding both to the benign characterizations of slave owners that were so common in 1890s and to the fact that old symbols and themes appeared to have lost their dramatic impact. He chose his white characters carefully, adding the details that still might have the power to shock the reader and call into question the depictions of the genial master appearing in fiction. In a jarring revelation, Fairbank described one owner who had indulged in sexual relations first with one woman, and then with her daughter, granddaughter, great-granddaughter, and great-great-granddaughter. In other anecdotes, two slaveholders failed to recognize their fugitive slaves when they were "disguised" in genteel clothing, mistaking one for a lady and the other for a young southern gentleman. So much for the intimate knowledge slave owners supposedly had of their slaves. The master of the male slave actually exchanged some words with his slave, who, of course, spoke in dialect. But as Fairbank reminded the reader, despite the belief that dialect signaled the debased character of blacks, "most [white] Southern people" spoke "with the same provincialism—anent-dialect and tone" as their slaves.[37]

Of all the incidents designed to compel the reader's attention, the description of the slave auction was surely the most effective. It was just this symbol of the horrors of slavery that some feared no longer elicited feelings of shock and disapproval. Fairbank took great care in dramatizing his scene. Eliza, the young woman to be sold, was not only "accomplished," "beautiful," and the daughter of her master but "only one sixty-fourth African." How Fairbank came up with this figure was unclear, but the fraction had the potential of arousing a stronger reaction from the reader than that elicited by the usual abolitionist comment that a slave was "virtually" white. The auction itself attracted 2,000 people, another astonishing figure. The attendees represented "the wealth and culture" of cities ranging from Boston and New York to New Orleans and Louisville. To make the story more compelling and to emphasize the horror of the slave auction, Fairbank explained that the auctioneer attempted to attract high bids by emphasizing Eliza's suitability as "a mistress for any gentleman" in "the most insinuating and vile manner, outraging human decency." As the bidding continued, "the fiend" unbuttoned the top of her dress, crying out, "'Who is going to lose such a chance as this? Here is a girl fit to be the mistress of a king!'" Even southerners in the crowd were ashamed. But worse was yet to come. A "scene [followed] at which civilization blushed, and angels wept, and the human heart sickened and turned away." The auctioneer raised her skirts, slapped her "white flesh" and cried out for further bids. It was an "exhibition of a beautiful, helpless Caucasian girl," Fairbank explained, amidst "the shambles of Republican America." No matter what a white female reader might think of slavery, such a depiction was sure to shock.[38]

Fairbank's part in the auction was a triumphant one. Having raised over $2,200 from antislavery friends, he made the winning bid of $1,485 and presented Eliza with her freedom. His role in this story was consistent with the picture he painted of himself as resourceful, brave, and energetic. The accounts of the rescues included in the book typically showed Fairbank initiating a rescue that the slave was unable to carry off on his or her own. Sam Johnson, the first slave Fairbank helped escape, established the pattern. When Fairbank encountered Johnson, he was walking along the Ohio River singing. Fairbank asked him why he didn't run away, and when Johnson answered that he did not know where to go, Fairbank told him that he could show him. Johnson was uncertain, but Fairbank "argued the case" and engineered his escape.[39]

While Fairbank claimed the credit for liberating slaves, he did not indulge in the racial stereotyping so common in the 1890s. It is true that he showed Sam Johnson shuffling "a jig upon free frozen soil" and recalled that when he met up with Johnson twelve years later, he "danced about in glee." But these slaves were not cheerful "darkies" or loving servants but fully human men and women eager for and capable of independence. John Hamilton thirsted for freedom. Lewis Hayden, asked why he wanted to be free, replied, "'Because I'm a man.'" And Fairbank also made clear that these fugitives were very capable of living in freedom. When he visited Sam Johnson, he found that he owned a "good farm well improved and stocked" and that his family "were well educated and promising." Others had similar stories of success, and one even "'shouldered arms' for the Union."[40]

Many of the fugitives Fairbank chose to write about in the autobiography were light-skinned or almost white. One could see Fairbank's fascination with light-skinned slaves as merely a repetition of an old pattern established by abolitionist writers, but in the context of southern segregation, his choices called into question the idea of any definitive color line based on ancestry. The "color line" was a flawed idea and, in fact, permeable. Eliza, the woman so humiliated at the slave auction, later married a white man, and only a few friends and her husband realized that she had been a slave. Quite unlike the heroine of "Was It an Exceptional Case?," Eliza had no difficulty in filling a position "of honor and usefulness in [white] society." Other examples diminished the importance of a bloodline and suggested the brotherhood of man Fairbank proclaimed in the dedication. One of Fairbank's fellow prisoners in jail was "to all intents and purposes, white, though of African extraction." While other abolitionists had emphasized the fugitive Ellen Craft's whiteness, Fairbank described her as "just a dark-skinned women, though of African extraction."

Despite the extensive cutting of his manuscript, Fairbank included an account of "one of the most extraordinary meetings that come to mortals during a lifetime." The meeting was held to protest segregation on Philadelphia streetcars, and Fairbank quoted approvingly from the eloquent speech made by Robert Purvis questioning the policy of segregation in public transport.[41]

A significant portion of the book covered Fairbank's arrests, trials, and prison experiences. He considered the prison sentences and the carefully noted 1,003 floggings as the basis of his claim of martyrdom for "the American Slave." While there was little doubt that he suffered for his cause, his narrative glossed over the arrests for aiding fugitives and trials. The details would have weakened the heroic self-image he was trying to create. Negligence contributed to both his arrests, while, despite the claim that there was no legitimate evidence against him during his first trial, he actually pleaded guilty and, more astonishingly, renounced his abolitionist beliefs. In another serious omission, Fairbank did not mention that the former slave Lewis Hayden had actually paid a considerable sum to obtain Fairbank's pardon and release from prison.[42]

By the time Fairbank published his book, it is likely that few remembered what had happened at the trials so many years earlier or were very interested in learning about Fairbank's exploits, even though the *Chicago Tribune* plugged the book as a story that would "stir the blood" and ran an excerpt in the paper in January 1893. Who paid for publishing his manuscript, how many copies were printed, and how they were sold is unknown. The Patriotic Publishing Company and the printer, R. R. McCabe, who produced the book, specialized in religious works and perhaps did not have an appropriate way to distribute it. Fairbank, who was living in New York State and in poor health at the time, probably was not up to hustling the volume. While the stories he included did not lack excitement, his commitment to the broader goals of abolitionism and his refusal to adopt a gentler view of the South and its past must have made the story objectionable to some readers. In 1893, the *Chicago Tribune* suggested lackluster sales when it commented on Fairbank's struggle against poverty, noting that he was "dependent for support upon the sale of his book." The book did not sell well even in the black community, although Laura Haviland had written an enthusiastic endorsement for the black newspaper the *Cleveland Gazette*. Fairbank's book belonged "in the hand of every lover of home, country, and native land," she insisted. The prominence of Fairbank's role at the expense of black agency perhaps contributed to black indifference. Perhaps, too, Fairbank's selection of light-skinned fugitives did not resonate with black buyers.[43]

Some readers, of course, were interested in Fairbank's story and thought it worthy of preservation. William Birney, son of abolitionist James G. Birney, donated a copy of the book to the Johns Hopkins University library, where it still remains. At the end of the decade, the *Boston Transcript* published parts of the narrative. "Among the people, so multitudinous in these days, eager to claim antislavery descent and to aver that their parents and grandparents were assistants on the Underground Railroad," the paper asserted, "there ought to be sufficient customers for Calvin Fairbank's book to exhaust the edition in a week." Despite positive comments, the fact was that the first and only edition was still not sold out.[44]

In 1891, 1892, and 1893, three women published accounts of their lives as abolitionists. In comparison to books previously published, these reminiscences were brief. Publishers were not interested in manuscripts that were too long for a magazine article and too short to be remunerative. Thus two of the authors, Elizabeth Buffum Chace and Sarah Southwick, paid for the publications themselves and distributed copies to friends, acquaintances, and to libraries. The costs of printing and giving copies away for free may have encouraged the two women to control length. Lucy Colman secured a Buffalo publisher for her book, and her book seems to have been for sale.

While any sales offered the possibility of recouping some of the initial investment to produce the book, the poor performance of abolitionist memoirs suggested the wisdom of brevity.[45]

Chace and Colman touched upon some of the themes animating Fairbank's work, while Southwick described the "small and personal incidents" that she remembered from her youth in antislavery circles in Boston. Few male autobiographies had given much space to women's participation in antislavery, and all three women wanted to ensure that female contributions to abolitionism were not forgotten. Each captured a different aspect of women's antislavery work. Southwick's modest book touched upon the rich associational life that accompanied an antislavery commitment and provided a picture of what it was like to be a female abolitionist in Boston. Chace portrayed women's efforts within a domestic setting. For Colman, who had taught African American students, lectured on abolitionism, and been involved in assisting freed people in Washington D.C., the emphasis was on labor in the public sphere. "Private sorrows," she asserted, were not "for public ears." All three women concentrated their stories on the period of their lives during which they had been actively engaged in abolitionism. That focus made it clear that, no matter what some might say about the importance or value of abolitionism, these women believed that their reform commitment had been significant on both the personal and national level and that their experiences still had something to say to their contemporaries. As Chace explained, when she reviewed her past from the vantage point of her eighty-five years, she recognized that the abolitionist "portion" of her life had provided "the most entire satisfaction." In telling her story, she, like so many other abolitionist writers, hoped to provide "some lessons" about the importance of holding on to principles and devoting oneself to duty "at whatever cost of worldly prospect and advancement."[46]

Before her autobiography was published, Chace had already been engaged in speaking and writing about the contributions and sacrifices of abolitionist women. In 1888, she had prepared a paper on Abby Kelley Foster, who had died the year before, for the meeting of the International Council of Women in Washington, D.C. At the 1889 meeting of the Rhode Island Woman Suffrage Association, Chace not only spoke of the sacrifices prominent women like Kelley Foster, Maria Weston Chapman, and Lucretia Mott, but she also drew attention to "the great army of women throughout the Northern States who enlisted under the anti-slavery banner, and in quiet unappreciated, but effective way[s] did noble service to the cause despite loss of reputation in society, in the church, and sometimes in their own families, so strong and bitter was the pro-slavery spirit of that day!"[47]

In her forty-seven-page narrative Chace did not claim any special credit for her abolitionism, pointing out that she had been born into an antislavery Quaker family that had strenuously rejected the "vile system" of slavery. She did, however, show the consequences of that commitment. They did not include the mobs and violence so often described but social and religious ostracism. Challenging contemporary arguments that insisted that churches had played a significant part in antislavery, Chace succinctly accused the Friends of being proslavery in spirit and hostile to her family's abolitionist activities. In a condemning comparison, Chace suggested that no Catholic believed more fervently in papal infallibility than the Quakers, who were convinced that they could do no wrong. Eventually, Chace had resigned from the Society. No doubt aware of the old accusation, still occasionally repeated, that abolitionist had been infidels, Chace pointed out that she had struggled and agonized over the decision but that, in the end, she had had to respond to her conscience.[48]

Although Chace had engaged in antislavery activities outside of her home, her reminiscences emphasized activism within the domestic setting. She described the comfortable "resting place" that she had provided for visiting abolitionists and the creation of an "anti-slavery" spirit that affected household servants as well as her own children. Her most important contribution to emancipation lay in offering her home as a refuge to fugitives and using her domestic skills to ready them for the trip that lay ahead.[49]

Chace's account of housing and clothing fugitives made the obvious point that slaves wanted to flee from bondage, "so cruel was slavery in this country, less than 40 years ago." She gave no details of their sufferings, no names, no long exciting tales of their flight. But she provided them with fully human identities. As she pointed out, the fugitives were intelligent and sharp-sighted, with a lively moral sense, which was surprising to northerners, who expected to see the blighting influence of slavery. Acknowledging that those escaping from the South represented the brightest and best, she insisted that they were "far" superior to proslavery northern whites. The contrast called into question a range of historical and racial assumptions.[50]

Chace's brief fugitive stories also reversed the usual story line that juxtaposed trembling fugitives and resolute Underground Railroad conductors. In Chace's narrative, the whites bolted doors and windows, always anxious "in this so-called Land of Liberty," always in "hourly fear and expectation of the arrival of the slave-catcher." The only heroism that she was willing to claim for her white household was reserved for the children, who bravely discussed what they would do if their parents were arrested.[51]

In almost every regard, Chace rejected the prevailing characterizations of abolitionists and the negative assessments of their historical importance. As far as the coming of the war was concerned, the South had initiated the "rebellion." Far from having contributed to bringing on the conflict, abolitionists had worked to avoid bloodshed by holding meetings in favor of emancipation. Once the war had broken out, abolitionists, understanding that slavery was its fundamental cause, petitioned Abraham Lincoln to make emancipation a war goal. By making emancipation a war goal, they believed, the president could shorten the war. Lincoln, however, persisted in the position that if he could end the rebellion without eliminating slavery he would do so. Thus he, not the abolitionists, had prolonged the bloodshed and suffering. When he finally embraced emancipation, he received the praise that was actually due the abolitionists. But they graciously allowed him to have the credit: "We rejoiced . . . and made no resistance to the honor it gave him, as the emancipator."[52]

Chace's anecdotes about her own struggles against prejudice highlighted the abolitionist commitment to racial equality and challenged the popular view of blacks as an inferior race. Her examples suggested her commitment to both civil and social rights for blacks. She and her family had refused to abide by discrimination in transportation and had ridden in the railway car reserved for blacks, who were "intelligent, agreeable companions." And as a member of the Female Anti-Slavery Society of Fall River, Chace had invited a black woman to join the group, to the consternation of some. Race prejudice had survived the war, as Chace's narrative made clear. In 1877, Chace and her daughters had resigned from the Rhode Island Women's Club because it had not allowed a "highly responsible well-educated" black woman to join the club.[53]

The pervasive nature of prejudice shaped Chace's recollection of the past. Ignoring the disagreements over abolitionist goals that had accompanied the dissolution of the antislavery societies, she argued that only abolitionists had realized that emancipation by itself was insufficient. The root problem was the belief that blacks were inferior to whites, and all abolitionists recognized "the necessity of all removal of race prejudice." Espousing what was a now minority view, Chace rejected segregation in "any charitable or educational institution" and called for the citizenship that had been conferred on blacks and was now being denied. "The sooner they are admitted to all the privileges of citizenship, and estimated solely by their merits and qualifications, the better for all concerned," she wrote. "It is a baneful policy to undertake to support two distinct nationalities or municipalities in one commonwealth, or two distinct social fabrics, on any basis except that of mental or moral fitness."[54]

Many Americans, if not most, would disagree with her conclusions. Most, of course, would never encounter her "pamphlet," available in both a hard and soft cover, since it was not for sale. Yet Chace did make an effort to put the book in the hands of readers who would be likely to be receptive to her positions. Despite feeling "queer about *peddling*" copies around, she told Frank Garrison that "as I have undertaken it, I do it boldly and have sent off by mail about two hundred." She distributed the book to English abolitionists, colleagues in the suffrage struggle, friends, and family and sent extra copies to people to give to their acquaintances. William Lloyd Garrison Jr. received thirteen copies, one for him and his wife, the others for him "to distribute as thee likes." Of course, this method of disseminating her work put it in the hands of what was likely to be an appreciative audience.[55]

At least fifty people wrote Chace to thank her for the book. Some went beyond the obligatory appreciative phrases to describe their responses to the book. Their comments suggest that they understood and were sympathetic to Chace's interpretation of the past and its relevance for the present. The recollections certainly revived personal memories. One individual remembered being in Chace's house and having a meal with Wendell Phillips and "colored friends from New Bedford," and others recalled the social rejection that went along with being an abolitionist. Still others recalled the famous "old antislavery people." Lorenza Haynes, who was hopeful that "antislavery literature" would one day become more valuable "than Greek and Roman writings . . . for us today," understood the historic significance of abolitionism. The "struggle commenced by a few men and women willing to sacrifice anything *every thing* to crush the infamous system, and to help the enslaved to freedom," she declared, "had in it the undying elements of true greatness and goodness."[56]

Readers also grasped the contemporary messages embedded in Chace's text. Caroline Jones realized the value of this "personal account of those antislavery times" for "the present generation [that] knows so little of the struggle, and sacrifice made by those noble men and women for the cause of Liberty." "Born too late to participate in those struggles," Mary Arnold recognized that "oppression in some form, knows not time or season." Some correspondents linked Chace's book with specific causes like temperance and woman's suffrage. Sophia Little, who had been active in abolitionism for decades, made the connections between Chace's discussion of racial equality and what was happening in the South. *Anti-Slavery Reminiscences* was "just the book for the time because the Southern Question is before the nation," she wrote. It was "well calculated to awaken the thinking people who are to decide whether the former slaves shall be really free citizens."[57]

At seventy, Colman was considerably younger than Chace and probably not in a financial position to subsidize her reminiscences. With "the reputation of an earnest Abolitionist," she had tested reader interest in her past with some articles for *Freethinkers Magazine*. Predictably, she claimed that "friends," who considered her recollections "worthy of record," encouraged her to embark upon a more ambitious project. She revealed, however, that at least one person had some reservations about whether Colman would produce something that would please an audience. A cousin had advised her to stick to abolitionism and to "keep out . . . any reference to 'woman's rights'" that "would make . . . [the] reminiscences unpopular." Colman cavalierly disregarded the advice.[58]

The picture of an elderly, respectably attired Colman with an inscription in her own handwriting, "Yours truly, Lucy N. Colman," appeared at beginning of the book. The ensemble suggested sincerity and gentility, but the impression was misleading. Colman was a feisty author with forceful views not only about race but also about the wrongs done to women. "In a life of so many years a reformer cannot be too narrow," she explained. Quick to claim credit for her achievements and gleeful about besting opponents, she argued that the autobiographical form called for frankness rather than modesty. "If I were not writing an Autobiography," she explained, "I should feel that there was a good deal of egotism in many of my anecdotes, but I was in them, and my *experience* is what I am writing."[59]

Amy Post, a prominent abolitionist and friend of Colman, wrote the preface for the book. In it, she referred to one of Colman's great achievements: "Mrs. Colman, by her own exertions, without any help from any one, removed from our city of Rochester the blot of the *colored* school, thereby giving to our colored people equal rights in our public schools, and helping to remove the prejudice so harmful to both races." Colman herself mentioned the incident only briefly, but the theme that Post suggested, the struggle against racial prejudice, was one that dominated Colman's account of her life. While most abolitionists emphasized their rejection of prejudice, this theme took on increased importance during a decade that insisted that blacks were a defective and degenerate species.[60]

Colman dated her sensitivity to the plight of slaves to her early childhood, but not until she was a mother was she able to sympathize fully with the slave mother's "agony." The recognition of the evils of slavery carried with it the realization that the North as well as the South was guilty because both regions shared the ideas about black inferiority that made slav-

This picture of Lucy Colman in her book, *Reminiscences*, reveals nothing of her fiery personality or the frank and energetic character of her narrative. This image of respectability would soon fade for most of her readers as they read her life story. (Courtesy Library of Congress)

ery possible. Colman recalled wondering what a woman might do to help the slave. Although the means were unclear, she wrote, "I was determined to find some way to work for the slave's deliverance." The fact that she was widowed and needed to earn a living probably also played a major part in encouraging her to pursue a public career as an abolitionist. Her first job opportunity was at a segregated black school in Albany, where she was determined that she would be the last teacher and that the school would die within the year.[61]

It was not long before Colman moved into the lecture field, leaving her parents to care for her child. In the description of her public work in the Midwest, Pennsylvania, and New York, Colman stressed the difficulty of her life as an abolitionist lecturer. Beyond the predictable challenges of learning to speak before an audience, she had faced arduous traveling conditions, uncomfortable or dirty accommodations, and unsympathetic fellow agents. She also described the malicious gossip and the accusations of sexual misconduct that swirled around her. But underlying all the personal trials was the reality of pervasive racial prejudice, even among some of her abolitionist hosts. In one case, the arrival of Colman and her companion, the daughter of a fugitive, took their hostess aback. "'I am greatly embarrassed,'" Mrs. A. said, "'for I have only one guest-room.'" Colman replied that she had consulted her companion, who had "no prejudice against *white* people" and would not mind sharing the room. Mrs. A., much surprised, grasped Colman's point and later said that the "lesson she had learned" was one she never forgot. In another case, a young woman refused to eat with Colman and her companion, a man of color, declaring, "'I don't eat with niggers.'" When Colman held a mock slave auction during the evening meeting and "sold" the young woman's baby, "she was fully converted." While Colman introduced these incidents to show the hold of prejudice, they also indicated that it was possible to overcome it, at least with the assistance of a skillful teacher.[62]

Colman's story of her lecturing days not surprisingly emphasized the hostility that greeted the abolitionist message. The Midwest Colman described was not the one filled with Underground Railroad conductors. She described the residents of Michigan, Ohio, Indiana, Illinois, and Pennsylvania as stupid, ignorant, and quick to resort to violence (a characterization hardly likely to win over her many readers in those states). "In Ohio, Indiana, and Illinois, we were constantly in jeopardy," Colman recalled. "And whom do you suppose were the leaders in these riots?" Colman asked her readers. "Always ministers, or leaders of the Republican party."[63]

Colman's "discovery" of the role ministers played in opposing abolitionism was foreshadowed by her early comments about religion. As a young woman, she had "given up the Church, more because of its complicity with slavery than from a full understanding of the foolishness of its creed." Her text mocked the recent argument that the churches had been in the forefront of the antislavery struggle. Readers were meant to be shocked to learn that the Methodist minister, along with a doctor and a lawyer, in one Ohio village in which Colman spoke urged the crowd to tar and feather Colman, who was, after all, a lady. As far as Colman was concerned, the war had not changed the basic character of the churches. Scorning churches' claim of good deeds among the freed people, Colman described the cruelty of the Christian resident teacher at the National Colored Orphan's Asylum in Washington, D.C. The woman starved and abused the children "under the name of Christian care." This was only one case of many "where the poor colored people were used to profit some broken-down teacher or clergyman." Asserting that Secretary of War Edwin Stanton had told her of his continuing trouble with clergy who mistreated contrabands, Colman concluded, "The North had so many superannuated ministers to care for, that it seemed a Godsend to be able to send them where they would be able to obtain a salary for doing something that was worse than nothing."[64]

The inclusion of Republicans in her list of racist opponents certainly tarnished the party's association with emancipation. Perhaps her accusation stemmed as much from their more recent failure to keep faith with southern blacks as from their actions before the war or during the 1860s and 1870s. In any case, she certainly challenged the idea that devotion to the Union was the noblest achievement of the party and the president. The party was "made upon the subject of preserving the Union, no matter how low they should be required to stoop to their lords of the South," she declared. Only when the South initiated the war did the Republicans, along with the Democrats, realize their own "degradation."[65]

In a biting anecdote, Colman called into question Lincoln's reputation as the great emancipator. During her period in Washington, Colman met Sojourner Truth, whom she found a "remarkable" woman. Truth was eager to meet the man who had issued the Emancipation Proclamation, but when she had tried to attend a White House reception, the doorkeeper had turned her away. Colman decided to get Truth into the White House, and using Mary Todd Lincoln's black dressmaker as her contact, managed to arrange an appointment with the president. While the two women were waiting, another black woman entered the waiting room. She had no appointment and little chance of seeing the president, so Colman decided to escort her, along with Truth. Although at the time Truth had revealed that Lincoln had "showed [her] as much consideration" as he would have to a white person and Colman wrote that the president had greeted Truth with "pleasing cordiality," now, in retrospect, the meeting was hardly a success. As Colman recalled in her text, Lincoln had been very uncomfortable. He was without his usual humorous story and called Truth "aunty, as he would his washerwomen." When Truth praised him for being the first antislavery president, Colman claimed, Lincoln replied that he was not an abolitionist but had only emancipated the slaves because it was the only way to save the Union. Lincoln's behavior demonstrated to Colman that "he was not glad that the war had made him the emancipator of four million slaves. Perhaps he came to rejoice over it, when he realized by the logic of events his name would be immortal through that act, but at that time he did not see it. He believed in the white race, not in the colored, and did not want to put them on an equality."[66]

Colman obviously did believe in "an equality," and her narrative demonstrated not only the work that she did for African Americans but also the associations she had with them. She described staying in the home of fugitives before the war and finding the house attractive, with "many elegancies." In Richmond, after the war, a black woman gave a party for Colman and her fellow teachers and invited several black guests. "We had a very nice dinner, with all the *et ceteras*, and in the evening ice-cream and cake — all excellent and everything in good taste," Colman recalled.[67]

These recollections demonstrated the ability of blacks to succeed (the woman's family had several cows and was in the "business" of selling milk and eggs) and to achieve not merely respectability but also gentility. From the vantage point of the 1890s, however, she recognized that in the first years after the war, "we expected altogether too much of them."

Yet Colman did not backtrack from her commitments. Toward the end of her narrative, she asked questions that anticipated discussions a century later of reparations for descendants of slaves: "Who pays the slave for his sufferings? In this interminable talk of compensating the slave-owner for his losses, who ever thought of paying the slave for the loss of a lifetime? We are none of us very patient of wrongs done by those whom our race defrauded of everything but life itself, and often of that." Her theme of the "most bitter prejudice against color" in the North and her rejection of racial separation offered both an explanation and condemnation of the northern indifference to the fate of the freed people.[68]

———•———

Aaron Powell's *Personal Reminiscences* appeared in 1899 and was one of the last personal recollections to be published by an abolitionist. Powell had spent his life as a reformer and had planned to provide an overview of his entire career in his autobiography. But he had died suddenly in 1899, having only completed the account of his activities as an abolitionist. His widow, Anna Powell, decided to go ahead with publication and secured the Caulon Press, a minor publishing company, to do the printing.[69]

In his autobiography, Powell dismissed critical views of the abolitionists or the notion that they were historically irrelevant. While he believed that Americans were still "too near the historic antislavery conflict for it to be seen generally in its true perspective," he emphatically gave credit to Garrison for making "Lincoln later a possibility." He was confident that the abolitionist view of slavery "in the sight of the impartial historian of the future" would "put to shame the much lauded statesmanship" of men like Webster, whose reputation was on the upswing. His laudatory vignettes of prominent abolitionists like May, Garrison, Phillips, the Motts, and the Posts (many of whose portraits appeared as illustrations in the book) suggested that the older generation dazzled him. The men were noble and manly, the women gifted and gracious. While he was willing to note an occasional flaw — he conceded that Garrison appeared critical and cold in public but that in private he was warm — he provided some memorable pictures of the reformers. His description of Garrison's visit to the Fifty-fifth Massachusetts Regiment's camp outside Charleston after the war conveyed a touching scene that could have become the basis for a statue of Garrison as the great emancipator. He described the "ragged, most forlorn looking company" of former slaves, "a striking object lesson of the misery and degradation begotten by slavery! . . . The poor creatures . . . seemed intuitively drawn to Mr. Garrison as their friend and deliverer. It was most pathetic to see them gather about him, and, approaching timidly, touch his garment. As a picture, photographed upon my brain more than thirty years ago, it is still vivid in memory and will be indelible."[70]

Powell was in his twenties when he began to lecture in the late 1850s, and his recollections of his lecturing experiences, like Colman's, touched upon difficult traveling conditions, antagonistic audiences, and hostility from church leaders. But he also remembered "kindly welcomes in hospitable homes, . . . valued new friendships," and "helpful co-operation in confessedly difficult, but most needy fields for the labor of the abolitionist." He recalled with pride that many of the meetings he had held had been the first in that place. He also questioned whether "at this distance of time, with slavery abolished, and the whole attitude of the public mind changed towards it," his work might seem "inconsequential," but he rejected the idea that abolitionist agitation had been futile and insisted that it had provided the basis for emancipation. "New converts were won and . . . finally," he concluded, "public sentiment was so educated and revolutionized as to make the abolition of slavery a possibility."[71]

Toward the end of his narrative, Powell described the days leading up to the war. The mobs that attacked the abolitionists," Powell wrote, "proved to be the forerunner of the slaveholders' rebellion" that after "a great expenditure of blood and treasure" ended slavery "as a legalized institution." His choice of words was revealing: slavery might have ended as a legal institution, but the other abolitionist goal remained unfulfilled.[72]

While Powell did not emphasize the persistence of prejudice as an evil to the extent that Colman did, he condemned the "still prevalent . . . unchristian color prejudice." It was a theme he had sounded many times in his life. During a commemoration of John Brown in 1879, he had decried the "present disgraceful persecution" of southern blacks and declared that the spirit of slavery still existed. Four years later, at the meeting honoring the founding of the American Anti-Slavery Society, he had argued that the country should not be allowed to step backward and give in to "the spirit of oppression and race prejudice." In his book Powell provided past examples of segregated cemeteries and hotels that had such obvious parallels in the present, and he declared the beliefs that barred blacks from public spaces as "cruel," "heartless and vulgar." He recalled one "educated, refined and sensitive" black lecturer remarking, "'to the colored people it is the same as having the small-pox all the time.'"[73]

One of the illustrations in Powell's book was a photograph of the Quaker abolitionist Joseph Carpenter. Carpenter not only sheltered fugitives in his home, but he also arranged speaking engagements for Powell. Because whites barred local blacks from being interred in white cemeteries, Carpenter donated one of the fields on his farm to be used as a burial ground. When Powell visited him shortly before his death, Carpenter told Powell that he planned for his own body to be buried alongside his black neighbors. Powell reproduced the photograph that gave visual form to Carpenter's beliefs. The setting for the picture may have been Carpenter's own house, for a flowered carpet and the wall of the room are visible. Seated with his legs comfortably crossed, Carpenter has one arm around a small very black boy standing beside him. His other arm rests on his lap, where his hand clasps the boy's. Powell approvingly noted that Carpenter gave this picture to those who requested his photograph, "feeling that he was at the same time conveying silently the lesson he so much desired to teach concerning the cruel and unjust color prejudice."[74]

Three decades after emancipation, Powell seems to have been trying to make some sense of what went wrong. One of the problems he identified was the organizational vacuum that occurred after the war. Years before, he had supported disbanding the AAS, although he had also favored forming a new organization with more effective methods of operation. Now Powell regretted the dissolution of the AAS, "with its funded moral capital." In Great Britain, he noted, the British and Foreign Anti-Slavery Society had continued on after emancipation in the West Indies. "If only an Independent committee of competent men and women, kept wholly distinct from all partisan political alliances" had survived in the United States, he wrote; "its effective moral censorship of public men and measures, especially as involving the rights of the colored people, would even now thirty years after emancipation, be most valuable and timely, in view of the monstrous outrages to which, as in the Carolinas, Louisiana and elsewhere, they have been, in the long interim, and yet are, subjected."[75]

Powell's sense of regret and his attempt to analyze problematic decisions abolitionists had made after the war showed the vast changes that had occurred since the confident assertions some expressed in the 1860s that the entire country was now one big antislavery society. Especially for those who wrote during the 1890s about their lives as abolitionists, it was almost impossible to look back on the past and capture that heady moment when it appeared possible that Americans might support freedom for former slaves and move beyond racial prejudice. As the writer of the final section of Powell's book, titled "In Memoriam," observed, Powell had discovered, as he was working on his book, that "there was much in the retrospect that was of necessity saddening." Perhaps this sense of sadness was what Calvin Fairbank had in mind when he pictured himself at the end of his book as "old and lonely." Yet abolitionist autobiographers also had the conviction that the history they were preserving, and the lofty ideals of racial justice it reflected, was important for Americans to remember. And for some writers, surely there was another reward that accompanied the hard work of recording their experiences. As the author of Powell's "In Memoriam" suggested, "There was also the glow of enthusiasm awakened by living again, in memory, with the great souls whom he pictured with sincere and sympathetic hand. The record of the labors of the past, looked at for the first time, as a whole, was a surprise to him. And he loved to bear the testimony, as many others have done, that whatever he had been able to do for the anti-slavery cause, it had done immeasurably more for him."[76]

Afterword

Mary Grew had never undertaken to write the story of her life. But she did compose the history of the Philadelphia Female Anti-Slavery Society and participate in the process of collective reminiscences when she attended antislavery reunions. At the age of seventy-nine, she was still appearing and speaking in public. She told her old friend Elizabeth Gay in 1893 that she had gone to a meeting of Philadelphia's New Century Club, "where reminiscences of Anti-Slavery days were told to a large audience by Dr. Furness, Harriet Purvis & myself. How new & strange & exciting it was to most of them! A very few of 'the old guard,' who survive unto this day, were there."[1]

Grew had been elated by her reception. But the comment that her audience was unacquainted with the history that she and others were presenting hints at the obstacles facing abolitionists as they tried to keep their understanding of the past alive. It is hardly surprising that so few abolitionists took on the task of writing and publishing their life stories. Those stories were increasingly at odds with what Americans believed had happened in the decades leading up to and following the Civil War. And, because the act of recollection itself is necessarily shaped by all that happens since the events being described, the understanding of the past was transformed as each autobiographer attempted to make sense of his or her life. Even Samuel J. May had the uneasy sense that the long-sought goal of emancipation had results more limited than abolitionists had imagined during the many years of struggle. And as the significance of the past seemed to change, so too could the value of the individual life that had been devoted to that struggle.

For all the reassessment that accompanied the process of composing life narratives, however, abolitionist autobiographers refused to accept the ever more negative evaluations of their movement and their own participation in reform. Increasingly regarding their work as unfinished, most maintained their basic commitment to a more just society and the values that had fueled their struggles against the political and cultural currents of the day. Their books explicitly or implicitly encouraged their readers to follow their example. African Americans who wrote about their own involvement in liberating the enslaved during the antebellum years insisted upon the agency of black people in the struggle for freedom.[2]

It must have been disappointing for them to learn how few people were interested in reading their books and to realize how many would rather read about quaint slaves and kindly masters than the evils of slavery. It was disheartening, surely, to see the reemergence of the old stereotype of abolitionists as misguided fanatics. It was hard to find the money to finance the publication of their recollections and then perhaps to lose it on the venture. It may have felt demeaning for some to peddle their own books. But for all the frustrations that writing may have entailed, they preferred those to silence.

As this work has pointed out, however, it was not just changing cultural attitudes toward the past that made abolitionist autobiographies of so little general interest; it was also the ways in which they were written. Readers were not enthusiastic about the type of earnest personal accounts that abolitionists produced: autobiographies that put in "much of what [was] better left out" or appeared to be a "narrative of bitter theological [or other] controversies long since the driest of dust." Over time, it became difficult to provide a story with content "not already familiar." Even recollections focusing on Harriet Beecher Stowe were seen as commercially "hopeless" by the mid-1890s, for her day had "gone by, and Mrs. Stowe does not stand in the minds of people as an oracle."

Instead, publishers, critics, and presumably readers hailed reminiscences that were "really charming," with a natural, unassuming style, and writers who exhibited no "ill-disguised vanity." Summing up a largely successful autobiographical manuscript, a Houghton Mifflin reader praised its picture of "remarkable social, business, religious and patriotic activity" and its avoidance of "moralizing."[3]

The enthusiastic critical reception and impressive sales of Thomas Wentworth Higginson's 1898 autobiography reveal how far most other abolitionist memoirs diverged from cultural expectations. Higginson had been an active abolitionist before the war but had subsequently enjoyed a successful and long career as a literary man. He saw his experiences as an abolitionist as only a small piece of his life, now particularly interesting for the adventure they yielded.[4]

With the exception of Henry Stanton, no abolitionist since Samuel J. May had published with a major eastern publishing house. On the other hand, not only had Higginson's reminiscences been published by the prestigious firm of Houghton Mifflin, Higginson had been asked to write them.

The agreement was that Higginson would first produce several articles (for which he was to be paid $150 apiece) for the *Atlantic Monthly*. Then the complete reminiscences would appear in book form, with very generous royalties for Higginson. The title for both the articles and book was *Cheerful Yesterdays*. Chosen by Higginson's wife, the title established the upbeat mood for the recollections.[5]

Perhaps with an eye to ensuring the future success of the book, the journal articles were enthusiastically advertised. The glowing descriptions suggest how well Higginson understood the autobiographical formula. "Colonel" Higginson's career was characterized as "unique," and his personal record "contribute[d] an entertaining and valuable series of personal recollections" for the reader. "There is not an important movement or event, and hardly an important personage, in war, in politics, or in literature for the last half-century that does not come into these personal recollections." There were many signs that Higginson knew what pleased readers. He described the difficulties he had experienced as a young man struggling to find direction, a personal emphasis on "the inner life and its changing phases" that was beginning to come into fashion. The two chapters on his European sojourn and the people he met there provided "a kind of gossip always in demand."[6]

Early in the finished narrative, Higginson declared that he had "deeply . . . cast in my lot with the black race." In fact, his experiences as an abolitionist only occupied a small part of the reminiscences (no doubt good for sales) and hardly provided the picture of devotion to the black cause that Higginson boasted. His understanding of abolitionism, based on the simple idea that one man could not own another, suggested a commitment to emancipation but little else. He had supported the Fourteenth and Fifteenth Amendments, but this part of his story did not appear in his book, nor did he discuss his views on Reconstruction. In a discussion of Levi Coffin's *Reminiscences*, which was written almost twenty years before his own book, Higginson suggested the kind of abolitionism that he admired and that shaped his own self-representation. Coffin had given readers "a wholly different aspect of the great contest," Higginson had remarked. "Readers fond of personal adventure will find [it] much more entertaining than any memoir of Mr. Garrison." The same comment could certainly be applied to his own discussion of his abolitionist activities.[7]

When Higginson looked back on the past, he saw himself as a young man with "radical tendencies" and a "voracious desire for all knowledge and action." This vision of manly activism knit the phases of his exciting but relatively short career as abolitionist together. The first opportunity

Cheerful Yesterdays

BY

THOMAS WENTWORTH HIGGINSON

Author of

"Oldport Days," "Margaret Fuller Ossoli"
(in the Series of American Men of Letters), etc.

1 vol. 12mo, $2.00

CONTENTS: A CAMBRIDGE BOYHOOD; A CHILD
OF THE COLLEGE; THE PERIOD OF THE NEWNESS;
THE REARING OF A REFORMER; THE FUGITIVE SLAVE
EPOCH; THE BIRTH OF A LITERATURE; KANSAS AND
JOHN BROWN; CIVIL WAR; LITERARY LONDON
TWENTY YEARS AGO; LITERARY PARIS TWENTY
YEARS AGO; ON THE OUTSKIRTS OF PUBLIC LIFE;
EPILOGUE.

A BOOK giving the reader glimpses of the
home life and character of those men and
women whom the world rightly calls "great"
is never more welcome than when written by
one within the charmed circle. In Colonel
Higginson's "Cheerful Yesterdays" (just published by Messrs. Houghton, Mifflin & Co.) the
reader is irresistibly lured on by his own experiences and those of his friends as they actually
lived, worked, and played. The book itself is
the very flower of autobiography. It gives the
most interesting experiences of a singularly
interesting life, in the most attractive manner.
A fine, discriminating optimism pervades it,
and the impression produced is that life is un-
speakably worth living, and that opportunity

This fulsome advertisement for Thomas Wentworth Higginson's life story, *Cheerful Yesterdays*, gives a good idea of the kind of autobiography publishers were interested in and the extensive publicity that Houghton Mifflin provided for the book. The contrast between how this book was advertised and sold and how most of the other and the delight of noble effort await every manly spirit.

The table of contents gives only hints of the riches of this book. It describes his boyhood in Cambridge; his years and associates in Harvard College, following the careers of his comrades there as they realize or disappoint the early expectations of their friends; the period of the Transcendental movement; the observations and experiences which made him a reformer; the storm and stress of the time when the Fugitive Slave Law excited the country; the development of literature and his own literary work in the fifties; the stirring episode of the Kansas conflicts, and the daring and doom of John Brown; and the Civil War, with a very modest account of his share in it. Later chapters describe literary London and Paris twenty years ago, and some of the notable persons he met in those capitals.

The intrinsic and widely varied interest of the book, the close and accurate knowledge of the people and events described, the noble and cheerful tone that pervades it, and the exquisite literary style which is a constant delight, — these give the book a very uncommon charm and value.

HOUGHTON, MIFFLIN & COMPANY
4 Park St., Boston; 11 East 17th St., New York
378-388 Wabash Ave., Chicago
FOR SALE BY ALL BOOKSELLERS

narratives penned by abolitionists were is dramatic. (Thomas Wentworth Higginson Collection, fMS Am 2030 [243], p. 44, used by permission of the Houghton Library, Harvard University)

Higginson had to act "forcibly" came when the fugitive Anthony Burns was recaptured and jailed in Boston in 1854. The effort on the part of some abolitionists to break into the jail and free Burns, dramatically described by Higginson, resulted in one death. Higginson interpreted the bloodshed as evidence that the war against slavery had begun. Now he was a "private soldier" in that war. Higginson's second opportunity to experience the "tonic of life" occurred during the struggle over whether Kansas was to allow slavery, which Higginson dubbed the rehearsal for war. Not only was Higginson involved in sending weapons to antislavery emigrants in Kansas, but he also spent six weeks there. Higginson described the letdown that he felt when he left Kansas: "It seemed as if all vigor had suddenly gone out of me, and a despicable effeminacy had set in." According to Higginson, the final stage of his abolitionist career was Higginson's service as the commander of a company of black slaves during the war.[8]

Higginson described himself and those who agreed with him as men who meant business. The majority of abolitionists who rejected violence for most of the prewar period came up short. While antislavery conventions offered "picturesque" sights like women knitting during speeches and men sporting the new style of beards, and could offer some excitement, they could also be "torpid." Organizations like the Boston Vigilance Committee were "almost exasperating" because of "the placid way" the pacifist members "looked beyond the rescue of an individual to the purifying of a nation." Political abolitionists who wanted to stay within the law also did not measure up to Higginson's manly standards. In Higginson's opinion, it was better to take action and fail than to "acquiesce tamely." This view meshed easily with the admiration of manly virility and action so common in the 1890s.[9]

Higginson had already written a book about his war service. Anyone who had read *Army Life in a Black Regiment* would find a similar characterization of the men under Higginson's command in *Cheerful Yesterdays*. But the racial climate of 1898 was quite different from the racial climate of 1870, making this section of the book the closest he came to being an advocate for African Americans. The view he gave of his soldiers was mixed. On the one hand, he emphasized their childlike qualities: "They were certainly more docile than white soldiers, more affectionate, and more impulsive . . . and were less individually self-reliant." They were also gregarious and fond of singing as they marched. On the other hand, those who had doubted "the warlike" capability of black troops had been proved wrong. Blacks were the equal of whites in terms of courage, and, since they were fighting for freedom, "the most potent of all motives," they had much greater investment in the fighting than their white officers or white soldiers.[10]

While Higginson's acknowledgment of blacks' contributions to victory and their desire for freedom might have raised uncomfortable questions about their situation in the present, readers soon could forget them. Higginson's account of his army service ended the part of the book devoted to abolitionism. He moved onto his literary career, suggesting that emancipation had solved the black man's problem or that he did not care. He was silent about his activities during Reconstruction, his waning support for the rights of freed people, and his shifting political allegiances. While news from the South would occasionally prompt Higginson to publish a response that recalled older abolitionist values, for the most part, Higginson, along with most Americans accepted the racial status quo. His book offered little challenge to contemporary racial views.[11]

In its advertising for the book, Houghton Mifflin emphasized the interesting and noncontroversial character of *Cheerful Yesterdays*. It was "a most delightful autobiographical book," announced one advertisement, "giving the most interesting experiences of Colonel Higginson's remarkably interesting life." The book represented "the very flower of autobiography" and had a "noble and cheerful tone" and an "exquisite literary style." Unlike most abolitionist memoirs, the charming and delightful volume was available in bookstores for $2.[12]

Even before Higginson's work came out in book form, the *New York Times* promoted it as an enjoyable book: "It will be ideal reading for the middle-aged dreamer, recalling the days that are no more hard days, but pleasant to remember." The comment suggested the dramatic difference in tone and intention between *Cheerful Yesterdays* and other abolitionist recollections. In its review of the book, the *Times* praised Higginson for giving a "pleasant but unexaggerated description" of Boston and Cambridge life half a century before and quoted approvingly a passage in which Higginson noted the humble social background of many abolitionist supporters, who, he claimed, lacked the education of "modern" civil service reformers. All in all, Higginson's book was the kind of autobiography that won easy critical approval. It had "variety . . . and charm of manner," and its author "has nothing to conceal; . . . [his] unconscious self-betrayals are always to his advantage."[13]

Not surprisingly, the book did very well. Between 1898 and 1904, 3,907 copies of the book were sold, bringing Higginson almost $2,250 in royalties. A comparison of the sales figures for Higginson's recollections and a book on James and Lucretia Mott also published by Houghton Mifflin is telling. Between 1891, the year the Mott book appeared, and 1907, only 218 copies were sold.[14]

For most abolitionists, writing had been a form of activism rather than income. Perhaps this is one reason why their autobiographies lacked the literary qualities critics praised. This activism still had power for John F. Hume, who, in 1905, published one of the very last firsthand accounts of abolitionist activity. Hume had not been at the center of abolitionism and, indeed, described as one of his antislavery credentials schoolyard fights, complete with black eyes and bloody noses. But, unlike *Cheerful Yesterdays*, his narrative insisted on the importance of what abolitionists had done and the necessity of continuing that work. Like Aaron Powell, he saw the dissolution of antislavery societies after the Civil War as a serious error because it stripped abolitionists of the institutional basis that would have sustained the movement for decades despite its unpopularity. The contrast between the situation of antislavery in Great Britain, where the antislavery society pursued new goals, lobbied government, mounted petition drives, attended international antislavery conferences, and published a newspaper, and the isolation felt by American abolitionists was striking. Hume insisted that "what this country now needs" was "a revival of Abolitionism" and of its national organization, the American Anti-Slavery Society. "Unfurl the old standard" he urged. Restate the vital principles that blacks as well as whites must enjoy political and personal rights and that all servitude, including the denial of self-government, must end. Rather than providing hours of pleasant reading, Hume was calling his readers to act.[15]

This call to organize resonated with a few Americans, who established the NAACP as an institutional base for carrying on the old abolitionist struggle. Initially, few Americans were aware of the organization's existence, and, if they were aware, they hardly were supportive of its goals. Like the original abolitionists, these workers for racial justice labored as a minority. The situation changed with the emergence of the modern civil rights movement in the 1950s. Then, activists and historians could look back to the roots of the new effort and rediscover their ancestors, whose recollections provided an inspiring historical record.[16]

N O T E S

ABBREVIATIONS

BHL   Bentley Historical Library, University of Michigan, Ann Arbor, Mich.
CCCA   Cleveland-Colby-Colgate Archives, Susan Colgate Cleveland Library,
       Colby Sawyer College, New London, N.H.
CUL   Cornell University Library, Ithaca, N.Y.
HL   Houghton Library, Harvard University, Cambridge, Mass.
HSP   Historical Society of Pennsylvania, Philadelphia, Pa.
LC   Library of Congress, Washington, D.C.
NAM   *North American Review*
NAS   *National Anti-Slavery Standard*
WCL   Whittier College Library, Whittier, Calif.

INTRODUCTION

1. John G. Whittier, "The Anti-Slavery Convention of 1833," *Atlantic Monthly* 33 (1874): 171.

2. "Editor's Easy Chair," *Harper's* 36 (1868): 813; Whittier, "Convention," 169. See also Eugene Exman, *The House of Harper: One Hundred and Fifty Years of Publishing* (New York: Harper & Row, 1967), 259.

3. "Topics of the Times," *Scribner's* 8 (1874): 374; Thomas L. Connelly and Barbara L. Bellows, *God and General Longstreet: The Lost Cause and the Southern Mind* (Baton Rouge: Louisiana State University Press, 1982), 48.

4. Michael Kammen, *Mystic Chords of Memory: The Transformation of Tradition in American Culture* (New York: Alfred A. Knopf, 1991), 3, 4–14.

5. This is the point that Kathleen Diffley makes in *Where My Heart Is Turning Ever: Civil War Stories and Constitutional Reform, 1861–1876* (Athens: University of Georgia Press, 1992), xviii.

6. The scholarship on Civil War memory is large. Some of the more important works include David W. Blight, *Race and Reunion: The Civil War in American Memory* (Cambridge, Mass.: Harvard University Press, 2001) and *Frederick Douglass' Civil War: Keeping the Faith in Jubilee* (Baton Rouge: Louisiana State University Press, 1989); W. Fitzhugh Brundage, ed., *Where These Memories Grow: History, Memory, and Southern Identity* (Chapel Hill: University of North Carolina Press, 2000); Gary W. Gallagher and Alan T. Nolan, eds., *The Myth of the Lost Cause and Civil War History* (Bloomington: Indiana University Press, 2000); Matthew J. Grow, "The Shadow of the Civil War: A Historiography of Civil War Memory," *American Nineteenth Century History* 4 (Summer 2003): 77–103; Mitchell A. Kachun, "The Faith that the Dark Past Has Taught Us: African-American Commemorations in the North and West

and the Construction of a Usable Past, 1808–1915" (Ph.D diss., Cornell University, 1997), and *Festivals of Freedom: Memory and Meaning in African American Emancipation Celebrations, 1808–1915* (Amherst: University of Massachusetts Press, 2003); Kirk Savage, *Standing Soldiers, Kneeling Slaves: Race, War, and Monument in Nineteenth-Century America* (Princeton: Princeton University Press, 1997); Paul A. Shackel, *Memory in Black and White: Race, Commemoration, and the Post-Bellum Landscape* (Walnut Creek, Calif.: AltaMira Press, 2003); Nina Silber, *The Romance of Reunion: Northerners and the South, 1865–1900* (Chapel Hill: University of North Carolina Press, 1993); and John David Smith, "The Evil that Americans Did," *Chronicle of Higher Education*, March 9, 2007. The scholar is Steven Mintz.

7. See Grow, "Shadow of the Civil War," 96–97, and Carol Reardon, "Why We Should Still Care: The Civil War and Memory," Dwight D. Eisenhower Lectures in War and Peace, biennial series no. 9, Kansas State University, 1991. See also John R. Neff, *Honoring the Civil War Dead: Commemoration and the Problem of Reconciliation* (Lawrence: University Press of Kansas, 2005), 5–6, 13. As Neff remarks, the emphasis on reconciliation in scholarship is too narrow and certainly minimizes the feelings of grief that many northerners continued to feel for those lost in the war: "The documentation of the era has been skewed largely to give pride of place to that effort that in hindsight seems the proper course for history to have taken. . . . [The effort] does an injustice to all those who mourned and would not be reconciled in their grief" (205).

For the purposes of this study, I consider all who embraced the antislavery cause abolitionists even though they disagreed upon strategies and approaches to ending slavery. I clearly am disagreeing with the view presented by William B. Hixson Jr., in *Moorfield Storey and the Abolitionist Tradition* (New York: Oxford University Press, 1972), 201, that "caught between an increasingly complacent middle class, which regarded the Negro as an object of charity, and an increasingly articulate working class, which regarded him with suspicion, the abolitionists . . . had nothing to say. And so they withdrew to the memories of great battles fought and won, or spent their time in working on pallid copies of their prewar agitation." My interpretation dovetails with the work of Jane Dailey, who shows that historians have neglected the various interracial political movements in the South during the 1880s, thus making the movement toward segregation seem inevitable. See her *Before Jim Crow: The Politics of Race in Postemancipation Virginia* (Chapel Hill: University of North Carolina Press, 2000).

8. Blight, *Frederick Douglass' Civil War*.

9. Ibid.

10. Henry Mayer, *All on Fire: William Lloyd Garrison and the Abolition of Slavery* (New York: St. Martin's Press, 1998), 602; Dorothy Sterling, *Ahead of Her Time: Abby Kelley and the Politics of Anti-Slavery* (New York: W. W. Norton, 1991), 374, 383.

11. For discussions of memoirs, see Timothy Dow Adams, *Telling Lies in Modern American Autobiography* (Chapel Hill: University of North Carolina Press, 1990), 40; Marcus Billson, "The Memoir: New Perspectives on a Forgotten Genre," *Genre* 10 (Summer 1977): 259–82, especially 261, 265; and John D. Barbour, *The Conscience of the Autobiographer: Ethical and Religious Dimensions of Autobiography* (London: Mac-

millan, 1992), 14. While some literary scholars make distinctions between autobiographies and memoirs, I will use both words interchangeably. I also use the descriptive terms that the authors themselves chose for their works. Susanna Egan provides an analysis of autobiography after the Civil War in "'Self'-Conscious History: American Autobiography after the Civil War," in Paul John Eakin, ed., *American Autobiography: Retrospective and Prospect* (Madison: University of Wisconsin Press, 1991), 70–94.

12. Paul John Eakin, in *Touching the World: Reference in Autobiography* (Princeton: Princeton University Press, 1992), 66, talks of the dialectic relationship between past and present.

13. James M. McPherson, *The Abolitionist Legacy: From Reconstruction to the NAACP* (Princeton: Princeton University Press, 1975), 54.

14. Shackel, *Memory in Black and White*, 16; Laura Marcus, "The Face of Autobiography," in *The Uses of Autobiography*, ed. Julia Swindell (London: Taylor & Francis, 1995), 17; Nancy Wood, "Memory's Remains: *Les lieux de mémoire*," *History and Memory* 6 (Spring/Summer 1994): 126.

15. Quoted in Silber, *Romance of Reunion*, 62. See also Ednah Dow Cheyney, *Reminiscences of Ednah Dow Cheyney* (Boston: Lee & Shepard, 1902), 154–55.

16. Rosamond Gilder, ed., *Letters of Richard Watson Gilder* (Boston: Houghton Mifflin, 1916), 395, 392.

17. For the British situation, see Howard Temperley, *British Antislavery, 1833–1870* (Columbia: University of South Carolina Press, 1972), 66, 68, 79–84, and chap. 6.

RITUAL REMEMBRANCES I

1. "Editor's Easy Chair," *Harper's* 31 (1865): 265–66; Eugene Exman, *The House of Harper: One Hundred and Fifty Years of Publishing* (New York: Harper & Row, 1967), 72.

2. For discussions of celebrations and rituals, see Amitai Etzioni, "Holiday and Rituals: Neglected Seedbeds of Virtue," 7–11, 20, and David E. Procter, "Victorian Days: Performing Community through Local Festival," 135–40, in Amitai Etzioni and Jared Bloom, eds., *We Are What We Celebrate: Understanding Holidays and Rituals* (New York: New York University Press, 2004); and James Combs, "Celebrations: Rituals of Popular Veneration," *Journal of Popular Culture* 22 (Spring 1989): 72.

3. *NAS*, May 29, 1869; Procter, "Victorian Days," 132–36, 141; *Brooklyn Eagle*, April 15, 1870; *New York Times*, January 28, 1868.

4. *National Era*, May 12, 1870; *Brooklyn Eagle*, April 15, 1870; David Herbert Donald, Jean H. Baker, and Michael F. Holt, *The Civil War and Reconstruction* (New York: W. W. Norton, 2001), 617–21; David Blight, *Race and Reunion: The Civil War in American Memory* (Cambridge, Mass.: Harvard University Press, 2001), 122–28; *National Era*, May 23, 1872.

5. Quoted in Paul Goodman, *Of One Blood: Abolitionism and the Origins of Racial Equality* (Berkeley: University of California Press, 1998), 58, 54–64.

6. For violence in the South, see Eric Foner, *A Short History of Reconstruction, 1863–1877* (New York: Harper & Row, 1990), chap. 9. For the Fifteenth Amendment, see ibid., 191–92. James Brewer Stewart, in *Wendell Phillips: Liberty's Hero* (Baton

Rouge: Louisiana State University Press, 1986), 248–69, points out that these discussions and the disagreements they produced went back to 1864.

7. Ira V. Brown, *Mary Grew: Abolitionist and Feminist (1813–1896)* (Selinsgrove, Pa.: Susquehanna University Press, 1991), 119, 120; *NAS*, February 27, 1869, February 12, 1870. For a sense of the hopefulness of the Executive Committee of the Pennsylvania Anti-Slavery Society that the 1869 anniversary meeting be its last, see *NAS*, October 30, 1869.

8. *NAS*, January 2, 1869, March 27, 1869, April 16, 1870, March 6, 1869; Stewart, *Wendell Phillips*, 249, 255, 263, 290. Stewart argues that Phillips's faith in legislation dated back to 1864. He suggests that Phillips adjusted "emotionally to this terrible defeat" of failing to secure land confiscation by finally declaring "that the proposed franchise amendment itself represented the last and most necessary of all the abolitionists' victories and the key to solving all the other social issues to which he had become so heavily committed" (*Wendell Phillips*, 290).

9. *NAS*, May 15, 22, 1869, November 27, 1869, February 5, 1870. As James M. McPherson noted about another abolitionist, George Julian, Phillips had a view of the future that was definitely non-Darwinian and allowed space for moral reform to have an impact on events. See *The Abolitionist Legacy: From Reconstruction to the NAACP* (Princeton: Princeton University Press, 1975), 55. Stewart, in *Wendell Phillips*, 284, notes that Phillips's confidence was, in fact, not very strong. In 1867, he despaired that racism would soon end and was not hopeful of the Republicans's commitment to "absolute equality of blacks." At that point, he said that abolitionists must continue to agitate.

10. Stewart, *Wendell Phillips*, 289; *NAS*, April 17, 1869, February 13, 1869. Stewart, *Wendell Phillips*, 278–79, shows how Phillips acted as the party's "conscience," although his views went "far beyond the acceptable limits" of party policy. McPherson, *Abolitionist Legacy*, appendix A, gives some biographical information on abolitionists like Haven.

11. *NAS*, May 15, 22, 1869, June 5, 12, 1869. Cora Tappan was a prominent spiritualist and abolitionist. See <http://en.wikipedia.org/wiki/Samuel_F._Tappan>.

12. Stewart, *Wendell Phillips*, 289; *NAS*, June 5, 1869, May 29, 1869, February 5, 1870, June 12, 1869, December 25, 1869, January 29, 1870, April 16, 1870; Stewart, *Wendell Phillips*, 286; Foner, *Short History*, 194, 202. Eric Foner, *Reconstruction: America's Unfinished Revolution, 1863–1877* (New York: Harper & Row, 1988), 246, 568. As Foner points out, the Southern Homestead Act was repealed in 1876.

13. The analysis of the last meeting is drawn from *NAS*, April 2, 1870; *New York Times*, April 10, 1870; and *NAS*, April 16, 1870. McPherson, *Struggle for Equality*, appendix A, gives information on John Sargent.

14. Ira V. Brown, *Mary Grew*, 128, 129. The Pennsylvania Historical Society holds the records of both the PFAS and the Pennsylvania Anti-Slavery Society.

15. Ibid., 126–32; *NAS*, April 2, 1870.

16. Ira V. Brown, *Mary Grew*, 126–32; *NAS*, April 2, 1870.

17. *NAS*, April 2, 1870.

18. Stewart, *Wendell Phillips*, 281; *NAS*, April 2, 1870, November 27, 1869.

19. Ira V. Brown, *Mary Grew*, 127, chap. 7; *NAS*, April 2, 1870.

20. *NAS*, April 16, 1870.

21. *Harper's Weekly*, August 31, 1872.

22. *NAS*, April 16, 1870, May 13, 1871, December 1872. As the paper pointed out on December 28, 1871, it had never been self-supporting and had depended on funds from antislavery activities to continue publication. Stewart explains in *Wendell Phillips*, 251–61, that for Wendell Phillips temperance was not an extraneous issue. The republic he hoped to see emerge with the end to slavery could be ruined by alcohol as it could by racism. McPherson, *Struggle for Equality*, 14, reveals some of the achievements of the National Reform League.

23. *Brooklyn Daily Eagle*, January 28, 1870, April 11, 15, 1870, May 6, 1870.

24. Ibid., May 6, 1870.

25. *NAS*, November 27, 1869; *National Standard*, n.s., June 1870, 81–84.

26. *National Era*, May 12, 1870; W. Fitzhugh Brundage, "Introduction: No Deed but Memory," in W. Fitzhugh Brundage, ed., *Where These Memories Grow: History, Memory, and Southern Identity* (Chapel Hill: University of North Carolina Press, 2000), 4.

1. "Editor's Easy Chair," *Harper's* 31 (1865): 265–66; Eugene Exman, *The House of Harper: One Hundred and Fifty Years of Publishing* (New York: Harper & Row, 1967), 72.

2. "William Lloyd Garrison," *The Living Age* 94 (1867): 253–54; "Editor's Easy Chair," *Harper's* 35 (1867): 256–57.

3. "Editor's Easy Chair," *Harper's* 31 (1865): 398.

4. "Editor's Easy Chair," *Harper's* 35 (1867): 665–66.

5. "Editor's Easy Chair," *Harper's* 36 (1868): 813; V. B. Denslow, "Thirteen Years of the Nation, 1854–1867," *Putnam's Magazine* 11 (1868): 8–19, and "The Situation and the Candidates," *Putnam's Magazine* 12 (1868): 373–78. Van Buren Denslow was a frequent contributor to magazines, commenting on political and economic events. He also wrote fiction, including a 1857 piece titled *Owned, Disowned; or, The Chattel Child: A Tale of Southern Life*. In 1862, he also published a pamphlet about John Charles Frémont and George McClellan.

6. Ira V. Brown, *Mary Grew: Abolitionist and Feminist (1813–1896* (Selinsgrove, Pa.: Susquehanna University Press, 1991), 127; *NAS*, April 2, 1870.

7. Samuel J. May, *Some Recollections of Our Antislavery Conflict* (Miami: Mnemosyne Pub. Co., 1969), 210–11.

8. Daniel Yacovone has written a study of May titled *Samuel Joseph May and the Dilemmas of the Liberal Persuasion, 1797–1871* (Philadelphia: Temple University Press, 1991).

9. Samuel J. May Diary, January 17, March 9, April 25, 1867; January 22, February 12, 24, March 10, 11, May 25, 24, 27, September, 23, 1868; January 21, February 2, 10, 1869, May Papers, CUL.

10. For examples of his activities regarding freed people, see ibid., March 11, 19, April 30, 1867; January 8, February 3, 29, March 17, June 5, October 12, 14, 23, November 24, 28, 1868.

11. Ibid., February 26, May 26, 27, October 8, 30, 1868; March 2, April 20, May 12, 1869.

12. May, *Some Recollections*, iii; George Baker to Samuel May, December 9, 1867, in back of 1868 May diary, May Papers, CUL.

13. May, *Some Recollections*, 404; Justice to Samuel May, April 1868 in back of 1868 May diary, May Papers, CUL. May, who gave only excerpts of this letter in his recollections, omitted altogether "Justice's" comment about the "slightly self complacent tone" of May's work.

14. May, *Some Recollections*, 404, iii, v.

15. May diary, March 5, 1869, May Papers, CUL.

16. May diary, March 5, April 13, 1869; record of letters sent and received in 1869 diary, May Papers, CUL.

17. Fields & Osgood to Samuel J. May, May 13, 1869; and Pressed Letterbook, September 1866–February 1877, Records of Ticknor & Fields and Related Firms, in Houghton Mifflin Co. Records, HL; Ellen B. Ballou, *The Building of the House: Houghton Mifflin's Formative Years* (Boston: Houghton Mifflin Co., 1970), 165; Hellmut Lehmann-Haupt, *The Book in America* (New York: R. R. Bowker Co., 1939), 181; Augusta Rohrbach, *Truth Stranger than Fiction: Race, Realism, and the U.S. Literary Marketplace* (New York: Palgrave Press, 2002), 55.

18. Lawrence Buell, "Autobiography in the American Renaissance," in *American Autobiography: Retrospect and Prospect*, ed. Paul John Eakin (Madison: University of Wisconsin Press, 1991), 48. Scott E. Casper has written a valuable study of nineteenth-century biography titled *Constructing American Lives: Biography and Culture in Nineteenth-Century America* (Chapel Hill: University of North Carolina Press, 1999).

19. May diary, May 7, 11, 13, 20, 21, 31; June 3, 8, 9, 18, 26, 28, 29; July 1, 9, 12, 14, 19, 21, 22, 26, 27, 31, 1869.

20. In his discussion of fiction, James L. Machor suggests that reviews in popular journals reveal both the dissemination and assimilation of ideas about fiction and how to read it. It seems likely that his point about public interpretive practices could apply to autobiography as well. See his "Historical Hermeneutics and Antebellum Fiction: Gender, Response Theory, and Interpretive Contexts," in *Readers in History: Nineteenth-Century American Literature and the Contexts of Response*, ed. James L. Machor (Baltimore: Johns Hopkins University Press, 1993), 63–64. Nancy Glazener makes similar points in *Reading for Realism: The History of a U.S. Literary Institution, 1850–1910* (Durham: Duke University Press, 1997), 3, 14. She stresses the importance of the reviews published in the monthly periodicals in discussing genre, shaping reading practices, and providing recognition to authors and their works (see 24–26). For May's reading, see May diary, January 23, 1867; September 23, December 8, 1868; August 21, September 3, 1869. The following discussion about critical expectations of autobiography is drawn from "Autobiography of General Scott," *NAM* 100 (1865): 242–44; "Life and Times of Gardiner Spring," *NAM* 103 (1866): 269–76; "Horace Greeley's Recollections of a Busy Life," *Scientific American*, n.s., 19 (1868): 265–66; "Literature — At Home," *Putnam's Magazine* 14 (1869): 377–81; "Reviews and Literary Notices," *Atlantic Monthly* 23 (1869): 260–62; "Editor's Book

Table," *Harper's* 39 (1869): 146–51, 610–15; and "Stickney's Autobiography of Amos Kendall," *NAM* 116 (1873): 166–76.

21. "Editor's Book Table," *Harper's* 39 (1869): 614.

22. Quotations are from "Horace Greeley's Recollections," 265, and "Life and Times of Gardiner Spring," 275. Howard Helsinger's "Credence and Credibility: The Concern for Honesty in Victorian Autobiography," in *Approaches to Victorian Autobiography*, ed. George P. Landow (Athens: Ohio University Press, 1979), 40, argues that Victorians saw autobiography as a public discourse and were, therefore, aware of issues of propriety. This concern led them to avoid introspection.

23. "Literature—At Home," 379; "Books and Authors at Home and Abroad," *Scribner's* 1 (1871): 461; Horace Greeley's Recollections," 265. Greeley may well have composed his memoir with an eye to its possible utility as a political document. He was the candidate in 1872 of the Liberal Republicans. See "Reviews and Literary Notices," 260; Casper discusses the shift away from interest in the self-made and Christian man in biography in *Constructing American Lives*, 7.

24. "Stickney's Autobiography," 167; "Autobiography of General Scott," *NAM* 100 (1865): 243.

25. "Reviews and Literary Notices," 261; "Stickney's Autobiography," 167, 173; "Editor's Book Table," *Harper's* 39 (1869): 149; "Life and Times of Gardiner Spring," 276.

26. Brief mentions of family include references to his father (23–24), his "precious" wife (235), and his eldest son (298) in May, *Some Recollections*.

27. Ibid., 19–20, 89.

28. "Autobiography of Elder Jacob Knapp," *New Englander and Yale Review* 27 (1868): 612; May, *Some Recollections*, 39, 62–64; see also 356, 363. May implied that much of the credit for managing the Crandall affair was due to Charles Burleigh, an able young law student, who later became a major abolitionist figure in his own right. At the very least, May could have claimed credit for recruiting Burleigh for the abolitionist cause. Instead, his lavish praise of Burleigh suggested that anyone could have seen his future value to abolitionism. "I do not believe that Samuel of old saw . . . the man whom the Lord would have him anoint, more clearly that I saw in C. C. Burleigh the man whom I should choose to be my assistant in that emergency," May wrote. "So soon as I had told him what I wanted of him his eye kindled as if eager for conflict" (May, *Some Recollections*, 64).

29. Yacovone, *Samuel Joseph May*, 178–80; Carol Faulkner, *Women's Radical Reconstruction: The Freedman's Aid Movement* (Philadelphia: University of Pennsylvania Press, 2004), 46; Kathleen Diffley, *Where My Heart Is Turning Ever: Civil War Stories and Constitutional Reform, 1861–1876*, (Athens: University of Georgia Press, 1992), 134; Howard N. Rabinowitz, "Segregation and Reconstruction," in *The Facts of Reconstruction: Essays in Honor of John Hope Franklin*, ed. Eric Anderson and Alfred A. Moss Jr. (Baton Rouge: Louisiana State University Press, 1991), 91–93; David Herbert Donald, Jean H. Baker, and Michael F. Holt, *The Civil War and Reconstruction* (New York: W. W. Norton, 2001), 543–48.

30. Elizabeth W. Bruss points to the important clues that titles of autobiographies provide in *Autobiographical Acts: The Changing Situation of a Literary Genre* (Bal-

timore: Johns Hopkins University Press, 1976), 22. May's view that the war was not yet over is one that Richard Nelson Current has proposed in *Arguing with Historians: Essays on the Historical and the Unhistorical* (Middletown, Conn.: Wesleyan University Press, 1987), 79.

31. May, *Some Recollections*, 305.

32. Ibid., iii, iv, 126, 373. May suggested that Garrison's personal modesty might well prevent him from properly assessing his own role, and, like May, would be unable to provide "ample justice" for those "fellow-laborers" whom he did not know personally.

33. Ibid., iii, 2, 3, 79, 256, 33. As Marcus Billson would have it in "The Memoir: New Perspectives on a Forgotten Genre," *Genre* 10 (Summer 1977): 261, 264, May was arguing for the truth of his version of history. See also Timothy Dow Adams, *Telling Lies in Modern American Autobiography* (Chapel Hill: University of North Carolina Press, 1990), 30.

34. See Julie Roy Jeffrey, "'No Occurrence in Human History Is More Deserving of Commemoration Than This': Abolitionist Celebrations of Freedom," in *Prophets of Protest: Reconsidering the History of American Abolitionism*, ed. John Stauffer and Timothy Patrick McCarthy (New York: New Press, 2006), 200–219. The emphasis on sacred documents was not just an extension of prewar rhetoric but must be related to the emphasis at this time on amending the constitution. See May, *Some Recollections*, 1, 4.

35. May, *Some Recollections*, 1, 4, 126.

36. Ibid., 85, 87, 4, 89, 318–19, 349. In a similar manner, opposition to the Fugitive Slave Act in the 1850s represented another "proud episode" in the nation's history.

37. Ibid., v, 238–39, 126–27.

38. Ibid., 185.

39. Ibid., 1, 3–5, 15–16, 18–19, 33–35, 229, 332. The nearest May came to recognizing a human flaw in his hero was Garrison's extreme language. May was not the only abolitionist who worried that Garrison's rhetoric might be counterproductive. Yet the anecdote he included in his book about this issue suggested his initial criticism had been misplaced. Not long after the *Liberator* was founded, May reported, he had urged Garrison to "moderate" his indignation, to "keep more cool." "Why," he exclaimed to Garrison, "you are all on fire." Garrison acknowledged that May was right but pointed out that he "had mountains of ice" to melt. May concluded his story by pointing out that he had never brought the topic up again "from that hour to this. . . . I am more than half satisfied now that he was right then, and we who objected were mistaken" (ibid., 36–37).

40. For some examples, see ibid., 94, 63–65, 43, 66, 169, 205, 230, 222, 290. See also Martha Watson, *Lives of Their Own: Rhetorical Dimensions in Autobiographies of Women Activists* (Columbia: University of South Carolina Press, 1999), 105, 109.

41. May, *Some Recollections*, 253–56, 189, 64–66, 96. Carol Faulkner in *Women's Radical Reconstruction*, 35, suggests that male abolitionists after the war were attempting to masculinize reform. Clearly, May was not part of this effort. See also George M. Frederickson, *The Inner Civil War: Northern Intellectuals and the Crisis of Union* (New York: Harper & Row, 1965), 176; R. Anthony Rotundo, "Learning About Manhood:

Gender Ideas and the Middle Class Family in Nineteenth Century America," in *Manliness and Morality: Middle-Class Masculinity in Britain and America, 1800–1940*, ed. J. A. Mangan and James Walvin (New York: St. Martin's Press, 1987), 36–38; and Alice Fahs, *The Imagined Civil War: Popular Literature of the North and South, 1861–1865* (Chapel Hill: University of North Carolina Press, 2001), 94, 106.

42. May, *Some Recollections*, 19–20. Paul John Eakin in *Touching the World: Reference in Autobiography* (Princeton: Princeton University Press, 1992), 72, 76, 77, 89, points out that people adopt the models of identity available in their culture as they are growing up.

43. Eakin, *Touching the World*, 245, 97, 230–37, 244, 245, 91–92, 97–100; Yacovone, *Samuel Joseph May*, 181.

44. May, *Some Recollections*, 127, 134, 214, 94.

45. Ibid., 65, 79.

46. Ibid., 35, 157, 152–53, 156–57, 221–30, 391–95. Despite May's intention to write about material and people that he knew firsthand, he included "infamous" events that he had only heard about in order to strengthen his narrative: for example, the destruction of Garrison's antislavery office in Boston; the 1835 riot in Utica, New York; and the murder of Rev. Elijah P. Lovejoy in Alton, Illinois, in 1837.

47. For mentions of war see ibid., iii, 50, 100, 263, 328, 331, 344, 384, 395. See also Frederickson, *Inner Civil War*, 81–82; Fahs, *Imagined Civil War*, 289, 292, 294, 296; and Matthew J. Grow, "The Shadow of the Civil War: A Historiography of Civil War Memory," *American Nineteenth Century History* 4 (Summer 2003): 94.

48. May, *Some Recollections*, 317, 313; Heather Cox Richardson, *The Death of Reconstruction: Race, Labor, and Politics in the Post–Civil War North, 1865–1901* (Cambridge, Mass.: Harvard University Press, 2001), 30, 71.

49. May, *Some Recollections*, 137, 185; Earl J. Hess, *Liberty, Virtue, and Progress: Northerners and Their War for Union* (New York: New York University Press, 1988), 104.

50. May, *Some Recollections*, 225, 136, 128–29.

51. Ibid., 177, 128, 329.

52. Ibid., 344, 333, iv.

53. Ibid., 239–41, 329, 331.

54. Ibid., 147–50, 336–37.

55. Ibid., 337.

56. Ibid., 266–67. Edward J. Blum, in *Reforging the White Republic: Race, Religion, and American Nationalism, 1865–1898* (Baton Rouge: Louisiana State University Press, 2005), 22–45, argues that the clergy played an important role after the Civil War in supporting new and more egalitarian racial arrangements. This interpretation would suggest that at least part of May's narrative contributed to this effort.

57. May, *Some Recollections*, 328, 268–69. May gave a moving description of his own emotional rejection of prejudice when he recalled having to tell Crandall's students that the school was about to be closed. "The words almost blistered on my lips," he recalled. "My bosom glowed with indignation. I felt ashamed of Canterbury, ashamed of Connecticut, ashamed of my country, ashamed of my color" (ibid., 71).

58. Ibid., 25, 271–72, 285–96.

59. Ibid., 285–96, 303–4. As Carol Faulkner points out in *Women's Radical Reconstruction*, 94, worries about black dependency were widespread during Reconstruction.

60. May, *Some Recollections*, 297–98.

61. Ibid., 296–303, 278–85.

62. Ibid., 279–83.

63. Ibid., 271–77.

64. Ibid., 233, 82, 352, 293, 97, 266, 312, 102–3; Linda H. Peterson, "Audience and the Autobiographer's Art: An Approach to the *Autobiography* of Mrs. M. O. W. Oliphant," in *Approaches to Victorian Autobiography*, ed. George P. Landow (Athens: Ohio University Press, 1979), 158; Stephen Railton, "The Address of *The Scarlet Letter*," in Machor, ed., *Readers in History*, 138–39; Barbara Hochman, *Getting at the Author: Reimagining Books and Reading in the Age of American Realism* (Amherst: University of Massachusetts Press, 2001), 12, 22, 36.

65. *Brooklyn Eagle*, August 10, 1869; John D. Barbour, *The Conscience of the Autobiographer: Ethical and Religious Dimensions of Autobiography* (London: Macmillan, 1992), 23.

66. May, *Some Recollections*, 367, 234, 271, 337–38. For another example of moderation and balance see his treatment of Horace Mann, 312. As Marcus Billson points out in "Memoir," 264, claiming reliability is more of a rhetorical device to influence readers than a scientific approach to the facts.

67. May, *Some Recollections*, 227–28. Alice Fahs, in *Imagined Civil War*, 122, points out the importance of feeling in a sentimental culture. May was trying to make the reader feel along with him.

68. For an example of a re-created conversation, see May, *Some Recollections*, 49–50, 23. See also Heather Cox Richardson, *Death of Reconstruction*, 124–25.

69. May, *Some Recollections*, 260, 235–36, 64, 269.

70. Ibid., 227, 157, 150, 335, 336, 337, 407.

71. Casper, *Constructing American Lives*, 237; May diary, July 6, August 6, September 14, 1869, May Papers, CUL; *New York Times*, September 8, 1869; *American Literary Gazette and Publishers' Circular* 13 (September 15, 1869): 314.

72. May diary, September 18, October 8, December 10, 1869, May Papers, CUL; *NAS*, December 25, 1869.

73. Beverly Wilson Palmer, ed., *Selected Letters of Lucretia Coffin Mott* (Urbana: University of Illinois Press, 2002), 436; *NAS*, December 25, 1869.

74. Thomas J. Pressly, *Americans Interpret Their Civil War* (New York: Collier Books, 1962 ed.), 58, 60; Nina Silber, *The Romance of Reunion: Northerners and the South, 1865–1900* (Chapel Hill: University of North Carolina Press, 1993), 124–26; Kirk Savage, *Standing Soldiers, Kneeling Slaves: Race, War, and Monument in Nineteenth-Century America* (Princeton: Princeton University Press, 1997), 89–103; Thomas L. Connelly and Barbara L. Bellows, *God and General Longstreet: The Lost Cause and the Southern Mind* (Baton Rouge: Louisiana State University Press, 1982), 48. Since the monthlies were in stiff competition with one another it seems likely that what they

chose to include in the journals reflected messages that their middle-class audience found acceptable.

75. "Editor's Easy Chair," *Harper's* 36 (1868): 812; Diffley, *Where My Heart Is Turning Ever*, xviii; Louise L. Stevenson, *The Victorian Homefront: American Thought and Culture, 1860–1880* (Ithaca: Cornell University Press, 2001), 137. For a discussion of novels, see Lyde Cullen Sizer, *The Political Work of Northern Women Writers and the Civil War, 1850–1872* (Chapel Hill: University of North Carolina Press, 2000), 231–44.

76. Elizabeth Stuart Phelps, "Too Late," *Harper's* 32 (1866): 468–74; "Elizabeth Stuart Phelps (Ward)," <http: www.readseries.com/auth-oz/phelps-daught.html>; Donald Edward Liedel, "The Antislavery Novel, 1836–1861" (Ph.D. diss., University of Michigan, 1961), 6. For Phelps's views on teaching freed people, see Elizabeth Stuart Phelps, "Why Shall They Do It?" *Harper's* 36 (1868): 220–21.

77. Phelps, "Too Late," 469.

78. Liedel, "Antislavery Novel," 164–95; Fahs, *Imagined Civil War*, 171.

79. "Reviews and Literary Notices," *Atlantic Monthly* 24 (1869): 644; Fahs, *Imagined Civil War*, 169.

80. M. Schele DeVere, "The Freedman's Story," *Harper's* 33 (1866): 647–50, 652, 654–57; *Cyclopedia of American Literature* (Philadelphia: Baxter Publishing Co., 1881), 747.

81. Robert M. Copeland, "My Man Anthony," *Putnam's Magazine* 13 (1869): 452–53.

82. Ibid., 454–55; Heather Cox Richardson, *Death of Reconstruction*, 7. A different form of success story appeared in "Uncle Gabriel's Account of His Campaigns," also published in 1869 in *Atlantic Monthly*. This was purportedly the true story of Gabriel Edwards's war service with the two sons of his Confederate mistress, Miss Flora. Gabriel is the faithful family retainer who has "loved Miss Flora from the very first time I saw her." In this story, it is Gabriel rather than the mistress or her sons who is the figure of strength. He understands the dangers of war as the rash young men do not. He brings the dead body of one son home and saves the life of the other who was terribly wounded. He lies to the pale and wasted Flora who wants to know if her dead son had read his Bible the night before being killed. The young man had spent his evening drinking wine, but Gabriel assures his mistress that her son had held a prayer meeting. At the end of the story, Gabriel receives twenty-five acres and a house from Miss Flora rather than forty acres and a mule from the federal government as a reward for his fidelity. The resolution of this story held out the promise of economic independence for blacks in the South in a painless manner for northerners. See "Uncle Gabriel's Account of His Campaigns," *Atlantic Monthly* 24 (1869): 207–8, 210–14.

83. In one 1866 story, however, the St. Leons from New Orleans move north and become neighbors and friends of the white narrator. But both of the St. Leons are very light skinned. See D. H. Castleton, "The St. Leons," *Harper's* 33 (1866): 373–84; see also N. W. Sikes, "Absalom Mather," *Harper's* 33 (1866): 466, and Fahs, *Imagined Civil War*, 175.

84. William M. Baker, "The New Timothy," *Harper's* 37 (1868): 391–93.

85. Phelps, "Why Shall They Do It?" 212–22; Phelps, "Too Late," 468; Copeland, "My Man Anthony," 444, 446; Sikes, "Absalom Mather," 466–67.

86. "A Pioneer Editor," *Atlantic Monthly* 17 (1866): 747; V. B. Denslow, "Chief-Justice Chase," *Putnam's Magazine* 12 (1868): 111; "Official Life of Governor Andrew," *Putnam's Magazine* 12 (1868): 250; Eugene Benson, "New York Journalists: Parke Godwin, of the Evening Post," *Galaxy* 7 (1869): 230–31.

87. V. B. Denslow, "Thirteen Years of the Nation, 1854–1867," *Putnam's Magazine* 11 (1868): 10, 16. Information on Denslow's publications can be found at <http://www.abebooks.com/servlet/SearchResults?bx=off&sts=t&ds=30&bi=0&an=denslow%2Cvan+buren&y=10&x=63&sortby=2>.

88. "New Aspects of the American Mind," *Harper's* 34 (1867): 793, 799.

89. J. W. De Forest, "Drawing Bureau Rations," *Harper's* 36 (1868): 795, 798; "Drawing Bureau Rations, ii," *Harper's* 37 (1868): 76.

90. J. W. De Forest, "Lieutenant Barker's Ghost Story," *Harper's* 39 (1869): 713–14.

91. Joshua Emett Brown, "*Frank Leslie's Illustrated Newspaper*: The Pictorial Press and the Representations of America, 1855–1889" (Ph.D. diss., Columbia University, 1993), 199–202; Fahs, *Imagined Civil War*, 165; "Editor's Easy Chair," *Harper's* 36 (1868): 812.

92. Randolph B. Marcy, "Border Reminiscences," *Harper's* 39 (1869): 483–88. The illustration appears on page 485.

93. "The Usurpation" by George S. Boutwell, which appeared in *Atlantic Monthly* 18 (1866): 506–7, had decried Andrew Johnson for failure to uphold ideals of black civic equality. V. B. Denslow, "The Situation and the Candidates," *Putnam's Magazine* 12 (1868): 374–76.

94. "Editor's Book Table," *Harper's* 38 (1868): 148; "Reviews and Literary Notices," *Atlantic Monthly* 23 (1869): 134–35.

95. "Uncle Gabriel's Account," 207, 214.

96. Phillips quoted in David W. Blight, *Race and Reunion: The Civil War in American Memory* (Cambridge, Mass.: Harvard University Press, 2001), 50; Liedel, "Antislavery Novel," 231–32; J. W. De Forest, "Chivalrous and Semi-Chivalrous Southrons," *Harper's* 38 (1869): 192, 197–98, 345, 200, 339–40.

97. Donald, Baker, and Holt, *Civil War and Reconstruction*, 559, 594–97; quotations, 594, 595.

98. May, *Some Recollections*, 266, 134, 289, 211.

99. Ibid., 20, 395–96; Frederickson, *Inner Civil War*, 122. As Roy Pascal says in *Design and Truth in Autobiography* (New York: Garland, 1985 ed.), 11, the significance of an autobiography rests in its "revelation of the present situation" rather than "the uncovering of the past."

100. "Editor's Literary Record," *Harper's* 43 (1871): 301; "Publishers' Department," *Scribner's* 4 (1874): 6.

101. May diary, 10 December 1869, May Papers, CUL; Copyright Accounts, 1860–76, Records of Ticknor & Fields and Related Firms, in Houghton Mifflin Co. Records, HL. For help in interpreting this information, as well as materials in his microfilmed Houghton Mifflin records, I am indebted to Professor Michael Winship at the University of Texas. See e-mails between the author and Winship, Janu-

ary 17, 18, 2007. Winship provided me with cost figures that suggest that for the publisher to break even, over 2,000 copies of the book would have to be sold.

102. Frank Garrison to Parker Pillsbury, June 20, 1883, Pillsbury Papers, WCL. For an overview of the changing nature of Fields & Osgood (by 1871 called James R. Osgood & Company), see Ellery Sedgwick, *The Atlantic Monthly, 1857–1909: Yankee Humanism at High Tide and Ebb* (Amherst: University of Massachusetts Press, 1994), 71, 82, 19, 108–10. Frank Garrison began his career at Houghton Mifflin in 1871 at the Riverside Press. See Harriet Hyman Alonso, *Growing Up Abolitionist: The Story of the Garrison Children* (Amherst: University of Massachusetts Press, 2002), 239.

103. May diary, November 26, 27, 30, 1870, May Papers, CUL. See the description of the Cornell holdings at <http://www.library.cornell.edu/mayantislavery.history_p2.htm>.

CHAPTER TWO

1. *Harper's Weekly*, February 26, 1870, April 8, 1871. For information about Rogers, see the following website and its links: <http:dlxs.library.cornell.edu/m/mayantislavery/collection.html>, <http://www.johnrogers.org/vendors.htm>, and <http://78.1911encyclopedia.org/R/RO/ROGERS_JOHN_1829_1904_.htm>. See also Henry Mayer, *All On Fire: William Lloyd Garrison and the Abolition of American Slavery* (New York: St. Martin's Press, 1998), 618.

2. *National Standard*, n.s., June 1870, 83–84; William Still, *The Underground Rail Road* (Philadelphia: Porter and Coates, 1872; reprint, New York: Arno Press, 1978), 1.

3. Fergus M. Bordewich, *Bound for Canaan: The Underground Railroad and the War for the Soul of America* (New York: Harper Collins, 2005), 355–56, 431, 435.

4. For a copy of Still's letter to the New York *Tribune*, see Still, *Underground Rail Road*, 87–91; for examples of letters to Still, see ibid., 252–53, 120, 234, 323, 497–98. In a letter to the *New National Era*, March 21, 1872, Still commented that the book was to be published within a few days.

5. Still, *Underground Rail Road*, pictures opposite 400, 83, 329, 385, 611–12.

6. Ibid., title page and portrait facing title page, 1.

7. Ibid., 4–5, 101, 132, 202, 531, 417, 419.

8. Ibid., 3, 6, 584, 241, 648, 75.

9. Ibid., 272, 494, 321.

10. Ibid., 79, 146, 121, 653, 6; James McKim to Still, March 15, 1872, Still Papers, HSP.

11. Still, *Underground Rail Road*, 214, 5, 343. For his sense that he was providing a historical record where none existed, see Still to W. G. Fields, June 5, 1873, Still Letterbook, Still Papers, HSP.

12. Eric Foner, *A Short History of Reconstruction, 1863–1877* (New York: Harper & Row, 1990), 194–98, 213–16; quotation, 197. For other accounts of the split in the Republican Party and the election of 1872, see Michael Les Benedict, "Reform Republicans and the Retreat from Reconstruction," in *The Facts of Reconstruction: Essays in Honor of John Hope Franklin*, ed. Eric Anderson and Alfred A. Moss Jr. (Baton Rouge: Louisiana State University Press, 1991), 53–77, and Gary W. Gallagher, "Shaping Public Memory of the Civil War: Robert E. Lee, Jubal A. Early, and Douglas South-

all Freeman," in *The Memory of the Civil War in American Culture*, ed. Alice Fahs and Joan Waugh (Chapel Hill: University of North Carolina Press, 2004), 39–63.

13. Still to Edward, October 13, 1873; Still to W. L. Leister, June 10, 1873, Still Letterbook, Still Papers, HSP; *Christian Recorder*, April 27, 1872.

14. Still, *Underground Rail Road*, 23–38.

15. Ibid., 157.

16. Ibid., 137, 223, 336, 419, 610.

17. Ibid., 81.

18. Robert B. Stepto, "Narration, Authentication, and Authorial Control in Frederick Douglass's *Narrative* of 1845," in William L. Andrews, ed., *African American Autobiography: A Collection of Critical Essays* (Englewood Cliffs, N.J.: Prentice Hall, 1993), 26; Still, *Underground Rail Road*, 133, 147; for another example of direct testimony that probably comes from interview questions, see Still, *Underground Rail Road*, 204.

19. For other examples, see Still, *Underground Rail Road*, 242, 239–40, 306, 317.

20. Ibid., 239, 494, 76, 111, 40, 56, 342–43.

21. William L. Andrews, "The Representation of Slavery and the Rise of Afro-American Literary Realism, 1865–1920," in Andrews, ed., *African American Autobiography*, 78; Still, *Underground Rail Road*, 6.

22. Raymond Hedin, "Probable Readers, Possible Stories: The Limits of Nineteenth-Century Black Narrative," in *Readers in History: Nineteenth-Century American Literature and the Contexts of Response*, ed. James L. Machor (Baltimore: Johns Hopkins University Press, 1993), 186; Still, *Underground Rail Road*, 444, 425, 464, 209, 497, 495, 414, 419.

23. Still, *Underground Rail Road*, 52, 416, 76, 123, 393, 301, 317, 447, 73, 473, 504.

24. Ibid., 48, 54–55, 107, 97, 72–73.

25. Ibid., 2, 62, 66, 136, 81, 99, 121, 203, 71, 232, 140.

26. Ibid., 326, 37–38, 177–89, 80.

27. Ibid., 66, 190, 319, 52, 65, 55, 76, 127, 161, 211, 273.

28. Ibid., 121, 2.

29. Ibid., 67, 100, 134, 260.

30. Ibid., 100, 142, 201.

31. Ibid., 126, 79, 140, 487. Andrews, "Representation of Slavery," 79, points out that slave narratives emphasized brutality to show the necessity of escape.

32. Andrews, "Representation of Slavery," 81; Still, *Underground Rail Road*, 265–66, 112–17, 431, 433, 435, 440.

33. Still, *Underground Rail Road*, pictures opposite 50, 102, 125, and on 302, 424, 425, 495, 538. Other examples of these kinds of images are a young black woman shooting her gun seemingly pushing armed white men to retreat and blacks and whites in separate boats battling it out with their oars.

34. Ibid., 558–59.

35. Ibid., 678.

36. Ibid., 34–35.

37. Ibid., 125.

38. Ibid., 100, 113, 129–30, 211–12, 294, 71, 378, 383, 293, 414, 434, 441, 414, 397.

39. Ibid., 399.

40. Ibid., 397, 378.

41. Ibid., 480, 225, 456, 174.

42. Ibid., 481–85.

43. Still to Rev. E. L. Jones, June 14, 1873, Still Letterbook, Still Papers, HSP; Still, *Underground Rail Road*, 271–72.

44. Still, *Underground Rail Road*, 191, 332, 445, 474, 539, 541, 257–58.

45. Ibid., 448, 439.

46. Ibid., 540–47.

47. Ibid., title page, 283.

48. For a telling comparison, see the scene of slaves disembarking from a vessel at night, opposite 561, with the four heads titled "Faithful Workers in the Cause," opposite 623, in ibid.

49. Ibid., 637, 623–41.

50. Ibid., 680–88. See 723 for similar comments from Charles D. Cleveland's son, who knew his father would "forbid any detailed account of what he accomplished and endured."

51. Ibid., 659, 665, 668, 689–90.

52. Ibid., 755. For an idea of Harper's efforts during Reconstruction, see 768–71.

53. Ibid., 779–80.

54. Ibid., 770–78.

55. Frank Luther Mott, *Golden Multitudes: The Story of Best Sellers in the United States* (New York: Macmillan, 1947), 158; Scott E. Casper, *Constructing American Lives: Biography and Culture in Nineteenth-Century America* (Chapel Hill: University of North Carolina Press, 1999), 241; Walter Sutton, *The Western Book Trade: Cincinnati as a Nineteenth-Century Publishing and Book-Trade Center* (Columbus: Ohio State University Press, 1961), 229; John Tebbel, *A History of Book Publishing in the United States*, vol. 2 (New York: R. R. Bowker, 1975), 365, 511–12, 517; Nancy Cook, "Reshaping Publishing and Authorship in the Gilded Age," in *Perspectives on American Book History*, ed. Scott E. Casper, Joanne D. Chaison, and Jeffrey D. Groves (Amherst: University of Massachusetts Press, 2002), 245; "Editor's Literary Record," *Harper's* 41 (1870): 300. The Reader's Report of September 1, 1883, for a manuscript submitted to Houghton Mifflin (Houghton Mifflin Co. Records, HL) suggests the wariness of publishers toward very long books. In this case the manuscript would have resulted in a 600-page book, a length that the report suggested would be "fatal" to its chances of success.

56. William Still to Rev. W. S. Lowry, January 26, 1874, Still Letterbook, Still Papers, HSP; Agreement and Supplemental Agreement between Porter & Coates and William Still, January 29, 1872, Still Papers, HSP.

57. Although dissatisfaction with sales was not Still's major reason for ending the arrangement, he may not have been pleased with how Porter & Coates was handling that part of the operation. In a July 25, 1873, letter to V. A. Bell (Still Letterbook, Still Papers, HSP), responding to Bell's comment that California and the adjoining states had been pretty thoroughly canvassed, Still suggested that, except for Virginia City, previous canvassers had only skimmed the area. Possibly Porter

& Coates used only white canvassers, and this, too, probably presented a problem for Still. For Still's goals, see letter from Still to S. S. Grinell, June 9, 1873, Still Letterbook, Still Papers, HSP, and also his letter to the *New National Era*, June 26, 1873. Donald Sheehan, in *This Was Publishing: A Chronology of the Book Trade in the Gilded Age* (Bloomington: Indiana University Press, 1952), 29–30, states that between 1880 and 1882, only 20 percent of first books published by Scribner's sold more than 1,500 copies. These figures highlight Still's ambitious goal. The 1883 copy of the book merely says "Philadelphia, William Still publisher." This information comes from a copy of the 1883 edition, viewed at <http://www.abebooks.com/servlet/SearchResults?bx=off&sts=t&ds=30&bi=0&an=still%2C+william&y=10&tn=underground+railroad&x=74&sortby=2> (accessed July 27, 2006).

58. Still letters to W. H. Jones, June 3, 1873; to William Perry, June 5, 1873; to Thomas E. Franklin, April 9, 1874; to Rev. E. C. Joiner, August 8, 1873; to Charles Irving, October 30, 1873, Still Letterbook, Still Papers, HSP.

59. Still letters to W. H. Jones, June 3, 1873, and to Christopher Furness, June 20, 1873, Still Letterbook, Still Papers, HSP. In a January 20, 1874, communication with Rev. Jones (ibid.), Still said that he gave a 50 percent discount while the normal rate was 40 percent. So he may have changed what he offered agents. In any case, he claimed that his personal profits were small. See also letter from Still to Rev. W. S. Lowry, January 26, 1874, ibid.; and *New National Era*, June 26, 1873.

60. Still letters to E. C. Greer, June 3, 1873; to Dr. J. Holmes, June 10, 1873; to W. G. Fields, June 5, 1873; to W. L. Leister, June 10, 1873; to Rebecca S. Travel, June 23, 1873, Still Letterbook, Still Papers, HSP; Cook, "Reshaping Publishing," 245. In *This Was Publishing*, 151, Sheehan suggests that $3.50 was expensive for a cloth-bound book in the mid-1880s. If he is correct, then even the cheapest version of Still's book was costly.

61. Information about how Still hoped his agents would sell the book come from the following letters in Still Letterbook, Still Papers, HSP: to E. C. Greer, June 3, 1873; to S. S. Grinell, June 9, 1873; to Robert Furnas, June 18, 1873; to J. C. Price, June 23, 1873; to Mrs. A. W. Viney, June 26, 1873; to N. W. Curry, July 21, 1873; to Mrs. Mary Young, August 7, 1873; to Edward, October 8, 1873; to William Maben, October 9, 1873; to Rev. W. H. Day, December 17, 1873. See also Tebbel, *History of Book Publishing*, 522; *Christian Recorder*, March 3, 1872, September 10, 1874; and letter to Rev. E. C. Jones, January 20, 1874, Still Letterbook, Still Papers, HSP.

62. *New National Era*, June 26, 1873.

63. Still letters to Brown, December 23, 1873; to Rev. E. C. Jones, January 20, 1874; to Dungie, February 20, 1874; to J. C. Price, June 12, 1873; to D. W. Boxley, September 1, 1873; to John P. Green, June 17, 1873, Still Letterbook, Still Papers, HSP. In his letter to Brown, Still commiserated over the disappointing sales of Brown's book and urged him not to be disheartened. The most faithful workers in reform, he suggested, always faced struggle and difficulties in reaching their goals. See also *New National Era*, June 26, 1873.

64. Still letters to Wm. Jones, June 5 and 12, 1873; to Wm. H. Steward, June 17, 1873; to Rev. W. S. Lowry, January 8, 26, 1874, Still Letterbook, Still Papers, HSP.

65. Still letters to Dr. Henry Charles, June 6, 1873; to Rev. E. C. Joiner, August 8, 1873; to W. L. Leister, June 10, 1873, ibid.

66. Notice from Library of Congress, April 11, 1872, Still Papers, HSP; Still letters to Mary, June 28, 1873; to N. W. Curry, July 21, 1873; to E. C. Greer, June 3, 1873; to Rev. W. D. Harris, June 5, 1873; to S. S. Grinell, August 4, 1873; to Edward, October 13, 1873, Still Letterbook, Still Papers, HSP; anonymous letter to Still, March 4, 1874, Still Papers, HSP.

67. Oliver Johnson to Still, April 11, 1872, Still Papers, HSP.

68. For information on the critical response, see *Christian Recorder*, September 10, 1874; *New York Times*, April 18, 1872; and "Editor's Literary Record," *Harper's* 45 (1872): 302; for indications of qualities that reviewers and publishers looked for in a good autobiography, see "Publishers' Department," *Scribner's* 4 (1872): 6; "Culture and Progress," *Scribner's* 5 (1872): 271; "Stickney's Autobiography of Amos Kendall," *NAM* 116 (1873): 166–76; Reader's Report, January 15, 1883, Houghton Mifflin Co. Records, HL; and Still to Rev. G. C. Jones, January 20, 1874, Still Letterbook, Still Papers, HSP.

69. Still letters to Edward, October 2, 1873; to Mary, November 11, 1873; to Rev. R. Jones, November 12, 1873; to Mrs. Mary Jackson, December 11, 1872; to Rev. W. H. Day, December 17, 1873; to Rev. J. B. Caldwell, April 16, 1874, Still Letterbook, Still Papers, Still Papers, HSP; Still to W. H. Stanton, January 15, 1878, Still Papers, HSP. For a brief account of the depression's impact, see Foner, *Short History*, 217–22.

70. *New York Times*, September 9, 1877; *Christian Recorder*, September 19, 1878; Larry Gara, "William Still," in John A. Garraty and Mark C. Carnes, eds., *American National Biography* (New York: Oxford University Press, 1999), 20:776; P. L. Lamont to Still, October 7, 1886, Still Papers, HSP. I learned of the volume acquired by Mark Twain on the Abebooks site mentioned below, which I viewed on July 26, 2006. The seller of the book described this volume in the following way:

Book Description: Philadelphia: Wm. Still, Publishers, 1883. Hardcover. Book Condition: Very Good. Original deluxe maroon cloth gilt-extra, all edges gilt, the deluxe premium binding. Engraved frontispiece portrait of the author, numerous wood-engraved plates and text illustrations. Inner hinges tender, a few leaves slightly pulled. An excellent copy. Half maroon morocco case. A splendid association copy, from Mark Twain's library, with a lengthy anecdote in his hand about an escaped slave on the front flyleaf. . . . This fabulous copy of Still's Underground Railroad bears a full-page, 146-word anecdote in Twain's handwriting recording a slave's escape similar to those described by Still. Twain, who heard the heart-wrenching story from his mother-in-law, Olivia Lewis Langdon, writes: Mrs. Luckett was a slave in Richmond, with a daughter 3 years old. Her brother, Jones, an escaped slave, lived in Elmira (1844.) He cut two duplicate hearts out of pink paper, & wrote on one, "When you see this again, you will know." No other word accompanied it. After a while a white man went [to] Richmond with the other heart, called on the woman's mistress on some pretext which brought in the slaves: Mrs. L. saw & recognized the duplicate heart; she escaped, with her child in the night, joined the man at a place appointed, (Annapolis,) & thence got through safely to Elmira. She lives in Canada, now (whither she had to flee when the fugitive slave law was passed (1850,) & the child is also married & lives in Binghamton, N.Y., (1884.) This account given by Mother, who knew the several parties. Twain had great interest in the problem of slavery. In Huckleberry Finn, Jim escapes from slavery and travels down the Mississippi River on a raft with Huck, and in Pudd'nhead Wilson, Twain explores the absurdity of slavery. In this volume Twain has also closely marked Still's section on Seth Concklin (pages 24–38) with marginal rules. Mrs. Luckett's adventure shares many elements in common with Clemens's celebrated dialect narrative . . . A True Story Repeated Word for Word as I Heard It . . . (1874), and he may have written the present sketch concerning the escape of Mrs. Luckett and her daughter in anticipation of expanding it to a full short story. Gribben, Mark Twain's Library 666. Bookseller Inventory # ABE-697709820. (<http://www.abebooks.com/servlet/SearchResults?bx= off&sts=t&ds=30&bi=0&an=still%2C+william&y=10&tn=underground+ railroad&x=74&sortby=2>)

71. Still to J. L. Evans, February 20, 1874, Still Letterbook, Still Papers, HSP.

72. The narratives are John Quincy Adams, *Narrative of the Life of John Quincy Adams, When in Slavery, and Now as a Freeman* (Harrisburg, Pa.: Sieg, Printer and Stationer, 1872), 3, and William Webb, *The History of William Webb, Composed by Himself* (Detroit: Egbert Hoekstra, 1873). See also William L. Andrews, "The Spirit of Friday Jones" (Greenville, N.C.: J. Y. Joyner Library, East Carolina University, 1999), 2–3, at the Documenting the American South website of the University of North Carolina at Chapel Hill Libraries, <http://docsouth.unc.edu/neh/fjones/support2.html>.

73. Reader's Report, April 11, 1885, Houghton Mifflin Co. Records, HL. The book was a told-to narrative and was eventually published. The white minister who "authored" the story explained,

The following narrative was prepared without intention of publication; but I have been led to think that it may be of use, not only as a reminiscence of the "war of secession," but as a fair presentation of slavery in the Border States for the twenty or thirty years preceding the outbreak of hostilities. I am confirmed in this view by the fact, that, on submitting the manuscript to a leading publishing-house in a Northern city, it was objected to, among other reasons, as too tame to satisfy the public taste and judgment. But, from equally intelligent parties in a city farther south, the exactly opposite criticism was made, as if a too harsh judgment of slavery and slave-holders was conveyed, so that its publication would be prejudicial to those undertaking it.

I therefore asked the opinion of several friends, who, like myself, had lived all those years under the shadow of the "peculiar institution," in one or other of the northern tier of the slave States, and who labored faithfully for its abolition, giving the best service of their lives to the cause of freedom, "possessing their souls in patience" while contending against what seemed to be an irresistible power. Their concurrence has confirmed me in the opinion, that, however feebly drawn, a true picture, so far as it goes, is given in these pages of the relation between master and slave, and of the social condition of slave-holding communities. Without claiming to be more than a plain story plainly told, it shows things as they were, and how they were regarded by intelligent and thoughtful people at the time. (William G. Elliot, *From Slavery to Freedom: The Story of Archer Alexander* [Boston: Cupples, Upham & Co., 1885], 5–6.)

74. Ann Fabian, *The Unvarnished Truth: Personal Narratives in Nineteenth-Century America* (Berkeley: University of California Press, 2000), 17–18, 51–52, 120–21, 124–25; John Quincy Adams, *Life*, 3; Webb, *History*, page opposite title page.

75. John Quincy Adams, *Life*, 3, 16, 21, 39; Webb, *History*, page opposite title page, 37, 45, 70, 77.

76. John Quincy Adams, *Life*, 12, 15, 40–44; Webb, *History*, 76, 48–62.

77. John Quincy Adams, *Life*, 4, 21–22, 46–48.

78. Ibid., 43, 48, 52–55; Webb, *History*, 72–74, 67–68.

79. John Quincy Adams, *Life*, 47, 14–15; Webb, *History*, 66, 68–70.

80. Ellwood Griest, *John and Mary; or, The Fugitive Slaves, a Tale of South-Eastern Pennsylvania* (Lancaster: Inquirer Printing and Publishing Co., 1873), 5.

81. Ibid., 42, 56, 83, 137, 149, 156–58, 160, 175–90, 201–2.

82. Ibid., 201, 187, 198–99, 217–18, 225–26.

83. Ibid., 32–34, 117–18, 140.

84. Ibid., 63, 51, 113, 121–23, 89.

85. *Harper's Weekly*, August 31, 1872; *New National Era*, March 21, 1872.

86. Michael P. Johnson, "Rebellious Slaves and Slave Rebellions in North America: Reflections on Contexts, Sources, and Written History," Paper delivered on July 22 at the 2006 annual meeting of the Society for the History of the Early Republic.

87. *Harper's Weekly*, August 31, 1872.

RITUAL REMEMBRANCES II

1. Paul Connerton, *How Societies Remember* (Cambridge: Cambridge University Press, 1989), 38, 40. Connerton notes the importance of what he calls transfer ceremonies as the means for passing along collective memories.

2. *Brooklyn Eagle*, June 10, 1874.

3. *Chicago Tribune*, June 9, 10, 1874; Larry Gara, "A Glorious Time: The 1874 Abolitionist Reunion in Chicago," *Journal of Illinois State Historical Society* 65 (1972): 280; *New York Times*, June 10, 1874.

4. *Chicago Tribune*, June 10, 1874.

5. Ibid., *New York Times*, June 10, 1874.

6. *Brooklyn Eagle*, January 20, 1873.

7. *Chicago Tribune*, June 10, 11, 12, 1874.

8. Ibid., June 10, 11, 1874.

9. These were not the only newspapers to report on the reunion. See *Christian Recorder*, June 25, 1874, and *New York Times*, June 10, 1874.

10. *New York Times*, June, 11, 12, 13, 1874; *Chicago Tribune*, June 12, 21, 1874.

11. *Chicago Tribune*, June 10, 1874.

12. Ibid., June 12, 1874.

13. *Chicago Tribune*, June 12, 1874; *New York Times*, June 12, 1874.

14. *Chicago Tribune,* June 13, 1874; *New York Times,* June 13, 1874; Gara, "A Glorious Time," 291. Amasa Walker was a political economist and political abolitionist connected with the Free Soil and Republican Parties. See Virtual American Biographies, at <http: www.famousamericans.net/amasawalker>.

15. *New York Times,* June 12, 1874.

16. Ibid., *Chicago Tribune,* June 12, 1874; Gara, "A Glorious Time," 283.

17. *Chicago Tribune,* June 13, 1874.

18. Ibid., June 11, 13, 1874; *New York Times,* June 11, 1874.

19. *Chicago Tribune,* June 10, 13, 1874.

20. Ibid., June 13, 1874.

21. *Centennial Anniversary of the Pennsylvania Society for Promoting the Abolition of Slavery, the Relief of Free Negroes Unlawfully Held in Bondage: and For Improving the Condition of the African Race* (Philadelphia: Grant, Faires & Rodgers, Printers, 1875), 67. Still sent the book to George Curtis, *Harper's* editor, who thanked him for "the handsome copy of your book," calling it "a unique chapter of our history" (*Christian Recorder,* March 25, 1875).

22. *Christian Recorder,* April 22, 1875; *Centennial Anniversary,* 6–7.

23. *Centennial Anniversary,* 3.

24. Ibid., 12–18. He gave few details of the society's work, perhaps because its reliance on tactics like court litigation and petitions lacked dramatic potential. For an overview of the work of the society, see Richard S. Newman, *The Transformation of American Abolitionism: Fighting Slavery in the Early Republic* (Chapel Hill: University of North Carolina Press, 2002).

25. *Centennial Anniversary,* 16–18.

26. Ibid., 4.

27. Ibid., 6–7, 25.

28. Ibid., 7–8. 35.

29. Ibid., 8–10.

30. Ibid., 21–25, 73.

31. Ibid., 25–26. For a brief overview of the violence against blacks, see David Herbert Donald, Jean H. Baker, and Michael F. Holt, *The Civil War and Reconstruction* (New York: W. W. Norton, 2001), 602–4.

32. *Centennial Anniversary,* 29–30.

33. Ibid., 29–31.

34. Ibid., 31–33.

35. Joseph Moreau, *Schoolbook Nation: Conflicts over American History Textbooks from the Civil War to the Present* (Ann Arbor: University of Michigan Press, 2003), 36–41; Connerton, *How Societies Remember,* 38.

36. David Turley, *The Culture of English Antislavery, 1780–1860* (New York: Routledge, 1991), 56, 90–91; Suzanne Miers, *Britain and the Ending of the Slave Trade* (New York: Holmes and Meier, 1975), 30–33.

37. *Christian Recorder,* May 28, 1874; *New York Times,* June 1, 1878.

38. *Brooklyn Eagle,* March 21, 1871, June 21, 1873, May 25, 1879.

39. *New York Times,* March 4, 1878. Already in 1875 the newspaper was making a similar point, saying about antislavery congressional leaders in the 1850s that the

events of their era read "like ancient history now," and commenting that the issues had "utterly . . . faded" (ibid., December 7, 1875).

CHAPTER THREE

1. The title of this chapter comes from an epithet that was hurled at Laura Haviland by a furious southerner. See Laura Haviland, *A Woman's Life-Work: Labors and Experiences of Laura S. Haviland* (Chicago: Publishing Association of Friends, 1881; reprint, Salem: Ayer Co., 1984), 76.

2. Joseph Gibbons to William Still, December, 1871, Still Papers, HSP; William Still, *The Underground Rail Road* (Philadelphia: Porter & Coates, 1872; reprint, New York: Arno Press, 1978), 5.

3. *Chicago Tribune*, June 11–13, 1874; *New York Times*, June 11, 13, 1874.

4. *New York Times*, November 2, 1874.

5. *Chicago Tribune*, June 21, 1874; see Levi Coffin, *Reminiscences* (Cincinnati: Robert Clarke & Co., 1880; reprint, New York: AMS Press, 1971), 658, for one of several references about his reluctance to speak in public; see also preface comments for an understanding of his decision to write: i, iii. Coffin had already indicated what kind of book he might write in terms of the content and purpose in a letter he sent to a Tennessee newspaper in 1860: "If I were to write a book, I might expose some of the abominations of slavery, that would not be pleasant to thy ear. The extent of the evils of slavery, and its demoralizing effect upon the white population of the South, can not be written even by a Southerner" (591–92). Of course, emancipation modified Coffin's conception of how he might handle a book. See David W. Blight, *Race and Reunion: The Civil War in American Memory* (Cambridge, Mass.: Harvard University Press, 2001), 130; and *New York Times*, December 7, 1875. For hints of Coffin's finances and the hope that the reminiscences would help to support his wife, see *Christian Worker*, June 9, 1881, and *Friends' Intelligencer* 36 (1880): 722. The latter publication notes, "Owing to his many pecuniary sacrifices in the great cause to which his life was dedicated, Levi Coffin died a poor man, and his widow, who shared his labors and his dangers for more than 40 years, is to some extent dependent on the sale of this volume." Coffin may have had substantial help in composing his narrative. An insert, dated December 14, 1962, in the Earlham College Library's copy of Coffin's book, a gift of a descendant, says that "the story . . . was actually written by my husband's mother, then Louise Coffin (later Mrs. Louise Coffin Jones) in the fall and winter of 1875 at the home of 'Uncle Levi,' where he recounted his experiences and she wrote them out and read them back to him for his approval." Thanks to Professor Thomas Hamm of Earlham College for sharing materials about Coffin with me.

6. Coffin, *Reminiscences*, i, ii, 386. Marcus Belson made the observation about the autobiography and moral vision, and he is quoted in Timothy Dow Adams, *Telling Lies in Modern American Autobiography* (Chapel Hill: University of North Carolina Press, 1990), 129–30.

7. Coffin, *Reminiscences*, ii–iii; James M. McPherson, *The Abolitionist Legacy: From Reconstruction to the NAACP* (Princeton: Princeton University Press, 1975), 13–23.

8. *Brooklyn Eagle*, January 20, 1873. For a brief biography of Woolson and her lit-

erary work, see <http://college.hmco.com/english/lauter/heath/5e/resources/author_pages/late_nineteenth/woolson_co.html>.

9. *Brooklyn Eagle*, January 20, 1873; Constance F. Woolson, "Jeanette," *Scribner's* 9 (1874): 233, 240–41. I do not mean to imply that all references to abolitionists were negative, for there were various positive depictions as well. Obituaries were generally respectful. Coffin frequently referred to *Uncle Tom's Cabin* in his book and made other general references to fiction.

10. Coffin, *Reminiscences*, 386, 344–45. For an incident in which Coffin's suspicions turned out to be false, see 381 ff.

11. Ibid., 72–75, 225, 230, 232, 265–96, 649.

12. Ibid., title page.

13. Ibid., 103, 79–99, 106, 129–37, 269–76, 296, 575. As one writer noted in the *Atlantic Monthly*, "When a man sets about any autobiographical work, he ought to remember that he cannot be too personal." Such a statement should be consistent with the autobiographer's modesty and restraint about personal matters. See "Recent Literature," *Atlantic Monthly* 35 (1875): 237–38; and "Editor's Easy Chair," *Harper's* 55 (1877): 142.

14. In *The Conscience of the Autobiographer: Ethical and Religious Dimensions of Autobiography* (London: Macmillan, 1992), 1–9, John D. Barbour discusses the importance of moral assessment in autobiography; conscience, he argues, is part of the "autobiographical act." It can act to prompt a person to write his life story and entails a consideration of how moral ideals and ambitions have shaped that life. See also Candy Gunther Brown, *The Word in the World: Evangelical Writing, Publishing, and Reading in America, 1789–1880* (Chapel Hill: University of North Carolina Press, 2004), 88–89.

15. Coffin, *Reminiscences*, 12–14.

16. Ibid., 46, 49, 52, 58, provide examples of the emotional character of these early exploits; for early efforts for slaves, see 71, 108, 113, 118.

17. Ibid., 224, 227–28, 234–43, 577, 594.

18. Ibid., 201, 247, 481, 490, 619–29, 655–711.

19. Ibid., 227, 229, 586, 596. Chapter 15 (524–41) covers Cincinnati mobs. Julian quotation in McPherson, *Abolitionist Legacy*, 55.

20. "Editor's Easy Chair," *Harper's* 42 (1871): 617; Coffin, *Reminiscences*, 428–46, 279–84, 502. The moderation that characterized Coffin's approach was just the kind of moderation lavishly praised by a critic reviewing a book on John Woolman and his antislavery work. See Rev. O. E. Daggett, "John Woolman," *New Englander* 31 (1872): 225, 230.

21. Coffin, *Reminiscences*, 383–84.

22. Ibid., 568, 349.

23. Ibid., 298, 403, 197, 272–74, 403, 489.

24. Ibid., 13, 59, 127–28, 633, 490, 578–79. While, for the most part, Coffin seems to have felt that emotion was fruitful, on one occasion, he suggested that his response to a former fugitive's tears "quite unmanned me for a time" (ibid., 169). Marcus Billson makes the point about helping readers to share the writer's experiences in "The Memoir: New Perspectives on a Forgotten Genre," *Genre* 10 (Summer 1977):

270. Nina Silber describes the reaction against sentimental reform in *The Romance of Reunion: Northerners and the South, 1865–1900* (Chapel Hill: University of North Carolina Press, 1993), 20, as does Louise L. Stevenson, *The Victorian Homefront: American Thought and Culture, 1860–1880* (Ithaca: Cornell University Press, 2001), 179, 181.

25. Coffin, *Reminiscences*, 46, 49, 116, 118–19, 188–89, 191, 108, 227, 603.

26. Ibid., 677, 651–52, 655, 658–59.

27. Ibid., i, 660–61, 669, 243–44, 677, 680.

28. Ibid., 108–11.

29. Ibid., 118, 608, 296, 67, 150–51.

30. Ibid., 506.

31. Ibid., 275, 328, 398, 27–28, 280, 283–84.

32. Ibid., 346, 353, 391–92, 126–27. Interestingly, Coffin included a letter he had sent to a newspaper in 1860, in which he wrote, "I should not suppose for a moment that thou wouldst desire me to write a book. I am a Southern man, born and raised in the State of North Carolina; have traveled in most of the Southern States, and have connections and acquaintances in several of them; and, if I were to write a book, I might expose some of the abominations of slavery, that would not be pleasant to thy ear. The extent of the evils of slavery . . . can not be written even by a Southerner" (591–92). It seems that Coffin had not softened his views but had come upon an effective way both to condemn the system of slavery and those who had supported it and to use language that would best make his case.

33. Ibid., 481–89, 328, 409, 422–23. Coffin did include, however, the story of a young woman of color who had been sent to Oberlin but wanted to return to New Orleans, where she had been the mistress of a merchant. Coffin tried to change her mind: "I endeavored to impress upon her mind a sense of the sinfulness of living in such a way; I told her that the merchant who kept her as his wife was not her husband legally, that he could not be in Louisiana, and probably had no intention of making her his wife by coming North. . . . This case gives us a glimpse into the customs and state of morals that existed in the South, and shows the demoralizing influences of slavery" (ibid., 479–80). See also W. H. Ruffner, "The Co-Education of the White and Colored Races," *Scribner's* 8 (1874): 88.

34. Coffin, *Reminiscences*, 619, 630.

35. Ibid., 186, 342–45, 366–73.

36. *Harper's Weekly*, July 20, 1872, and January 9, 1875.

37. Coffin, *Reminiscences*, 515–23.

38. Ibid., 596–99; Blight, *Race and Reunion*, 151.

39. Coffin, *Reminiscences*, 596–99; *Scribner's* 8 (1874): 374.

40. Coffin, *Reminiscences*, 601, 606–8, 627, 637, 509. Coffin recalled a conversation with an intelligent slaveholder whom he advised to free his slaves. This man, and others like him, Coffin said, "were relieved of responsibility in the matter, a few years later, by the proclamation of President Lincoln." For another brief reference to Lincoln, see ibid., 626. For a discussion of the monuments erected to Lincoln, see Kirk Savage, *Standing Soldiers, Kneeling Slaves: Race, War, and Monument in Nineteenth-Century America* (Princeton: Princeton University Press, 1997), 65–66, 72.

41. Coffin, *Reminiscences*, 604–5, 636–37, 646. Some examples included an Ala-

bama regiment composed of former slaves who were "the most orderly and best behaved regiment in camp; it was the first time their manhood had been recognized, and they were anxious to prove that they were worthy of the confidence reposed in them" (637). Many of the soldiers in another regiment were eager to learn how to read. Black troops also distinguished themselves in combat. At a fierce battle at Helena, Arkansas, Coffin heard that "the final victory [was] won by the valor of a regiment of colored soldiers who had been kept in reserve till the last, and fought with desperation when ordered into action" (646).

42. Ibid., 630, 599.

43. Ibid., 662–63, 667, iii. Coffin may have been somewhat old-fashioned in thinking that religion had a role to play in resolving worldly problems. He pointed out that the Bible was oblivious to differences of color and made love of neighbor a moral duty. He realized, however, that change was not easy and felt blessed that "my wife and I had been favored to overcome prejudice against color or caste." See ibid., 108, 481.

44. McPherson, *Abolitionist Legacy*, 14–15; Coffin, *Reminiscences*, 155–57, 203–4, 338, 440–41, 30–31, 218–19, 407, 411, 427.

45. Coffin, *Reminiscences*, 121–25, 157–59. Compare Coffin's view to the one expressed by the superintendent of the Virginia Board of Public Instruction, W. H. Ruffner, in "Co-Education," 90: "Is it too much to hope that profound thinkers may yet rebuke the vulgar spirit of miscegenation in all its forms, and evolve a scheme of preserving and improving the separate races of man in their purity?"

46. Coffin, *Reminiscences*, 323–24, 183, 577–78.

47. Ibid., 578, 144, 153, 146, 167, 379, 391, 333–34.

48. McPherson, *Abolitionist Legacy*, 64, discusses the discouragement that grew in the 1870s because of the slow progress of former slaves.

49. Coffin, *Reminiscences*, 67, 143, 366, 369, 582, 150, 250–53. Canadian land policy is described on 252–53. Coffin's treatment of the situation in Canada suggests that he would disagree with the view that the government had no responsibility to freed people. See also Heather Cox Richardson, *The Death of Reconstruction: Race, Labor, and Politics in the Post–Civil War North, 1865–1901* (Cambridge, Mass.: Harvard University Press, 2001), 140.

50. Coffin, *Reminiscences*, 328, 407, 156.

51. Ibid., 160, 473, 174, 562–63.

52. Ibid., 262–63, 256, 259, 254, 138, 165, 413.

53. Ibid., 165–67, 141–43, 213–15.

54. Ibid., 189–90, 107, 297–99, 382, 306–7, 299, 300, 184, 320.

55. Ibid., 113–14, 120. There were occasional vignettes of blacks foiling slavehunters on their own. See 174–75.

56. Ibid., 628, 632, 633, 711. Paul Eakin discusses the dialectic relationship between the past and the present and suggests the ways in which the beginning of an autobiography is connected with its ending. See his *Touching the World: References in Autobiography* (Princeton: Princeton University Press, 1992), 66–67.

57. Coffin, *Reminiscences*, ii.

58. Walter Sutton, *The Western Book Trade: Cincinnati as a Nineteenth-Century*

Publishing and Book-Trade Center (Columbus: Ohio State University Press, 1961), 151, 161–62; Coffin, *Reminiscences*, 653; Candy Gunther Brown, *The Word in the World*, 54–55, 88–93.

59. Sutton, *Western Book Trade*, 299–300, 304; *The British Friend*, March 1, 1879, 68; *Christian Worker*, June 9, 1881.

60. In a bizarre example of the interest in Underground Railroad activities, *Harper's Weekly*, November 1, 1879, reported that a South Carolinian had come north with his pack of hounds to demonstrate that northern views of the way fugitives were hunted down were exaggerated. His "exhibition," intended to make money, featured the "slave" Sam trying to "escape" from the hounds.

61. Haviland, *A Woman's Life-Work*, 14–15.

62. Ibid., 28–29, 32–33.

63. Ibid., 34–47. The disease was identified as erysipelas, a fever and inflammation caused by streptococcus erysipelas.

64. Laura Haviland, *A Woman's Life-Work*, 1st edition, at The Project Gutenberg EBook, <http://www.gutenberg.org/dirs/etext05/wlwrk10.txt>.

65. Haviland, *A Woman's Life-Work* (1984), 372–73, 85, 227, 76–79. Lyde Cullen Sizer, in *The Political Work of Northern Women Writers and the Civil War, 1850–1872* (Chapel Hill: University of North Carolina Press, 2000), 194, argues that women's historical contributions to the war effort were contested. Certainly, the activist role that Haviland claimed for herself was unusual, especially since no other women had yet written a full-length account of their lives as abolitionists. See also Elizabeth Elkin Grammer, *Some Wild Visions: Autobiographies by Female Itinerant Evangelists in Nineteenth-Century America* (New York: Oxford University Press, 2003). Grammer suggests that women like Haviland wrote "subversive" stories (see 44 and elsewhere).

66. Haviland, *A Woman's Life-Work* (1984), 163–66, 180, 183–85, 189–90, 193–96. The following notes refer to the 1984 edition unless otherwise noted.

67. Ibid., 242–44, 265–66, 279.

68. Ibid., 360, 125, 339, 160; scrapbook, clipping of 1885, clipping of 1894, Haviland Papers, BHL.

69. Haviland, *A Woman's Life-Work*, preface to fourth edition, no page, included in the 1984 edition. Haviland's emphasis on active Christianity stands in dramatic contrast to the view of some clergymen. The prominent evangelist Dwight Moody proclaimed, "Don't flatter yourselves that the world is going to get any better. . . . [T]he world is on the rocks." See Edward J. Blum, *Reforging the White Republic: Race, Religion, and American Nationalism, 1865–1898* (Baton Rouge: Louisiana State University Press, 2005), 128.

70. Her conversion is described in *A Woman's Life-Work*, 15–32; for dreams, see 38, 48, 106–7; for prayer, see 60. The deathbed scene appears on 121. Haviland continued to have dreams and visions until the end of her life. In her scrapbook, there is an account given of her death when "visions of angels came to her again and again. During one of these her physicians was present. He was not a professed believer but he said the scene impressed him with the truth of the immortality of the soul" (Scrapbook, Haviland Papers, BHL). Grammer points out in *Some Wild Vi-*

sions (63–64) how quickly Haviland gets through her conversion experience and on to her work. Haviland's insistence on the connection between her religious com mitment and her hardline view of the South sets her apart from many northern religious leaders, who were promoting reconciliation and forgiveness. See Blum, *Reforging the White Republic*, 86–112.

71. *New York Times* quotation from McPherson, *Abolitionist Legacy*, 49; *Brooklyn Eagle*, October 9, 1874, November 15, 1876; *Harper's Weekly*, October 14, 1876.

72. *Christian Recorder*, May 10, 1877, July 25, November 21, 1878; *New York Times*, May 5, June 2, 1877. Huber Winton Ellingsworth ("Southern Reconciliationist Orators in the North, 1868–1899" [Ph.D. diss., Florida State University, 1955], 12) suggests that in 1877 *Harper's Weekly* began to treat the South more sympathetically but the *Nation* and the *New York Times* shifted more slowly to a more favorable treatment of the South. See also McPherson, *Abolitionist Legacy*, 99, 102. Kenneth M. Price and Susan Belasco Smith, eds., in "Introduction: Periodical Literature in Social and Historical Context," in *Periodical Literature in Nineteenth-Century America* (Charlottesville: University Press of Virginia, 1995), 14, call the monthly periodicals the central component of American culture. For the Kansas migration, see Nell Irvin Painter, *Exodusters: Black Migration to Kansas After Reconstruction* (New York: Alfred A. Knopf, 1976).

73. *New York Times*, May 5, 1877.

74. Thomas L. Connelly and Barbara L. Bellows, *God and General Longstreet: The Lost Cause and the Southern Mind* (Baton Rouge: Louisiana State University Press, 1982), 47–48; Edward E. Chielens, ed., *American Literary Magazines: The Eighteenth and Nineteenth Centuries* (New York: Greenwood Press, 1986), 365; Price and Smith, eds., *Periodical Literature*, 7, 14; comments of David Blight in "What's American about American Memory," at the annual meeting of the Organization of American Historians, March 31, 2007.

75. Connelly and Bellows, *God and General Longstreet*, 51; Ellery Sedgwick, *The Atlantic Monthly, 1857–1909: Yankee Humanism at High Tide and Ebb* (Amherst: University of Massachusetts Press, 1994), 2–5, 38. Wayne Mixon, in *Southern Writers and the New South Movement, 1865–1913* (Chapel Hill: University of North Carolina Press, 1980), 7, suggests that more northerners read these magazines than southerners.

76. Chielens, ed., *American Literary Magazines*, 365; Michael Flusche, "The Private Plantation: Versions of the Old South Myth, 1880–1914" (Ph.D. diss., Johns Hopkins University, 1973), 24; Mixon, *Southern Writers*, 7; Frank Luther Mott, *A History of American Magazines*, 5 vols. (Cambridge, Mass.: Harvard University Press, 1957), 3:48–49.

77. D. R. Castleton, "Linda's Young Lady," *Harper's* 40 (1870): 703; William M. Baker, "The New Timothy," *Harper's* 37 (1868): 393; Ruffner, "Co-Education," 87; Jane Dailey, *Before Jim Crow: The Politics of Race in Postemancipation Virginia* (Chapel Hill: University of North Carolina Press, 2000), 25, 180 n. 58. I do not mean to suggest that journals carried only articles and stories that romanticized the prewar South and undermined positive views of blacks. George Washington Cable's novel *The Grandissimes* was serialized in *Scribner's* in 1878, and it condemned slavery and made it clear that blacks valued freedom. For a discussion of the novel, see Daniel

Aaron, *The Unwritten War: American Writers and the Civil War* (New York: Alfred A. Knopf, 1973), 278–82.

78. "Topics of the Times," *Scribner's* 9 (1874): 8; Connelly and Bellows, *God and General Longstreet*, 50–57; Stanley J. Kunitz and Howard Haycraft, eds., *American Authors, 1600–1900: A Biographical Dictionary of American Literature* (New York: H. W. Wilson Co., 1938), 439; Arthur John, *The Best Years of the Century: Richard Watson Gilder, Scribner's Monthly, and Century Magazine, 1870–1909* (Urbana: University of Illinois Press, 1981), 39–40; Robert Underwood Johnson, *Remembered Yesterdays* (Boston: Little, Brown, and Co., 1923), 96–97.

79. John, *Best Years*, 41; Edward King, "The Great South," *Scribner's* 7 (1873–74): 1–2, 15, 26–27, 134, 145, 148, 645–48, 654, 664; 8 (1874): 10, 26, 137, 141, 522, 532. Other articles include Albert F. Webster, "Southern Home Politics," *Atlantic Monthly* 36 (1875): 464–67; Harriet Beecher Stowe, "Our Florida Plantation," *Atlantic Monthly* 43 (1877): 641–49; Thomas Wentworth Higginson, "Fourteen Years Later," in *The Magnificent Activist: The Writings of Thomas Wentworth Higginson (1823–1911)*, ed. Howard N. Meyer (New York: Da Capo Press, 2000), 162–74; William C. Lodge, "Among the Peaches," *Harper's* 41 (1870): 511–18; Mrs. M. P. Handy, "In a Tobacco Factory," *Harper's* 47 (1873): 713–19; Helen W. Ludlow, "The Hampton Normal and Agriculture Institute," *Harper's* 47 (1873): 672–85; Edwin DeLeon, "The New South," *Harper's* 48 (1874): 270–80, 406–22; 49 (1874): 555–68; General T. M. Logan, "The Southern Industrial Prospect," *Harper's* 52 (1876): 589–90; and R. W. Wright, "Richmond Since the War," *Scribner's* 14 (1877): 303–12.

80. Charles D. Deshler, "Ab'm: A Glimpse of Modern Dixie," *Harper's* 57 (1878): 489–95. Not surprisingly, Deshler also wrote sentimental pieces about the prewar world. In one he praised "the old-time favored and trusted family domestic" who was, alas, fast fading out of sight. See "Daddy Will," *Harper's* 57 (1878): 238–46.

81. T. L. M. M'Cready, "Uncle Zeke's Conscience," *Harper's* 54 (1877): 706–10; Lizzie W. Champney, "Polly Pharaoh," *Harper's* 53 (1876), 196; "Topics of the Times," *Scribner's* 9 (1874): 9.

82. Dailey, *Before Jim Crow*, 48; George Ward Nichols, "Six Weeks in Florida," *Harper's* 41 (1870): 663; Isabella T. Hopkins, "In the M.E. African," *Scribner's* 20 (1880): 422–23, 425–28; and "Editor's Drawer," *Harper's* 61 (1880): 647. For basic biographical information, see "George Ward Nichols," in Virtual American Biographies, at <http://famousamericans.net/georgewardnichols/>.

83. "Editor's Drawer," *Harper's* 52 (1876): 790–91; 53 (1876): 769; William M. Baker, "Two Couples: A White and a Yellow," *Scribner's* 18 (1879): 379–81; Kunitz and Haycraft, *American Authors*, 48.

84. "Editor's Drawer," *Harper's* 49 (1874): 904. In *Strange Talk: The Politics of Dialect Literature in Gilded Age America* (Berkeley: University of California Press, 1999), 10–12, Gavin Jones suggests that the use of black dialect was one means of conveying black inferiority but that it also could "encode" resistance and weaken the linguistics of white English.

85. King, "The Great South," 12–14.

86. John G. Whittier, "The Antislavery Convention of 1833," and Ralph Keeler, "Owen Brown's Escape from Harper's Ferry," *Atlantic Monthly* 33 (1874): 166–72,

342–65; Connelly and Bellows, *God and General Longstreet*, 70; George Eggleston, "A Rebel's Recollections," *Atlantic Monthly* 33 (1874): 730; 36 (1875): 603; 34 (1874): 669; "George Cary Eggleston" at <http://patriot.net/crouch/southsoldier.html>.

87. Clarence Gordon, "The Gentle Fire-Eater," *Atlantic Monthly* 41 (1878): 43–44, 49–50; "Clarence Gordon," Virtual American Biographies, at <http://www.famousamericans.net/clarencegordon/>.

88. T. N. Page, "Uncle Gabe's White Folks," *Scribner's* 13 (1877): 882; Irwin Russell, "Mahar John," *Scribner's* 14 (1877): 127; A. S. Miller, "Crow-Which?" *Scribner's* 14 (1877): 127, 416; Alfred Young Wolff Jr., "The South and the American Imagination: Mythical Views of the Old South, 1865–1900" (Ph.D. diss., University of Virginia, 1971), 127.

89. Irwin Russell, "Christmas-Night in the Quarters," *Scribner's* 15 (1877): 445–46; A. C. Gordon, "Dis Ole 'Oman an' Me," *Scribner's* 15 (1878): 752; "Editor's Drawer," *Harper's* 56 (1878): 478–79; George Cary Eggleston, "My Friend Phil," *Galaxy* 20 (1875): 739–42. Amazingly, the November 25, 1875, issue of the *Christian Recorder*, praised this story for its use of black dialect and appreciated its flow of humor.

90. Haviland, *A Woman's Life-Work*, 121, chaps. 3–6. On 515, she refers to a particular issue of *Scribner's* that carried an article on Prudence Crandall. It is interesting to note that at the same time Haviland was emphasizing the fugitive slave, blacks were less interested in telling the stories of flight. Rather, as William L. Andrews notes, blacks chose to tell the stories of slaves who remained in the South and who demonstrated their character by performing ably there. See "The Representation of Slavery and the Rise of Afro-American Literary Realism, 1865–1920," in William L. Andrews, ed., *African American Autobiography: A Collection of Critical Essays* (Englewood Cliffs, N.J.: Prentice Hall, 1993), 80–82. Haviland, of course, was telling the story of her own involvement with fugitive slaves and was addressing a white audience.

91. Haviland, *A Woman's Life-Work*, 112–17, 213–14.

92. Ibid., 53, 94, 98–99, 125, 134.

93. M'Cready, "Uncle Zeke's Conscience," 707; Haviland, *A Woman's Life-Work*, 91–92, 59–81, 203.

94. Haviland, *A Woman's Life-Work*, 78, 215, 150–51. Haviland repeated the claim to impartial judgment on 232.

95. Ibid., 321.

96. Ibid., 463–65, 439–49. Haviland had written a "long sketch" of Uncle Phil's life and sent it to the prominent temperance reformer John Gough. At that time (probably 1865), she was not considering publishing the vignette. See copy of letter from Laura Haviland to George Whipple, June 4, 1868, Haviland Papers, BHL.

97. Haviland, *A Woman's Life-Work*, 255.

98. Ibid., 255, 274, 370–71.

99. Ibid., 254, 276, 272, 292, 293, 307. The picture of Haviland and the slave irons is found opposite 292. Gaines M. Foster, in *Ghosts of the Confederacy: Defeat, the Lost Cause, and the Emergence of the New South, 1865–1913* (New York: Oxford University Press, 1987), 24–25, points out the efforts on the part of southerners to deny any guilt for the past.

100. Haviland, *A Woman's Life-Work*, 297, 310, 311, 309.

101. Ibid., 482, 494, 505, 492, 490, 493. For a study of those who opposed reconcili-ation, like Haviland, see John R. Neff, *Honoring the Civil War Dead: Commemoration and the Problem of Reconciliation* (Lawrence: University Press of Kansas, 2005).

102. Haviland, *A Woman's Life-Work*, 490, 495, 500, 501.

103. *New York Times*, March 4, 1878.

104. Sutton, *Western Book Trade*, 157, 342; letter from Laura Haviland probably to Professor S. Williams, May 24, 1882, Haviland Papers, BHL.

105. Laura Haviland to Professor S. Williams, July 10, 1883; postcard from Laura Haviland to Revs. Walden & Stowe, October 27, 1883; and Laura Haviland to Mr. S. Williams, November 5, 1883, Haviland Papers, BHL. David Blight, in "What's American about American Memory," highlights the role that big business played in promoting reconciliation. Certainly, publishing houses were big business.

106. Letters from Laura Haviland to Professor S. Williams, April 27, 1882, July 10, 1882, November 5, 1883; postcard from Laura Haviland to Revs. Walden & Stowe, October 27, 1883, Haviland Papers, BHL.

107. Haviland, *A Woman's Life-Work*, unpaginated material following the book's conclusion. The *Chicago Tribune*, March 15, 1882, also reviewed the work and praised its exciting and thrilling character.

108. Haviland, *A Woman's Life-Work* (Chicago: C. V. Waite & Co., 1887), 538; Mott, *American Magazines*, 3:6. With the fourth edition, Haviland was to receive a royalty. For a discussion of the critical preference for subdued realism, see Nancy Glazener, *Reading for Realism: The History of a U.S. Literary Institution, 1850–1910* (Durham: Duke University Press, 1997), 48.

109. Timothy Dow Adams, in *Telling Lies*, 29, calls the practice of describing what one has not seen or heard a "telling invention."

110. *North Into Freedom: The Autobiography of John Malvin, Free Negro, 1795–1880*, ed. Allan Peskin (Kent: Kent State University Press, 1988), 44, 86, chaps. 4, 6, 7; Kenneth L. Kusmer, "John Malvin," in John A. Garraty and Mark C. Carnes, eds., *American National Biography* (New York: Oxford University Press, 1999), 14:392.

111. *North Into Freedom*, 86.

112. Ibid., 20; William L. Andrews, "The Spirit of Friday Jones" (Greenville, N.C.: J. Y. Joyner Library, East Carolina University, 1999), 1–3, at Documenting the American South website of the University of North Carolina at Chapel Hill Libraries, <http://docsouth.unc.edu/neh/fjones/support2.html>.

113. Stuart Seely Sprague, ed., *His Promised Land: The Autobiography of John P. Parker, Former Slave and Conductor on the Underground Railroad* (New York: W. W. Norton, 1996), 35, 40, 60–62; Garrison quoted in the *New York Times*, November 18, 1876.

114. Sprague, ed., *His Promised Land*, 66–70.

115. Ibid., 74, 89, 95, 100, 132, 134, 138, 103.

116. *Harper's Weekly*, November 1, 1879. Stories treating blacks as dignified char-acters were rare. Julia E. Dodge, in "An Island of the Sea," *Scribner's* 14 (1877): 652–61, adopts an unusual stance, describing a Florida plantation owner marrying one of his slaves, a "dusky princess" with "none of the usual negro characteristics."

117. Lorien Foote, *Seeking the One Great Remedy: Francis George Shaw and Nineteenth-Century Reform* (Athens: Ohio University Press, 2003), 144; "Mozley's Reminiscences," *Atlantic Monthly* 50 (1882): 411; Blight, *Race and Reunion*, 231–37.

CHAPTER FOUR

1. Stanley J. Kunitz and Howard Haycraft, eds. *American Authors, 1600–1900: A Biographical Dictionary of American Literature* (New York: H. W. Wilson Co., 1938), 26.

2. James Lane Allen, "Mrs. Stowe's 'Uncle Tom' at Home in Kentucky," *Century* 34 (1887): 855–56, 858, 860, 862–63, 866–67. On 861, Allen did admit that slavery was an evil institution, but he claimed it had inspired a nobility of character in white owners.

3. Joan Waugh, "Ulysses S. Grant, Historian," in *The Memory of the Civil War in American Culture*, ed. Alice Fahs and Joan Waugh (Chapel Hill: University of North Carolina Press, 2004), 6–8, 15, 22, 27, 30–31.

4. J. G. Nicolay and John Hay, "Abraham Lincoln: A History," *Century* 34 (1887): 203, 206, 516–19, 523; Henry Goddard Thomas, "The Colored Troops at Petersburg," *Century* 34 (1887): 778, 781; "Topics of the Times," *Century* 34 (1887): 155. Quotation from Sarah E. Gardner, *Blood and Irony: Southern White Women's Narratives of the Civil War, 1861–1937* (Chapel Hill: University of North Carolina Press, 2004), 81.

5. Quotation from Gardner, *Blood and Irony*, 81; Annie Porter, "My Life as a Slave," *Harper's* 69 (1884): 730–38; Walter B. Hill, "Uncle Tom Without a Cabin," *Century* 27 (1884): 859–61; Thomas Nelson Page, "Unc' Edinburg's Drownden," *Harper's* 72 (1886): 304. See David W. Blight, *Race and Reunion: The Civil War in American Memory* (Cambridge, Mass.: Harvard University Press, 2001), 222–27. Albion Tourgée, in a piece for *Forum* in 1888, criticized the typical fictional depictions of former slaves: "About the Negro as a man, with hopes, fears, and aspirations like other men, our literature is nearly silent." See Peter Rawlings, ed., *Americans on Fiction, 1776–1900*, vol. 3 (London: Pickering & Chatto, 2002), 236–37. On Hill, see <http://www.libs.uga.edu/hargrett/pexhibit/presiden/wbhill.html>. D. Bruce Dickson Jr. analyzes black fiction in *Black American Writing from the Nadir: The Evolution of a Literary Tradition, 1877–1915* (Baton Rouge: Louisiana State University Press, 1989).

6. Blight, *Race and Reunion*, 216–17; "A Georgia Plantation," *Scribner's* 21 (1881): 830–36; C. H. Jones, "Sectional Fiction" in Rawlings, ed., *Americans on Fiction*, 47, 50–51; Virginia S. Imlia, "Dictation Exercises," *Scribner's* 19 (1880): 478; W. W. Blacknall, "The New Departure in Negro Life," *Atlantic Monthly* 52 (1883): 681, 683; "Studies in the South," *Atlantic Monthly* 49 (1882): 76–91, 179–95, 673–84, 740–52; 50 (1882): 99–110, 194–205, 349–61, 476–88, 623–33, 750–63; 51 (1883): 89–99; Charles Dudley Warner, "Impressions of the South," *Harper's* 71 (1885): 546–52, and "The South Revisited," 74 (18[87]): 634–40; Rebecca Davis Harding, "Here and There in the South," *Harper's* 75 (1887): 421–43, 593–605, 747–60, 914–25. For a detailed look at the policies of two journals, see Janet Habler-Hover, "The North-South Reconciliation Theme and the 'Shadow of the Negro'" in *Century Illustrated Magazine*, and Kenneth M. Price, "Charles Chesnutt, The *Atlantic Monthly* and the Intersection of African-American Fiction and Elite Culture," in Kenneth M. Price and Susan Belasco Smith, eds., *Periodical Literature in Nineteenth-Century America* (Charlottes-

ville: University Press of Virginia, 1995), 239–74. Robert Underwood Johnson, one of *Century's* editors, considered the period to be the golden age of southern fiction "with the diverting traits of the negro holding the centre of the stage" (*Remembered Yesterdays* [Boston: Little, Brown, and Co., 1923], 121).

7. "Studies in the South," *Atlantic Monthly* 49 (1882): 76–77, 186–87, 678–79; 50 (1882): 100, 753.

8. Ibid., 49 (1882): 188–90.

9. See Jane Dailey, *Before Jim Crow: The Politics of Race in Postemancipation Virginia* (Chapel Hill: University of North Carolina Press, 2000). For examples of these views, see "Topics of the Times," *Century* 25 (1883): 787; H. H. Chalmers, "Effects of Negro Suffrage," *NAM* 132 (1881): 239–48; Warner, "The South Revisited," 635; "Topics of the Times," *Scribner's* 21 (1880): 311; Hill, "Uncle Tom Without a Cabin," 862–63; and "Topics of the Times," *Century* 28 (1884): 461–62. The *NAM* published a piece in 1879 titled "Ought the Negro Be Disenfranchised? Ought He to Have Been Enfranchised?" 128 (1879): 225–84. Both southern and northern writers debated the question of black suffrage, suggesting the unsettled nature of black political rights. For a list of journal editors, see Daniel A. Wells, comp., *The Literary Index to American Magazines, 1850–1900* (Westport, Conn.: Greenwood Press, 1996), xi.

10. Warner, "Impressions of the South," 549; "Studies in the South," 30 (1882): 110; J. A. Macon, "Politics at the Log-Pulling," *Scribner's* 20 (1880): 952; Frank R. Stockton, "The Cloverfield Carriage," *Century,* 31 (1886): 389–95; Eva M. De Jarnette, "An Old Vote for 'Young Master,'" *Century* 28 (1884): 958–59. For information on Warner, see <http://www.1911encyclopedia.org/Charles_Dudley_Warner>.

11. As Dickson, in *Black American Writing,* 32, points out, it was not clear that the worsening racial situation was permanent. *Century* stimulated a debate over civil rights when it published George W. Cable's "A Freedman's Case in Equity," 29 (1885): 409–18, and Henry W. Grady's "In Plain Black and White: A Reply to Mr. Cable," in the same issue, 909–17. Cable supported black civil rights but pressed for social separation. See Paul Gaston, *The New South Creed: A Study in Southern Mythmaking* (Montgomery, Ala.: New South Books, 2002), 138–56, for a discussion of the racial views of the New South proponents. See also Walter Allen, "Two Years of President Hayes," *Atlantic Monthly* 44 (1879): 194; Rawlings, ed., *Americans on Fiction,* 40–43; "Studies in the South," *Atlantic Monthly* 50 (1882): 103–10; Warner, "Impressions of the South," 546–48; and Charles Dudley Warner, "The South Revisited," 634–35.

12. "The Political Attitude of the South," *Atlantic Monthly* 45 (1880): 817–20; Theodore Bacon, "The End of the War," *Atlantic Monthly* 47 (1881): 394–400. The same point about the magnitude of change in the South appeared in an article in *Harper's Weekly,* June 6, 1885.

13. "Topics of the Times," *Century* 30 (1885): 164–65; *Harper's Weekly,* June 6, 1889; "Impressions of the South," *Harper's* 71 (1885): 550; "Topics of the Times," *Scribner's* 19 (1879): 302–5: 28 (1884): 461; "Studies in the South," *Atlantic Monthly* 51 (1883): 92–93.

14. "Studies in the South," 93; Davis, "Here and There in the South," 441.

15. Roosevelt quoted in John F. Hume, *Abolitionists: Together with Personal Mem-*

ories of the *Struggle for Human Rights, 1830–1864* (New York: G. P. Putnam's Sons, 1905), 1; Henry Cabot Lodge, "William H. Seward," *Atlantic Monthly* 53 (1884): 682–84.

16. Leonard Woolsey Bacon, "A Good Fight Finished," *Century* 25 (1883): 657–58.

17. Lydia Maria Child, "William Lloyd Garrison," *Atlantic Monthly* 44 (1879): 234–35.

18. "William Lloyd Garrison," *Atlantic Monthly* 57 (1886): 121–22, 124.

19. Leonard Woolsey Bacon, "William Lloyd Garrison," *New Englander and Yale Review* 45 (1886): 3, 5, 8, 11, 13, 16. See also Benjamin B. Babbitt, "William Lloyd Garrison and Emancipation," *American Church Review* 139 (1882): 237–42. For a rare positive view of Garrison, see Edmund C. Stedman, "Whittier," *Century* 30 (1885): 38–50.

20. Harriet Prescott Spofford, "The Quaker Poet," *Harper's* 68 (1884): 175; "Editor's Study," *Harper's* 76 (1888): 477; "Editor's Easy Chair," *Harper's* 68 (1884): 804; "Abraham Lincoln," *Century* 38 (1889): 284–86; *Harper's Weekly*, January 31, 1885; "Abraham Lincoln," *Century* 36 (1888): 299.

21. "Van Holst's Constitutional History of the United States," *Atlantic Monthly* 49 (1882): 279. See also Francis Parkman, "The Failure of Universal Suffrage," *NAM* 127 (1878): 19.

22. Arthur John, *The Best Years of the Century: Richard Watson Gilder, and Scribner's Monthly, and Century Magazine, 1870–1909* (Urbana: University of Illinois Press, 1981), 203; Nicolay and Hay, "Abraham Lincoln," *Century* 33 (1887): 685–86; George Lowell Austin, "The Grimké Sisters," *Bay State Monthly* 3 (1885): 183; Theodore Bacon, "End of the War," 395–96; "Letter from a Southern Democrat," *Century* 29 (1885): 471–72. As Joan Waugh argues in "Ulysses S. Grant, Historian," in *The Memory of the Civil War in American Culture*, ed. Alice Fahs and Joan Waugh (Chapel Hill: University of North Carolina Press, 2004), 5–38, Grant's very successful autobiography, published in 1885, presented the antislavery view of the coming of the war.

23. Michael Flusche, "The Private Plantation: Versions of the Old South Myth, 1880–1914" (Ph.D. diss., Johns Hopkins University, 1973), 24; Blight, *Race and Reunion*, 173–75. In his memoirs published in 1885, former president Grant challenged these sorts of historical memories by stating baldly that "the cause of the great War of the Rebellion . . . will have to be attributed to slavery" (Waugh, "Ulysses S. Grant," 8–9). For the significance of Grant's work, see the entire article, 5–38. See also Gardner, *Blood and Irony*, 82–85.

24. "The Contributors' Club," *Atlantic Monthly* 41 (1878): 121; "Culture and Progress," *Scribner's* 18 (1879): 466–73; "Editor's Easy Chair," *Harper's* 59 (1879): 944–45.

25. Reader's Reports, October 22, 25, 1883, Houghton Mifflin Co. Records, HL; "Recollections of a Naval Officer," *Atlantic Monthly* 52 (1883): 835–37; "Two Journalists," *Atlantic Monthly* 52 (1883): 411, 414, 416; "Two English Men of Letters," *Atlantic Monthly* 56 (1885): 124; "Editor's Literary Record," *Harper's* 70 (1885): 813, "Autobiography of Frith," *NAM* 146 (1888): 351–52.

26. "Editor's Easy Chair," *Harper's* 59 (1879): 945; Reader's Reports, January 15, April 3, 1883, Houghton Mifflin Co. Records, HL; "Two Journalists," *Atlantic Monthly* 52 (1883): 418.

27. Reader's Reports, October 12, 13, 1882; April 25, September 1, 1883; June 12, July 2, 1884, Houghton Mifflin Co. Records, HL.

28. Ibid., May 5, June 13, October 20, 1883.

29. "The Jubilee of Emancipation," *American Missionary* 39 (1885): 132. I do not mean to suggest that all former abolitionists were silent or indifferent to the problems of southern blacks. Atticus G. Haygood, in "The South and the School Problem," *Harper's* 79 (1889): 235, itemized the substantial financial contributions of various organizations and individuals to black education. See also James M. McPherson, *The Abolitionist Legacy: From Reconstruction to the NAACP* (Princeton: Princeton University Press, 1975). On the reader's response to Mott's biography, see Reader's Report, January 17, 1884, Houghton Mifflin Co. Records, HL. Houghton Mifflin eventually did publish the book despite the reader's misgivings.

30. Kathleen Clark, in "Celebrating Freedom: Emancipation Day Celebrations and African American Memory in the Early Reconstruction South," in *Where These Memories Grow: History, Memory, and Southern Identity,* ed. W. Fitzhugh Brundage (Chapel Hill: University of North Carolina Press, 2000), 132 n. 58, suggests that scholars see the 1880s as the pivotal period in which northern and southern whites were eliminating slavery as a cause of the war.

31. Frederick Douglass, *Life and Times of Frederick Douglass* (New York: Collier Books ed., 1962); Reader's Report, October 12, 1882, Houghton Mifflin Co. Records, HL; "Two Journalists," *Atlantic Monthly* 52 (1883): 416; "Recollections of a Naval Officer," 837; "Grant's Memoirs, Second Volume," *Atlantic Monthly* 58 (1886): 423. Houghton Mifflin also found manliness an important component of a good autobiography. As one Reader's Report of July 5, 1887, noted, if the author "were more of a man the book might possibly pass muster" (Houghton Mifflin Co. Records, HL).

32. Frederick Douglass, "My Escape from Slavery," *Century* 23 (1881): 125–31; Douglass, *Life and Times,* second part, chaps. 1, 8, 10, 16. All of the following citations to Douglass's *Life and Times* refer to the second part.

33. Douglass, *Life and Times,* 213, 223–24, 226–27, 230, 268–71, 292–95, 301, 328, 351–55, 380–81.

34. Henry Mayer, *All on Fire: William Lloyd Garrison and the Abolition of Slavery* (New York: St. Martin's Press, 1998), 371. Douglass, *Life and Times,* 257, 259–61, 329, chap. 18.

35. Douglass, *Life and Times,* 480–81.

36. See ibid., 226, 228, 229, 256, 260, 264, 288, for some examples.

37. Ibid., 400–403, 407, 415, 424–28, 442.

38. "The Life of Bayard Taylor," *Atlantic Monthly* 54 (1884): 568; Douglass, *Life and Times,* 226, 232, 235, 259, 342, 359, chap. 18, 479.

39. "Agreement of April 7, 1881," Douglass Papers, LC; Benjamin Quarles, *Frederick Douglass* (Washington, D.C.: Associated Publishers, 1948), 337.

40. Letters from Frederick Douglass to Park Publishing Company, October 30, 1881, January 28. 1882; Park Publishing Company to Douglass, November 11, 1881, Douglass Papers, LC. Some of Douglass's friends thought that the pictures would actually be effective with readers. See R. L. Carpenter to Douglass, February 2, 1882, and Mary Carpenter to Douglass, February 27, 1882, Douglass Papers, LC.

41. Information on handling the book can be found in letters from Park Publishing Company to Frederick Douglass, November 11, December 22, 1881; April 3, July 19, 1882; and Park Publishing Company to Mrs. M. M. Greene, December 16, 1881, Douglass Papers, LC.

42. Park Publishing Company to Frederick Douglass, April 3, 1882; John Lobb to Douglass, September 28, 1882, Douglass Papers, LC.

43. Park Publishing Company to Frederick Douglass, July 19, 1889, December 22, 1881; Park Publishing Company to Mrs. M. M. Greene, December 16, 1881; John Lobb to Douglass, September 28, 1882, Douglass Papers, LC; "Grant's Memoirs: Second Volume," 422. The numbers of volumes purchased in the United States and Great Britain are not definitive evidence of the total number of volumes sold since not all the correspondence from Park has necessarily survived.

44. *Chicago Tribune*, June 12, 1874; *New York Times*, June 12, 1874; Jane Grey Swisshelm, *Half a Century* (New York: Source Book Press, 1970 ed.), 363. For an overview of her career as an abolitionist, see Frederick J. Blue, *No Taint of Compromise: Crusaders in Antislavery Politics* (Baton Rouge: Louisiana State University Press, 2004), chap. 7. For her travels, see Sylvia D. Hoffert, *Jane Grey Swisshelm: An Unconventional Life, 1815–1884* (Chapel Hill: University of North Carolina Press, 2004), 170–75, 204–5.

45. Swisshelm, *Half a Century*, 3–4. Kathleen Clark, "Celebrating Freedom," 132. Blight, *Race and Reunion*, 217, notes that the understanding of the ideological character of the war was fading in the 1880s.

46. Swisshelm, *Half a Century*, 4.

47. The following reviews of Martineau's book that reveal how critics approached a female-authored autobiography appeared at different points in the 1880s, but I am assuming that the views expressed were not new and were widely shared by critics: "Editor's Literary Record," *Harper's* 61 (1880): 477; 66 (1883): 961; "Two American Memoires," *Atlantic Monthly* 60 (1887): 127, 129; "Literature," *Century* 25 (1883): 471; "Culture and Progress," *Scribner's* 15 (1877): 137.

48. "Editor's Literary Record," *Harper's* 70 (1885): 813–14.

49. Swisshelm, *Half a Century*, 8, 26–38.

50. For insights into the marriage, see ibid., 40–46, 50, 64, 70, 83, 86–87, 164–65, 168. Later in the autobiography, Swisshelm described how Christ appeared to her in a dream that made her realize that she had made a mistake to lecture for pay. See ibid., 220–21. For her ongoing struggle over property and money, see Hoffert, *Swisshelm*, 73.

51. Swisshelm, *Half a Century*, 34. The modern reader cannot help thinking there are connections between Swisshelm's marital problems and her hatred of southern slaveholders. See Gardner, *Blood and Irony*, 91, 95, 103.

52. Swisshelm, *Half a Century*, 52–53. She notes the destruction of personal papers on 164.

53. Ibid., 58–61, 64.

54. Ibid., 55–56.

55. Ibid., 56–57. While Swisshelm's portrayal of black slaves was sympathetic, it would have been hard to imagine these abused men and women living a life of

freedom. Haviland was far more forceful in her depiction of blacks who had vigor and energy.

56. Ibid., 91–93, 97, 105–15; Peter F. Walker, *Moral Choices: Memory, Desire, and Imagination in Nineteenth-Century Abolition* (Baton Rouge: Louisiana State University Press, 1979), 136. To avoid any hint of sexual impropriety, she emphasized her refusal to rely on her good looks. "When a women starts out in the world on a mission, secular or religious," she insisted, "she should leave her feminine charms at home" (Swisshelm, *Half a Century*, 110).

57. Swisshelm, *Half a Century*, chaps. 23–24, 26–28, 31; 173, 194. See Hoffert, *Swisshelm*, 112–16, for the more complex account of her struggle with the local boss.

58. Swisshelm, *Half a Century*, 91, 112, 122–23. Blue, *No Taint of Compromise*, 154.

59. Swisshelm, *Half a Century*, 122–23, 161.

60. Ibid., 184–89.

61. Ibid., 196, 198, 200–201.

62. Ibid., 184, 211–12.

63. Ibid., 236–37, 211–12, 331.

64. Ibid., 311, 340, 343, 345, 259, 292, 352. Some of the scenes she described were surely meant to shock: "lady nurses" allowing surgeons to hold them around their waists in "full view of the wounded men," Union commissaries issuing "delicacies" to rebels when Union soldiers were starving, surgical "stupidity" that led to unnecessary amputations. See also Stuart McConnell, *Glorious Contentment: The Grand Army of the Republic, 1865–1900* (Chapel Hill: University of North Carolina Press, 1992), 167, 169.

65. For examples, see Swisshelm, *Half a Century*, 273–80, 295, 322, 327, 351, 239, 350.

66. Ibid., 360–63; Blue, *No Taint of Compromise*, 159–60.

67. Swisshelm, *Half a Century*, 360–61, 363. Blue, *No Taint of Compromise*, 160, points out that Swisshelm agitated for a harsh Reconstruction policy, but she says nothing of this in her autobiography.

68. John Tebbel, *A History of Book Publishing in the United States*, vol. 2 (New York: R. R. Bowker, 1975), 427–28, 441; "1872—Jansen, McClurg & Co." at <http://paperbarn.www1.50megs.com/publishers/i.html>; information on the 1880 books from <http://dogbert.abebooks.com/servlet/SearchResults?bx=off&sts=t&ds=30&bi=h&an=swisshelm> (accessed June 24, 2005). Hellmut Lehmann-Haupt, in *The Book in America* (New York: R. R. Bowker Co., 1939), 216, 247, wrote that A. C. McClurg and Co. was the largest bookseller in the Midwest and that the firm operated the most famous bookstore in the West.

69. *New York Times*, August 8, 1880.

70. Ibid.

71. "Julian's Political Recollections," *Atlantic Monthly* 53 (1884): 560. See also "Editor's Easy Chair," *Harper's* 59 (1879): 945; and 55 (1877): 143; and George Julian, *Political Recollections, 1840 to 1872* (Chicago: Jansen, McClurg & Co., 1884), 38, 11–29. Blue, *No Taint of Compromise*, chap. 8, gives some of the personal details missing in Julian's recollections.

72. Julian, *Recollections*, 3, 251. Julian had already worked out some of his ideas in articles for the *NAM*: "The Death-Struggle of the Republican Party" and "Is the Reformer Any Longer Needed?" 126 (1878): 237–60 and 262–92.

73. Julian, *Recollections*, 113, 16, 22, 36, 64, 95, 97, 105, 112, 122.

74. Ibid., 23, 29, 32, 51, 95, 97, 158, 159, 172, 180.

75. Ibid., 23, 25, 42.

76. Ibid., 43, 55, 58, 122, 137, 32, 150, 154. According to Julian, the plank of the Free-Soil platform of 1848 stating that since the federal government was responsible for the existence of slavery, it had the duty of eliminating it wherever it had the power to do so, was perhaps the most "admirable declaration of party principles ever promulgated by any party" (58). Free-Soilers' antipathy to slavery was a matter of principle not of policy. The Republican campaign of 1856, with a platform that rejected slavery in the territories (a position that undermined slavery) offered a stark choice between Democracy and Absolutism. It represented the "first great national struggle for liberty" (154).

77. Ibid., 43, 73–74, 130, 152, 154. The "immortal nine" were Julian, David Wilmot, Preston King, "Jo Root," Charles Allen, Charles Durkee, Amos Tuck, John W. Howe, and Joshua Giddings.

78. Ibid., 38, 65, 67, 73–74, 88–89, 123, 149, 321, 251.

79. Ibid., 177, 199–210, 226–27, 262–63.

80. Ibid., 338, 346, 246, 242; Blue, *No Taint of Compromise*, 181.

81. Julian, *Recollections*, 262, 264–72. Paul Gaston, in *The New South Creed; A Study in Southern Mythmaking* (Montgomery, Ala.: New South Books, 2002), 226, reminds us that the 1880s represented a time "of uncertainty and flux in which no monolithic pattern of race relations emerged." At such a time, it made sense to restate the importance of black suffrage, as Julian was doing.

82. Julian, *Recollections*, 330–31. He did criticize military Reconstruction, which he believed fostered sectional hostilities, but he seemed most concerned about corruption in "practical administration," a problem that he did not see as confined merely to the Reconstruction South.

83. Ibid., 322, 345–46.

84. Ibid., 336, 333–43.

85. Ibid., 347, 346.

86. Walker, *Moral Choices*, 90–91.

87. Julian, *Recollections*, 373–74.

88. *Chicago Tribune*, December 15, 1883; "Julian's Political Recollections," 560–61.

89. "Julian's Political Recollections," 562–63.

90. Henry B. Stanton, *Random Recollections* (New York: Harper & Bros., 1887), preface; <http://dogbert.abebooks.com/servlet/SearchResults?bx=off&sts=t&ds =30&bi=0&an=stant . . .> (accessed June 24, 2005).

91. "Editor's Study," *Harper's* 75 (1887): 642; "Mr. Stanton's Random Recollections," *Monthly Review of Current Literature* 18 (1887): 182. It is also worth noting that Stanton's book received reviews in several monthly magazines, whereas I have been unable to find any notice in these magazines of the work of Haviland, Coffin, Still, or Swisshelm.

92. "Editor's Study," *Harper's* 75 (1887): 642; Stanton, *Random Recollections*, 191.

93. Stanton, *Random Recollections*, 5, 46; it is noteworthy that Stanton did not really explain his support of Greeley or why that campaign represented the culmination of his antislavery work. He merely said, "I was ready to say with one of old, 'Now lettest Thou thy servant depart in peace . . . for mine eyes have seen thy salvation.'" See also ibid., 47–53. In a similar fashion, Stanton noted that he wrote for antislavery publications, stressing that he usually received no pay. See ibid., 61. For Samuel J. May's account of the Lane Debates in which Stanton participated and their importance, see *Some Recollections of Our Antislavery Conflict* (Miami: Mnemosyne Pub. Co., 1969), 102–5.

94. Stanton, *Random Recollections*, 162, 127, 166, 184–85.

95. Ibid., 65–72.

96. Swisshelm, *Half a Century*, 112, 197; Julian, *Recollections*, 22–24.

97. "Editor's Study," *Harper's* 75 (1887): 642.

98. Stanton, *Random Recollections*, 278–79.

99. Leonard Woolsey Bacon, "Open Letter," and Oliver Johnson, "Open Letter," *Century* 26 (1883): 636–37, 153–55; "Notices of New Books," *New Englander and Yale Review* 40 (1881): 544. The *Christian Recorder*, April 22, 1880, noted an exchange in a Chicago newspaper between Johnson and S. W. Coggshall, D.D., in which Coggshall defended the Methodists on the slavery question. *The American Church Review* 37 (1882): 284, reported that Oliver Johnson's book had been attacked by the religious press for its claim that the northern churches were apathetic about slavery. On Bacon and other moderates, see Kenneth P. Minkema and Harry S. Stout, "The Edwardsean Tradition and the Antislavery Debate, 1740–1865," *Journal of American History* 92 (June 2005): 66–72.

100. Parker Pillsbury, *Acts of the Anti-Slavery Apostles* (Concord, N.H.: Clague, Wegman, Schlicht & Co., 1883), iii–v; Parker Pillsbury to James Miller McKim, January 17, 1883, Department of Rare Books, CUL.

101. Pillsbury, *Acts*, iii–v. See 41, 47; Parker Pillsbury to James Miller McKim, January 17, 1883, Department of Rare Books, CUL.

102. Pillsbury, *Acts*, iii, 379–80; Parker Pillsbury to James Miller McKim, January 17, 1883, Department of Rare Books, CUL; George W. Putnam to Parker Pillsbury, March 25, 1883, Pillsbury Papers, WCL.

103. Pillsbury, *Acts*, 9, 156, 263, 319, 353, 364, 386. Another example of how Pillsbury was aware of some of the flaws in his approach but persisted: "It need not be told again that he (Stephen Foster) differed at that time from most of his fellow christians in modes of worship" (ibid., 265).

104. Ibid., 364, 166, 233, 130.

105. Ibid., 18, 87, iii; for examples of meetings and resolutions, see 209–15, 251–63.

106. Ibid., 247–49, 75–76, 491–93.

107. Ibid., 46, 11–27.

108. Ibid., 31, 28–29, 35, and the rest of chap. 2.

109. Ibid., 129, 131–34, 143, 145. Pillsbury described one Sabbath when Foster was thrown out of Concord's South Church for interrupting the morning service. Undeterred, Foster reappeared for the afternoon service. As he began speaking, some

young men "ferociously seized him . . . in the very spirit of malignant murder," threw him down the stairs, kicked him, and pulled his hair. The graphic violent detail shifted attention from Foster's challenging behavior to the brutal retaliation. When Pillsbury compared this incident to the ejection of Christ from the temple, he further reinforced the picture of the persecution of the righteous. Pillsbury praised the "utility" of Foster's "method." "Nothing like or unlike it, before or afterward, so stirred the whole people," Pillsbury declared, until John Brown's raid on Harpers Ferry.

110. Ibid., 88, 496, 251, 253–54.

111. Ibid., 10, 88.

112. Ibid., 104, 111, 149, 152, 155, 169–70, 339–40, 343, 205, chap. 14. For the part played by the church and prominent laymen in promoting reconciliation in the postwar period, see Edward J. Blum, *Reforging the White Republic: Race, Religion, and American Nationalism, 1865–1898* (Baton Rouge: Louisiana University Press, 2005), 89–107, 112–14, 123–28.

113. Pillsbury, *Acts*, 43–44, 105, 171–79, 167. Pillsbury gave no specific evidence to back up his claim that ministers instigated mobs, but it is interesting that May also made a related point. "The most violent conflicts we had, and the most outrageous mobs we encountered," he wrote, "were led on or instigated by persons professing to be religious" (May, *Our Antislavery Conflict*, 331).

114. Pillsbury, *Acts*, chap. 15; "Editor's Literary Record," *Harper's* 61 (1880): 477.

115. Pillsbury, *Acts*, iii, 122, chap. 3. His specific accusations against slavery included the charge that it was blasphemous because it reduced human beings to the level of animals. By stealing men, it was a form of robbery. Since slave marriages were not recognized, slavery fostered adultery. It was also murder, for under law, slaves were to be put to death for more than seventy offenses, including hitting a white person. Slavery was cruel, its punishments more severe than death by hanging.

116. Ibid., 70, 120–21. At times in his book Pillsbury almost seemed to glory in the carnage of the war. Describing a disrespectful audience of Dartmouth students who whistled and snickered at Foster's remarks, Pillsbury wrote, "Possibly on some battle-field in the Rebellion, they learned their mistake" (ibid., 211).

117. Ibid., 496, 501.

118. Blight, *Race and Reunion*, 309; Parker Pillsbury to Frederick Douglass, November 13, 1883, Douglass Papers, Yale University Library.

119. Frank Garrison to Parker Pillsbury, June 20, 1883. Pillsbury Papers, WCL.

120. Ibid.

121. Reader's Report, July 10, 1883, Houghton Mifflin Co. Records, HL.

122. The book was printed by a printer in Concord, New Hampshire, as well as by Clague in Rochester, New York. The book was reprinted in Boston. See <http://dogbert.abebooks.com/servlet/BookSearchPL?an=pillsburyh%2C+parker&tn=&ph=2&s>o> (accessed February 4, 2003). See also Frank Garrison to Parker Pillsbury, November 13, 1883, Pillsbury Papers, WCL.

123. J. C. Frémont to Parker Pillsbury, April 29, 1884, CCCA; Parker Pillsbury to Frederick Douglass, November 13, 1883, Douglass Papers, Yale University Library;

Abby Kelley Foster to Parker Pillsbury, January 20, 1884, Concord Public Library Historical Materials Collection, New Hampshire Historical Society, Concord; Wendell Phillips to Parker Pillsbury, January 4, 1884, CCCA; John Brown Jr. to Parker Pillsbury, February 1, 1884, Pillsbury Papers, WCL. I wish to thank Stacey Robertson for her generosity in allowing me to look at these materials that she collected.

124. Wendell Phillips to Parker Pillsbury, January 4, 1884, CCCA; Abby Kelley Foster to Parker Pillsbury, January 20, 1884, Concord Public Library Historical Materials Collection, New Hampshire Historical Society, Concord; Elizur Wright to Parker Pillsbury, February 19, 1884, Pillsbury Papers, WCL. In the 1880s, an author needed to sell at least 1,000 copies of his or her book just to cover costs. See Tebbel, *History of Book Publishing*, 12.

125. Parker Pillsbury to Sydney Gay, April 19, 1884, Sydney Howard Gay Collection, Columbia University Library, New York; Stacey M. Robertson, *Parker Pillsbury: Radical Abolitionist, Male Feminist* (Ithaca: Cornell University Press, 2000), 182.

RITUAL REMEMBRANCES III

1. *New York Times*, December 3, 1879.

2. Ibid.

3. *Commemoration of the Fiftieth Anniversary of the Organization of the American Anti-Slavery Society in Philadelphia* (Philadelphia: Thomas S. Dando & Co., 1884), 4.

4. Ibid., 49, 3, 34, 96.

5. Ibid., 7–8.

6. John G. Whittier, "The Antislavery Convention of 1833," *Atlantic Monthly* 33 (1874): 166–72; *Commemoration*, 23, 42.

7. *Commemoration*, 22–25; Ira V. Brown, *Mary Grew: Abolitionist and Feminist (1813–1896)* (Selinsgrove, Pa.: Susquehanna University Press, 1991), 156.

8. *Commemoration*, 25–28, 31, 36; James M. McPherson, *The Abolitionist Legacy: From Reconstruction to the NAACP* (Princeton: Princeton University Press, 1975), 54–55.

9. *Commemoration*, 33, 4.

10. Ibid., 21, 38–41, 49; *New York Times*, December 5, 1883.

11. *Commemoration*, 47–48, 50–51.

12. While the British and Foreign Anti-Slavery Society adopted new antislavery goals that imperialism made relevant, the existence of the organization ensured the survival of antislavery ideas and action. As Suzanne Miers points out in *Britain and the Ending of the Slave Trade* (New York: Holmes and Meier, 1975), 30–33, the antislavery society, with only a few hundred members, was able to exert influence out of proportion to its size.

13. *Commemoration*, 51–52, 29–30.

14. *New York Times*, December 5, 1883; Dorothy Sterling, *Ahead of Her Time: Abby Kelley and the Politics of Anti-Slavery* (New York: W. W. Norton, 1991), 385, picture facing 277; quotation from Elizabeth Cooke Stevens, "'From Generation to Generation': The Mother and Daughter Activism of Elizabeth Buffum Chace and Lillie Chace Wyman" (Ph.D. diss., Brown University, 1993), 325.

15. *Old Anti-Slavery Days: Proceedings of the Commemoration Meeting, Held by the Danvers Historical Society at the Town Hall, Danvers, April 26, 1893* (Danvers, Mass.: Danvers Historical Society, 1893), 42; *New York Times*, March 7, 1886.

16. *New York Times*, May 9, 1886; William Howe Downes, "Monuments and Statues in Boston," *New England Magazine* 17 (1894): 364–65.

17. Edwin Mead, "A Monument to Wendell Phillips," *New England Magazine* 9 (1890): 535–36, 537–38.

18. Archibald H. Grimké, "Anti-Slavery Boston," *New England Magazine* 9 (1890): 441–59; Nina Moore Tiffany, "Stories of the Fugitive Slaves," *New England Magazine* 7 (1890): 524–31; 8 (1890): 280–83, 569–77; Sidney H. Morse, "An Anti-Slavery Hero," *New England Magazine* 10 (1891): 486–96.

19. "Anti-Slavery History and Biography," *Atlantic Monthly* 72 (1893): 268, 271–72, 275–76; for a discussion of how far Rhodes's history had diverged from more traditional antislavery treatments of the coming of the Civil War, see Thomas J. Pressly, *Americans Interpret Their Civil War* (New York: Collier Books, 1962 ed.), 171–75.

20. *Old Anti-Slavery Days*, viii.

21. Ibid., viii, ix; "Circular," July 15, 1893, in *Old Anti-Slavery Days*, Subject File, Douglass Papers, LC.

22. *Old Anti-Slavery Days*, x, vii, xiii, 1.

23. Ibid., ix, x, xxiv–xxv.

24. Ibid., 50, vii, 42–43, 70, 71–72.

25. Ibid., picture, 27–29.

26. Ibid., ix, xxv.

27. Ibid., 6–7, 11, xxiii, 51.

28. Ibid., 31, 55.

29. Ibid., 53–54, 66–67, 72, 82–83.

30. Ibid., 63–65.

31. Ibid., 63, 72.

CHAPTER FIVE

1. The title of this chapter comes from Caroline H. Dall, "At Whittier's Funeral," *New England Magazine* 13 (1893): 652.

2. "Topics of the Times," *Century* 47 (1894): 470; 52 (1896): 471. I do not mean to suggest that abolitionists like George Julian did not embrace such new reforms, merely that the new reforms lacked the moral meaning of abolitionism.

3. As William B. Hixson Jr. pointed out in *Moorfield Storey and the American Abolitionist Tradition* (New York: Oxford University Press, 1972), 104, whether blacks sided with the Redeemers in this decade of political conflict or supported protest groups, their choice was politically fatal and resulted in disenfranchisement. See also ibid., 106–7; Jane Dailey, *Before Jim Crow: The Politics of Race in Postemancipation Virginia* (Chapel Hill: University of North Carolina Press, 2000), 201 n. 132; Charles H. Levermore, "Impressions of a Yankee Visitor in the South," *New England Magazine* 9 (1890): 316; James M. McPherson, *The Struggle for Equality: Abolitionists and the Negro in the Civil War and Reconstruction* (Princeton: Princeton University Press, 1964), 303; and *American Missionary*, 46 (1892): 145–46.

4. In "Topics of the Times," the editor of *Century* pointed out that there was opposition to lynching in the South and cited the address of Georgia's governor to the state legislature as one example. See *Century* 55 (1898): 474–77. See also McPherson, *Struggle for Equality*, 304–6; and "Topics of the Time," *Century* 57 (1899): 474.

5. David W. Blight, *Race and Reunion: The Civil War in American Memory* (Cambridge, Mass.: Harvard University Press, 2001), 271; Patrick J. Kelly, "The Election of 1896 and the Restructuring of Civil War Memory," in *The Memory of the Civil War in American Culture*, ed. Alice Fahs and Joan Waugh (Chapel Hill: University of North Carolina Press, 2004), 181, and his article "The Election of 1896 and the Restructuring of Civil War Memory," *Civil War History* 49 (September 2003): 255–72; Noah Brooks, "When Slavery Went out of Politics," *Scribner's* 17 (1895): 351. The *Chicago Tribune*, quoted in Kelly's article in *Civil War History*, 272, encouraged veterans to "recognize the danger which confronts the country from an anarchical . . . mob" and urged them to "do their duty in 1896 as they did it from 1861 to 1865" and to vote Republican.

6. Arthur John, *The Best Years of the Century: Richard Watson Gilder, Scribner's Monthly, and Century Magazine, 1870–1909* (Urbana: University of Illinois Press, 1981), 120; "Topics of the Times," *Century* 42 (1891): 950; 51 (1895): 155; 42 (1891): 313; 55 (1898): 476–77; 57 (1899): 474; Charles Foster Smith, "The Negro in Nashville," *Century* 42 (1891): 154–56; letter from S. W. Powell, *Century* 49 (1895): 956–58; letter from Robert A. McGuinn, *Century* 56 (1898): 316; Thomas Wentworth Higginson, "Colored Troops Under Fire," *Century* 54 (1897): 199–200. As Kenneth Price points out in "Charles Chesnutt, The *Atlantic Monthly* and the Intersection of African-American Fiction and Elite Culture," in *Periodical Literature in Nineteenth-Century America*, ed. Kenneth M. Price and Susan Belasco Smith (Charlottesville: University Press of Virginia, 1995), 258, the magazine cut back on its coverage of African Americans in the 1880s, having decided that readers were no longer interested in reading about them. The magazine had few readers in the South, in contrast to *Century*. See Ellery Sedgwick, *The Atlantic Monthly, 1857–1909: Yankee Humanism at High Tide and Ebb* (Amherst: University of Massachusetts Press, 1994), 248. The articles published in the *American Missionary* were an exception to these trends.

7. Frank Luther Mott, *A History of American Magazines*, 5 vols. (Cambridge, Mass.: Harvard University Press, 1957), 4:20, 43; Price, "Charles Chesnutt," 274 n. 36; Richard Malcolm Johnston, "Travis and Major Jonathan Wilby," *Century* 40 (1890): 127, 129, 133; Grace King, "A Crippled Hope," *Century* 46 (1893): 377–79. In "A Southern Study," *New England Magazine* 10 (1891): 527, Lillie B. Chace Wyman differed with the dominant view by noting how many black people told stories about the cruelty and misery of slavery.

8. Letter from Starnes, *Century* 50 (1895): 155; Virginia Frazer Boyle, "Old 'Bias's Vision," *Century* 48 (1894): 516; Matt Crim, "Was It an Exceptional Case?" *Century* 42 (1891): 821–28; Michael D. Pierson, "'Slavery Cannot Be Covered up with Broadcloth or a Bandanna': The Evolution of White Abolitionist Attacks on the 'Patriarchal Institution,'" *Journal of the Early Republic* 25 (Fall 2005): 412–13. As D. Bruce Dickson Jr. points out in *Black American Writing from the Nadir: The Evolution of a Literary Tradition, 1877–1915* (Baton Rouge: Louisiana State University Press, 1989),

136–37, 149–51, segregation made the issue of the color line significant for both black and white writers. Interracial marriage suggested the possibility of assimilation, a possibility rejected in Crim's story.

9. Maurice Thompson, "A Race Romance," *Century* 41 (1891): 895–98; Harry Stillwell Edwards, "Captain Jerry," *Century* 47 (1894): 478–80; see also Edwards's story "Mas'Craffud's Freedom," *Century* 52 (1896): 88. A brief biography of Edwards is available at <http://myweb.wvnet.edu/~jelkins/lp-2001/Edwards.html>. See also "Abolitionists and Prohibitionists; or, Moral Reform Embarrassed by Ultra-Ism," *New Englander and Yale Review* 56 (1892): 7. Even Lillie B. Chace Wyman, daughter of abolitionist Elizabeth Chace, gave a mixed picture of free blacks in her articles for *New England Magazine*. See "A Southern Study," *New England Magazine* 10 (1891): 521–31, and Elizabeth Cooke Stevens, "'From Generation to Generation': The Mother and Daughter Activism of Elizabeth Buffum Chace and Lillie Chace Wyman" (Ph.D. diss., Brown University, 1993), 358–69.

10. Harry Stillwell Edwards, "The Gum Swamp Debate," *Century* 50 (1895): 798–800; Wade Hall, *The Smiling Phoenix: Southern Humor from 1865 to 1914* (Gainesville: University of Florida Press, 1965), 198, 219, 228–30; Gavin Jones, *Strange Talk: The Politics of Dialect Literature in Gilded Age America* (Berkeley: University of California Press, 1999), 10–11.

11. Henry M. Stanley, "The Story of the Development of Africa," *Century* 51 (1896): 506, and "Slavery and the Slave Trade in Africa," *Harper's* 86 (1893): 614, 622, 628. See also Herbert Ward, "Life Among the Congo Savages," *Scribner's* 7 (1890): 135–57.

12. G. W. Cable, "The Gentler Side of Two Great Southerners," *Century* 47 (1894): 292; Wilbur Fisk Vanderbilt Tillett, "Southern Womanhood as Affected by the War," *Century* 43 (1891): 9–16. In one rare article for the decade, Grace Blanchard depicted the southern slaveholder who had fathered a child with Black Jenny as a weakling. See "Two Union Men," *New England Magazine* 8 (1890): 624–25.

13. Thomas J. Pressly, *Americans Interpret Their Civil War*, (New York: Collier Books, 1962 ed.), 187; Tillett, "Southern Womanhood as Affected by the War," 14; Harry Stillwell Edwards, "A Helping Hand," *Century* 56 (1898): 478–79; Johnston, "Travis and Major Wilby," 127 (When Wilby attempts to go to work, his former slave is against the idea, and Wilby earns little more than his expenses [see 129]); F. Hopkinson Smith, "Colonel Carter of Cartersville," *Century* 41 (1890–91): 62–73, 227–38, 426–31, 593–99, 733–38, 885–91.

14. Johnston, "Travis and Major Wilby," 128.

15. Janet Habler-Hover, "The North-South Reconciliation Theme and the 'Shadow of the Negro' in *Century Illustrated Magazine*," in Price and Smith, eds., *Periodical Literature*, 239–42; Brander Matthews, "A Decoration Day Revery," *Century* 40 (1890): 103.

16. Pressly, *Civil War*, 183–211; John Coleman Adams, "Lincoln's Place in History," *Century* 47 (1894): 594–95. Histories written by black authors presented a very different interpretation of the past than that produced by the white, university-trained historians. See Laurie F. Maffly-Kipp, "Redeeming Southern Memory: The Negro Race History, 1874–1915," in *Where These Memories Grow: History, Memory, and South-*

ern Identity, ed. W. Fitzhugh Brundage (Chapel Hill: University of North Carolina Press, 2000), 169–89. On Adams, see <http://www.hds.harvard.edu/library/bms/bms00193.2.html>.

17. Mellen Chamberlain, "A Glance at Daniel Webster," *Century* 46 (1893): 710. See also "A Seventy-Niner" and "An Anecdote of Webster," *Century* 47 (1893): 477–78; "Topics of the Times," *Century* 53 (1896): 313; and Joseph S. Auerbach, "The Legal Aspects of Trusts," *NAM* 169 (1899): 395. *Century* published a portrait of Webster as its frontispiece for the September 1896 issue.

18. Steven Mintz is quoted in John David Smith, "The Evil Americans Did," *Chronicle of Higher Education*, March 9, 2007.

19. Alfred Serene Hudson, "The Home of Lydia Maria Child," *New England Magazine* 8 (1890): 402–14; Charlotte Forten Grimké, "Personal Recollections of Whittier," *New England Magazine* 14 (1893): 468–76; Benjamin Penhallow Shillaben, "Experiences during Many Years," *New England Magazine* 15 (1894): 625–31; John White Chadwick, "Samuel May of Leicester," *New England Magazine* 20 (1899): 201–14; "Editor's Table," *New England Magazine* 24 (1898): 509–10.

20. "A Political Abolitionist," *Atlantic Monthly* 71 (1893): 701–2; Gamaliel Bradford Jr., "The American Idealist," *Atlantic Monthly* 70 (1892): 89–90; "Emerson, Sixty Years After," *Atlantic Monthly* 79 (1897): 223; J. T. Trowbridge, "Some Confessions of a Novel-Writer," *Atlantic Monthly* 75 (1895): 317, 320. See also Charles Dudley Warner, "The Story of Uncle Tom's Cabin," *Atlantic Monthly* 78 (1896): 311–21; and John Jay Chapman, "Between Elections," *Atlantic Monthly* 85 (1900): 26–37. The magazine also published parts of Thomas Wentworth Higginson's autobiography and the reminiscences of Julia Ward Howe. Ellery Sedgwick, in *The Atlantic Monthly, 1857–1909: Yankee Humanism at High Tide and Ebb* (Amherst: University of Massachusetts Press, 1994), 202, 213–15, 248, 264, discusses the monthly during the 1890s, when it was under the direction of Horace Elisha Scudder. Sedgwick credits Scudder with publishing admiring articles of antislavery workers with the hope that his readers would gain greater understanding of the present by seeing parallels with the past. I see the articles as more ambiguous.

21. Harold Frederic, "The Copperhead," *Scribner's* 14 (1893): 113, 115–16, 199, 202, 350, 518–19, 524, 630–31. On Frederic, consult the brief biography at <http://helios.acomp.usf.edu/rrogers/biooffrederic.html>.

22. "Abolitionists and Prohibitionists," 1–25.

23. King, "A Crippled Hope," 375–76; George Howe, "The Last Slave Ship," *Scribner's* 8 (1890) 113–28; "Point of View," *Scribner's* 10 (1891): 657. See also Hudson, "Home of Lydia Maria Child," 402.

24. "Point of View," *Scribner's* 8 (1890): 657–58.

25. Frederick Douglass, *Life and Times of Frederick Douglass Written by Himself* (New York: Collier Books ed., 1962), 513. De Wolfe, Fiske and Co. to Helen Douglass, March 26, 1895, Douglass Papers, LC.

26. Douglass, *Life and Times*, 512, 518–19.

27. Ibid., 523, 536–37, 554.

28. Ibid., 514–16.

29. Benjamin Quarles, *Frederick Douglass* (Washington, D.C.: Associated Publish-

ers, Inc., 1948), 337; De Wolfe, Fiske and Co. to Helen Douglass, March 26, 1895, and Frederick Douglass to De Wolfe, Fiske and Co., November 18, 1892, Douglass Papers, LC.

30. De Wolfe, Fiske and Co. to Helen Douglass, March 26, 1895; De Wolfe, Fiske and Co. Monthly Statement, March 1895; unattributed newspaper review, 1890s, in Frederick Douglass, General, Folder 8, Douglass Papers, LC.

31. Students from Raisin Institute, the biracial school started by the Havilands, held reunions with "Aunt Laura" from 1885 on. The reunions emphasized the school's abolitionist character and allowed former students to reminisce. These events may well have persuaded Haviland that there was still an audience for her book. See news clipping in Scrapbook, Haviland Papers, BHL, and E. P. Powell, "New England in Michigan," *New England Magazine* 19 (1895): 426. The website <http://www.abebooks.com/servlet/SearchResults?an=levi+coffin&bi=o&bx= off&ds=30&sortby=2&sts=t&x=o&y=o> provides information on the 1899 edition of Coffin's book. David W. Blight discusses the work of Wilbur Siebert in collecting Underground Railroad stories in *Race and Reunion*, 231–37. Blight suggests that narrators wanted to lay claim to a place in historical memory and to bask in the moral glow of having helped undermine slavery. He also sees the effort as part of the move toward reconciliation, with some of the stories relying on racial stereotypes and others implying that with the end of slavery, the race problem had been solved. The works of Haviland, Coffin, and Calvin Fairbank do not support this interpretation.

32. Calvin Fairbank, *During Slavery Times: How He "Fought the Good Fight" to Prepare "The Way"* (Chicago: Patriotic Publishing Co., 1890), 7–8, 10, 50–57, 105, 162–70, 174.

33. Ibid., preface.

34. Fairbank, *During Slavery Times*, 193, 207. In a letter to the *Cleveland Gazette*, March 21, 1891, Laura Haviland explained that McCabe, who must have been related to the book's printer, had done the final condensation.

35. Fairbank, *During Slavery Times*, 144, dedication page, 26, 19, 21, 60, 68–69.

36. Fairbank, *During Slavery Times*, 181, 183, 187, 189–90. I am not sure whether Fairbank coined the term "Africo-Americans". He is the only one of the abolitionists discussed in this study that used this phrase.

37. Ibid., 18–19, 22–23, 40–42.

38. Ibid., 26–30.

39. Ibid., 12–13. See also 13–17 for other accounts that cast Fairbank in the active role.

40. Ibid., 12, 15, 23, 46, 44.

41. Ibid., 33, 88–89, 79, 170–72.

42. Ibid., 105, 112, 137, 140, 147, 150. Michael B. Chesson points out Fairbank's carelessness and behavior during the first trial in his "Review of Randolph Paul Runyon. *Delia Webster and the Underground Railroad*," http://www.h-net.org/reviews/showpdf.cgi?path=15581857574286. According to Fergus Bordewich, many abolitionists accused Fairbank of being a hypocrite. See Fergus M. Bordewich, *Bound for Canaan: The Underground Railroad and the War for the Soul of America* (New York:

Harper Collins, 2005), 362–63. For a good discussion of the trial and Fairbank's "re-cantation" of his abolitionist conviction, see Randolph Paul Runyon, *Delia Webster and the Underground Railroad* (Lexington: University Press of Kentucky, 1996), 62, 121–22, 131.

43. *Chicago Tribune*, January 23, December 24, 1893; Chesson, "Review"; *Cleveland Gazette*, March 21, 1891. For R. R. McCabe and Co., see <http:www3.sympatico.ca/dmckilli/whc/bib.htm>.

44. For Birney, see <http://en.wikipedia.org/wiki/William_Birney>; quota-tion in Blight, *Race and Reunion*, 233.

45. Reader's Report, July 14, 1884, Houghton Mifflin Co. Records, HL. Elizabeth Chace's *Anti-Slavery Reminiscences* was originally published in 1891 by E. L. Free-man & Sons, State Printers, in Central Falls, Rhode Island. I am using the edition edited by Lucille Salitan and Eve Lewis Perera: *Virtuous Lives: Four Quaker Sisters Remember Family Life, Abolitionism, and Women's Suffrage* (New York: Continuum, 1994). Sarah H. Southwick's *Reminiscences of Early Anti-Slavery Days* was privately printed in Cambridge by Riverside Press, in 1893. Lucy N. Colman's *Reminiscences* was published by H. L. Green in 1891).

46. Southwick, *Reminiscences*, frontispiece; Salitan, *Virtuous Lives*, 85. Southwick's reminiscences described associational life with its meetings, picnics, and fairs. She provided admiring vignettes of George Thompson and Wendell Phillips and some of the key antislavery women. Her book gives a good sense of what it was like to be a female abolitionist in Boston. See also Colman, *Reminiscences*, 79.

47. Stevens, "'From Generation to Generation,'" 328–32; quotation, 332.

48. Salitan, *Virtuous Lives*, 97, 101–2.

49. Ibid., 102, 109, 111, 107. Stacey Robertson discusses the connection between home and female activism in "Remembering Antislavery Women Abolitionists in the Old Northwest," paper delivered at the annual meeting of the Organization of American Historians, 2001.

50. Salitan, *Virtuous Lives*, 105–6, 110.

51. Ibid., 108–9.

52. Chace did not explain how promoting emancipation would prevent the con-flict. See ibid., 112–14.

53. Ibid., 98–100; Joseph Moreau, *Schoolbook Nation: Conflicts over American His-tory Textbooks from the Civil War to the Present* (Ann Arbor: University of Michigan Press, 2003), 143–45.

54. Salitan, *Virtuous Lives*, 114–15. Oddly enough, Chace followed this affirma-tion with a statement that slavery was over and that blacks had "the diadem of citizenship. It is too late to be an Abolitionist now," she wrote, and then promoted woman suffrage. These sentiments hardly conformed to the underlying theme of her narrative. Stevens ("'From Generation to Generation,'" 338) suggests that her comments about suffrage were intended to demonstrate to her readers her high sense of moral purpose.

55. Stevens, "'From Generation to Generation,'" 333, 338, 338 nn. 39 and 63.

56. Ibid., 339, 341, 341 n. 65.

57. Ibid., 340–41, 338, 338 n. 61.

58. Colman, *Reminiscences*, 12, 40, 70; John A. Garraty and Marks C. Carnes, eds., *American National Biography* (New York: Oxford University Press, 1999), 5, 260.

59. Colman, *Reminiscences*, frontispiece, 12, 16–17, 38. Augusta Rohrbach, in *Truth Stranger than Fiction: Race, Realism, and the U.S. Literary Marketplace* (New York: Palgrave Press, 2002), 88–89, discusses the growing importance of the photographs of authors in helping to shape readers' responses to books and to promote them.

60. Colman, *Reminiscences*, preface; Nina Silber, *The Romance of Reunion: Northerners and the South, 1865–1900* (Chapel Hill: University of North Carolina Press, 1993), 136–37.

61. Colman, *Reminiscences*, 5, 12, 16.

62. Ibid., 20–21, 24–25, 32–38, 47, 50–51, 54–55.

63. Ibid., 29–30, 38, 43, 47–48.

64. Ibid., 13, 34–35, 60–63.

65. Ibid., 29, 58.

66. Ibid., 65–67. Nell Irvin Painter thinks that Colman's later assessment in the text was likely more accurate than the earlier comments since they meshed with Lincoln's racial attitudes. See her *Sojourner Truth: A Life, a Symbol* (New York: W. W. Norton, 1996), 206. See also Carleton Mabee with Susan Mabee Newhouse, *Sojourner Truth: Slave, Prophet, Legend* (New York: New York University Press, 1993), 118–24.

67. Colman, *Reminiscences*, 23, 79; John David Smith, "Evil Americans Did."

68. Colman, *Reminiscences*, 79, 51.

69. Aaron M. Powell, *Personal Reminiscences of the Anti-Slavery and Other Reforms and Reformers* (Westport, Conn.: Negro Universities Press, 1970).

70. Ibid., 37, 7, 11, 40, 51, 77, 84, 126, 129, 142, 158.

71. Ibid., 7, 73, 74, 108, 117, 122–24, 126, 136, 158.

72. Ibid., 177.

73. Ibid., 161, 170–71; *New York Times*, December 3, 1879; *Commemoration of the Fiftieth Anniversary of the Organization of the American Anti-Slavery Society in Philadelphia* (Philadelphia: Thomas S. Dando & Co., 1884), 47.

74. Powell, *Reminiscences*, 160–63, picture facing 164.

75. Ibid., 53–54; *NAS*, April 2, 1870.

76. Powell, *Personal Reminiscences*, 229–30; Fairbank, *During Slavery Times*, 181.

AFTERWORD

1. Ira V. Brown, *Mary Grew: Abolitionist and Feminist (1813–1896)* (Selinsgrove, Pa.: Susquehanna University Press, 1991), 166–67.

2. John T. Hume, *Abolitionists: Together with Personal Memories of the Struggle for Human Rights, 1830–1864* (New York: G. P. Putnam's Sons, 1905), 79.

3. The material in this and the preceding paragraph is based upon reviews and reader's reports: "The Contributors Club," *Atlantic Monthly* 48 (1881): 281; "Some Recent Biographies," *Atlantic Monthly* 48 (1881): 414; "Autobiography of Frith," *NAM* 146 (1888): 251; Reader's Reports, October 17, 1887, June 6, 1894, July 24, 1896, Houghton Mifflin Co. Records, HL.

4. A comparison of Colman's and Higginson's comments about light-skinned

blacks highlights the difference between Higginson's and other abolitionists' reminiscences. When Colman described her work at the National Colored Orphan's Asylum, she ironically noted of her charges' varied skin tones: "Surely such [children] had fathers destitute of prejudice against color, as far as the mothers of their children were concerned." The mixed-blood children revealed the hypocrisy that was at the heart of southern slavery. See Lucy N. Colman, *Reminiscences* (Buffalo: H. L. Green, Publisher, 1891), 60. Of the union that produced the light complexion of a female fugitive whom Samuel May had sent to Higginson many years earlier Higginson wrote, "It was one of those . . . romantic incident[s] which slavery yielded" (Thomas Wentworth Higginson, *Cheerful Yesterdays* [Boston: Houghton Mifflin, 1898], 146–47).

5. George Mifflin to Thomas Higginson, February 17, 1903; Contract for *Cheerful Yesterdays*, November 29, 1896, Contracts 1831–97, Houghton Mifflin Co. Records, HL. Higginson was offered 15 percent royalties on the retail price of every volume sold. See Thomas Higginson to Horace Scudder, March 1, April 5 and 11, 1896, ibid.

6. "Important Announcements for the Fall and Winter of 1896-7," booklet in Houghton Mifflin Scrapbook, 1895–97, Houghton Mifflin Co. Records, HL. The phrase about the inner life comes from a Reader's Report, November 15, 1893: "If the book [an autobiography of Annie Besant] is to be a real autobiography it must set forth the inner life in its changing phases." See Scott E. Casper, *Constructing American Lives: Biography and Culture in Nineteenth-Century America* (Chapel Hill: University of North Carolina Press, 1999), 323–31.

7. Higginson, *Cheerful Yesterdays*, 27, 121. Higginson had little to say about slavery itself, but he did describe how disturbing he found his one visit to a slave market (see ibid., 236); see also Higginson, *The Magnificent Activist: The Writings of Thomas Wentworth Higginson (1823–1911)*, ed. Howard N. Meyer (Cambridge: Da Capo Press, 2000), 33; and Thomas Wentworth Higginson, "Two Antislavery Leaders," *International Review* 9 (1880): 148. For a picture of Higginson's more radical racial views during and directly following the war, see Tilden G. Edelstein, *Strange Enthusiasm: A Life of Thomas Wentworth Higginson* (New Haven: Yale University Press, 1968), 291–304.

8. Higginson, *Cheerful Yesterdays*, 65, 70, 138, 147, 153, 160, 197–98, 214, 252.

9. Ibid., 139–40, 117–18, 149; Joseph A. Conforti, *Imagining New England: Explorations of Regional Identity from the Pilgrims to the Mid-Twentieth Century* (Chapel Hill: University of North Carolina Press, 2001), 221.

10. Edelstein, *Strange Enthusiasm*, 321–24; Higginson, *Cheerful Yesterdays*, 257–59, 254.

11. Edelstein, *Strange Enthusiasm*, 331, 375–78, 388–92, 396–97; James M. McPherson, *The Abolitionist Legacy: From Reconstruction to the NAACP* (Princeton: Princeton University Press, 1975), 131.

12. *Century* 55 (1898): miscellaneous back pages; *Atlantic Monthly* 82 (1898): miscellaneous back pages, and 78 (1896): miscellaneous back pages; *The Living Age* 211 (1896): 902; advertisement for *Cheerful Yesterdays*, Houghton Mifflin Scrapbook, 1897–99, Houghton Mifflin Co. Records, HL.

13. *New York Times*, February 26, March 19, 1898.

14. Records of Book Sales, 1891–1907, and Records of Book Earnings, 1887–1905, Houghton Mifflin Co. Records, HL.

15. Hume, *Abolitionists*, 22, 86–87.

16. James M. McPherson points out the connections between abolitionism (though not the role of abolitionist autobiographies) and the birth of the NAACP in *The Struggle for Equality: Abolitionists and the Negro in the Civil War and Reconstruction* (Princeton: Princeton University Press, 1964), 368, 391. For a useful account of the origins of the NAACP, see also William B. Hixson, *Moorfield Storey and the Abolitionist Tradition* (New York: Oxford University Press, 1972).

BIBLIOGRAPHY

PRIMARY SOURCES

Manuscript Collections

Bentley Historical Library, University of Michigan, Ann Arbor
    Laura Haviland Papers
Cleveland-Colby-Colgate Archives, Susan Colgate Cleveland Library,
    Colby Sawyer College, New London, New Hampshire
Cornell University Library, Ithaca, New York
    Samuel J. May Papers
Historical Society of Pennsylvania, Philadelphia
    William Still Papers
Houghton Library, Harvard University, Cambridge, Massachusetts
    Houghton Mifflin Co. Records
    Papers of Thomas Wentworth Higginson
Library of Congress, Washington, D.C.
    Frederick Douglass Papers
Whittier College Library, Whittier, California
    Parker Pillsbury Papers

Periodicals and Newspapers

American Missionary
Atlantic Monthly
Brooklyn Eagle
Century Illustrated Magazine
Chicago Daily Tribune
Christian Recorder
Galaxy
Harper's Monthly Magazine
Harper's Weekly
National Anti-Slavery Standard
National Era
National Standard
New Englander and Yale Review
New England Magazine
New National Era
New York Times
North American Review

Putnam's Magazine
Scribner's
Scribner's series II

Published Primary Sources

Adams, John Quincy. *Narrative of the Life of John Quincy Adams, When in Slavery, and Now as a Freeman.* Harrisburg, Pa.: Sieg, Printer and Stationer, 1872.

Bearse, Austin. *Reminiscences of Fugitive-Slave Law Days in Boston.* 1880. New York: Arno Press, 1969.

Centennial Anniversary of the Pennsylvania Society for Promoting the Abolition of Slavery, the Relief of Free Negroes Unlawfully Held in Bondage: and for Improving the Condition of the African Race. Philadelphia: Grant, Faires & Rodgers, Printers, 1875.

Chace, Elizabeth Buffum. *Anti-Slavery Reminiscences.* Central Falls, R.I.: E. L. Freeman & Son, State Printers, 1891.

Cheyney, Ednah Dow. *Reminiscences of Ednah Dow Cheyney.* Boston: Lee & Shepard, 1902.

Chielens, Edward E., ed. *American Literary Magazines: The Eighteenth and Nineteenth Centuries.* New York: Greenwood Press, 1986.

Clarke, James Freeman. *Anti-Slavery Days: A Sketch of the Struggle Which Ended in the Abolition of Slavery in the United States.* New York: John W. Lovell Co., 1883.

Coffin, Levi. *Reminiscences.* Cincinnati: Robert Clarke & Co., 1880.

Colman, Lucy N. *Reminiscences.* Buffalo: H. L. Green, Publisher, 1891.

Commemoration of the Fiftieth Anniversary of the Organization of the American Anti-Slavery Society in Philadelphia. Philadelphia: Thomas S. Dando & Co., 1884.

Conway, Moncure Daniel. *Autobiography, Memories and Experiences of Moncure Daniel Conway.* Boston: Houghton, Mifflin & Co., 1904.

Douglass, Frederick. *Life and Times of Frederick Douglass Written by Himself.* New York: Collier ed., 1962.

Fairbank, Calvin. *During Slavery Times. How He "Fought the Good Fight" to Prepare "The Way."* Chicago: Patriotic Publishing Co., 1890.

Furness, William Henry. *Recollections of Seventy Years: A Discourse Delivered to the First Unitarian Church in Philadelphia, January 1895.* N.p., n.d.

Gilder, Rosamond, ed. *Letters of Richard Watson Gilder.* Boston: Houghton Mifflin, 1916.

Griest, Ellwood. *John and Mary; or, The Fugitive Slaves, a Tale of South-Eastern Pennsylvania.* Lancaster: Inquirer Printing and Publishing Co., 1873.

Haviland, Laura. *A Woman's Life-Work: Labors and Experiences of Laura S. Haviland.* Chicago: Publishing Association of Friends, 1881. Reprint, Salem, N.H.: Ayer Co., 1984.

Higginson, Thomas Wentworth. *Cheerful Yesterdays.* Boston: Houghton Mifflin, 1898.

———. *The Magnificent Activist: The Writings of Thomas Wentworth Higginson (1823–1911).* Edited by Howard N. Meyer. New York: Da Capo Press, 2000.

Howe, Julia Ward. *Reminiscences, 1819–1899.* Boston: Houghton Mifflin, 1910.

Hume, John F. *Abolitionists: Together with Personal Memories of the Struggle for Human Rights, 1830–1864.* New York: G. P. Putman's Sons, 1905.

Johnson, Oliver. *The Abolitionists Vindicated in a Review of Eli Thayer's Paper on the New England Emigrant Aid Company.* Worcester, Mass.: Worcester Society of Antiquity, 1887.

Johnson, Robert Underwood. *Remembered Yesterdays.* Boston: Little, Brown, and Co., 1923.

Julian, George. *Political Recollections, 1840 to 1872.* Chicago: Jansen, McClurg & Co., 1884.

———. "The Truth of Anti-Slavery History." N.p., 1882, 437–54. Xerox copy in Johns Hopkins University Archives, Baltimore, Md.

Knapp, John I., and R. I. Bonner. "Mrs. Laura S. Haviland." In *Illustrated History and Biographical Record of Lenawee County, Michigan.* Adrian: The Times Printing Co. Xerox in Friends Historical Library, Swarthmore College, Swarthmore, Pa.

Lovell, Malcolm, ed. *Two Quaker Sisters: From the Original Diaries of Elizabeth Buffum Chace and Lucy Buffum Lovell.* New York: Liveright Publishing Co., 1937.

May, Samuel J. *Some Recollections of Our Antislavery Conflict.* Miami: Mnemosyne Pub. Co., 1969.

North Into Freedom: The Autobiography of John Malvin, Free Negro, 1795–1880. Edited by Allan Peskin. Kent: Kent State University Press, 1988.

Old Anti-Slavery Days: Proceedings of the Commemoration Meeting, Held by the Danvers Historical Society at the Town Hall, Danvers, April 26, 1893. Danvers, Mass.: Danvers Historical Society, 1893.

Palmer, Beverly Wilson, ed. *Selected Letters of Lucretia Coffin Mott.* Urbana: University of Illinois Press, 2002.

Pillsbury, Parker. *Acts of the Anti-Slavery Apostles.* Concord, N.H.: Clague, Wegman, Schlicht & Co., 1883.

Porter, Mary H. *Eliza Chappell Porter: A Memoir.* Chicago: Fleming H. Revell Co., 1892.

Powell, Aaron M. *Personal Reminiscences of the Anti-Slavery and Other Reforms and Reformers.* Westport, Conn.: Negro Universities Press, 1970.

Rawlings, Peter, ed., *Americans on Fiction, 1776–1900.* Vol. 3. London: Pickering & Chatto, 2002.

Ross, Alexander Milton. *Recollections and Experiences of an Abolitionist: From 1855 to 1865.* Northbrook, Ill.: Metro Books, 1972 ed.

Salitan, Lucille, and Eve Lewis Perera, eds. *Virtuous Lives: Four Quaker Sisters Remember Family Life, Abolitionism, and Women's Suffrage.* New York: Continuum, 1994.

Siebert, Wilbur H. *The Underground Railroad from Slavery to Freedom.* New York: Macmillan, 1898.

Southwick, Sarah H. *Reminiscences of Early Anti-Slavery Days.* Cambridge, Mass.: Privately printed, 1893.

Sprague, Stuart Seely, ed. *His Promised Land: The Autobiography of John P. Parker, Former Slave and Conductor on the Underground Railroad.* New York: W. W. Norton, 1996.

Stanton, Henry B. *Random Recollections*. New York: Harper & Bros., 1887.

Still, William. *The Underground Rail Road*. Philadelphia: Porter & Coates, 1872. Reprint, New York: Arno Press, 1978.

Swisshelm, Jane Grey. *Half A Century*. New York: Source Book Press, 1970 ed.

Thompson, John W. *An Authentic History of the Douglass Monument*. Freeport, N.Y.: Books for Libraries Press, 1971 ed.

Webb, William. *The History of William Webb, Composed by Himself.* Detroit: Egbert Hoekstra, 1873.

Willey, Austin. *The History of the Anti-Slavery Cause in State and Nation*. Portland, Me.: Brown Thurston and Hoyt, Fogg & Donham, 1886.

Wyman, Lillie Buffum Chace. *American Chivalry*. Boston: W. B. Clarke Co., 1913.

SECONDARY SOURCES

Aaron, Daniel. *The Unwritten War: American Writers and the Civil War*. New York: Alfred A. Knopf, 1973.

Adams, Timothy Dow. *Telling Lies in Modern American Autobiography*. Chapel Hill: University of North Carolina Press, 1990.

Alexander, Roberta Sue. "Presidential Reconstruction: Ideology and Change." In *The Facts of Reconstruction: Essays in Honor of John Hope Franklin*, edited by Eric Anderson and Alfred A. Moss Jr., 29–51. Baton Rouge: Louisiana State University Press, 1991.

Alonso, Harriet Hyman. *Growing Up Abolitionist: The Story of the Garrison Children*. Amherst: University of Massachusetts Press, 2002.

Altman, Janet Gurkin. *Epistolarity: Approaches to a Form*. Columbus: Ohio State University Press, 1982.

Anderson, David. "Down Memory Lane: Nostalgia for the Old South in Post–Civil War Plantation Reminiscences." *Journal of Southern History* 21 (February 2005): 105–36.

Anderson, Eric, and Alfred A. Moss Jr., eds. *The Facts of Reconstruction: Essays in Honor of John Hope Franklin*. Baton Rouge: Louisiana State University Press, 1991.

Andrews, William L., ed. *African American Autobiography: A Collection of Critical Essays*. Englewood Cliffs, N.J.: Prentice Hall, 1993.

————. "Forgotten Voices of Afro-American Autobiography, 1865–1930." *Auto/Bio Studies* 2 (Fall 1986): 21–27.

————. "The Spirit of Friday Jones." Greenville, N.C.: J. Y. Joyner Library, East Carolina University, 1999. At Documenting the American South website of the University of North Carolina at Chapel Hill Libraries.

Aptheker, Herbert. *Abolitionism: A Revolutionary Movement*. Boston: Twayne Publishers, 1989.

Ayers, Edward L., Patricia Nelson Limerick, Stephen Nissenbaum, and Peter S. Onuf. *All Over the Map: Rethinking American Regions*. Baltimore: Johns Hopkins University Press, 1996.

Ballou, Ellen B. *The Building of the House: Houghton Mifflin's Formative Years*. Boston: Houghton Mifflin Co., 1970.

Barbour, John D. *The Conscience of the Autobiographer: Ethical and Religious Dimensions of Autobiography*. London: Macmillan, 1992.

Belz, Herman. "The Constitution and Reconstruction." In *The Facts of Reconstruction: Essays in Honor of John Hope Franklin*, edited by Eric Anderson and Alfred A. Moss Jr., 189–228. Baton Rouge: Louisiana State University Press, 1991.

Benedict, Michael Les. "Reform Republicans and the Retreat from Reconstruction." In *The Facts of Reconstruction: Essays in Honor of John Hope Franklin*, edited by Eric Anderson and Alfred A. Moss Jr., 53–77. Baton Rouge: Louisiana State University Press, 1991.

Bethel, Elizabeth Rauh. *The Roots of African-American Identity: Memory and History in Antebellum Free Communities*. New York: St. Martin's Press, 1997.

Billson, Marcus. "The Memoir: New Perspectives on a Forgotten Genre." *Genre* 10 (Summer 1977): 259–82.

Bishir, Catherine W. "Landmarks of Power: Building a Southern Past in Raleigh and Wilmington, North Carolina, 1885–1915." In *Where These Memories Grow: History, Memory, and Southern Identity*, edited by W. Fitzhugh Brundage, 139–68. Chapel Hill: University of North Carolina Press, 2000.

Bland, Sterling Lecater, Jr. *Voices of the Fugitives: Runaway Slave Stories and Their Fictions of Self-Creation*. Westport, Conn.: Greenwood Press, 2000.

Blatt, Martin H., Thomas J. Brown, and Donald Yacovone, eds. *Hope and Glory: Essays on the Legacy of the Fifty-Fourth Massachusetts Regiment*. Amherst and Boston: University of Massachusetts Press and Massachusetts Historical Society, 2001.

Blight, David W. *Beyond the Battlefield: Race, Memory, and the American Civil War*. Amherst: University of Massachusetts Press, 2002.

———. "Decoration Days: The Origins of Memorial Day in North and South." In *The Memory of the Civil War in American Culture*, edited by Alice Fahs and Joan Waugh, 94–129. Chapel Hill: University of North Carolina Press, 2004.

———. "Fifty Years of Freedom: The Memory of Emancipation at the Civil War Semicentennial, 1911–1915." *Slavery & Abolition* 21 (August 2000): 117–34.

———. *Frederick Douglass' Civil War: Keeping Faith in Jubilee*. Baton Rouge: Louisiana State University Press, 1989.

———. *Race and Reunion: The Civil War in American Memory*. Cambridge, Mass.: Harvard University Press, 2001.

———. "The Shaw Memorial in the Landscape of Civil War Memory." In *Hope and Glory: Essays on the Legacy of the Fifty-Fourth Massachusetts Regiment*, edited by Martin H. Blatt, Thomas J. Brown, and Donald Yacovone, 79–93. Amherst and Boston: University of Massachusetts Press and Massachusetts Historical Society, 2001.

———. "Why the Underground Railroad, and Why Now? A Long View." In *Passages to Freedom: The Underground Railroad in History and Memory*, edited by David W. Blight, 233–47. Washington, D.C.: Smithsonian Books, 2004.

Blockson, Charles L. *African Americans in Pennsylvania; A History and Guide*. Baltimore: Black Classics Press, 1994.

————. *The Underground Railroad*. New York: Prentice Hall, 1987.

Blue, Frederick J. *No Taint of Compromise: Crusaders in Antislavery Politics*. Baton Rouge: Louisiana State University Press, 2004.

Blum, Edward J. *Reforging the White Republic: Race, Religion, and American Nationalism, 1865–1898*. Baton Rouge: Louisiana State University Press, 2005.

Bodnar, John, ed. *Bonds of Affection: Americans Define their Patriotism*. Princeton: Princeton University Press, 1996.

————. "Introduction: The Attractions of Patriotism." In *Bonds of Affection: Americans Define their Patriotism*, edited by John Bodnar, 3–17. Princeton: Princeton University Press, 1996.

————. *Remaking America: Public Memory, Commemoration, and Patriotism in the Twentieth Century*. Princeton: Princeton University Press, 1992.

Bordewich, Fergus M. *Bound for Canaan: The Underground Railroad and the War for the Soul of America*. New York: Harper Collins, 2005.

Borome, Joseph A. "The Vigilant Committee of Philadelphia." *The Pennsylvania Magazine of History and Biography* 92 (July 1968): 320–51.

Braham, Jeanne. *Crucial Conversations: Interpreting Contemporary American Literary Autobiographies by Women*. New York: Teachers College Press, 1995.

Brown, Candy Gunther. *The Word in the World: Evangelical Writing, Publishing, and Reading in America, 1789–1880*. Chapel Hill: University of North Caroline Press, 2004.

Brown, Ira V. *Mary Grew: Abolitionist and Feminist (1813–1896)*. Selinsgrove, Pa.: Susquehanna University Press, 1991.

Brown, Thomas J. "Reconstructing Boston: Civic Monuments of the Civil War." In *Hope and Glory: Essays on the Legacy of the Fifty-Fourth Massachusetts Regiment*, edited by Martin H. Blatt, Thomas J. Brown, and Donald Yacovone, 130–55. Amherst and Boston: University of Massachusetts Press and Massachusetts Historical Society.

Brundage, W. Fitzhugh. "Introduction: No Deed but Memory." In *Where These Memories Grow: History, Memory, and Southern Identity*, edited by W. Fitzhugh Brundage, 1–28. Chapel Hill: University of North Carolina Press, 2000.

————, ed. *Where These Memories Grow: History, Memory, and Southern Identity*. Chapel Hill: University of North Carolina Press, 2000.

Bruss, Elizabeth W. *Autobiographical Acts: The Changing Situation of a Literary Genre*. Baltimore: Johns Hopkins University Press, 1976.

Buell, Lawrence. "Autobiography in the American Renaissance." In *American Autobiography: Retrospect and Prospect*, edited by Paul John Eakin, 47–69. Madison: University of Wisconsin Press, 1991.

Casper, Scott E. *Constructing American Lives: Biography and Culture in Nineteenth-Century America*. Chapel Hill: University of North Carolina Press, 1999.

————. "Defining the National Pantheon: The Making of Houghton Mifflin's Biographical Series, 1880–1900." In *Reading Books: Essays on the Material Text and Literature in America*, edited by Michele Moylan and Lane Stiles, 179–222. Amherst: University of Massachusetts Press, 1996.

Casper, Scott E., Joanne D. Chaison, and Jeffrey D. Groves, eds. *Perspectives on American Book History: Artifacts and Commentary*. Amherst: University of Massachusetts Press, 2002.

Clark, Kathleen. "Celebrating Freedom: Emancipation Day Celebrations and African American Memory in the Early Reconstruction South." In *Where These Memories Grow: History, Memory, and Southern Identity*, edited by W. Fitzhugh Brundage, 107–32. Chapel Hill: University of North Carolina Press, 2000.

Combs, James. "Celebrations: Rituals of Popular Veneration." *Journal of Popular Culture* 22 (Spring 1989): 71–77.

Conforti, Joseph A. *Imagining New England: Explorations of Regional Identity from the Pilgrims to the Mid-Twentieth Century*. Chapel Hill: University of North Carolina Press, 2001.

Connelly, Thomas L., and Barbara L. Bellows. *God and General Longstreet: The Lost Cause and the Southern Mind*. Baton Rouge: Louisiana State University Press, 1982.

Cook, Nancy. "Finding His Mark: Twain's *The Innocents Abroad* as a Subscription Book." In *Reading Books: Essays on the Material Text and Literature in America*, edited by Michele Moylan and Lane Stiles, 151–78. Amherst: University of Massachusetts Press, 1996.

―――. "Reshaping Publishing and Authorship in the Gilded Age." In *Perspectives on American Book History: Artifacts and Commentary*, edited by Scott E. Casper, Joanne D. Chaison, and Jeffrey D. Groves, 223–54. Amherst: University of Massachusetts Press, 2002.

Coultrap-McQuin, Susan. *Doing Literary Business: American Writers in the Nineteenth Century*. Chapel Hill: University of North Carolina Press, 1990.

Cox, James M. *Recovering Literature's Lost Ground: Essays in American Autobiography*. Baton Rouge: Louisiana State University Press, 1989.

Crane, Gregg D. *Race, Citizenship, and Law in American Literature*. Cambridge, U.K.: Cambridge University Press, 2002.

Crane, Susan A. "(Not) Writing History: Rethinking the Intersections of Personal History and Collective Memory with Hans von Aufsess." *History and Memory* 8 (Spring/Summer 1996): 5–29.

Cravens, Hamilton. "Scientific Racism in Modern American, 1870s–1990s." *Prospects* 21 (1996): 471–90.

Cullen, Jim. *The Civil War in Popular Culture: A Reusable Past*. Washington, D.C.: Smithsonian Institution Press, 1995.

Culley, Margo. "What a Piece of Work Is 'Woman'! An Introduction." In *American Women's Autobiography: Fea(s)ts of Memory*, edited by Margo Culley, 3–31. Madison: University of Wisconsin Press, 1992.

―――, ed., *American Women's Autobiography: Fea(s)ts of Memory*. Madison: University of Wisconsin Press, 1992.

Current, Richard Nelson. *Arguing with Historians: Essays on the Historical and the Unhistorical*. Middletown, Conn.: Wesleyan University Press, 1987.

Dailey, Jane. *Before Jim Crow: The Politics of Race in Postemancipation Virginia*. Chapel Hill: University of North Carolina Press, 2000.

Danahay, Martin. "Class, Gender, and the Victorian Masculine Subject." *Auto/Bio Studies* 5 (Fall 1990): 99–113.

Davidson, Cathy N., ed. *Reading in American Literature and Social History.* Baltimore: Johns Hopkins University Press, 1989.

Delombard, Jeannine Marie. "Turning Back the Clock: Black Antislavery Literary Studies." *New England Quarterly* 75 (December 2002): 647–55.

Dickson, D. Bruce, Jr. *Black American Writing from the Nadir: The Evolution of a Literary Tradition, 1877–1915.* Baton Rouge: Louisiana State University Press, 1989.

Diffley, Kathleen. "Home from the Theatre of War: The *Southern Magazine* and Recollections of the Civil War." In *Periodical Literature in Nineteenth-Century America*, edited by Kenneth M. Price and Susan Belasco Smith, 185–201. Charlottesville: University Press of Virginia, 1995.

———. "Home on the Range: Turner, Slavery, and the Landscape Illustrations in *Harper's New Monthly Magazine*, 1861–1876." *Prospects* 14 (1989): 175–202.

———. *Where My Heart Is Turning Ever: Civil War Stories and Constitutional Reform, 1861–1876.* Athens: University of Georgia Press, 1992.

Donald, David Herbert, Jean H. Baker, and Michael F. Holt. *The Civil War and Reconstruction.* New York: W. W. Norton, 2001.

Dormon, James H. "Shaping the Popular Image of Post-Reconstruction American Blacks: The 'Coon Song' Phenomenon of the Gilded Age." *American Quarterly* 40 (December 1988): 450–71.

Eakin, Paul John. *Touching the World: Reference in Autobiography.* Princeton: Princeton University Press, 1992.

———, ed. *American Autobiography: Retrospect and Prospect.* Madison: University of Wisconsin Press, 1991.

Edelstein, Tilden G. *Strange Enthusiasm: A Life of Thomas Wentworth Higginson.* New Haven: Yale University Press, 1968.

Edwards, Rebecca. *Angels in the Machinery: Gender and American Party Politics from the Civil War to the Progressive Era.* New York: Oxford University Press, 1997.

Egan, Susanna. "'Self'-Conscious History: American Autobiography after the Civil War." In *American Autobiography: Retrospect and Prospect*, edited by Paul John Eakin, 70–94. Madison: University of Wisconsin Press, 1991.

Ernest, John. *Resistance and Reference in Nineteenth-Century African-American Literature: Brown, Wilson, Jacobs, Delany, Douglass, and Hunter.* Jackson: University of Mississippi Press, 1995.

Etzioni, Amitai. "Holidays and Rituals: Neglected Seedbeds of Virtue." In *We Are What We Celebrate: Understanding Holidays and Rituals*, edited by Amitai Etzioni and Jared Bloom, 1–40. New York: New York University Press, 2004.

Etzioni, Amitai, and Jared Bloom, eds. *We Are What We Celebrate: Understanding Holidays and Rituals.* New York: New York University Press, 2004.

Exman, Eugene. *The House of Harper: One Hundred and Fifty Years of Publishing.* New York: Harper & Row, 1967.

Fabian, Ann. *The Unvarnished Truth: Personal Narratives in Nineteenth-Century America.* Berkeley: University of California Press, 2000.

Fahs, Alice. "The Feminized Civil War: Gender, Northern Popular Literature, and the Memory of the War, 1861–1900." *Journal of American History* 85 (March 1999): 1461–94.

——— . *The Imagined Civil War: Popular Literature of the North and South, 1861–1865.* Chapel Hill: University of North Carolina Press, 2001.

——— . "Remembering the Civil War in Children's Literature of the 1880s and 1890s." In *The Memory of the Civil War in American Culture*, edited by Alice Fahs and Joan Waugh, 79–93. Chapel Hill: University of North Carolina Press, 2004.

Fahs, Alice, and Joan Waugh. "Introduction." In *The Memory of the Civil War in American Culture*, edited by Alice Fahs and Joan Waugh, 1–4. Chapel Hill: University of North Carolina Press, 2004.

——— , eds. *The Memory of the Civil War in American Culture.* Chapel Hill: University of North Carolina Press, 2004.

Faulkner, Carol. *Women's Radical Reconstruction: The Freedmen's Aid Movement.* Philadelphia: University of Pennsylvania Press, 2004.

Finkelman, Paul. "Rehearsal for Reconstruction: Antebellum Origins of the Fourteenth Amendment." In *The Facts of Reconstruction: Essays in Honor of John Hope Franklin*, edited by Eric Anderson and Alfred A. Moss Jr., 1–27. Baton Rouge: Louisiana State University Press, 1991.

Fitzpatrick, Ellen. *History's Memory: Writing America's Past, 1880–1980.* Cambridge, Mass.: Harvard University Press, 2002.

Foner, Eric. *Reconstruction: America's Unfinished Revolution, 1863–1877.* New York: Harper & Row, 1988.

——— . *A Short History of Reconstruction, 1863–1877.* New York: Harper & Row, 1990.

Foote, Lorien. *Seeking the One Great Remedy: Francis George Shaw and Nineteenth-Century Reform.* Athens: Ohio University Press, 2003.

Foote, Stephanie. *Regional Fictions: Culture and Identity in Nineteenth-Century American Literature.* Madison: University of Wisconsin Press, 2001.

Foster, Gaines M. *Ghosts of the Confederacy: Defeat, the Lost Cause, and the Emergence of the New South, 1865–1913.* New York: Oxford University Press, 1987.

——— . *Moral Reconstruction: Christian Lobbyists and the Federal Legislation of Morality, 1865–1920.* Chapel Hill: University of North Carolina Press, 2002.

Fox-Genovese, Elizabeth. "Between Individualism and Fragmentation: American Culture and the New Literary Studies of Race and Gender." *American Quarterly* 42 (March 1990): 7–34.

Frank, Gelya. "Myths of Creation: Construction of Self in an Autobiographical Account of Birth and Infancy." In *Imagined Childhoods: Self and Society in Autobiographical Accounts*, edited by Marianne Gillestad, 63–90. Oslo: Scandinavian University Press, 1996.

Franklin, V. P. *Living Our Stories, Telling Our Truths: Autobiography and the Making of the African-American Intellectual Tradition.* New York: Scribner, 1995.

Frederickson, George M. *The Arrogance of Race: Historical Perspectives on Slavery, Racism, and Social Inequality.* Middletown, Conn.: Wesleyan University Press, 1988.

————. *The Black Image in the White Mind: The Debate on Afro-American Character and Destiny, 1817–1914.* New York: Harper & Row, 1971.

————. *The Inner Civil War: Northern Intellectuals and the Crisis of Union.* New York: Harper & Row, 1965.

Frerichs, Sarah C. "Elizabeth Missing Sewell: Concealment and Revelation in a Victorian Everywoman." In *Approaches to Victorian Autobiography*, edited by George P. Landow, 175–99. Athens: Ohio University Press, 1979.

Gallagher, Gary W. "Shaping Public Memory of the Civil War: Robert E. Lee, Jubal A. Early, and Douglas Southall Freeman." In *The Memory of the Civil War in American Culture*, edited by Alice Fahs and Joan Waugh, 39–63. Chapel Hill: University of North Carolina Press, 2004.

Gallagher, Gary W., and Alan T. Nolan, eds. *The Myth of the Lost Cause and Civil War History.* Bloomington: Indiana University Press, 2000.

Gallman, J. Matthew. "Is the War Ended? Anna Dickinson and the Election of 1872." In *The Memory of the Civil War in American Culture*, edited by Alice Fahs and Joan Waugh, 157–79. Chapel Hill: University of North Carolina Press, 2004.

Gara, Larry. "Friends and the Underground Railroad." *Quaker History* 51 (Spring 1962): 3–19.

————. "A Glorious Time: The 1874 Abolitionist Reunion in Chicago." *Journal of Illinois State Historical Society* 65 (1972): 280–92.

————. *The Liberty Line: The Legend of the Underground Railroad.* Lexington: University of Kentucky Press, 1967.

Gardner, Sarah E. *Blood and Irony: Southern White Women's Narratives of the Civil War, 1861–1937.* Chapel Hill: University of North Carolina Press, 2004.

Gaston, Paul. *The New South Creed: A Study in Southern Mythmaking.* Montgomery, Ala.: New South Books, 2002.

Gelfant, Blanche. "Speaking Her Own Piece: Emma Goldman and the Discursive Skeins of Autobiography." In *American Autobiography: Retrospect and Prospect*, edited by Paul John Eakin, 235–66. Madison: University of Wisconsin Press, 1991.

Gienapp, William E. *The Origins of the Republican Party, 1852–1856.* New York: Oxford University Press, 1987.

Gillestad, Marianne. "Modernity, Self, and Childhood in the Analyses of Life Stories." In *Imagined Childhoods: Self and Society in Autobiographical Accounts*, edited by Marianne Gillestad, 1–39. Oslo: Scandinavian University Press, 1996.

Gillis, John R. "Gathering Together: Remembering Memory Through Ritual." In *We Are What We Celebrate: Understanding Holidays and Rituals*, edited by Amitai Etzioni and Jared Bloom, 89–103. New York: New York University Press, 2004.

Ginzberg, Lori D. *Women and the Work of Benevolence: Morality, Politics, and Class in the Nineteenth-Century United States.* New Haven: Yale University Press, 1990.

Glazener, Nancy. *Reading for Realism: The History of a U.S. Literary Institution, 1850–1910.* Durham: Duke University Press, 1997.

Glesner, Anthony Patrick. "Laura Haviland: Neglected Heroine of the Underground Railroad." *Michigan Historical Review* 21 (Spring 1995): 19–48.

Goodman, Paul. *Of One Blood: Abolitionism and the Origins of Racial Equality.* Berkeley: University of California Press, 1998.

Gordon, Ann D. "The Political Is the Personal: Two Autobiographies of Woman Suffragists." In *American Women's Autobiography: Fea(s)ts of Memory*, edited by Margo Culley, 111–27. Madison: University of Wisconsin Press, 1992.

Gordon, Lesley J. "'Let the People See the Old Life as It Was': LaSalle Corbell Pickett and the Myth of the Lost Cause." In *The Myth of the Lost Cause and Civil War History*, edited by Gary W. Gallagher and Alan T. Nolan, 170–89. Bloomington: Indiana University Press, 2000.

Grammer, Elizabeth Elkin. *Some World Visions: Autobiographies by Female Itinerant Evangelists in Nineteenth-Century America.* New York: Oxford University Press, 2003.

Gravely, William B. "The Dialectic of Double-Consciousness in Black American Freedom Celebrations, 1808–1863." *Journal of Negro History* 67 (Winter 1982): 302–17.

Griffler, Keith. *Front Line of Freedom: African Americans and the Forging of the Underground Railroad in the Ohio Valley.* Lexington: University Press of Kentucky, 2004.

Groves, Jeffrey D. "Judging Literary Books by Their Covers: House Styles, Ticknor and Fields, and Literary Promotion." In *Reading Books: Essays on the Material Text and Literature in America*, edited by Michele Moylan and Lane Stiles, 75–100. Amherst: University of Massachusetts Press, 1996.

Grow, Matthew J. "The Shadow of the Civil War: A Historiography of Civil War Memory." *American Nineteenth Century History* 4 (Summer 2003): 77–103.

Gullestad, Marianne, ed. *Imagined Childhoods: Self and Society in Autobiographical Accounts.* Oslo: Scandinavian University Press, 1996.

Hackenberg, Michael, ed. *Getting the Books Out: Papers of the Chicago Conference on the Book in Nineteenth-Century America.* Washington, D.C.: Library of Congress, 1987.

———. "The Subscription Publishing Network in Nineteenth-Century America." In *Getting the Books Out: Papers of the Chicago Conference on the Book in Nineteenth-Century America*, edited by Michael Hackenberg, 45–75. Washington, D.C.: Library of Congress, 1987.

Hall, Jacqueline Dowd. "'You Must Remember This': Autobiography as Social Critique." *Journal of American History* 85 (September 1998): 439–65.

Hall, Wade. *The Smiling Phoenix: Southern Humor from 1865 to 1914.* Gainesville: University of Florida Press, 1965.

Harris, Susan K. "Responding to the Text(s): Women Readers and the Quest for Higher Education." In *Readers in History: Nineteenth-Century American Literature and the Contexts of Response*, edited by James L. Machor, 259–82. Baltimore: Johns Hopkins University Press, 1993.

Hart, James D. *The Popular Book: A History of America's Literary Taste.* New York: Oxford University Press, 1950.

Hedin, Raymond. "Probable Readers, Possible Stories: The Limits of Nineteenth-Century Black Narrative." In *Readers in History: Nineteenth-Century American*

Literature and the Contexts of Response, edited by James L. Machor, 180–205. Baltimore: Johns Hopkins University Press, 1993.

Hedrick, Joan D. *Harriet Beecher Stowe: A Life*. New York: Oxford University Press, 1994.

Helsinger, Elizabeth K. "Ulysses to Penelope: Victorian Experiments in Autobiography." In *Approaches to Victorian Autobiography*, edited by George P. Landow, 3–25. Athens: Ohio University Press, 1979.

Helsinger, Howard. "Credence and Credibility: The Concern for Honesty in Victorian Autobiography." In *Approaches to Victorian Autobiography*, edited by George P. Landow, 39–63. Athens: Ohio University Press, 1979.

Hess, Earl J. *Liberty, Virtue, and Progress: Northerners and the War for the Union*. New York: New York University Press, 1988.

Hixson, William B., Jr. *Moorfield Storey and the Abolitionist Tradition*. New York: Oxford University Press, 1972.

Hobson, Fred. *Tell About the South: The Southern Rage to Explain*. Baton Rouge: Louisiana State University Press, 1983.

Hochman, Barbara. *Getting at the Author: Reimagining Books and Reading in the Age of American Realism*. Amherst: University of Massachusetts Press, 2001.

Hoffert, Sylvia D. *Jane Grey Swisshelm: An Unconventional Life, 1815–1884*. Chapel Hill: University of North Carolina Press, 2004.

Holly, Carol. "Nineteenth-Century Autobiographies of Affiliation: The Case of Catharine Sedgwick and Lucy Larcom." In *American Autobiography: Retrospect and Prospect*, edited by Paul John Eakin, 216–34. Madison: University of Wisconsin Press, 1991.

Horton, James Oliver. "Defending the Manhood of the Race: The Crisis of Citizenship in Black Boston at Midcentury," In *Hope & Glory: Essays on the Legacy of the Fifty-Fourth Massachusetts Regiment*, edited by Martin H. Blatt, Thomas J. Brown, and Donald Yacovone, 7–20. Amherst: University of Massachusetts Press and Massachusetts Historical Society.

Hunter, Carol M. *To Set the Captives Free: Reverend Jermain Wesley Loguen and the Struggle for Freedom in Central New York 1835–1872*. New York: Garland, 1993.

Hutler-Hover, Janet. "The North-South Reconciliation Theme and the 'Shadow of the Negro' in *Century Illustrated Magazine*." In *Periodical Literature in Nineteenth-Century America*, edited by Kenneth M. Price and Susan Belasco Smith, 239–56. Charlottesville: University Press of Virginia, 1995.

Isenberg, Nancy. "Second Thoughts on Gender and Women's History." *American Studies* 36 (Spring 1995): 93–103.

Jacobson, Marcia. "Howell's *Literary Friends and Acquaintances*: An Autobiography Through Others." *American Literary Realism* 27 (Fall 1994): 59–73.

Jeffrey, Julie Roy. "'No Occurrence in Human History Is More Deserving of Commemoration Than This': Abolitionist Celebrations of Freedom." In *Prophets of Protest: Reconsidering the History of American Abolitionism*, edited by John Stauffer and Timothy Patrick McCarthy, 200–219. New York: New Press, 2006.

Jelinek, Estelle C. *The Tradition of Women's Autobiography: From Antiquity to the Present*. Boston: Twayne Publishers, 1986.

Joannou, Maroula. "Gender, Militancy, and Wartime." In *The Uses of Autobiography*, edited by Julia Swindells, 31–44. London: Taylor & Francis, 1995.

John, Arthur. *The Best Years of the Century: Richard Watson Gilder, Scribner's Monthly, and Century Magazine, 1870–1909*. Urbana: University of Illinois Press, 1981.

Jones, Gavin. *Strange Talk: The Politics of Dialect Literature in Gilded Age America*. Berkeley: University of California Press, 1999.

Kachun, Mitchell A. *Festivals of Freedom: Memory and Meaning in African American Emancipation Celebrations, 1808–1915*. Amherst: University of Massachusetts Press, 2003.

Kammen, Michael. *Mystic Chords of Memory: The Transformation of Tradition in American Culture*. New York: Alfred A. Knopf, 1991.

Kanner, Barbara Penny, et al. eds. *Women in Context: Two Hundred Years of British Women*. New York: G. K. Hall & Co., 1997.

Kaplan, Justin. "A Culture of Biography." *Yale Review* 82 (October 1994): 1–12.

Kearns, Michael. "The Material Melville: Shaping Readers' Horizons." In *Reading Books: Essays on the Material Text and Literature in America*, edited by Michele Moylan and Lane Stiles, 52–74. Amherst: University of Massachusetts Press, 1996.

Keller, Frances Richardson. *Fictions of U.S. History: A Theory and Four Illustrations*. Bloomington: Indiana University Press, 2002.

Kelly, Patrick J. "The Election of 1896 and the Restructuring of Civil War Memory." *Civil War History* 49 (September 2003): 254–80.

———. "The Election of 1896 and the Restructuring of Civil War Memory." In *The Memory of the Civil War in American Culture*, edited by Alice Fahs and Joan Waugh, 180–212. Chapel Hill: University of North Carolina Press, 2004.

Landow, George P., ed. *Approaches to Victorian Autobiography*. Athens: Ohio University Press, 1979.

Lehmann-Haupt, Hellmut. *The Book in America*. New York: R. R. Bowker, 1939.

Lehuu, Isabelle. *Carnival on the Page: Popular Print Media in Antebellum America*. Chapel Hill: University of North Carolina Press, 2000.

Leonard, Elizabeth D. *Yankee Women: Gender Battles in the Civil War*. New York: W. W. Norton, 1994.

Lively, Robert A. *Fiction Fights the Civil War: An Unfinished Chapter in the Literary History of the American People*. Chapel Hill: University of North Carolina Press, 1957.

Machor, James L. "Historical Hermeneutics and Antebellum Fiction: Gender, Response Theory, and Interpretive Contexts." In *Readers in History: Nineteenth-Century American Literature and the Contexts of Response*, edited by James L. Machor, 54–84. Baltimore: Johns Hopkins University Press, 1993.

———, ed. *Readers in History: Nineteenth-Century American Literature and the Contexts of Response*. Baltimore: Johns Hopkins University Press, 1993.

Madison, Charles A. *Book Publishing in America*. New York: McGraw-Hill Book Co., 1966.

Maffly-Kipp, Laurie F. "Redeeming Southern Memory: The Negro Race History, 1874–1915." In *Where These Memories Grow: History, Memory, and Southern Identity*, edited by W. Fitzhugh Brundage, 169–89. Chapel Hill: University of North Carolina Press, 2000.

Mailloux, Steven. "Misreading as a Historical Act: Cultural Rhetoric, Bible Politics, and Fuller's 1845 Review of Douglass's *Narrative*." In *Readers in History: Nineteenth-Century American Literature and the Contexts of Response*, edited by James L. Machor, 3–31. Baltimore: Johns Hopkins University Press, 1993.

Marcus, Laura. "The Face of Autobiography." In *The Uses of Autobiography*, edited by Julia Swindells, 13–30. London: Taylor & Francis, 1995.

Mayer, Henry. *All on Fire: William Lloyd Garrison and the Abolition of Slavery*. New York: St. Martin's Press, 1998.

McBride, Dwight A. *Impossible Witnesses: Truth, Abolitionism, and Slave Testimony*. New York: New York University Press, 2001.

McConnell, Stuart M. "Epilogue: The Geography of Memory." In *The Memory of the Civil War in American Culture*, edited by Alice Fahs and Joan Waugh, 258–66. Chapel Hill: University of North Carolina Press, 2004.

———. *Glorious Contentment: The Grand Army of the Republic, 1865–1900*. Chapel Hill: University of North Carolina Press, 1992.

———. "Reading the Flag: A Reconsideration of the Patriotic Cultures of the 1890s." In *Bonds of Affection: Americans Define their Patriotism*, edited by John Bodnar, 102–19. Princeton: Princeton University Press, 1996.

McGlone, Robert E. "Deciphering Memory: John Adams and the Authorship of the Declaration of Independence." *Journal of American History* 85 (September 1998): 411–38.

McInerney, Daniel J. *The Fortunate Heirs of Freedom: Abolitionism and Republican Thought*. Lincoln: University of Nebraska Press, 1994.

McPherson, James M. *The Abolitionist Legacy: From Reconstruction to the NAACP*. Princeton: Princeton University Press, 1975.

———. *Ordeal by Fire: The Civil War and Reconstruction*. 2nd ed. New York: McGraw-Hill, 1993.

———. *The Struggle for Equality: Abolitionists and the Negro in the Civil War and Reconstruction*. Princeton: Princeton University Press, 1964.

Melman, Billie. "Gender, History and Memory: The Invention of Women's Past in the Nineteenth and Early Twentieth Centuries." *History and Memory* 5 (Spring/Summer 1993): 5–41.

Menendez, Albert J. *Civil War Novels: An Annotated Bibliography*. New York: Garland, 1986.

Merish, Lori. *Sentimental Materialism: Gender, Commodity Culture, and Nineteenth-Century American Literature*. Durham: Duke University Press, 2000.

Miers, Suzanne. *Britain and the Ending of the Slave Trade*. New York: Holmes and Meier, 1975.

Minkema, Kenneth P., and Harry S. Stout. "The Edwardsean Tradition and the Antislavery Debate, 1740–1865." *Journal of American History* 92 (June 2005): 47–74.

Mixon, Wayne. *Southern Writers and the New South Movement, 1865–1913.* Chapel Hill: University of North Carolina Press, 1980.

Moneyhon, Carl H. "The Failure of Southern Republicanism, 1867–1876." In *The Facts of Reconstruction: Essays in Honor of John Hope Franklin,* edited by Eric Anderson and Alfred A. Moss Jr., 99–119. Baton Rouge: Louisiana State University Press, 1991.

Moody, Jocelyn K. "Twice Other, Once Shy: Nineteenth-Century Black Women Autobiographers and the American Literary Tradition of Self-Effacement." *Auto/Bio Studies* 7 (Spring 1992): 46–61.

Moreau, Joseph. *Schoolbook Nation: Conflicts over American History Textbooks from the Civil War to the Present.* Ann Arbor: University of Michigan Press, 2003.

Morris, Robert C. "Educational Reconstruction." In *The Facts of Reconstruction: Essays in Honor of John Hope Franklin,* edited by Eric Anderson and Alfred A. Moss Jr., 141–66. Baton Rouge: Louisiana State University Press, 1991.

Mott, Frank Luther. *Golden Multitudes: The Story of Best Sellers in the United States.* New York: Macmillan, 1947.

———. *A History of American Magazines.* 5 vols. Cambridge, Mass.: Harvard University Press, 1957.

Moylan, Michele, and Lane Stiles, eds. *Reading Books: Essays on the Material Text and Literature in America.* Amherst: University of Massachusetts Press, 1996.

Nasstrom, Kathryn. "Down to Now: Memory, Narrative, and Women's Leadership in the Civil Rights Movement in Atlanta, Georgia." *Gender and History* 11 (April 1999): 113–44.

Neff, John R. *Honoring the Civil War Dead: Commemoration and the Problem of Reconciliation.* Lawrence: University Press of Kansas, 2005.

Newman, Richard S. *The Transformation of American Abolitionism: Fighting Slavery in the Early Republic.* Chapel Hill: University of North Carolina Press, 2002.

Nissenbaum, Stephen. "New England as Region and Nation." In *All Over the Map: Rethinking American Regions,* edited by Edward L. Ayers, Patricia Nelson Limerick, Stephen Nissenbaum, and Peter S. Onuf, 38–61. Baltimore: Johns Hopkins University Press, 1996.

Nolan, Alan T. "The Anatomy of the Myth." In *The Myth of the Lost Cause and Civil War History,* edited by Gary W. Gallagher and Alan T. Nolan, 11–24. Bloomington: Indiana University Press, 2000.

Nord, David Paul. "Religious Reading and Readers in Antebellum America." *Journal of the Early Republic* 15 (Summer 1995): 241–72.

O'Leary, Cecilia Elizabeth. "'Blood Brotherhood': The Racialization of Patriotism, 1865–1918." In *Bonds of Affection: Americans Define their Patriotism,* edited by John Bodnar, 53–81. Princeton: Princeton University Press, 1996.

Pascal, Roy. *Design and Truth in Autobiography.* New York: Garland, 1985 ed.

Perman, Michael. "Counter Reconstruction: The Role of Violence in Southern Redemption." In *The Facts of Reconstruction: Essays in Honor of John Hope Franklin,* edited by Eric Anderson and Alfred A. Moss Jr., 121–40. Baton Rouge: Louisiana State University Press, 1991.

Peterson, Linda H. "Audience and the Autobiographer's Art: An Approach to the *Autobiography* of Mrs. M. O. W. Oliphant." In *Approaches to Victorian Autobiography*, edited by George P. Landow, 158–74. Athens: Ohio University Press, 1979.

———. *Traditions of Victorian Women's Autobiography: The Poetic and Politics of Life Writing*. Charlottesville: University Press of Virginia, 1999.

Peterson, Merrill D. *John Brown: The Legend Revisited*. Charlottesville: University Press of Virginia, 2002.

———. *Lincoln in American Memory*. New York: Oxford University Press, 1994.

Pierson, Michael D. "'Slavery Cannot Be Covered Up with Broadcloth or a Bandanna': The Evolution of White Abolitionist Attacks on the 'Patriarchal Institution.'" *Journal of the Early Republic* 25 (Fall 2005): 383–415.

Pressly, Thomas J. *Americans Interpret Their Civil War*. New York: Collier Books, 1962 ed.

Price, Kenneth M. "Charles Chesnutt, the *Atlantic Monthly*, and the Intersection of African-American Fiction and Elite Culture." In *Periodical Literature in Nineteenth-Century America*, edited by Kenneth M. Price and Susan Belasco Smith, 257–74. Charlottesville: University Press of Virginia, 1995.

Price, Kenneth M., and Susan Belasco Smith. "Introduction: Periodical Literature in Social and Historical Context." In *Periodical Literature in Nineteenth-Century America*, edited by Kenneth M. Price and Susan Belasco Smith, 3–16. Charlottesville: University Press of Virginia, 1995.

———, eds. *Periodical Literature in Nineteenth-Century America*. Charlottesville: University Press of Virginia, 1995.

Procter, David E. "Victorian Days: Performing Community through Local Festival." In *We Are What We Celebrate: Understanding Holidays and Rituals*, edited by Amitai Etzioni and Jared Bloom, 131–48. New York: New York University Press, 2004.

Quarles, Benjamin. *Frederick Douglass*. Washington, D.C.: Associated Publishers, Inc., 1948.

Rabinowitz, Howard N. "Segregation and Reconstruction." In *The Facts of Reconstruction: Essays in Honor of John Hope Franklin*, edited by Eric Anderson and Alfred A. Moss Jr., 79–97. Baton Rouge: Louisiana State University Press, 1991.

Raffo, Steven M. *A Biography of Oliver Johnson, Abolitionist and Reformer, 1809–1889*. Lewiston, N.Y.: Edwin Mellen Press, 2002.

Railton, Stephen. "The Address of *The Scarlet Letter*." In *Readers in History: Nineteenth-Century American Literature and the Contexts of Response*, edited by James L. Machor, 138–63. Baltimore: Johns Hopkins University Press, 1993.

Rather, Lorman A., and Dwight L. Teeter Jr. *Fanatics and Fire-eaters: Newspapers and the Coming of the Civil War*. Urbana: University of Illinois Press, 2003.

Reardon, Carol. "Why We Should Still Care: The Civil War and Memory." Dwight D. Eisenhower Lectures in War and Peace, biennial series no. 9. Kansas State University, 1991.

Richardson, Heather Cox. *The Death of Reconstruction: Race, Labor, and Politics in the Post–Civil War North, 1865–1901*. Cambridge, Mass.: Harvard University Press, 2001.

Richardson, Joe M. *Christian Reconstruction: The A.M.A. and Southern Blacks, 1861–1890*. Athens: University of Georgia Press, 1986.

Robertson, Stacey M. *Parker Pillsbury: Radical Abolitionist, Male Feminist*. Ithaca: Cornell University Press, 2000.

Rohrbach, Augusta. *Truth Stranger than Fiction: Race, Realism, and the U.S. Literary Marketplace*. New York: Palgrave Press, 2002.

Rose, Anne C. *Victorian America and the Civil War*. New York: Cambridge University Press, 1992.

Rotundo, R. Anthony. "Learning About Manhood: Gender Ideas and the Middle-Class Family in Nineteenth Century America." In *Manliness and Morality: Middle-Class Masculinity in Britain and America, 1800–1940*, edited by J. A. Mangan and James Walvin, 35–51. New York: St. Martin's Press, 1987.

Rubin, Louis D., Jr. "Southern Local Color and the Black Man." *Southern Review*, n.s., 6 (Fall 1970): 1011–30.

Runyon, Randolph Paul. *Delia Webster and the Underground Railroad*. Lexington: University Press of Kentucky, 1996.

Russo, David J. *Keepers of Our Past: Local Historical Writing in the United States, 1820s–1930s*. Westport, Conn.: Greenwood Press, 1988.

Ryan, Barbara, and Amy M. Thomas, eds. *Reading Acts: U.S. Readers' Interactions with Literature, 1800–1950*. Knoxville: University of Tennessee Press, 1992.

Ryan, Susan. "Acquiring Minds: Commodified Knowledge and the Positioning of the Reader in McClure's Magazine, 1893–1903." *Prospects* 22 (1997): 211–38.

Sartwell, Crispin. *Act Like You Know: African-American Autobiography and White Identity*. Chicago: University of Chicago Press, 1998.

Savage, Kirk. *Standing Soldiers, Kneeling Slaves: Race, War, and Monument in Nineteenth-Century America*. Princeton: Princeton University Press, 1997.

Scholnick, Robert J. "*Scribner's Monthly* and the 'Pictorial Representation of Life and Truth' in Post–Civil War America." *American Periodicals* 2 (Fall 1991): 46–69.

Sedgwick, Ellery. *The Atlantic Monthly, 1857–1909: Yankee Humanism at High Tide and Ebb*. Amherst: University of Massachusetts Press, 1994.

Sengupt, Gunja. "Elites, Subalterns, and American Identities: A Case Study of African-American Benevolence." *American Historical Review* 109 (October 2004): 1104–39.

Shackel, Paul A. *Memory in Black and White: Race, Commemoration, and the Post-Bellum Landscape*. Walnut Creek, Calif.: AltaMira Press, 2003.

Shaw, Christopher, and Malcolm Chase. "The Dimensions of Nostalgia." In *The Imagined Past: History and Nostalgia*, edited by Christopher Shaw and Malcolm Chase, 1–17. Manchester: Manchester University Press, 1989.

———, eds. *The Imagined Past: History and Nostalgia*. Manchester: Manchester University Press, 1989.

Sheehan, Donald. *This Was Publishing: A Chronology of the Book Trade in the Gilded Age*. Bloomington: Indiana University Press, 1952.

Sicherman, Barbara. "Reading and Middle-Class Identity in Victorian America: Cultural Consumption, Conspicuous and Otherwise." In *Reading Acts: U.S. Readers' Interactions with Literature, 1800–1950*, edited by Barbara Ryan and Amy M. Thomas, 137–60. Knoxville: University of Tennessee Press, 2002.

Silber, Nina. *The Romance of Reunion: Northerners and the South, 1865–1900*. Chapel Hill: University of North Carolina Press, 1993.

Silver, Andrew. "Making Minstrelsy of Murder: George Washington Harris, the Ku Klu Klan, and the Reconstruction Aesthetic of Black Fright." *Prospects* 25 (2000): 339–62.

Simpson, Brooks D. "Continuous Hammering the Mere Attrition: Lost Cause Critics and the Military Reputation of Ulysses S. Grant." In *The Myth of the Lost Cause and Civil War History*, edited by Gary W. Gallagher and Alan T. Nolan, 147–69. Bloomington: Indiana University Press, 2000.

Sizer, Lyde Cullen. *The Political Work of Northern Women Writers and the Civil War, 1850–1872*. Chapel Hill: University of North Carolina Press, 2000.

Smethurst, James. "'Those Noble Sons of Ham': Poetry, Soldiers, and Citizens at the End of Reconstruction." In *Hope and Glory: Essays on the Legacy of the Fifty-Fourth Massachusetts Regiment*, edited by Martin H. Blatt, Thomas J. Brown, and Donald Yacovone, 168–87. Amherst and Boston: University of Massachusetts Press and Massachusetts Historical Society, 2001.

Smith, Mark M. *Listening to Nineteenth-Century America*. Chapel Hill: University of North Carolina Press, 2001.

Smith, Sidonie. "The Impact of Critical Theory on the Study of Autobiography: Marginality, Gender, and Autobiographical Practice." *Auto/Bio Studies* 3 (Fall 1987): 1–12.

———. "Resisting the Gaze of Embodiment: Women's Autobiography in the Nineteenth Century." In *American Women's Autobiography: Fea(s)ts of Memory*, edited by Margo Culley, 75–110. Madison: University of Wisconsin Press, 1992.

Sterling, Dorothy. *Ahead of Her Time: Abby Kelley and the Politics of Anti-Slavery*. New York: W. W. Norton, 1991.

Stern, Madeleine B. "Dissemination of Popular Books in the Midwest and Far West during the Nineteenth Century." In *Getting the Books Out: Papers of the Chicago Conference on the Book in Nineteenth-Century America*, edited by Michael Hackenberg, 76–97. Washington, D.C.: Library of Congress, 1987.

Stevenson, Louise L. *The Victorian Homefront: American Thought and Culture, 1860–1880*. Ithaca: Cornell University Press, 2001.

Stewart, James Brewer. *Wendell Phillips: Liberty's Hero*. Baton Rouge: Louisiana State University Press, 1986.

Stull, Heidi I. *The Evolution of Autobiography, 1770–1850: A Comparative Study and Analysis*. New York: Peter Lang, 1985.

Sutton, Walter. *The Western Book Trade: Cincinnati as a Nineteenth-Century Publishing and Book-Trade Center*. Columbus: Ohio State University Press, 1961.

Sweet, Leonard I., ed. *Communication and Change in American Religious History*. Grand Rapids: William B. Eerdmans Publishing Co., 1993.

Swindells, Julia. "The Tradition of Autobiography, or Egoists and Interlopers." In *The Uses of Autobiography*, edited by Julia Swindells, 1–12. London: Taylor & Francis, 1995.

———, ed. *The Uses of Autobiography*. London: Taylor & Francis, 1995.

Symes, Ruth A. "The Educative 'I' in Nineteenth-Century Women's Autobiographies." In *The Uses of Autobiography*, edited by Julia Swindells, 128–37. London: Taylor & Francis, 1995.

Tang, Edward. "Rebirth of a Nation: Frederick Douglass as Postwar Founder in *Life and Times*." *Journal of American Studies* 39 (2005): 19–39.

Tebbel, John. *A History of Book Publishing in the United States*. Vol. 2. New York: R. R. Bowker, 1975.

Temperley, Howard. *British Antislavery, 1833–1870*. Columbia: University of South Carolina Press, 1972.

Thomas, Amy M. "'There Is Nothing So Effective as a Personal Canvass': Revaluing Nineteenth-Century American Subscription Books." *Book History* 1 (1998): 140–55.

Turley, David. *The Culture of English Antislavery, 1780–1860*. New York: Routledge, 1991.

Turner, Lorenzo Dow. *Anti-Slavery Sentiment in American Literature Prior to 1865*. Washington, D.C.: Association for the Study of Negro Life and History, 1929.

Van Deburg, William C. "The Battleground of Historical Memory: Creating Alternative Culture Heroes in Postbellum America." *Journal of Popular Culture* 20 (Summer 1986): 49–62.

Verduin, Kathleen. "Dante in America: The First Hundred Years." In *Reading Books: Essays on the Material Text and Literature in America*, edited by Michele Moylan and Lane Stiles, 16–51. Amherst: University of Massachusetts Press, 1996.

Walker, Peter F. *Moral Choices: Memory, Desire, and Imagination in Nineteenth-Century American Abolition*. Baton Rouge: Louisiana State University Press, 1979.

Walther, Luann. "The Invention of Childhood in Victorian America." In *Approaches to Victorian Autobiography*, edited by George P. Landow, 64–83. Athens: Ohio University Press, 1979.

Walvin, James. *Questioning Slavery*. New York: Routledge, 1996.

Watson, Martha. *Lives of Their Own: Rhetorical Dimensions in Autobiographies of Women Activists*. Columbia: University of South Carolina Press, 1999.

Waugh, Joan. "'It Was a Sacrifice We Owed': The Shaw Family and the Fifty-Fourth Massachusetts Regiment." In *Hope and Glory: Essays on the Legacy of the Fifty-Fourth Massachusetts Regiment*, edited by Martin H. Blatt, Thomas J. Brown, and Donald Yacovone, 52–75. Amherst and Boston: University of Massachusetts Press and Massachusetts Historical Society, 2001.

———. "Ulysses S. Grant, Historian." In *The Memory of the Civil War in American Culture*, edited by Alice Fahs and Joan Waugh, 5–38. Chapel Hill: University of North Carolina Press, 2004.

Williams, Susan S. "Manufacturing Intellectual Equipment: The Tauchnitz Edition of *The Marble Faun*." In *Reading Books: Essays on the Material Text and Literature in America*, edited by Michele Moylan and Lane Stiles, 117–50. Amherst: University of Massachusetts Press, 1996.

Wilson, Matthew. "Charles W. Chesnutt's *The Colonel's Dream*: The Failure of Critical Realism." *Prospects* 25 (2000): 363–89.

Winship, Michael. *Ticknor and Fields: The Business of Literary Publishing in the United States of the Nineteenth Century*. Chapel Hill: Hanes Foundation, 1992.

Wood, Marcus. *Blind Memory: Visual Representations of Slavery in England and America, 1780–1865*. New York: Routledge, 2000.

Wood, Nancy. "Memory's Remains: *Les lieux de mémoire*." *History and Memory* 6 (Spring/Summer 1994): 123–49.

Yacovone, Donald. *Samuel Joseph May and the Dilemmas of the Liberal Persuasion, 1797–1871*. Philadelphia: Temple University Press, 1991.

Zboray, Ronald J. *A Fictive People: Antebellum Economic Development and the American Reading Public*. New York: Oxford University Press, 1993.

Zboray, Ronald J., and Mary Saracino Zboray. "Books, Reading, and the World of Goods in Antebellum New England." *American Quarterly* 48 (December 1996): 587–622.

UNPUBLISHED SOURCES

Atkin, Andrea M. "Converting America: The Rhetoric of Abolitionist Literature." Ph.D. dissertation, University of Chicago, 1995.

Brown, Joshua Emett. "*Frank Leslie's Illustrated Newspaper*: The Pictorial Press and the Representations of America, 1855–1889." Ph.D. dissertation, Columbia University, 1993.

Ellingsworth, Huber Winton. "Southern Reconciliation Orators in the North, 1868–1899." Ph.D. dissertation, Florida State University, 1955.

Flusche, Michael. "The Private Plantation: Versions of the Old South Myth, 1880–1914." Ph.D. dissertation, Johns Hopkins University, 1973.

Gruner, Mark Randall. "Letters of Blood: Antislavery Fiction and the Problem of Unjust Laws." Ph.D. dissertation, UCLA, 1993.

Herbig, Katherine Lydigsen. "Friends for Freedom: The Lives and Careers of Sallie Holley and Caroline Putnam." Ph.D. dissertation, Claremont Graduate School, 1977.

Kachun, Mitchell A. "The Faith that the Dark Past Has Taught Us: African-American Commemorations in the North and West and the Construction of a Usable Past, 1808–1915." Ph.D. dissertation, Cornell University, 1997.

Liedel, Donald Edward. "The Antislavery Novel, 1836–1861." Ph.D. dissertation, University of Michigan, 1961.

Robertson, Stacey. "Remembering Antislavery: Women Abolitionists in the Old Northwest." Paper delivered at the annual meeting of the Organization of American Historians, 2001.

Stevens, Elizabeth Cooke. "'From Generation to Generation': The Mother and

Daughter Activism of Elizabeth Buffum Chace and Lillie Chace Wyman."
Ph.D. dissertation, Brown University, 1993.

Wolff, Alfred Young, Jr. "The South and the American Imagination: Mythical
Views of the Old South, 1865–1900." Ph.D. dissertation, University of Virginia,
1971.

Canada, as fugitive slave haven, 74, 117, 121, 127, 143

Canvassers, 84–88, 89, 148, 169, 171

Carpenter, Joseph, 244

Caulon Press, 242

Centennial Exhibition (1876, Philadelphia), 87, 89–90

Century (magazine), 156, 192, 193, 217; openness to southern writers of, 9, 155, 218–19; post–Civil war prominence of, 137, 151; first-person accounts in, 163–64, 167, 173; black inferiority portrayed in, 220–21; Civil War series in, 221–22

Chace, Elizabeth Buffum, 211, 226, 233–38

Channing, William, 41

Chapman, Maria Weston, 39, 234

Charles (fugitive slave), 73, 79

Charley (slave), 128

Chesnutt, Charles, 219

Chester, John, 144

Cheyney, Ednah Dow, 7, 214, 215

Chicago abolitionist reunion (1874), 97–104, 108–9, 111–12, 131, 173

Chicago Tribune (newspaper), 97, 98, 100, 103, 112, 150, 189, 233

Child, Lydia Maria, 30, 39, 48, 153, 161, 223

Chinese Exclusion Act of 1882, 207

Chinese immigrants, 207

Christian Cynosure (periodical), 150

Christian Recorder (newspaper), 89, 90, 109, 136

Christian Register (newspaper), 28, 30

Churches. *See* Religion; *and specific denominations*

Citizenship, black, 2, 3, 34, 62, 140, 221, 236

Civil and political rights, 135, 136, as abolitionist reunion issue, 101, 102, 107; journal articles on, 158–60; Supreme Court ruling against, 198–99; southern blacks denial of,

214, 217, 218, 228; Chace's commitment to, 236. *See also* Suffrage

Civil Rights Act of 1875, 113, 126, 138, 199

Civil rights movement, 9, 254

Civil service reform, 217

Civil War: causes of, 2, 3, 4, 40, 124, 125, 145–46, 162–63, 167, 180, 184, 222; historical memory of, 2–3, 5, 26, 99; magazine interpretations of, 5, 137, 163, 221–22, 224; monuments to, 26, 209; May's view of, 40; slaves' poor treatment during, 123; emancipation and, 124, 163, 167, 222, 224, 236; Coffin (Levi) on, 124–25; black troops and, 125, 147, 156, 218, 220, 226, 252–53, 277–78 (n. 41); Haviland (Laura) and, 132, 133, 145–46; Swisshelm on, 174, 180–81; Julian on, 186, 189; Pillsbury on, 198; Republican 1890s view of, 218; historians' analysis of, 222–23; veterans of, 225; Fairbank on, 229; Higginson on, 252–53

Cleanliness, 44, 80

Clergy. *See* Preachers, black; Religion

Cleveland, Grover, 90

Cleveland Anti-Slavery Society, 152

Cleveland Gazette (newspaper), 233

Cleveland Leader (newspaper), 152

Coffin, Katy, 111, 115, 116, 117, 121, 126, 127, 131

Coffin, Levi, 148, 151, 155, 197; narrative by, 111–31, 135, 153–54, 228; Higginson on, 249

Coffin, Louise, 275 (n. 5)

Colfax (La.), 107

Colman, Lucy, 226, 233–34, 238–42, 243

Committee on the Conduct of the War, 186

Compromise of 1850, 184, 222

Concert Hall (Philadelphia), 104, 105

Concklin, Seth, 67–68, 78

Congregationalists, 194, 197

Congress, U.S., 16, 49, 101, 185, 186

Constitution, U.S., 92, 180. *See also*
Fifteenth Amendment; Four-
teenth Amendment; Thirteenth
Amendment
Conventions, 6, 11, 252
Conversion stories, 135, 175
Copeland, Robert M., 52–53
Cornell University, 59
Covenanter Church, 176
Craft, Ellen, 213, 232
Crandall, Prudence, 28, 34, 43, 263
(n. 57)
Curtis, George W., 1, 11, 25, 26, 55, 97,
164, 274 (n. 21)
Custer, Elizabeth, 174–75

Daniel (fugitive slave), 75
Danvers (Mass.) Historical Society,
210–15
Darwin, Charles, 108
Davis, Rebecca Harding, 158, 160
Debt, 217
Declaration of Independence, 2, 36,
92, 99
Declaration of Sentiments (AAS), 36,
205, 207
De Forest, J. W., 55, 57
Democratic Party, 26, 92, 113, 125,
213–14; as Greeley supporters, 13, 67,
95; in the South, 57, 136; Swisshelm
and, 179, 180; Julian's view of, 184,
185, 188; Bryan as presidential
nominee of, 218; Colman on, 241
Denslow, Van Buren, 26, 54, 56, 259
(n. 5)
"Desperate Conflict in a Barn"
(illustration), 76, 77
DeVere, M. Schele, 51–52
De Wolfe, Fiske and Company, 227
Dialect. *See* Black dialect
Diaz, Abby, 211
Dickinson, Anna, 39, 56
Discrimination, racial, 13, 34, 43–44,
81, 126, 139, 160, 232, 236. *See also*
Prejudice, racial; Segregation

Dishonesty, 144
Dix, Dorothea, 181
Dorsey, Luther, 75
Douglass, Frederick, 3, 44, 46, 192, 229;
American Anti-Slavery Society and,
12, 18, 25, 34; slave narrative by, 63,
167; abolitionist reunions and, 105,
106, 107; autobiography of, 156,
165, 166–73, 190, 201, 225, 226–28;
Pillsbury and, 199, 200
Downing, George T., 213–14
Dungy, John William, 81
Durkee, Charles, 290 (n. 77)

Eastman, Zebina, 98, 100, 101, 104
Education: freed blacks and, 16, 28, 81,
102, 107, 128, 159, 204, 220; school
segregation and, 138; magazine
writers' view of, 140
Edward, Harry Stillwell, 220
Edwards, Gabriel, 265 (n. 82)
Eggleston, George, 141, 145
Egotism, autobiographies and, 31, 169,
173, 196
Elder, William, 105
Eliza (slave), 230–31, 232
Emancipation, 59, 93, 95, 142, 217;
historical memory of, 3, 26–27; as
abolitionists' goal, 6, 13, 36, 40, 43,
115, 117, 124, 163, 222, 236; Lincoln
and, 21, 99, 105, 124, 209, 224, 236,
241; Frémont's proclamation of, 22,
162, 181, 186, 189; plantation owners
and, 57; Still's view of, 62, 66; Civil
War and, 124, 163, 167, 222, 224, 236
Emancipation Proclamation, 99, 173,
181, 186, 189, 241
Employment, 127, 158, 221
Endicott, Mrs., 211
Enforcement Acts of 1870–71, 67
England. *See* Great Britain
Equality, racial, 44–46, 153, 236, 241
Equal protection clause, 199
Evangelicals, 115–16; as publishers, 130

Garrison, William Lloyd, 48, 199, 223, 229; book advance returned by, 5; *New York Times* on, 7, 135; American Anti-Slavery Society's dissolution and, 11–12; public's embracement of, 25; May and, 27, 30, 33–34, 35, 36, 37–38, 59, 166, 262 (nn. 32, 39); annexation of Texas and, 36; magazine portrayals of, 54; monuments to, 61, 208, 209; Still and, 64, 67, 76–77; abolitionist reunions and, 98, 101, 106–7; death of, 109, 161; characterization of blacks by, 152; outlook (1880s) of, 160, 161–62, 165, 184, 191–92, 193, 195; Douglass and, 167–68; Julian on, 184, 191–92; Stanton (Henry) and, 191; Swisshelm on, 191; Pillsbury and, 195, 196; Grew and, 206; Powell on, 242–43; Higginson on, 249

Garrison, William Lloyd, Jr., 217, 237

Gay, Elizabeth, 247

Gay, Sidney, 201

Gibbons, Daniel, 64

Giddings, Joshua, 290 (n. 77)

Gilbert, Charles, 70

Gilded Age, 6, 117, 121, 128

Gilder, Richard Watson, 9, 137, 156, 158–59, 218, 221–22

Gordon, Clarence, 141

Gordon, Elizabeth, 79

Grant, Ulysses S., 15, 16, 28, 56, 92, 156, 286 (n. 23)

Great Britain, 9, 109, 171, 254; Coffin's (Levi) visits to, 120, 125, 130; anti-slavery society in, 244, 293 (n. 12)

"Great South, The" (King magazine series), 138–39, 141

Greeley, Horace: presidential candidacy of, 13, 67, 95, 123, 187–88, 190; autobiography of, 32, 33

Green, Beriah, 109

Greenwood, Grace, 136, 137

Grew, Mary, 13–14, 16, 19–20, 79, 205–6, 207, 247

Griest, Ellwood, 93–95

Grimké, Archibald, 209

Grimké sisters (Angelina and Sarah), 28, 39, 163, 209

Grover, Mr., 100, 101

Guilt, 3

Hale, John, 191

Half a Century (Swisshelm), 156, 165, 178–83, 184, 190, 201

Hall, John, 62

Hamilton, Elsie, 144

Hamilton, John, 231

Hamilton, Willis, 143, 144

Hardin, F. A., 135

Harper, Frances Watkins, 83, 105, 107–8

Harper & Brothers, 29–30, 190

Harpers Ferry raid, 167

Harper's Monthly Magazine, 1, 11, 118, 144; Civil War's aftermath and, 25, 49, 51–57, 137, 138, 140, 142; on Still's narrative, 89; on black inferiority, 138, 140, 158, 218; on Custer's auto-biography, 174–75; on Stanton (Henry), 190

Harper's Weekly (magazine), 21, 25, 50, 61, 95, 123, 136, 153

Haven, Gilbert, 15

Haviland, Charles, 131–32

Haviland, Laura, 137, 138, 165, 175, 190, 197; abolitionist reunion (1874) and, 103, 111–12, 131; "passing" by, 126; narrative by, 131–35, 142–51, 153–54, 155; reissues of narrative of, 131, 228; Fairbank and, 229, 233

Hayden, Lewis, 44, 231, 232

Hayes, Rutherford, 136, 206

Haynes, Lorenza, 237

Herald for Freedom (newspaper), 29, 195

"Here and There in the South" (Davis), 158

Higginson, Thomas Wentworth, 15, 16, 17, 98, 136, 218, 248–54; recollections of, 218, 248–54

Hill, Walter B., 157

Historical societies, 18
Historical Society of Pennsylvania, 20
Holland, Josiah, 1–2, 139
Home Affairs, Department of, 16
Horticultural Hall (Philadelphia), 204
Houghton Mifflin, 59, 91, 161, 164, 165, 167, 199, 248, 253, 254
Howe, John W., 290 (n. 77)
Hudson, E. D., 15
Human rights, 211
Hume, John F., 254
Humor, 118
Hunn, John, 82
Huxley, Thomas, 108

Imperialism, 218, 221
"Impressions of the South" (Warner), 158
Independent (periodical), 48
Indiana Yearly Meeting, 117
International Council of Women, 234
Inter Ocean (newspaper), 150
Interracial marriage, 51, 56, 126, 219–20
Isaac (fugitive slave), 71

Jack (fugitive slave), 121
Jackson, James C., 214
Jackson, Stonewall, 136, 137
James (fugitive slave), 79
James, Henry, 48
James R. Osgood & Company, 59
Jane (slave), 123
Jansen, McClurg & Co., 182, 189
Jefferson, Thomas, 198
Jerry (fugitive slave), 213
Jim (fugitive slave), 129
Joe (fugitive slave), 74
John (fugitive slave), 72, 81
Johns Hopkins University, 233
Johnson, Andrew, 17, 92, 181, 182
Johnson, Oliver, 88, 192, 199, 214
Johnson, Robert Underwood, 163
Johnson, Sam, 231, 232
Johnson, Samuel, 15
Joiner, Maria, 75

Jones, Caroline, 237
Jones, Robert, 80
Jones, Thomas, 74
Julian, George, 16, 117, 191–92, 226; abolitionist reunion (1874) and, 104; narrative by, 156, 165, 183–89, 190, 201

Kammen, Michael, 2
Kansas: southern blacks' exodus to, 132, 136, 147, 160, 169; antislavery emigrants to, 252
King, Edward, 138–39, 141
King, Preston, 290 (n. 77)
Ku Klux Klan, 41, 57
Ku Klux Klan Act of 1871, 67

Ladies' Anti-Slavery Societies and Sewing Circles of Philadelphia, 64
Lampson, Father, 191
Lancaster (Pa.) Inquirer (newspaper), 93
Landownership, 16–17, 127, 186, 217
Langston, John, 105
Leavitt, Joshua, 109
Lee, Robert E., 142, 221
Levermore, Charles, 217
Liberal Christian (periodical), 28
Liberal Republicans, 13, 67, 95, 187–88
Liberator (newspaper), 195
Liberty Guard, 229
Liberty Party, 179, 185
Library of Congress, 88
Life and Times of Frederick Douglass, The (Douglass), 156, 165, 166–73, 190, 201, 225, 226–28
Lincoln, Abraham, 49, 156, 163, 218, 222; emancipation and, 21, 99, 105, 124, 209, 224, 236, 241 (*see also* Emancipation Proclamation); Douglass's view of, 167; Swisshelm on, 180–81; Julian and, 186, 189; Pillsbury on, 195; Fairbank and, 228; Colman's criticism of, 241
Lincoln, Mary Todd, 180, 241
Lippincott (magazine), 142
Literacy, 220

Porter & Coates, 83–84, 87, 269–70
(n. 57)
Post, Amy, 238, 242
Poverty, 217
Powell, Aaron, 18, 20, 204, 207, 226,
242–45, 254
Powell, Anna, 242
Preachers, black, 140, 145, 158
Predo, Henry, 72
Prejudice, racial, 20, 55–56, 206, 207,
214; abolitionist efforts against, 6,
13–15, 17, 21, 43–44, 113, 125; public
transportation and, 81, 232, 236;
as abolitionist reunion issue, 101,
102, 106, 108; 1880s and, 160, 167,
173; 1890s and, 218, 226, 236; as
Colman theme, 238–39. See also
Discrimination, racial
Presbyterian Church, 176, 177, 197
"Present Crisis, The" (Lowell), 225
Press. See Magazines; Newspapers; and
specific publications
Public speaking: Coffin (Levi) and, 120;
Swisshelm and, 180; Colman and,
239–40; Powell (Aaron) and, 243
Public transportation, 81, 139, 232, 236
Publishing Association of Friends, 149
Publishing houses, 7, 29–30, 59;
subscription sales by, 83–88, 89,
148, 169; evangelicals and, 130;
autobiography criteria of, 164–65.
See also specific names
Purvis, Harriet, 247
Purvis, Robert, 105, 204–5, 232
Putnam, George W., 211
Putnam, Mrs., 211
Putnam's Magazine, 26, 52, 54

Quadroons, 128
Quakers. See Society of Friends

Racial justice, 6, 113, 245, 254. See also
Discrimination, racial; Equality,
racial
Racial prejudice. See Prejudice, racial

Railroads, discrimination and, 81, 236
Raisin Institute, 132, 298 (n. 31)
Recollections of a Busy Life (Greeley), 32
Reconciliation, 3, 222; Liberal
Republicans and, 13, 95, 123, 188;
Republicans and, 67, 218; Haviland's
(Laura) opposition to, 148; Julian's
support of, 186; Fairbank's rejection
of, 230
Reconstruction, 1–2, 57, 95, 121; end of,
4, 136; Liberal Republicans and, 13,
67; May's view of, 41; media on, 54,
135–36, 159; Republicans and, 57, 136;
Julian's criticism of, 186; 1890s view
of, 222
Redick, Willis, 73
Reform organizations, 11
Religion: slavery issue and, 11, 19–20,
42–43, 79, 116–17, 177, 192, 193, 194,
197–98, 235, 240; evangelicals and,
115–16; moral conduct and, 116–17;
conversion stories and, 135, 175;
blacks and, 139–40, 145, 158; social
prejudice vs., 139. See also specific
denominations
Reminiscences (Coffin), 111–31, 135,
153–54, 228
Reparations, 242
Republican Party, 26, 34, 88, 92, 210,
213; abolitionists and, 9, 21, 135, 152;
Grant and, 15, 28; Phillips and, 15,
135; Reconstruction and, 57, 136;
May's view of, 58; reconciliation
and, 67, 218; Swisshelm and, 179,
180, 226; Julian and, 185–89, 226;
corruption and, 187; Stanton
(Henry) and, 191; Pillsbury on,
195; black suffrage rights and, 218;
Douglass and, 226–27; Colman on,
240–41. See also Liberal Republicans
Resistance, slave, 95
Reunions, 6–7, 9, 97–110; Chicago
(1874), 97–104, 108–9, 111–12, 131, 173;
Pennsylvania Abolition Society,
104–8, 109

Tourgée, Albion, 157
Tract and American Bible Society, 197
Trowbridge, J. T., 223
Truth, Sojourner, 29, 241
Tuck, Amos, 290 (n. 77)
Turner, Mr., 111
Twain, Mark, 90, 271–72 (n. 70)

Uncle Dodson (preacher), 145
Uncle Phil (preacher), 145
Uncle Tim (slave), 146
Uncle Tom's Cabin (Stowe), 88, 151
Underground Railroad, 111–35, 166,
    207; May and, 28, 39, 44–45; Still's
    Underground Railroad narrative
    on, 61–91, 93, 95, 111, 115, 121, 129, 130,
    151, 168; Haviland's (Laura) account
    of, 112, 131–35, 142–51, 153–54, 155,
    165, 228; Coffin's (Levi) narrative
    of, 112–31, 151, 153–54, 155, 228; safe
    houses for, 130; black publications
    on, 151–53; 1890s interest in, 228;
    Chace and, 235
Unitarian Church, 42, 43
United States v. Stanley (1883), 198–99

Van Buren, Martin, 179
Veterans, Civil War, 225
Vicksburg, Miss., 107
Violence, 159, 196; mobs and, 40, 117,
    180, 197, 217, 292 (n. 113); against
    abolitionists, 40, 117, 240, 243;
    of slavery system, 74–76, 122,
    146–47, 184; slave hunters and,
    123; Douglass's view of, 167, 168;
    lynching and, 214, 217–18, 221
Virginia school segregation, 138
Voting rights. *See* Suffrage

Waite, Morrison R., 190
Walden & Stowe, 148
Walker, Amasa, 102, 274 (n. 14)
War Department, U.S., 181, 182
Warner, Charles Dudley, 158, 159

Warner, Olin L., 208
Webb, William, 90–91, 92–93, 95
Webster, Daniel, 47, 222, 242
Wesleyan Methodists, 132, 148
Western Freedman's Aid Commission,
    115
Western Methodist Book Concern, 148
Western Tract and Book Society, 130–31
Whig Party, 184, 185
Whipple, Charles, 214–15
White, John, 143
White League, 123
Whittier, John Greenleaf, 2, 30, 46,
    48, 141, 223; American Anti-Slavery
    Society and, 1, 205, 207; statue of, 61;
    abolitionist reunion (1874) and, 98;
    Haviland (Laura) and, 150
Willey, Austin, 208
Wilmot, David, 290 (n. 77)
Wilson, Henry, 59, 105, 106, 109, 199
Wilson, Woodrow, 210
Woman's Life-Work, A (Haviland), 131–35,
    142–51, 153–54, 155
Women: antislavery movement and, 4,
    13–14, 19, 38–39, 64, 83, 102–3, 107–8,
    118, 173–83, 191, 226, 233–42; voting
    rights for, 20, 34, 103, 204; as fugitive
    slaves, 73; treatment of slaves by,
    78–79, 144–45, 155, 177–78, 221;
    abolitionist reunions and, 102–3, 105,
    107–8, 173; slaveholder sexual abuse
    of, 122–23, 177, 184, 230; skin color
    and, 128; black chastity and, 158;
    autobiography criteria for, 174–75
Women's Christian Temperance Union
    (WCTU), 132
Women's rights, 102, 103, 174, 175
Women's suffrage, 20, 34, 103, 204
Woolson, Constance, 114
Wordsworth, William, 32
Wright, Elizur, 108, 201
Wright, Henry, 18

Yazoo City (Miss.), 123–240